T0301316

BEYOND THE
RESOURCE CURSE

BEYOND THE RESOURCE CURSE

Edited by

Brenda Shaffer

and Taleh Ziyadov

PENN

UNIVERSITY OF PENNSYLVANIA PRESS

PHILADELPHIA

Published by
University of Pennsylvania Press
Philadelphia, Pennsylvania 19104-4112

Printed in the United States of America
on acid-free paper
10 9 8 7 6 5 4 3 2 1

Library of Congress Cataloging-in-Publication Data
Beyond the resource curse / edited by Brenda Shaffer and
Taleh Ziyadov.—1st ed.
   p.   cm.
Includes bibliographical references and index.
   ISBN 978-0-8122-4400-7 (hardcover : alk. paper)
1. Resource curse. 2. Power resources. 3. Energy
policy. 4. Petroleum reserves. 5. Natural gas reserves.
6. International relations. I. Shaffer, Brenda.
II. Ziyadov, Taleh.
HD9502.A2B49   2011
333.7—dc23   2011033177

CONTENTS

BEYOND THE
RESOURCE CURSE

Introduction

Brenda Shaffer

Energy security is a fundamental challenge for major energy-exporting states. Most policymakers and many academics think of energy security solely in terms of the interests of energy importers. However, the constant volatility in energy prices and the permanent uncertainty of supply and consumption trends create energy security challenges for both importers *and* exporters. *Beyond the Resource Curse* examines a number of the challenges to energy-exporting states that emanate from this volatility and studies the various influences of oil and gas revenue on exporting states.

Energy production and transport is a highly capital-intensive industry. Creating new energy production also requires a long lead time, which means that energy supply and demand are frequently unsynchronized. This creates inherent energy price volatility and the subsequent boom and bust cycles characteristic of energy-exporting economies. Energy trade is the largest input in the world economy, and energy consumption and production trends directly influence and are influenced by the state of the world economy. Although the ebbs and flows of energy prices have a significant impact on the state of the world economy, those same ebbs and flows can translate into tsunamis and tidal waves for energy-exporting economies. This can be seen in the collapse of prices that took place with the onset of the current global financial crisis that began in 2008, when the price of oil fell to under $40 a barrel in January 2009. Just half a year earlier, oil prices had been at an all-time high of $147 a barrel.

Over the years, analysts have not been very good at predicting changes in oil prices, further complicating energy exporters' long-term planning. Oil prices fluctuate twice as frequently as other commodities.[1] In the last decade, oil prices have been especially volatile. In 2008, for example, daily oil prices increased or declined by at least 5 percent a total of thirty-nine times. This extreme unpredictability can wreak havoc with energy-exporting states' economic and budget projections. Oil producers may have enjoyed rising state revenues from 2004 to 2007, but the sudden collapse in oil prices in 2008 and 2009 left the state budgets and national economies of many oil exporters in turmoil.

States that rely predominately on revenues from energy export operate in an environment of constant uncertainty that creates a built-in challenge in state budgets on every level of government. This uncertainty leads to unstable state investments and thus often produces inadequately maintained infrastructures, such as roads and electricity grids. It also creates difficulty in building human capital over the long term. This often leads energy-exporting states to invest in policies that produce short-term, often ineffective, results, such as constructing new buildings and funding student scholarships instead of establishing comprehensive educational institutions and programs. This price uncertainty also affects exporters' ability to invest in and attract investments in oil and natural gas production, which affects the long-term productivity of the very source of their economic livelihoods.

The Resource Curse

In recent decades, scholars have found that exporting natural resources, such as oil and natural gas, tends to produce a distinctive set of political and economic qualities in major exporting states. This phenomenon is known as the resource curse. It refers to the tendency of natural-resource-exporting countries to underperform economically, have nondemocratic governments as well as poor governance, and a higher propensity for involvement in conflicts. *Beyond the Resource Curse* builds on the resource curse literature (which is surveyed in Chapter 2). It examines characteristics of energy exporters beyond these three main subjects that fall under the category of the resource curse and looks at a wider list of perils, including education, electricity infrastructure, and foreign policy.

Energy-exporting states are often categorized along the scale of "Norway or Nigeria," with these countries representing archetypical outcomes of the benefits and the detriments of hydrocarbon export. *Beyond the Resource Curse* shows that the fate of states may be much more nuanced: even Norway is plagued with some of the perils of energy exports (see Chapter 10). In addition, a number of the energy exporters, such as the United Arab Emirates, have benefited immensely from their oil wealth and have advanced their levels of human development despite the associated perils of the resource curse (see Chapter 3). The analysis of Norway in this volume claims that energy-exporting countries tend to develop powerful oligarchies, regardless of their regime type, that influence policy decisions beyond the narrow economic sector in which they operate.

Beyond the Resource Curse also looks at the strategies various states have adopted to circumvent the resource curse. This volume uses *peril* and not *curse* to refer to the consequences of energy export because the dangers from oil and gas export might not materialize. Appropriate policies may enable the state to avert or minimize these dangers. In addition, a number of variables can produce different influences on the resource revenue. These variables include the size of a state's population, how diverse it was economically as well as how entrenched the rule of law and good governance were before major energy exports came online, the ownership structure of the state's energy resources, and the degree of modernization the state and society had undergone prior to the onset of the energy export. The volume shows, for example, that the fiscal volatility associated with energy exports is affected by the size of the population of a state. Energy exporters with relatively large populations (such as Iran, Russia, and Venezuela) are less likely to maintain fiscal balance when energy export revenues are relatively low. Energy-exporting countries with small populations (such as the United Arab Emirates, Qatar, and Azerbaijan) are much less likely to encounter this problem.

Beyond the Resource Curse also examines a variety of cases where newer energy exporters initiated their major export activity while already aware of the potential perils of the resource. Most of these states have undertaken measures intended to avert these perils. Study of these states that benefited from the knowledge of the potential export perils of hydrocarbons may shed new light on the impact oil and natural gas exports can have on a country's economy and society.

This volume will, however, focus only on major energy exporters. The International Monetary Fund (IMF) defines major energy exporters as countries in which the average share of fuel exports exceeds 40 percent of total exports over a five-year period and the average value of fuel exports exceeds

$500 million. The remainder of this introductory chapter examines energy security from the perspective of major energy exporters and the perils energy exporters face in the international political system.

Energy Security

In recent decades, the term *energy security* has appeared frequently in policy debates and has become a major policy goal of many states. Yet discussions of energy security are often unclear about what the term means. Energy security is composed of three elements:[2]

- Reliability
- Affordability
- Environmental Sustainability

In discussions of energy policies, many people confuse the concepts of energy security and energy independence. The goal of achieving "energy independence" is a frequent rallying call of U.S. politicians from across the political spectrum. For instance, President Barack Obama articulates this goal in his speeches and programs related to U.S. energy policies (note that the comprehensive U.S. legislation on energy policy from 2007 is called the Energy Independence Security Act). However, achieving adequate energy security does not require a state to provide all of its long-term energy needs domestically. Aspiring to energy independence is about as reasonable as striving for "technology independence." Most states do not attempt to cut themselves off from technology exchange and trade. Likewise, seeking isolation in the energy sphere limits opportunities to enhance energy security. In integrated global markets for oil and coal, domestically produced supplies do not provide economic advantage over imported ones. Thus, focusing on energy independence can mar the ability to achieve one of the components of energy security: affordability.

Energy Security Challenges Faced by Energy Exporters

Energy importers and exporters both face energy security challenges. Almost counterintuitively, energy security challenges may be more acute for exporting states than importing states. Here is an overview of the energy security challenges major energy exporters face.

Reliability

For energy exporters, *reliability* means dependability of markets. An energy supplier is concerned about reliability of demand, just as an energy importer is concerned about reliability of supply. As Hasan Qabazard, director of the Research Division of the Organization of Petroleum Exporting Countries (OPEC), noted in the newspaper *Emirates Business 24/7*, "The security and predictability of demand are as important as the security of supply."[3]

Demand for fossil fuels is vulnerable to change, especially in response to policy measures that promote conservation, economic downturns, and technological advances. State policies, such as carbon or other taxes that aim to reduce fossil fuel consumption or vehicle and machine efficiency standards, affect demand for fossil fuels. Moreover, there is a direct correlation between economic growth rates and energy consumption rates. In addition, new technological developments can create alternative sources of energy or develop additional locations of production and thus deprive energy suppliers of markets for their oil and gas. For example, recent technological developments in the production of natural gas found in shale rock will most likely lead to natural gas replacing oil and coal in many functions. This development may also turn many current natural gas importers into exporters. The map of natural gas exporters will most likely change fundamentally in the coming decade. In response to the current prospects for production of natural gas from shale rock and other unconventional sources, the future of a number of liquefied natural gas (LNG) markets has also become radically uncertain.

Just as the reliability of supply can change, the reliability of markets can be challenged by potential obstructions and disruptions from energy transit states. Supply arrangements involving transit states are much more prone to disruption than arrangements in which exporters and importers have a direct relationship. Among the three types of states along the energy supply line—exporting states, transit states, and importing states—transit states have the most significant incentive and least risk from disrupting supply as a means to promote other goals. In recent decades, energy supply arrangements involving transit states have become more prevalent for three reasons: (1) rising consumption of natural gas, a commodity that is predominately supplied by pipelines; (2) initiation of oil and natural gas exports from a number of land-locked states (Chad, Kazakhstan, Azerbaijan, and Turkmenistan); and (3) expanded oil and natural gas exports from Russia to markets in Europe through supply networks involving transit states.

In addition, whereas the oil or "energy weapon" is seen as a tool in the hands of suppliers, it is more often utilized by consumers. In the case of oil, unless every supplier participates, a consumer cannot be denied supplies. However, export markets can effectively be denied to a state. In the last two decades, the United States and the UN have often used denial of oil markets and sanctions on investments in the oil and gas sector as a tool to moderate the behavior of oil- and gas-exporting states that include Iraq, Iran, Libya, and Sudan.

Furthermore, reliability of supply and markets is threatened by potential attacks on sea lanes and supply infrastructures. Both criminal and terrorist elements target energy export and transport infrastructure. Points of vulnerability include a number of narrow sea-lane passages that are potential choke points for major oil shipments, such as the Straits of Malacca, Hormuz, and Bosporus. Criminal elements are active in a number of major sea-lane passages. Terrorist elements can utilize this criminal infrastructure to obstruct oil transport as well.

A more fundamental challenge to energy exporters emanates from the fact that their main source of economic revenue is a commodity that in each location will at some point be depleted. In addition, on a global scale, technological advancement is likely to find a substitute for oil and other hydrocarbons even before they are exhausted. This bleak long-term outlook for energy exporters is compounded by the fact that major oil and natural gas exports tend to lead to the contracting of other sectors of the economy (a phenomenon commonly called "Dutch disease") that leaves exporters with little economic backup once those reserves are depleted or no longer in demand.

In recent decades, a number of energy exporters have undertaken policy measures to plan for their post-export period. One key policy instrument is the establishment of state oil funds. The guidelines governing a number of these funds deny the use of a large portion of the revenues for regular government budgetary expenditures and require saving them for investments in infrastructure and human capital.

Affordability

Affordability is an energy security concern for energy exporters and importers alike. Energy exporters face a complicated balancing act. On one hand, they must maintain a price that is high enough to attract continued investment in energy production and to maintain their national budgets. At the same time, energy exporters need energy prices to be moderate enough so that alternatives to fossil fuels do not become economically attractive and so that high energy prices do not lead to global economic recession and consequently a decline in demand for energy.

Maintaining oil and other energy prices that will attract investment in new production in the sector is a consistent energy security challenge. Investment trends are affected by prices and the general state of the economy, and so there is a trend toward underinvestment in future production when prices are low, which sets the stage for the next price spike and thus future volatility. Economic downturns generally lead to significant reduction in the demand for energy and thus lack of resources for investment in maintaining and expanding production of oil and natural gas. Although oil shocks have a negative impact on energy importers, they have an even greater negative impact on the economies of energy exporters over the long term. Each major oil shock during the last half century has led to long-term reduction in the growth of the global demand for oil.

In addition to maintaining a price that attracts investment in future production, major energy exporters require a price level that allows them to sustain their national budgets. Energy exporters are generally highly dependent on revenues from energy. Since the collapse of global oil prices in August 2008, most energy exporters with large populations have maintained a large gap between their budgets and their revenues from energy export. Iran, for instance, only maintains a balanced budget when oil prices are between $90 and $95 a barrel. Venezuela needs at least a similar oil price—if not a higher one—to maintain its budget.

State budgets of energy-exporting countries are particularly challenging to balance because most energy exporters maintain extensive subsidies for domestic consumption (see Chapter 5), especially subsidies for energy and energy products (vehicle fuels, electricity, and heating). Traditionally, energy exporters have conducted policies of maintaining low energy prices or even supplying free energy for their publics as a symbolic gesture of sharing the energy wealth. Domestic energy consumption in energy exporters is generally extremely high and energy efficiency is low.

However, when energy export revenues fall, domestic energy consumption patterns do not change because domestic prices are not linked to market trends. Thus, the state must continue to pay out large amounts of money on energy subsidies, even when its own revenues have fallen. States encounter great public resistance to the reduction or elimination of the domestic subsidies despite the great economic burden they impose. Moreover, publics are attached to these energy subsidies even though in most states they actually benefit the rich more than the poor. (Even at subsidized rates, the poor have limited means to consume the energy and often the subsidized products do not even reach those in need.) Due to its subsidies policies, Malaysia, for example, expends more on domestic energy subsidies than on health and education. Indonesia, even after becoming a net importer of oil in 2004, continues to subsidize domestic consumption of fuel, importing fuel at a higher price than the price at which it sells the fuel to the public. Iran spends over a quarter of its economic output on energy subsidies. Energy consumption subsidies also create additional costs to the state by stimulating consumption and thus pollution, which causes environmental and public health damage. The Obama Administration and the Group of 20 (G-20) have emphasized reducing energy subsides as a major plank in their policies to reduce fossil fuel consumption in the developing world, and these subsidies will be an issue of international political interest and on the domestic political agendas of energy exporters in coming years.

While striving to keep oil prices at a level that attracts investment and sustains states' budgets, energy exporters aspire to maintain an oil price that is low enough to discourage the development of alternative energy sources. In recent decades, OPEC, under Saudi Arabia's leadership, adopted a policy that favored maintenance of moderate oil prices in order to discourage transference to other energy sources. The most powerful disincentive for the development of alternative energy sources is lower oil prices. There is a correlation between investments in alternative and renewable energy technologies and the oil price: when the price is down, investments in alternative and renewable energy go down as well. Oil's main appeal is its low price relative to other energy sources. However, since the early part of the twenty-first century, OPEC has abandoned this policy of moderate world oil prices. Although keeping oil prices high brings revenue and investments to oil producers in the short run, it can lead to enduring reduction in demand in the long run. In order to maintain a price level that will ensure exporters' ability to meet their domestic commitments, OPEC producers often use their united production power to influence oil price trends. In 2009, OPEC cut production levels a number of times in order to prop up prices. This policy of maintaining higher prices, however, contains the peril of contributing to the demise of the long-term global demand for oil.

Environmental Sustainability

Environmental sustainability is a challenge for producers as well as consumers. Energy production poses dangers to public health and environmental sustainability. Most energy exporters rank high in pollution production and carbon emission. In addition, energy exporters tend to develop petrochemical industries that pose significant health and environmental risks.

Like all states, energy exporters are confronting the results of climate change. However, climate change creates an additional problem for energy exporters. If genuine steps are taken to address climate change and reduce global emission of carbon, demand will be greatly reduced or even eliminated for the very commodity that is the basis of these countries' economies. Many oil exporters view serious policies aimed at combating climate change as an existential threat. The December 2009 Copenhagen Conference failed to produce a binding agreement or defined targets for combating climate change. For those most concerned with the issue of climate change, this summit and the ensuing policy activity are considered a colossal failure. Still, major energy exporters expressed satisfaction regarding international inaction on climate change. On the closing day of the Copenhagen Conference, the chief negotiator from Saudi Arabia proclaimed that he was "satisfied" with the results of the Copenhagen Conference and that the adopted resolutions reflect "the interests of OPEC countries."[4]

Energy Exporters in the International Arena

Oil and natural gas exporters face a number of major perils in the international arena. Energy exporters are often presumed to possess significant geopolitical clout due to their energy riches. Despite the immense wealth transfer from energy importers to energy exporters, however, exporters have not been able to convert their revenues into significant geopolitical power. Furthermore, importing states view political action by energy exporters with caution and take collective action to undermine it. Since the energy crisis of the 1970s, importing states have taken a number of significant steps to offset the geopolitical power of the energy exporters, such as coordinating their policies vis-à-vis exporters, sharing information, and establishing extensive energy storage reserves. In addition, when energy-exporting countries change their policies to respond to changes in energy prices, it can lead to a lack of synchronization among energy-exporting states' foreign policies.

Leveraging Energy Revenues?

Each extended oil price boom brings immense revenue to major energy exporters. Despite this tremendous wealth, the geopolitical advantage acquired from this revenue is not clear. Major oil exports contribute to the longevity of ruling regimes in the exporting states, including their ability to receive security backing from major powers, chiefly the United States.[5] However, beyond this advantage, it appears that energy exporters have not been able to leverage their energy revenues significantly in the foreign policy arena. For example, energy exporters—with the exception of Russia, which benefits from significant sources of geopolitical power that do not derive from its energy wealth—have in many instances not succeeded in accomplishing their goals in the territorial conflicts that they champion. Azerbaijan believed that its role as an energy exporter and its acquired energy wealth would interest a number of global powers in the stability of the South Caucasus and thus a resolution of the Nagorno-Karabach conflict. Yet, in the years following Azerbaijan's initiation of major energy exports, the country had not come closer to resolution of the conflict in a manner favorable to Azerbaijan's position. At the same time, major Middle East producers have not succeeded in leveraging their energy wealth into resolution of the Palestinian-Israeli conflict according to their proclaimed goals.

Presumably, many of the same perils and curses that afflict major energy-exporting economies and the governance patterns of major energy exporters also affect their security and foreign policy capacity. As seen in *Beyond the Resource Curse*, major energy exports have an impact on diverse spheres, such as education reform and electricity provision. Accordingly, these same patterns can imperil additional spheres in the security and foreign policy realm, such as military acquisition patterns and security capacity building. Military capacity, like electricity infrastructures, requires long-term and consistent acquisitions and maintenance and is plagued by the inconsistencies of economic boom and bust cycles. In addition, energy exporters tend to acquire "white elephants" during boom cycles, which in the short term can create an impression of success but may not contribute to a sustainable policy in the long term. Military acquisition patterns in energy exporters will likely be a topic of further research.

An additional factor affecting the modest geopolitical clout of energy exporters is their lack of ability to operate as a coordinated force. Due to the commercial manner of the oil trade, OPEC did not succeed in conducting boycotts of states—even at the height of its power in the 1970s. The call of the Arab states in OPEC to embargo sales to the United States, the Netherlands, and Israel following the 1973 Yom Kippur War did not lead to the actual suspension of supplies to any states. The call to boycott did trigger an extreme price increase of more than 400 percent, but this was in light of the prevailing tight conditions in the world oil market.[6] Since the 1970s, however, OPEC member states have played a much smaller role in world oil production. In the 1970s, OPEC states produced 60 percent of the world oil output. In 2010, they are responsible for approximately 40 percent of global oil production.

In the field of natural gas, it seems that coordination between producers is even less attainable. In contrast to the dramatic statements of representatives from the Gas Exporting Countries Forum (GECF), this organization has not made any inroads in coordinating the policies of gas-exporting countries.[7] The core members of the group have conflicting interests, which dramatically decrease the prospects for coordinated action. Iran and Venezuela, for example, want to promote the forum to act as a "gas OPEC" regulating production and export among the member states, but Iran and Venezuela are not actually gas-exporting states.[8] The interests of these two countries diverge from those of Russia and Qatar, two other core states in the GECF. Russia is the largest exporter of the natural gas in the world, and Qatar is the largest exporter of LNG. In addition, as noted earlier, energy exporters are often more vulnerable to the perils of the "energy weapon" than consumers. Denial of markets to a specific producer is much more attainable and effective than attempts to boycott energy supplies to specific consumers.

The ability of energy exporters to leverage their energy revenue into geopolitical power has also been moderated by the united policy front by the major energy importers. As Richard Jones discusses in Chapter 10, the major energy importers have taken a number of steps since the oil crisis of the 1970s, including maintaining and coordinating energy supply storage, in order to minimize their vulnerability to the policies of the energy exporters. In fact, possessing substantial reserves—such as the U.S. Strategic Petroleum Reserve—give importers significant influence over market trends, including prices.

High-Risk Foreign Policy Perils?

The boom and bust revenue cycles resonate in the foreign policy patterns of many energy exporters. Among the manifestations in the sphere of foreign policy is the tendency of many energy exporters to adopt "resource nationalism" during periods of high oil and natural gas prices. As is discussed in Chapter 12, resource nationalism refers to the behavior of energy and other natural resource exporters to reopen contracts and nationalize production projects in an attempt to take advantage of their heightened power during periods of high prices. However, these policies often backfire in the long run, leading to a long-term decline in production and investments.

Another foreign policy manifestation of the boom and bust revenue cycles is the propensity for exporters to conduct foreign policies during periods of high prices that are unsustainable during periods of revenue decline. Revenue booms give these states a short-term increase in their power and thus encourage them to adopt hard-line foreign policy positions. These positions are not sustainable, however, due to the inevitable downward shift in oil prices and thus revenues and these states' power. Thus, oil and gas windfalls can lead to adoption of policies that are not effective in the long run and may be even very perilous for the exporters.

Organization of This Study

This volume presents the work of researchers from a variety of disciplines that range from economics and political science to international relations and sociology. The case studies examined in *Beyond the Resource Curse* cover a large number of geographic locations, including Iran, Azerbaijan, Venezuela, East Timor, Trinidad and Tobago, the United Arab Emirates, Norway, and Cambodia. A number of the case studies are devoted to post-Soviet energy producers. In contrast to the bulk of the leading oil and natural gas producers, the post-Soviet producers had diversified economies and had undergone extensive modernization prior to becoming major oil exporters. At the same time, these states did not have democratic governments or strong rule of law. With this unique combination of traits, these post-Soviet cases enhance our ability to study the variance of different factors on the influence energy exports can have on countries' economies and societies.

Beyond the Resource Curse opens with a survey of energy security from the perspective of major energy exporters. In Chapter 1, Jeffrey Frankel reviews the resource curse literature. Next, Patrick Clawson examines successful cases of utilization of energy export revenue in Chapter 2. In Chapter 3, Richard Auty looks at the case of Trinidad and Tobago's export revenue to discern if the state has succeeded in avoiding the resource curse. In Chapter 4, Ahmad Mojtahed focuses on the impact of domestic energy consumption subsidies on Iran. In Chapter 5, Elkin Nurmammadov looks at central bank institutions in energy-exporting states, highlighting the case of Azerbaijan. Next, Theresa Sabonis-Helf examines the challenge of electricity provision in energy-exporting states in Chapter 6. In the volume's section on energy and society, Murad Ismayilov opens Chapter 7 with a discussion on energy exports and collective identity. In Chapter 8, Regine Spector analyzes education reform in energy-exporting states. Next, in Chapter 9, Ole Andreas Engen, Oluf Langhelle, and Reidar Bratvold ask if Norway has indeed averted the problems found in so many other energy-exporting states. In the volume's third section, which focuses on energy exporters in the international system, Richard Jones discusses the relationship between energy exporters and the International Energy Agency in Chapter 10. In Chapter 11, Amy Jaffe reviews energy exporters' adoption of resource nationalism policies. Next, in Chapter 12, Elnur Soltanov looks at the interaction between energy export, domestic instability, and international conflicts. In Chapter 13, Naazneen Barma examines energy exporters' postconflict governance and politics. The volume concludes with an analysis by Taleh Ziyadov.

PART I

Economics and Infrastructures
of Energy Exporters

1

The Natural Resource Curse: A Survey

Jeffrey Frankel

It is striking how often countries with oil or other natural resource wealth have failed to show better economic performance than those without. This is the phenomenon known as the "natural resource curse." The pattern has been borne out in econometric tests across a comprehensive sample of countries. This paper considers seven aspects of commodity wealth, each of which is of interest in its own right but also a channel that some have suggested could lead to substandard economic performance. They are: long-term trends in world commodity prices, volatility, permanent crowding out of manufacturing, weak institutions, unsustainability, war, and cyclical Dutch disease.

Skeptics have questioned the natural resource curse. They point to examples of commodity-exporting countries that have done well and argue that resource exports and booms are not exogenous. Clearly, the relevant policy question for a country with natural resources is how to make the best of them. The paper concludes with a consideration of ideas for institutions that could help a country that is endowed with commodities overcome the pitfalls of the curse and achieve good economic performance. The most promising ideas include indexation of contracts, hedging of export proceeds, denomination of debt in terms of the export commodity, Chile-style fiscal rules, a monetary target that emphasizes product prices, transparent commodity funds, and lump-sum distribution.

The Resource Curse: An Introduction

It has been observed for decades that the possession of oil or other valuable mineral deposits or natural resources does not necessarily confer economic success. Many African countries—such as Angola, Nigeria, Sudan, and the Congo—are rich in oil, diamonds, or minerals, yet their peoples continue to experience low per capita income and a low quality of life. Meanwhile, the East Asian economies of Japan, Korea, Taiwan, Singapore, and Hong Kong have achieved Western-level standards of living despite being rocky islands (or peninsulas) with virtually no exportable natural resources. Richard Auty is apparently the one who coined the phrase "natural resource curse" to describe this puzzling phenomenon.[1] Its use spread rapidly.[2]

Figure 1.1 shows a sample of countries during the last four decades. Exports of fuels, ores, and metals as a fraction of total merchandise exports appear on the horizontal axis, and economic growth is on the vertical axis. Conspicuously high in growth and low in natural resources are China (CHN), Korea (KOR), and some other Asian countries. Conspicuously high in natural resources and low in growth are Gabon (GAB), Venezuela (VEN), and Zambia (ZMB). The overall relationship on average is slightly negative. The negative correlation is not very strong, masking almost as many resource successes as failures. But it certainly does not suggest a positive correlation between natural resource wealth and economic growth.

How could abundance of hydrocarbon deposits—or other mineral or agricultural products—be a curse? What would be the mechanism for this counterintuitive relationship? Broadly speaking, there are at least seven lines of argument. First, prices of such commodities could be subject to secular decline on world markets. Second, the high volatility of world prices for energy and other mineral and agricultural commodities could be problematic. Third, natural resources could be dead-end sectors in the sense that they may crowd out manufacturing, which might be the sector to offer dynamic benefits and spillovers that are good for growth. (It does not sound implausible that "industrialization" could be the essence of economic development.) Fourth, countries in which physical command of mineral deposits by the government or by a hereditary elite automatically confers wealth on the holders may be less likely to develop the institutions, such as rule of law and decentralization of decision making, that are conducive to economic development. These resource-rich countries suffer in contrast to countries in which moderate taxation of a thriving market economy is the only way the government can finance itself.

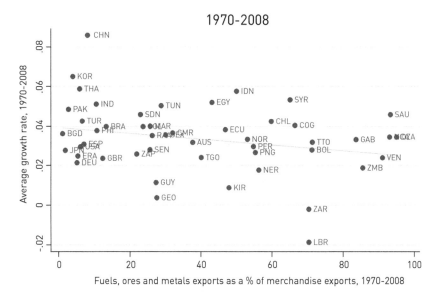

Figure 1.1 Statistical relationship between mineral exports and growth. World Development Indicators, World Bank.

Fifth, natural resources may be depleted too rapidly and leave the country with little to show for them, especially when it is difficult to impose private property rights on the resources, as under frontier conditions. Sixth, countries that are endowed with natural resources could have a proclivity for armed conflict, which is inimical to economic growth. Seventh, swings in commodity prices could engender excessive macroeconomic instability via the real exchange rate and government spending. This chapter considers each of these topics.

The conclusion will be that natural resource wealth does not necessarily lead to inferior economic or political development. Rather, it is best to view commodity abundance as a double-edged sword, with both benefits and dangers. It can be used for ill as easily as for good.[3] The fact that resource wealth does not in itself confer good economic performance is a striking enough phenomenon without exaggerating the negative effects. The priority for any country should be on identifying ways to sidestep the pitfalls that have afflicted other commodity producers in the past and to find the path of success. The last section of this chapter explores some of the institutional innovations that can help countries avoid the natural resource curse and achieve natural resource blessings instead.

Long-Term Trends in World Commodity Prices

Determination of the Export Price on World Markets

Developing countries tend to be smaller economically than major industrialized countries and more likely to specialize in the export of basic commodities. As a result, they are more likely to fit the small open economy model: they can be regarded as price takers, not just for their import goods, but for their export goods as well. That is, the prices of their tradable goods are generally taken as given on world markets. The price-taking assumption requires three conditions: low monopoly power, low trade barriers, and intrinsic perfect substitutability in the commodity between domestic and foreign producers—a condition usually met by primary products such as oil, and usually not met by manufactured goods and services. Literally speaking, not every barrel of oil is the same as every other and not all are traded in competitive markets. Furthermore, Saudi Arabia does not satisfy the first condition due to its large size in world oil markets.[4] But the assumption that most oil producers are price takers holds relatively well.

To a first approximation, then, the local price of oil is equal to the dollar price of oil on world markets times the country's exchange rate. It follows, for example, that a currency devaluation should push up the price of oil quickly and in proportion (leaving aside preexisting contracts or export restrictions). An upward revaluation of the currency should push down the price of oil in proportion.

Throughout this chapter, we will assume that the domestic country must take the price of the export commodity as given, in terms of foreign currency. We begin by considering the hypothesis that the given world price entails a long-term secular decline. The subsequent section of the paper considers the volatility in the given world price.

The Hypothesis of a Downward Trend in Commodity Prices
(Prebisch-Singer)

The hypothesis that the prices of mineral and agricultural products follow a downward trajectory in the long run, relative to the prices of manufactures and other products, is associated with Raul Prebisch and Hans Singer and what used to be called the "structuralist school."[5] The theoretical reasoning was that world demand for primary products is inelastic with respect to world income. That is, for every 1 percent increase in income, the demand for raw materials increases by less than 1 percent. Engel's Law is the (older) proposition that households spend a lower fraction of their income on food and other basic necessities as they get richer.

The Prebisch-Singer hypothesis, if true, would readily support the conclusion that specializing in natural resources is a bad deal. Mere "hewers of wood and drawers of water" (Deuteronomy 29:11) would remain forever poor if they did not industrialize. The policy implication that was drawn by Prebisch and the structuralists was that developing countries should discourage international trade with tariff and nontariff barriers to allow their domestic manufacturing sector to develop behind protective walls, rather than exploit their traditional comparative advantage in natural resources, as the classic theories of free trade would have it. This "import substitution industrialization" policy was adopted in most of Latin America and much of the rest of the developing world in the 1950s, 1960s, and 1970s. The trend reversed in subsequent decades, however.

Hypotheses of Upward Trends in Nonrenewable Resource Prices (Malthus and Hotelling)

There also exist persuasive theoretical arguments that we should expect prices of oil and other minerals to experience *upward* trends in the long run. The arguments begin with the assumption that we are talking about nonperishable, nonrenewable resources, that is, deposits in the earth's crust that are fixed in total supply and are gradually being depleted. (The argument does not apply as well to agricultural products.)

Let us add another assumption: whoever currently has claim to the resource, an oil company, for instance, can be confident that it will retain possession unless it sells to someone else, who then has equally safe property rights. This assumption excludes cases in which private oil companies fear that their contracts might be abrogated or their possessions nationalized.[6] It also excludes cases in which warlords compete over physical possession of the resource. Under such exceptions, the current owner has a strong incentive to pump the oil or extract the minerals quickly, because it might never benefit from whatever is left in the ground. One explanation for the sharp rise in oil prices between 1973 and 1979, for example, is that private Western oil companies had anticipated the possibility that newly assertive developing countries would eventually nationalize the oil reserves within their borders and thus had kept prices lower by pumping oil more quickly during the preceding two decades than they would have done had they been confident that their claims would remain valid indefinitely.

HOTELLING AND THE INTEREST RATE

At the risk of some oversimplification, let us assume for now also that the fixed deposits of oil in the earth's crust are all sufficiently accessible and that the costs of exploration, development, and pumping are small compared to the value of the oil. Harold Hotelling deduced from these assumptions the important theoretical principle that the price of oil in the long run should rise at a rate equal to the interest rate.[7]

The logic is as follows: At every point in time, an owner of the oil—whether a private oil company or a state—chooses how much to pump and how much to leave in the ground. Whatever is pumped can be sold at today's price (this is the price-taker assumption) and the proceeds invested in bank deposits or U.S. Treasury bills, which earn the current interest rate. If the value of the oil in the ground is not expected to increase in the future or not expected to increase at a sufficiently rapid rate, then the owner has an incentive to extract more of it today so that it can earn interest on the proceeds. As oil companies worldwide react in this way, they drive down the price of oil today, below its perceived long-run level. When the current price is below its perceived long-run level, companies will expect that the price must *rise* in the future. Only when the expectation of future appreciation is sufficient to offset the interest rate will the oil market be in equilibrium. That is, only then will oil companies be close to indifferent between pumping at a faster rate and a slower rate.

To say that oil prices are *expected* to increase at the interest rate means that they should do so on average; it does not mean that there will not be price fluctuations above and below the trend. But the theory does imply that, averaging out short-term unexpected fluctuations, oil prices in the long term should rise at the interest rate.

If there are constant costs of extraction and storage, then the trend in oil prices will be lower than the interest rate, by the amount of those costs; if there is a constant convenience yield from holding inventories, then the trend in prices will be higher than the interest rate, by the amount of the yield.[8]

MALTHUSIANISM AND THE "PEAK OIL" HYPOTHESIS

The idea that natural resources are in fixed supply and that as a result their prices must rise in the long run as reserves begin to run low is much older than Hotelling. It goes back to Thomas Malthus and the genesis of fears of environmental scarcity (albeit without interest rates necessarily playing a role).[9] Demand grows with population, and supply is fixed; what could be clearer in economics than the prediction that price will rise?[10]

The complication is that supply is not fixed. True, at any point in time there is a certain stock of oil reserves that have been discovered. But the historical pattern has long been that as the stock is depleted, new reserves are found. When the price goes up, it makes exploration and development profitable for deposits that are farther underground, underwater, or in other hard-to-reach locations. This is especially true as new technologies are developed for exploration and extraction.

During the two centuries since Malthus, or the seventy years since Hotelling, exploration and new technologies have increased the supply of oil and other natural resources at a pace that has roughly counteracted the increase in demand from growth in population and incomes.[11]

Just because supply has always increased in the past does not necessarily mean that it will always do so in the future. In 1956, oil engineer Marion King Hubbert predicted that the flow supply of oil within the United States would peak in the late 1960s and then start to decline permanently. The prediction was based on a model in which the fraction of the country's reserves that has been discovered rises through time, and data on the rates of discovery versus consumption are used to estimate the parameters in the model. Unlike myriad other pessimistic forecasts, this one came true on schedule and earned subsequent fame for its author.

The planet Earth is a much larger place than the United States, but it too is finite. A number of analysts have extrapolated Hubbert's words and modeling approach to claim that the same pattern will follow for extraction of the *world*'s oil reserves. Specifically, some of them claim the 2000 to 2011 run-up in oil prices confirmed a predicted global "Hubbert's Peak."[12] It remains to be seen whether we are currently witnessing a peak in world oil production, notwithstanding that forecasts of such peaks have proven erroneous in the past.

Evidence

STATISTICAL TIME SERIES STUDIES

With strong theoretical arguments on both sides, one must say that the question whether the long-term trend in commodity prices is upward or downard is an empirical one. Although specifics will vary depending on individual measures, it is possible to generalize somewhat across commodity prices.[13] Terms of trade for commodity producers had a slight upward trend from 1870 to World War I, a downward trend in the interwar period, an upward trend in the 1970s, a downward trend in the 1980s and 1990s, and an upward trend in the first decade of the twenty-first century.

What is the overall statistical trend in the long run? Some authors find a slight upward trend, some a slight downward trend.[14] The answer seems to depend, more than anything else, on the end date of the sample. Studies written after the commodity price increases of the 1970s found an upward trend, but those written after the 1980s found a downward trend, even when both kinds of studies went back to the early twentieth century. No doubt, when studies using data through 2011 are completed, some will again find a positive long-run trend. This phenomenon is less surprising than it sounds. When a real price undergoes large twenty-year cycles around a trend,[15] estimates of the long-term trend are very sensitive to the precise time period studied.[16]

THE WAGER OF PAUL EHRLICH AND JULIAN SIMON

Paul Ehrlich is a biologist who is highly respected among scientists but has a history of sensationalist doomsday predictions regarding population, the environment, and resource scarcity. Julian Simon was a libertarian economist frustrated by the failure of the public to hold Malthusians such as Ehrlich accountable for the poor track record of their predictions. In 1980, Simon publicly bet Ehrlich $1,000 that the prices of five minerals would decline between then and 1990. (Simon let Ehrlich choose the ten-year span and the list of minerals: copper, tin, nickel, chromium, and tungsten.)

Ehrlich's logic was Malthusian: because supplies were fixed while growth of populations and economies would raise demand, the resulting scarcity would continue to drive up prices. He, like most observers, was undoubtedly mentally extrapolating into the indefinite future what had been a strong upward movement in commodity prices during the preceding decade.

Simon's logic, on the other hand, is called cornucopian. Yes, the future would repeat the past. The relevant pattern from the past was not the ten-year trend, however, but rather a century of cycles: resource scarcity does indeed drive up prices, whereupon supply, demand, and (especially) technology respond with a lag, which drives the prices back down. Simon was precisely right. He won the bet handily. Not only did the real price of the basket of five minerals decline over the subsequent ten years, but also every one of the five real prices declined. Simon was also, almost certainly, right about the reasons: in response to the high prices of 1980, new technologies came into use, buyers economized, and new producers entered the market.

The Ehrlich-versus-Simon bet carries fascinating implications, for Malthusians versus cornucopians, environmentalists versus economists, extrapolationists versus contrarians, and futurologists versus historians. For present purposes, the main important point is slightly more limited. Simple extrapolation of medium-term trends is foolish. One must take a longer-term perspective. The review of the statistical literature in the preceding subsection illustrated the importance of examining as long a statistical time series as possible.

However, one should seek to avoid falling prey to *either* of two reductionist arguments at the philosophical poles of Malthusianism and cornucopianism. On one hand, the fact that the supply of minerals in the earth's crust is finite does not in itself justify the apocalyptic conclusion that we must necessarily run out. As Sheik Ahmed Zaki Yamani, the former Saudi oil minister, famously said, "The Stone Age came to an end not for a lack of stones, and the oil age will end, but not for a lack of oil." Malthusians do not pay enough attention to the tendency for technological progress to ride to the rescue. On the other hand, the fact that the Malthusian forecast has repeatedly been proven false in the past does not in itself imply the Panglossian forecast that this will always happen in the future. Rather, one must seek a broad perspective in which all relevant reasoning and evidence are brought to bear in the balance.

Medium-Term Volatility of Commodity Prices

Of course, the price of oil does not follow a smooth path, whether upward or downward. Rather, it experiences large short- and medium-term swings around a longer-term average. The world market prices for oil and natural gas are more volatile than those for almost any other mineral and agricultural commodities. (Copper and coffee are two major runners-up.) Most other mineral and agricultural commodity prices are also far more volatile than prices of most manufactured products or services.

Some have suggested that it is precisely the volatility of natural resource prices, rather than their long-term trends, that is bad for economic growth.[17]

Low Short-Run Elasticities

It is not hard to understand why the market price of oil is volatile in the short run or even the medium run. Because elasticities of supply and demand with respect to price are low, relatively small fluctuations in demand (due to weather, for example) or in supply (due to disruptions, for example) require a large change in price to re-equilibrate supply and demand. Demand elasticities are low in the short run largely because the capital stock at any point in time is designed physically to operate with a particular ratio of energy to output. Supply elasticities are also often low in the short run because it takes time to adjust output. Inventories can cushion the short-run impact of fluctuations, but they are limited in size. Some scope exists to substitute across different fuels, even in the short run. But this just means that the prices of oil, natural gas, and other fuels tend to experience their big medium-term swings together.

In the longer run, elasticities are far higher, both on the demand side and the supply side. This dynamic was clearly at work in the oil price shocks of the 1970s—the quadrupling of prices after the Arab oil embargo of 1973 and the doubling of prices after the Iranian revolution of 1979—which elicited relatively little consumer conservation or new supply sources in the short run but a lot of both after a few years had passed. People started insulating their houses and driving more fuel-efficient cars, and oil deposits were discovered and developed in new countries. This is a major reason why the real price of oil came back down in the 1980s and 1990s.

In the medium term, oil may be subject to a "cobweb cycle" due to the lags in response. Under this scenario, if the initial market equilibrium is a high price, the high price reduces demand after some years, which in turn leads to a new low price, which raises demand with a lag, which pushes the price back up again, and so on. In theory, if people have rational expectations, they should look ahead to the next price cycle before making long-term investments in housing or drilling. But the complete sequence of boom-bust-boom during the past thirty-five years looks suspiciously like a cobweb cycle nonetheless.

Is Volatility per se Detrimental to Economic Performance?

Gamblers aside, most people would rather have less economic volatility than more. But is variability necessarily harmful for long-run growth? Some studies and historical examples suggest that high volatility can accompany the rapid growth phase of a country's development (the United States before World War I).

Cyclical shifts of factors of production (labor, capital, and land) back and forth across sectors—mineral, agricultural, manufacturing, and services—may incur needless transaction costs. Frictional unemployment of labor, incomplete utilization of the capital stock, and incomplete occupancy of housing are true deadweight costs, even if they are temporary. Government policy-makers may not be better than individual economic agents at discerning whether a boom in the price for an export commodity is temporary or permanent. But the government cannot completely ignore the issue of volatility with the logic that the private market can deal with it. When it comes to exchange rate policy or fiscal policy, governments must necessarily make judgments about the likely permanence of shocks. Moreover, because commodities are inherently risky, a diversified country may indeed be better off than one that specializes in oil or a few other commodities, all other things being equal. However, the private sector dislikes risk as much as the government does and will take steps to mitigate it; thus, one must think where the market failure lies before assuming that a policy of deliberate diversification is necessarily justified.

Later parts of this chapter will consider the implications of the medium-term boom-bust cycle further, under the heading "Dutch Disease and Procyclicality" and will consider how to deal with short-term volatility further, under the heading "Institutions and Policies to Address the Natural Resource Curse."

More Possible Channels for the Natural Resource Curse

The natural resource curse is not confined to individual anecdotes or case studies but has been borne out in some statistical tests of the determinants of economic performance across a comprehensive sample of countries. Jeffrey Sachs and Andrew Warner (1995) kicked off the econometric literature and found that economic dependence on oil and minerals is correlated with slow economic growth, controlling for other structural attributes of the country. Sachs and Warner (2001) then summarized and extended previous research to show evidence that countries with great natural resource wealth tend to grow more slowly than resource-poor countries.[18] They say their result is not easily explained by other variables or by alternative ways to measure resource abundance. Their paper claims that there is little direct evidence that omitted geographical or climate variables explain the curse or that there is a bias in their estimates resulting from some other unobserved growth deterrent. Many other studies find a negative effect of oil in particular on economic performance.[19]

The result is by no means universal, especially when one generalizes beyond oil. Norway is conspicuous as an oil producer that is at the top of the international league tables for governance and economic performance.[20] As many have pointed out, Botswana and the Congo are both abundant in diamonds, yet Botswana is the best performer in continental Africa in terms of democracy, stability, and rapid growth of income[21] while the Congo is among the very worst.[22]

Among the statistical studies, Jacques Delacroix, Graham Davis, and Michael Herb all find no evidence of the natural resource curse.[23] Most recently, Michael Alexeev and Robert Conrad find that oil wealth and mineral wealth have *positive* effects on income per capita when controlling for a number of variables, particularly dummy variables for East Asia and Latin America.[24] In some cases, especially if the data do not go back to a time before oil was discovered, the reason different studies come to different results is that oil wealth may raise the *level* of per capita income while reducing or failing to raise the *growth rate* of income (or the end-of-sample level of income, if the equation conditions on initial income).[25]

In some cases, the crucial difference is whether "natural resource intensity" is measured by true endowments ("natural resource wealth") or by exports ("natural resource dependence"). The skeptics argue, in several different ways, that commodity exports are highly endogenous.[26]

On one hand, basic trade theory readily predicts that a country may show a high mineral share in exports, not necessarily because it has a higher endowment of minerals than other countries (*absolute* advantage) but because it does not have the ability to export manufactures (*comparative* advantage). This is important because it offers an explanation for negative statistical correlations between mineral exports and economic development, an explanation that would invalidate the common inference that minerals cause low growth.

On the other hand, the skeptics also have plenty of examples in which successful institutions and industrialization went hand in hand with rapid development of mineral resources. Economic historians have long noted that coal deposits and access to iron ore deposits (two key inputs into steel production) were geographic blessings that helped start the industrial revolutions in England, the vicinity of the lower Rhine, and the American Great Lakes region. Subsequent cases of countries that were able to develop their resource endowments efficiently as part of strong economy-wide growth include: the United States during its prewar industrialization period,[27] Venezuela from the 1920s to the 1970s, Australia since the 1960s, Norway since its oil discoveries of 1969, Chile since its adoption of a new mining code in 1983, Peru since its privatization program in 1992, and Brazil since it lifted restrictions on foreign mining participation in 1995.[28] Examples of countries that were equally well endowed geologically but failed to develop their natural resources efficiently include Chile and Australia before World War I and Venezuela since the 1980s.[29]

It is not that countries with oil wealth will necessarily achieve worse performance than those without. Few would advise a country with oil or other natural resources that it would be better off destroying them or refraining from developing them. Oil-rich countries can succeed. The question is how to make best use of the resource. The goal is to achieve the prosperous record of a Norway rather than the disappointments of a Nigeria. The same point applies to other precious minerals: the goal is to be a Botswana rather than a Bolivia, a Chile rather than a Congo.

Let us return to a consideration of various channels whereby oil wealth could lead to poor performance. Based on the statistical evidence, we have already largely rejected the hypothesis of a long-term negative trend in world prices while accepting the hypothesis of high volatility. But we have yet to spell out exactly how high price volatility might lead to slower economic growth. In addition, we have yet to consider the hypotheses according to which oil wealth leads to weak institutions—including in countries experiencing

military conflict and authoritarianism—that might in turn lead to poor economic performance.

Is Commodity Specialization per se Detrimental to Growth?

What are the possible negative externalities to specialization in natural resources, beyond volatility? What are the positive externalities to diversification into manufacturing?

Outside of classical economics, diversification out of primary commodities into manufacturing in most circles is considered self-evidently desirable. Several false arguments have been made for it. One is the Prebisch-Singer
hypothesis of secularly declining commodity prices, which we judged to
lack merit in Part I of this chapter. Another is the mistaken "cargo cult" inference that is based on the observation that advanced countries have heavy
industries such as steel mills and concludes that these visible monuments
must therefore be the route to economic development. But one should not
dismiss more valid considerations just because less valid arguments for diversification into manufacturing are sometimes made.

Is industrialization the sine qua non of economic development? Is encouragement of manufacturing necessary to achieve high income? Classical
economic theory says no; it is best for countries to produce whatever is their
comparative advantage, whether that is natural resources or manufacturing.
In this nineteenth-century view, attempts by Brazil to industrialize were as
foolish as it would have been for Great Britain to try to grow coffee and or-
anges in hothouses. But the "structuralists" mentioned early in this chapter
were never alone in their feeling that countries only get sustainably rich if
they industrialize (oil-rich sheikdoms notwithstanding). Nor were they ever
alone in feeling that industrialization in turn requires an extra push from
the government at least for latecomers, often known as industrial policy.

Kiminori Matsuyama provided an influential model formalizing this intuition: the manufacturing sector is assumed to be characterized by "learning by doing," yet the primary sector (agriculture, in his paper) is not.[30] This
is the channel through which the resource curse works in Sachs and Warner
(1995). The implication is that deliberate policy-induced diversification out
of primary products into manufacturing is justified and that a permanent
commodity boom that crowds out manufacturing can indeed be harmful.[31]

On the other side, it must be pointed out that there is no reason why "learning by doing" should be the exclusive preserve of manufacturing tradeables. Nontradeables can enjoy learning by doing.[32] Mineral and agricultural sectors can as well. Some countries have experienced tremendous productivity growth in the oil, mineral, and agricultural sectors. Since the late nineteenth century, American productivity gains have been aided by American public investment in such institutions of knowledge infrastructure as the U.S. Geological Survey, the Columbia School of Mines, the Agricultural Extension program, and land grant colleges. Although well-functioning governments can play a useful role in supplying these public goods for the natural resource sector, this is different than mandating government ownership of the resources themselves. In Latin America, for example, public monopoly ownership and prohibition on importing foreign expertise or capital has often stunted development of the mineral sector, whereas privatization has set it free.[33] Moreover, attempts by governments to force linkages between the mineral sector and processing industries have not always worked.[34]

Institutions

INSTITUTIONS AND DEVELOPMENT

A prominent trend in thinking regarding economic development is that the quality of institutions is the deep fundamental factor that determines which countries experience good performance and which do not[35] and that it is futile to recommend good macroeconomic or microeconomic policies if the institutional structure is not there to support them. Dani Rodrik, Arvind Subramanian, and Franceso Trebbi use as their measure of institutional quality an indicator of the rule of law and protection of property rights (taken from Daniel Kaufmann, Aart Kraay, and Pablo Zoido-Lobaton).[36] Daron Acemoglu, Simon Johnson, and James Robinson use a measure of expropriation risk to investors.[37] Acemoglu, Johnson, Robinson, and Yunyong Thaicharoen measure the quality of a country's "cluster of institutions" by the extent of constraints on the executive.[38] The theory is that weak institutions lead to inequality, intermittent dictatorship, and lack of constraints to prevent elites and politicians from plundering the country.

Institutions can be endogenous—the *result* of economic growth rather than the cause. (The same problem is encountered with other proposed fundamental determinants of growth, such as openness to trade and freedom from tropical diseases.) Many institutions, such as the structure of financial markets, mechanisms of income redistribution, social safety nets, tax systems, and intellectual property rules, tend to evolve *endogenously* in response to the level of income.

Econometricians address the problem of endogeneity by means of the technique of instrumental variables. What is a good instrumental variable for institutions, an exogenous determinant? Acemoglu, Johnson, and Robinson introduced the mortality rates of colonial settlers.[39] The theory is that out of all the lands that Europeans colonized, only those where Europeans actually settled were given good European institutions. These scholars chose their instrument on the reasoning that initial settler mortality rates determined whether Europeans subsequently settled in large numbers.[40] One can help justify this otherwise idiosyncratic-sounding instrumental variable by pointing out that there need not be a strong correlation between the diseases that killed settlers and the diseases that afflict natives, and that both are independent of the countries' geographic suitability for trade. The conclusion of Rodrik's study is that institutions trump everything else; the effects of both tropical geography and trade dim in the blinding light of institutions.

This is essentially the same result found by Acemoglu, Johnson, and Robinson; William Easterly and Ross Levine; and Robert Hall and Chad Jones: institutions drive out the effect of policies, and geography matters primarily as a determinant of institutions.[41] Clearly, institutions are important, whether the effect is merely one of several important deep factors or whether, as these papers seem to claim, it is the only important deep factor.

OIL, INSTITUTIONS, AND GOVERNANCE

Of the various possible channels through which natural resources could be a curse to long-run development, the quality of institutions and governance is perhaps the most widely hypothesized. Roland Hodler and Francesco Caselli are among those finding a natural resource curse via internal struggle for ownership.[42] Carlos Leite and Jens Weidmann find that natural resource dependence has a substantial statistical effect on measures of corruption in particular.[43] Elissaios Papyrakis and Rever Gerlach estimate effects via corruption but also via investment and other channels.[44] Others find a negative effect via inequality.[45] Gylfason reviews a number of possible channels that could explain natural resource dependence, as measured by labor allocation, that leads to worse average performance.[46]

It is not necessarily obvious, a priori, that endowments of commodities should lead to inequality or authoritarianism or bad institutions generally. Macartan Humphreys, Jeffrey Sachs, and Joseph Stiglitz point out that a government wishing to reduce inequality should in theory have an easier time of it in a country where much wealth comes from a nonrenewable resource in fixed supply because taxing it runs less risk of eliciting a fall in output.[47] This is in comparison to the more elastic supplies of manufactures and other goods or services, including agricultural goods, produced with a higher labor component. But the usual interpretation is that most governments in resource-rich countries have historically not been interested in promoting equality.

The "rent cycling theory" as enunciated by Richard Auty holds that economic growth requires recycling rents via markets rather than via patronage.[48] In high-rent countries, the natural resource elicits a political contest to capture ownership, but in low-rent countries the government must motivate people to create wealth, for example, by pursuing comparative advantage, promoting equality, and fostering civil society.

This theory is related to the explanation that economic historians Stanley Engerman and Kenneth Sokoloff make as to why industrialization first took place in North America and not Latin America (and in the U.S. Northeast rather than the South).[49] Lands endowed with extractive industries and plantation crops (mining, sugar, and cotton) developed institutions of slavery, inequality, dictatorship, and state control, whereas those climates suited to fishing and small farms (fruits, vegetables, grain, and livestock) developed institutions based on individualism, democracy, egalitarianism, and capitalism. When the industrial revolution came along, the latter areas were well suited to make the most of it. Those that had specialized in extractive industries were not, because society had come to depend on class structure and authoritarianism rather than on individual incentive and decentralized decision making. The theory is thought to fit Middle Eastern oil exporters especially well.[50]

Jonathan Isham and his coauthors find that the commodities that are damaging to institutional development, which they call "point-source" resources, are: oil, minerals, plantation crops, coffee, and cocoa (versus the same small-scale farm products identified by Engerman and Sokoloff).[51] Other authors find that the point-source resources which undermine institutional quality and thereby growth include oil and some particular minerals, but not agricultural resources.[52] Halvor Mehlum, Karl Moene, and Ragnar Torvik observe the distinction by designating them "lootable" resources.[53] Rabah Arezki and Markus Brückner find that oil rents worsen corruption.[54]

Some have questioned the assumption that oil discoveries are exogenous and institutions endogenous. In other words, they posit that oil wealth is not necessarily the cause and institutions the effect; rather, it is the other way around. Catherine Norman points out that the discovery and development of oil is not purely exogenous but rather is endogenous with respect to, among other things, the efficiency of the economy.[55] But many authors have argued that the important question is whether the country already has good institutions at the time that oil is discovered, in which case it is more likely to be put to use for the national welfare instead of the welfare of an elite.[56] Alexeev and Conrad find no evidence that oil or mineral wealth interacts positively with institutional quality.[57] But Rabah Arezki and Frederick Van der Ploeg use instrumental variables to control for the endogeneity of institutional quality and trade; they confirm that the adverse effect of natural resources on growth is associated with exogenously weak institutions and, especially, that it is associated with exogenously low levels of trade.[58] Pauline Jones Luong and Erika Weinthal, in a study of five former Soviet republics that have oil and similar initial conditions, conclude that the choice of ownership structure makes the difference as to whether oil turns out to be a blessing rather than a curse.[59] ·

Unsustainability and Anarchy

Two hundred years ago, much of the island of Nauru in the South Pacific consisted of phosphate deposits derived from guano. The substance is valuable in the fertilizer industry. As a result of highly profitable phosphate exports, Nauru in the late 1960s and early 1970s showed up globally with the highest income per capita of any country. Eventually, however, the deposits gave out. Not enough of the proceeds had been saved, let alone well invested, during the period of abundance. Today, the money is gone, and so is the tropical paradise: the residents are left with little more than an environmentally precarious rim of land circling a wasteland where the phosphates used to be.

What happens when a depletable natural resources is indeed depleted? This question is not only of concern to environmentalists. It is also one motivation for the strategy of diversifying the economy beyond natural resources into other sectors. The question is also a motivation for the "Hartwick Rule," which says that all rents from exhaustible natural resources should be invested in reproducible capital so that future generations do not suffer a diminution in total wealth (natural resource plus reproducible capital) and therefore in the flow of consumption.[60]

Sometimes, as in the Nauru example, it is the government that has control of the natural resource, and excessive depletion is another instance of a failure in governance. Robinson, Torvik, and Verdier (2006) show that politicians tend to extract at a rate in excess of the efficient path because they discount the future too much. They discount the future because they are more intent on surviving the next election or coup attempt.

Privatization would be a possible answer to the problem of excessive depletion, if a full assignment of property rights were possible, thereby giving the private sector owners adequate incentive to conserve the resource in question. But often this is not possible, either physically or politically. The difficulty in enforcing property rights over some nonrenewable resources creates a category of natural resource curse of its own.

UNENFORCEABLE PROPERTY RIGHTS OVER DEPLETABLE RESOURCES

Although one theory holds that the physical possession of point-source mineral wealth undermines the motivation for the government to establish a broad-based regime of property rights for the rest of the economy, another theory holds that some natural resources do not lend themselves to property rights whether the government wants to apply them or not. Overfishing, overgrazing, and overuse of water are classic examples of the so-called "tragedy of the commons" that applies to "open access" resources. Individual fishermen, ranchers, or farmers have no incentive to restrain themselves, even while the fisheries, pastureland, or water aquifers are being collectively depleted. The difficulty in imposing property rights is particularly severe when the resource is dispersed over a wide area, such as timberland. But even the classic point-source resource, oil, can suffer from this problem, especially when wells drilled from different plots of land hit the same underground deposit.

This unenforceability of property rights is the market failure that can invalidate some of the standard neoclassical economic theorems in the case of open access resources. One obvious implication of unenforceability is that the resource will be depleted more rapidly than the optimization of the Hotelling calculation calls for.[61] The benefits of free trade are another possible casualty: the country might be better off without the ability to export the resource, if doing so exacerbates the excess rate of exploitation.[62]

Common pool resources are (i) subtractable (as are private goods). At the same time, (ii) it is costly to exclude users from consuming them (as with public goods). Yet (iii) it is not impossible to exclude users from them.[63] Elinor Ostrom investigates ways that societies have dealt with water systems and other such common pool resources, institutions that lie between pure individual property rights and government management.[64]

Enforcement of property rights is all the more difficult in a frontier situation. The phrase "Wild West" captures the American experience, including legendary claim-jumping in the gold or silver rushes of the late nineteenth and early twentieth centuries. Typically, only when a large enough number of incumbents have enough value at stake are the transactions costs of establishing a system of property rights overcome.[65] Frontier rushes went on in many other parts of the world during this period as well.[66] Today, anarchic conditions can apply in the tropical forest frontiers of the Amazon Basin, Borneo, or the Congo.[67] Edward Barbier argues that frontier exploitation of natural resources can lead to unsustainable development characterized by a boom-bust cycle as well as permanently lower levels of income in the long term.[68]

DO MINERAL RICHES LEAD TO WARS?

Domestic conflict, especially when violent, is certainly bad for economic development. Factions are more likely to fight over a valuable resource such as oil or diamonds when it is there for the taking, rather than when production requires substantial inputs of labor and capital investment. James Fearon and David Laitin, Paul Collier, and Macartan Humphreys all find that economic dependence on oil and mineral wealth is correlated with civil war.[69] Chronic conflict in oil-rich countries such as Angola and Sudan comes to mind. Civil war is, in turn, very bad for economic development.

The conclusion is not unanimous: Christa Brunnschweiler and Erwin Bulte argue that the conventional measure of resource dependence is endogenous with respect to conflict and that instrumenting for dependence eliminates its significance in conflict regressions.[70] They find conflict increases dependence on resource extraction, rather than the other way around.

Oil and Democracy

Hussein Mahdavy was apparently the first to suggest—followed by Giacomo Luciani, Dirk Vandewalle, and many others—that Middle Eastern governments' access to rents, in the form of oil revenue, may have freed them from the need to tax their peoples and that this in turn freed them from the need for democracy. The need for tax revenue is believed to require democracy under the theory "no taxation without representation."[71]

Statistical studies across large cross-sections of countries followed. Michael Ross finds that economic dependence on oil and mineral wealth is correlated with authoritarian government.[72] So do others.[73] Some find that authoritarian regimes have lasted longer in countries with oil wealth.[74]

But Terry Karl points out that Venezuela had already been authoritarian when oil was developed and in fact transitioned to democracy at the height of its oil wealth.[75] None of the Central Asian states are democracies, even though Kazakhstan is the only one of them with major oil production. Inspired by such observations Stephen Haber and Victor Menaldo look at historical time series data for a link to democracy from the share of oil or minerals in the economy; they fail to find the statistically significant evidence that is typical of cross-section and panel studies.[76] Similarly, Marcus Noland finds that oil rents are not a robust factor behind lack of democracy in Middle Eastern countries.[77] When Thad Dunning introduces fixed effects to take into account country-specific differences within Latin America, he finds that the negative correlation between oil profits and democracy reverses.[78] Romain Wacziarg, too, finds no effect of oil prices on democracy.[79]

The question of whether oil dependence tends to retard democracy should probably not be regarded as a component of the causal relation between oil and economic performance. Some correlates of democracy—rule of law, political stability, openness to international trade, and initial equality of economic endowments and opportunities—do tend to be good for economic growth. But each of these other variables can also exist without democracy. Examples include predemocratic Asian economies such as Korea or Taiwan. Some believe that Lee Kwan Yew in Singapore and Augusto Pinochet in Chile could not have achieved their economic reforms without authoritarian powers (though the former was far more moderate and benevolent than the latter). On a bigger scale, it is said that China has grown so much faster than Russia since 1990 because Deng Xiaopeng chose to pursue economic reform before political reform while Mikhail Gorbachev did it the other way around.

The statistical evidence is at best mixed as to whether democracy per se is good for economic performance. Robert Barro finds that it is the rule of law, free markets, education, and small government consumption that are good for growth, not democracy per se.[80] Jose Tavares and Romain Wacziarg find that it is education, not democracy per se.[81] Alberto Alesina and his coauthors find that it is political stability.[82] Some scholars even find that, after controlling for important factors such as the rule of law and political stability, democracy has if anything a weak negative effect on economic growth. One *can* claim good evidence for the *reverse* causation—that economic growth leads to democracy, often assisted by the creation of a middle class—much more reliably than the other way around.[83] Examples include Korea and Taiwan.

Of course democracy is normally regarded as an end in itself, aside from whether it promotes economic growth. Even here, one must note that the benefits of the formalities of elections can be overemphasized. For one thing, elections can be a sham. Western-style or one-man, one-vote elections should probably receive less priority in developing countries than the fundamental principles of rule of law, human rights, freedom of expression, economic freedom, minority rights, and some form of popular representation.[84]

Dutch Disease and Procyclicality

The Macroeconomics of Dutch Disease

Dutch disease refers to some possibly unpleasant side effects of a boom in oil or other mineral and agricultural commodities.[85] The phenomenon arises when a strong, but perhaps temporary, upward swing in the world price of an export commodity causes:

- large real appreciation in the local currency (taking the form of nominal currency appreciation if the country has a floating exchange rate or the form of money inflows and inflation if the country has a fixed exchange rate[86]);
- an increase in spending (especially by the government, which increases spending in response to the increased availability of tax receipts or royalties—discussed below);
- an increase in the price of nontraded goods (goods and services such as housing that are not internationally traded) relative to traded goods (manufactures and other internationally traded goods other than the export commodity);

- resultant shift of labor and land out of non-export-commodity traded goods (pulled by the more attractive returns in the export commodity and in nontraded goods and services); and
- a possible current account deficit (thereby incurring international debt that may be difficult to service when the commodity boom ends).[87]

When the crowded-out, noncommodity tradable goods are in the manufacturing sector, the feared effect is deindustrialization. In a real-trade model, the reallocation of resources across tradable sectors—for example, from manufactures to oil—may be inevitable regardless of macroeconomics. But the movement into nontraded goods is macroeconomic in origin.

What makes Dutch disease a "disease"? One interpretation, particularly relevant if the complete cycle is not adequately foreseen, is that the process is all painfully reversed when the world price of the export commodity goes back down. A second interpretation is that, even if the perceived longevity of the increase in world price turns out to be accurate, the crowding out of non-commodity exports is undesirable, perhaps because the manufacturing sector is the locus of learning by doing.[88] The latter view is just another instance of the natural resource curse; it has nothing to do with cyclical fluctuations per se.

Dutch disease can arise from sources other than a rise in the commodity price. Other examples arise from commodity booms due to the discovery of new deposits or some other expansion in supply leading to a trade surplus via exports or to a capital account surplus via inward investment to develop the new resource. In addition, the term is also used by analogy for other sorts of inflows such as the receipt of transfers (foreign aid or remittances) or a stabilization-induced capital inflow. In all cases, the result is real appreciation and a shift into nontradeables and away from (nonbooming) tradeables. Again, the real appreciation takes the form of a nominal appreciation if the exchange rate is flexible or inflation if the exchange rate is fixed.

Procyclicality

Volatility in developing countries arises both from foreign shocks, such as the fluctuations in the price of the export commodity discussed above, and from domestic macroeconomic and political instability. Although most developing countries in the 1990s managed to control the chronic runaway budget deficits, money creation, and inflation that they had experienced in the preceding two decades, many are still subject to monetary and fiscal policy that is procyclical rather than countercyclical: they tend to be expansionary in booms and contractionary in recessions, thereby exacerbating the magnitudes of the swings. Ideally the aim should be to moderate them—to foster the countercyclical pattern, which the models and textbooks of the decades following the Great Depression originally hoped discretionary policy would accomplish. At a minimum, macroeconomic policy should not be procyclical. Often populist political economy underlies the observed procyclicality.

The fact that developing countries tend to experience larger cyclical fluctuations than industrialized countries do is only partly attributable to commodities. It is also in part due to the role of factors that "should" moderate the cycle but in practice seldom operate that way: procyclical capital flows, procyclical monetary and fiscal policy, and the related Dutch disease. If anything, they tend to exacerbate booms and busts instead of moderating them. The hope that improved policies or institutions might reduce this procyclicality makes this one of the most potentially fruitful avenues of research in emerging market macroeconomics.

The Procyclicality of Capital Flows to Developing Countries

According to the theory of intertemporal optimization, countries should borrow during temporary downturns to sustain consumption and investment and should repay or accumulate net foreign assets during temporary upturns. In practice, it does not always work this way. Capital flows are more often procyclical than countercyclical.[89] Most theories to explain this phenomenon involve imperfections in capital markets, such as asymmetric information or the need for collateral.

As developing countries evolve more market-oriented financial systems, the capital inflows during the boom phase show up increasingly in prices for land and buildings and in prices of financial assets. Prices of equities and bonds (or the reciprocal, the interest rate) reflect the extent of speculative enthusiasm, sometimes useful for predicting which countries are vulnerable to crises in the future.

In the commodity and emerging market boom of 2003–2011, net capital flows typically went to countries with current account surpluses, especially Asian countries and commodity producers in the Middle East and Latin America, where they showed up in record accumulation of foreign exchange reserves. This was in contrast to the two previous cycles, 1975–81 and 1990–97, when the capital flows into developing countries largely went to finance current account deficits.

One interpretation of procyclical capital flows is that they result from procyclical fiscal policy: when governments increase spending in booms, some of the deficit is financed by borrowing from abroad. When these governments are forced to cut spending in downturns, it is to repay some of the excessive debt that they incurred during the upturn. Another interpretation of procyclical capital flows to developing countries is that they pertain especially to exporters of agricultural and mineral commodities. We will consider procyclical fiscal policy in the next subsection and return to the commodity cycle (Dutch disease) in the one after.

The Procyclicality of Fiscal Policy

Many authors have documented that fiscal policy tends to be procyclical in developing countries, especially in comparison with industrialized countries.[90] Most studies look at the procyclicality of government spending, because tax receipts are particularly endogenous with respect to the business cycle. An important cause of procyclical spending is precisely that government receipts from taxes or royalties rise in booms and the government cannot resist the temptation or political pressure to increase spending proportionately, or more than proportionately.

Procyclicality is especially pronounced in countries that possess natural resources and in which income from those resources tends to dominate the business cycle. Commodity booms are found to be correlated with spending booms.[91]

Two large budget items that account for much of the increased spending from commodity booms are investment projects and government salaries. Regarding the first budget item, investment in infrastructure can have a large long-term payoff if it is well designed. In practice, however, it too often takes the form of white elephant projects, which are stranded without funds for completion or maintenance when the commodity price goes back down.[92]

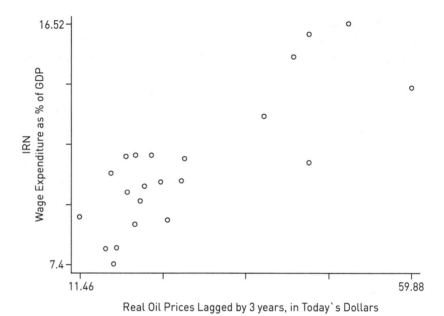

Figure 1.2 Iran's government wage bill is influenced by oil prices during the preceding three years (1974, 1977–1997).

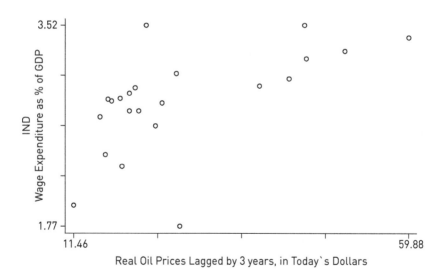

Figure 1.3 Indonesia's government wage bill is influenced by oil prices during the preceding three years (1974, 1977–1997).

Regarding the second budget item, Paolo Medas and Daria Zakharova point out that oil windfalls have often been spent on higher public sector wages.[93] They can also go to increasing the number of workers employed by the government. Either way, they raise the total public sector wage bill, which is hard to reverse when oil prices go back down. Figures 1.2 and 1.3 plot the public sector wage bill for two oil producers, Iran and Indonesia, against oil prices over the preceding three years. There is a clear positive relationship. That the relationship is strong with a three-year lag illustrates the problem: primary product prices may have fallen over three years, but it is not easy to cut public sector wages or lay off workers.[94]

Institutions and Policies to Address the Natural Resource Curse

A variety of measures have been tried to cope with the commodity cycle.[95] Some work better than others.

Institutions That Were Supposed to Stabilize but Have Not

A number of institutions have been implemented in the name of reducing the impact of volatility in world commodity markets on producer countries. Most have failed to do so, and many have had detrimental effects.

MARKETING BOARDS

Marketing boards were implemented around the time of independence in some East and West African countries. They required all sales of cocoa and coffee to pass through a government agency. The original justification was to stabilize the price to domestic producers and symmetrically set a price above world prices when the latter were low and a domestic price below world prices when the latter were high. That in turn would have required symmetrically adding to government stockpiles when world prices were low and running them down when world prices were high.

In practice, the price paid to cocoa and coffee farmers, who were politically weak, was always below the world price in the early decades of the marketing boards. The rationale eventually shifted from stabilization to taxation of the agricultural sector (which was thought to be inelastic in its supply behavior) and subsidization of the industrial sector. But industrialization did not happen. Rather, the coffee and cocoa sectors shrank. Commodity marketing boards were a failure.

TAXATION OF COMMODITY PRODUCTION

Some developing countries subject their mineral sectors to high levels of taxation and regulation, particularly where foreign companies are involved, which can discourage output. Of course, some taxation and regulation may be appropriate on environmental or safety grounds. One can understand, moreover, the desire to avoid past experiences where multinational companies were able to walk away with the lion's share of the profits. But when Bolivia, Mexico, and Venezuela, motivated by populist nationalism, explicitly prohibit or discourage foreign involvement in the development of their mineral resources, the danger is that they end up "killing the goose that lays the golden egg."

PRODUCER SUBSIDIES

More often in rich countries, the primary producing sector has political power on its side. Then stockpiles are used as a subsidy rather than a tax. An example is the Common Agricultural Policy in Europe. Subsidies also go to coal miners in Germany, oil companies with cheap leases on federal lands in the United States, and agricultural and energy sectors in many other countries.

GOVERNMENT STOCKPILES

Some governments maintain stockpiles under national security rationales, such as the U.S. Strategic Petroleum Reserve. One drawback is that decisions regarding the management of government stockpiles are made subject to political pressure, often failing to maximize the objective of insulating against the biggest shocks. Another drawback is that government stockpiles undermine the incentive for private citizens to hold inventories.

In some countries where the prices of fuel or food to consumers are a politically sensitive issue, the incentive for the private sector to maintain inventories is undercut in any case by the knowledge that in the event of a big increase in the price of the commodity, the inventory holder will probably not be allowed to reap the benefits. If this political economy structure is a given, then there is a valid argument for the government to do the stockpiling.

PRICE CONTROLS FOR CONSUMERS

In many developing countries, political forces seek to shield consumers from increases in basic food and energy prices through price controls. If the country is a producer of the crop or mineral in question, then the policy tool to insulate domestic consumers against increases in the world price may be export controls. (Examples include Argentina's wheat and India's rice in 2008, and Russia's wheat in 2010.) If the country is an importer of the crop or mineral in question, then either the commodity is rationed to domestic households or the excess demand at the below-market domestic price is made up by imports. Capped exports from the exporting countries and price controls in the importing countries both work to exacerbate the magnitude of the upswing of the price for the (artificially reduced) quantity that is still internationally traded. If the producing and consuming countries in the rice market could cooperatively agree to *refrain* from government intervention, volatility could be lower, rather than higher, even though intervention is rationalized in the name of reducing price volatility.

OPEC AND OTHER INTERNATIONAL CARTELS

In a world of multiple producers for a given commodity, efforts by producing countries to raise the price or reduce the volatility would logically require the cooperation of all or most of the producers. Each is strongly tempted to defect from the agreement and raise output to take advantage of the higher price. Most attempts at forming international cartels have failed within a few years.[96]

The institution that endures decade after decade is OPEC. It is not clear whether its attempts to raise the average price or reduce the variability of the international oil price have succeeded. Some of the most abrupt decreases and increases in the world oil price over the last half century have arguably been attributable to changes in OPEC's internal dynamics (increased collusion after the Arab Oil Embargo of 1973, followed by a breakdown in the 1980s when members stopped obeying their agreed-upon quotas). Meanwhile, many new oil producers have cropped up outside of OPEC, suggesting a diminution in its collective monopoly power even when the members act in unison.

Devices to Share Risks

It is probably best to accept that commodity prices will be volatile and to seek to establish institutions that will limit adverse effects that result from the volatility. In this section we will consider microeconomic policies to minimize exposure to risk, the sort of short-term volatility discussed earlier in the chapter. (We will shortly consider *macro*economic policies to minimize the costs of big medium-term swings of the sort associated with Dutch disease.)

Three devices for avoiding exposure to short-term volatility are promising. One is relevant for commodity exporters who sign contracts with foreign companies, another is relevant for producers who do their own selling, and a third for governments dependent on commodity revenues.

PRICE SETTING IN CONTRACTS WITH FOREIGN COMPANIES

Price setting in contracts between energy producers and foreign companies is often plagued by a problem that is known to theorists as "dynamic inconsistency."[97] A price is set by contract. Later the world price goes up, and then the government wants to renege. It does not want to give the company all the profits, and, in a sense, why should it? Certainly the political pressures are typically strong.

But this is a "repeated game." The risk that the locals will renege makes foreign companies reluctant to do business in the first place. It limits the amount of capital available to the country and probably raises the price of that capital. The process of renegotiation can have large transactions costs, such as interruptions in the export flow.

It has become such a familiar pattern that it seems more contracts ought to have been designed to be robust with respect to this inconsistency by making the terms explicitly dependent on future market conditions.[98] The simplest device would be indexed contracts in which the two parties agree ahead of time that "if the world price goes up 10 percent, then the gains are split between the company and the government" in some particular proportion. Indexation shares the risks of gains and losses, without the costs of renegotiation or the damage to a country's reputation from reneging on a contract.

HEDGING IN COMMODITY DERIVATIVES MARKETS

Producers, whether private or public, often sell their commodities on international spot markets. They are thus exposed to the risk that the dollar price of a given export quantity will rise or fall. In many cases, the producer can hedge the risk by selling that quantity on the forward or futures market.[99] As with indexation of the contract price, hedging means that there is no need for costly renegotiation in the event of large changes in the world price.

The adjustment happens automatically. One possible drawback, especially if it is a government ministry doing the hedging, is that the minister typically receives little credit for having saved the country from disaster when the world price plummets but will be excoriated for having sold out the national patrimony when the world price rises. Mexico has the best solution to this problem, a marriage of finance theory and political economy: it hedges by means of the options markets. Options allow the buyer to hedge the downside but retain the upside. The country is protected if the world price of oil falls, yet the finance minister is not put in a difficult position if the price of oil rises.

DENOMINATION OF DEBT IN TERMS OF COMMODITY PRICES

An excellent idea that has never managed to catch on is for a commodity-producing company or government to index its debt to the price of the commodity. Debt service obligations automatically rise and fall with the commodity price. This would save developing countries from the kinds of crises that Latin American countries faced in 1982 and Asian countries in 1997, when the dollar prices of their exports fell at the same time that the dollar interest rate on their debts went up. The result for many countries was an abrupt deterioration of their debt service ratios and a balance of payments crisis. This would not have happened if their debts had been indexed to their commodity prices—the oil price in the case of such borrowers as Ecuador, Indonesia, Iran, Mexico, Nigeria, and Russia. As with contract indexation and hedging, the adjustment in the event of fluctuations in the world price is automatic.

When officials in commodity-producing countries are asked why they have not tried indexing their bonds (or loans) to the price of their export commodity, the usual answer is that they believe there would not be enough demand from the market (or enough interest from banks). It is true that a market needs a certain level of liquidity in order to thrive and that it can be hard for a new financial innovation to get over the volume threshold. But it used to be said that foreigners would not buy bonds denominated in the currencies of emerging market countries.[100] Yet in recent years, more and more developing countries have found that they could borrow in their own currency if they tried. Investor receptivity to oil-denominated bonds is potentially larger. There are obvious natural ultimate customers for oil-linked bonds: electric utilities, airlines, and the other companies in industrialized countries who are as adversely affected by an increase in the world price of oil as the oil exporters are by a decrease. This is a market waiting to be born.

Monetary Policy

We will now move from ideas for institutions to address the risk created by short-term price volatility to ideas for macroeconomic management of medium-term swings. We will begin with monetary and exchange rate policy to manage Dutch disease.

FIXED VERSUS FLOATING EXCHANGE RATES

Fixed and floating exchange rates each have their advantages. The main advantages of a fixed exchange rate are, first, that it reduces the costs of international trade and finance and, second, that it is a nominal anchor for monetary policy that helps the central bank achieve low-inflation credibility. The main advantage of floating, for a commodity producer, is that it often provides automatic accommodation of terms of trade shocks. During a commodity boom, the currency tends to appreciate, thereby moderating what would otherwise be a danger of excessive inflows and overheating of the economy, and the reverse occurs during a commodity bust.

A reasonable balancing of these pros and cons, appropriate for many middle-size middle-income countries, is an intermediate exchange rate regime such as managed floating or a target zone (a band). In the booming decade that began in 2001, many countries followed the intermediate regime, in between a few commodity producers in the floating corner (Chile and Mexico) and a few in the firmly fixed corner (Gulf oil producers and Ecuador). Although these intermediate countries officially declared themselves as floating currency states (often as part of inflation targeting), in practice they intervened heavily, taking perhaps half the increase in demand for their currency in the form of appreciation but half in the form of increased foreign exchange reserves. Examples among commodity-producers include Kazakhstan, Peru, South Africa, and Russia.[101]

Particularly at the early stages of a commodity boom, when there is little idea whether it is permanent, there is a good case for intervention in the foreign exchange market—adding to reserves (especially if the alternative is abandoning an established successful exchange rate target) and perhaps for awhile attempting to sterilize the inflow of foreign currency to prevent rapid expansion in the money supply. In subsequent years, if the increase in world commodity prices looks to be long-lived, there is a stronger case for accommodating it through nominal and real appreciation of the local currency.

It is especially important in developing countries, where institutions tend to have lower credibility than in advanced countries, that the public's expectations of inflation be anchored by some nominal target by which the central bank asks to be judged. If the exchange rate is not to be that nominal target, then some other anchor variable should be chosen.

ALTERNATIVE NOMINAL ANCHORS

Three candidates for nominal anchor have had ardent supporters in the past but are no longer prominently in the running. They are: the price of gold, as under the nineteenth-century gold standard; the money supply (the choice of monetarists); and national income (the choice of many mainstream macroeconomists in the 1980s).

In recent years, central bankers and monetary economists alike have considered inflation targeting to be the preferred approach—or at least the preferred alternative to fixed exchange rates, which may be appropriate for very small, open countries. Although there are different interpretations of inflation targeting, some more flexible than others, they all tend to take the consumer price index (CPI) as the index to be targeted, and they tend to explicitly disavow the exchange rate, or domestic commodity prices or asset prices, as a target.[102]

Inflation targeting (IT) has a particular disadvantage for commodity producing countries: it is not robust with respect to changes in the terms of trade. Consider a fall in world market conditions for the export commodity, that is, a decrease in the dollar price. It has a negative impact on both the balance of payments and the level of economic activity. It would be desirable under these circumstances for monetary policy to loosen and the currency to depreciate to boost net foreign demand and thereby restore external and internal balance. But CPI targeting tells the central bank to keep monetary policy sufficiently tight so that the currency does not depreciate, because otherwise import prices will rise and push the CPI above its target. Conversely, if the world price for the export commodity goes *up*, a CPI target prevents a needed appreciation of the currency because it would lower import prices and push the CPI below its target.

I have in the past proposed for commodity producers a regime that I call "Peg the Export Price" (PEP). The proposal was that monetary policy be guided by the rule to keep the local currency price of the export commodity stable from day to day. For an oil exporter, every day that the dollar price of oil goes up 1 percent, monetary policy would allow the dollar price of the local currency to go up 1 percent, thereby keeping the local price of oil unchanged. The argument was that PEP combines the best of both worlds: it automatically accommodates terms of trade changes, as floating is supposed to do, while abiding by a preannounced nominal anchor, as IT is supposed to do.

Simulations show, for example, that if Indonesia and Russia had been on a PEP regime, they would have automatically experienced necessary depreciation in the late 1990s, when oil prices fell, without having to go through the painful currency crises that these two countries in fact experienced in 1998.[103] An additional selling point is that because PEP moderates swings in the real value of export revenue, expressed in terms of purchasing power over domestic goods and services, it would reduce the tendency for governments to increase spending excessively in boom times and symmetrically cut it in busts.

PEP in its pure form was a rather extreme proposal, which may account for the lack of guinea pigs willing to try it. If the noncommodity export sector is not small or if policy-makers want it to become larger, then PEP has the disadvantage of fully transferring the burden of exogenous fluctuations in world commodity prices to variability in domestic prices of noncommodity exports. It is not clear that this is an improvement over continuing to let the fluctuations show up as variability in domestic prices of the commodity export. A more practical version of the proposal would be to target a more comprehensive index of export prices rather than a single export price (Peg the Export Price Index).[104] Better still is the most recent version called PPT, for Product Price Targeting. It would target a comprehensive index of domestic production prices, including nontraded goods. Possibilities are the Producer Price Index, the GDP deflator, or a specially constructed index.[105] The important point is to include export commodities in the index and exclude import commodities, whereas the CPI does it the other way around.

Institutions to Make National Saving Procyclical

We have noted the Hartwick Rule, which says that rents from a depletable resource should be saved against the day when deposits run out. At the same time, traditional macroeconomics says that government budgets should be countercyclical: running surpluses in booms and spending in recessions. Commodity producers tend to fail in both these principles; they save too little on average and all the more so in booms. Thus some of the most important ways to cope with the commodity cycle are institutions to ensure that export earnings are put aside during the boom time into a commodity saving fund, perhaps with the aid of rules governing the cyclically adjusted budget surplus.[106] Jeffrey Davis and coauthors include under the rubric Special Financial Institutions three sorts of mechanisms: oil funds, fiscal rules and fiscal responsibility legislation, and budgetary oil prices.[107]

RULES FOR THE BUDGET DEFICIT: THE EXAMPLE OF CHILE

As of June 2008, the government of Chilean President Michele Bachelet had unusually low approval ratings. That it had resisted intense pressure to spend the soaring receipts from copper exports was widely resented. One year later, in the summer of 2009, Bachelet and her finance minister, Andres Velasco, had the *highest* approval ratings of any Chilean officials since the restoration of democracy. Why the change? In the meantime, the global recession had hit, and copper prices had fallen abruptly. But the government had increased spending sharply, using the assets that it had acquired during the copper boom, and thereby moderated the downturn. Saving for a rainy day made these officials heroes, now that the rainy day had come. Chile has achieved what few commodity-producing developing countries have achieved: a truly countercyclical fiscal policy. Some credit should go to previous governments, who initiated an innovative fiscal institution.[108] But much credit should go to the Bachelet government, which enshrined the general framework in law and abided by it when it was most difficult to do so politically.[109]

Chile's fiscal policy is governed by a set of rules. The first one is a target for the overall budget surplus—originally set at 1 percent of GDP, then lowered to 0.5 percent of GDP, and again to 0 percent in 2009. This may sound like the budget deficit ceilings that supposedly constrain members of Euroland (deficits of 3 percent of GDP under the Stability and Growth Pact) or like the occasional U.S. proposals for a Balanced Budget Amendment (zero deficit). But those attempts have failed because they are too rigid to allow the need for deficits in recessions, counterbalanced by surpluses in good times. The alternative of letting politicians explain away any deficits by declaring them the result of slower growth than expected also does not work because it imposes no discipline.

Under the Chilean rules, the government can run a deficit larger than the target when: (1) output falls short of trend, in a recession or (2) the price of copper is below its medium-term (ten-year) equilibrium. The key institutional innovation is two panels of experts that each mid-year make the judgments, respectively: what is the output gap and what is the medium-term equilibrium price of copper.

Thus in the copper boom of 2003–8 when, as usual, the political pressure was to declare the increase in the price of copper permanent and justify spending on par with export earnings, the expert panel ruled that most of the price increase was temporary so that most of the earnings had to be saved. As a result, Chile's fiscal surplus reached almost 9 percent when copper prices were high. The country paid down its debt to a mere 4 percent of GDP and saved about 12 percent of GDP in its the sovereign wealth fund. This allowed a substantial fiscal easing in the recession of 2009, when the stimulus was most sorely needed.

Any country, but especially commodity producers, could usefully apply variants of this Chilean fiscal device. Given that many developing countries are prone to weak institutions, a useful reinforcement of the Chilean idea would be to formalize the details of the procedure into law and give the expert panels legal independence. There could be a law protecting the members from being fired, as there is for governors of independent central banks. The principle of a separation of decision-making powers should be retained: the rules as interpreted by the panels determine the total amount of spending or budget deficits, but the elected political leaders determine how that total is allocated.

COMMODITY FUNDS OR SOVEREIGN WEALTH FUNDS

Many natural resource producers have commodity funds, often in global portfolios, to invest savings for future welfare. The oldest and biggest commodity funds are in the Persian Gulf and belong to Kuwait and the United Arab Emirates. Some highly successful noncommodity exporters in Asia have established such funds, too. When China joined the club in 2007, these funds received a new name—sovereign wealth funds—and a lot of new scrutiny.[110]

It has been pointed out that the mere creation of a commodity fund, in itself, does not necessarily do anything to ensure that politicians will not raid the fund when it is flush.[111] Two standard recommendations are that the funds be transparently and professionally run and that they be given clear instructions that politics should not interfere with their objective of maximizing the financial well-being of the country. The Norwegian State Petroleum Fund (now called the Norwegian Pension Fund) is often held up as a model.[112] But in fact Norway's legal system puts few restrictions on what policy makers can do, and the fund is managed with political objectives that sometimes go unnoticed when held up as an example for developing countries to emulate.[113] Botswana's Pula Fund is a more appropriate model.

For most countries, it would be best to have rules dictating the cap on spending from out of the fund. The commodity fund of São Tomé and Príncipe, established in 2004, includes extensive restrictions guiding how the oil revenues are to be saved, invested, or spent. Outflows legally cannot exceed the highest amount that could be sustained in perpetuity.

Macartan Humphreys and Martin Sandhu and Rolando Ossowski and co-authors sensibly recommend that commodity fund spending go through the regular budget so that these resources do not become any politicians' private "slush funds."[114] There can be advantages in earmarking the commodity funds for specific good causes such as education, health, or retirement support for a future generation (while seeking to avoid ad hoc extrabudgetary spending). If the political constituents know how the money is to be spent, they may be both more tolerant of the initiative to save it in the first place and more vigilant with respect to transgressions by politicians wishing to raid the kitty to spend on armies or palaces.

RESERVE ACCUMULATION BY CENTRAL BANKS

One way that countries save in the aggregate during booms, in order to be able to spend in busts, is for central banks to accumulate international reserves via foreign exchange intervention. Economists have regarded this as a suboptimal mechanism: if the goal is smoothing spending over time, as opposed to stabilization of the exchange rate, holding the assets in the form of foreign exchange reserves has disadvantages. First, the reserves (typically U.S. Treasury bills) do not earn a high return. Second, increases in reserves can lead to rapid monetary expansion (if not sterilized) and thereby to inflation. Thus a central bank that already has enough reserves, judged by precautionary and monetary criteria, should consider selling some of its foreign exchange reserves to the country's natural resource fund (NRF). But if the central bank has political independence and the NRF does not, that may be a reason to leave the reserves where they cannot be raided.

REDUCING NET PRIVATE CAPITAL INFLOWS DURING BOOMS

If foreign exchange reserves are piling up to excessive levels, there are other ways to reduce the balance of payments surplus and facilitate national saving. One is for the government to pay down debt deliberately, especially short-term debt. Another is to remove any remaining controls on the ability of domestic citizens to invest abroad. A third is to place controls on capital inflows, especially short-term inflows.

LUMP SUM DISTRIBUTION

The Alaska Permanent Fund saves earnings from the state's oil sector. Alaska state law says that the fund must distribute half of the investment earnings on an equal per capita basis. The theory is that the citizens know how to spend their money better than their government does. Certainly the system gives Alaskans a good reason to feel that they are full stakeholders in the fund. Xavier Sala-i-Martin and Arvind Subramanian suggest that Nigeria should similarly distribute its oil earnings on an equal per capita basis;[115] Nancy Birdsall and Subramanian make the same proposal for Iraq.[116]

Efforts to Impose External Checks

All these institutions can fail if, as in some countries, the executive simply ignores the law and spends what he wants. In 2000, the World Bank agreed to help Chad, a new oil producer, finance a new pipeline. The agreement stipulated that Chad would spend 72 percent of its oil export earnings on poverty reduction (particularly health, education, and road building) and put aside 10 percent in a "future generations fund." ExxonMobil was to deposit its oil revenues from Chad in an escrow account at Citibank, and the government was to spend them subject to oversight by an independent committee. But once the money started rolling in, the government (ranked by Transparency International as one of the two most corrupt in the world) reneged on the agreement.[117]

Evidently international financial institutions would have to go beyond the Chad model if local rulers are to be prevented from abusing natural resource funds. The Extractive Industries Transparency Initiative, launched in 2002, includes the principle "publish what you pay," under which international oil companies commit to make known how much they pay governments for oil so that the public at least has a way of knowing when large sums disappear. Legal mechanisms adopted by São Tomé and Principe void contracts if information relating to oil revenues is not made public. Further proposals would give extra powers, such as freezing accounts in the event of a coup, to a global clearing house or foreign bank where the natural resource fund is located.[118] Perhaps that principle could be generalized: it may be that well-intentioned politicians spend resource wealth quickly out of fear that their successors will misspend whatever is left, in which case the adoption of an external mechanism that constrains spending both in the present and in the future might not be an unacceptable violation of sovereignty.

Summary

Much theoretical reasoning and statistical evidence suggest that possession of natural resources, such as hydrocarbons, minerals, and perhaps agricultural endowments, can confer negative effects on a country along with the benefits. This chapter has considered seven channels whereby natural resources might possibly have negative effects on economic performance. The first—the Prebisch-Singer hypothesis of a negative long-term trend in commodity prices—is counteracted by theoretical arguments for a positive trend and empirical findings that there is no consistent trend either way.

But the other six channels each have at least some truth to them. (1) Commodity price volatility is high, which imposes risk and transactions costs. (2) Specialization in natural resources can be detrimental to growth if it crowds out the manufacturing sector and the latter is the locus of positive externalities. (3) Mineral riches can lead to civil war, an obstacle to development. (4) Endowments of "point-source" commodities (oil, minerals, and some crops) can lead to weak institutions, including corruption, inequality, class structure, chronic power struggles, and absence of the rule of law and property rights. Natural resource wealth can also inhibit the development of democracy though there is not good evidence that democracy per se (as opposed to openness, economic freedom, decentralization of decision making, and political stability) leads to economic growth. (5) Dutch disease, resulting from a commodity boom, entails real appreciation of the currency and increased government spending, both of which expand nontraded goods and service sectors such as housing and render noncommodity export sectors such as manufactures uncompetitive. If and when world commodity prices go back down, adjustment is difficult due to the legacy of bloated government spending, debt, and a shrunken manufacturing sector.

In recent years, revisionists have questioned each of these channels and the bottom line that natural resource wealth is detrimental for economic growth. Some differences in econometric findings are attributable to whether economic performance is measured as the level of income or the rate of growth of income during the sample period. Others are due to whether the equation conditions on related variables when it tests the influence of the channel in question. The revisionists often emphasize that resource extraction is endogenous and that it is wrong to treat data on mineral exports—the usual measure of "resource dependence"—as if they represent geographic endowments.

From a policy viewpoint, we do not necessarily need to settle these questions. It is clear that some resource-rich countries do surprisingly poorly economically while others do well. We have noted examples of both sorts: Norway, Botswana, and Chile, which have done very well with their endowments (oil, diamonds, and copper, respectively), versus Sudan, Bolivia, and the Congo, which have done much less well. The natural resource curse should not be interpreted as a rule that all resource-rich countries are doomed to failure. The question is which policies to adopt to increase the chances of prospering. It is safe to say that destruction or renunciation of resource endowments, to avoid dangers such as the corruption of leaders, will not be one of these policies. Even if such a drastic action would on average leave the country better off, which seems unlikely, who would be the policy maker to whom one would deliver such advice?

This chapter concludes with a list of ideas for institutions designed to address aspects of the resource curse and thereby increase countries' chances of economic success. Some of the ideas that most merit consideration by countries rich in oil or other natural resources are as follows.

1. In contracts with foreign purchasers, include clauses for automatic adjustment in the commodity price if world market conditions change.
2. Hedge export proceeds in commodity futures markets or, more pragmatically, options markets.
3. Denominate debt in terms of commodity prices.

4. Allow some nominal currency appreciation in response to an increase in world prices of the commodity, but also add to foreign exchange reserves under these circumstances, especially at the early stages of the boom when it may prove temporary.

5. If a country chooses inflation targeting as the monetary regime, consider using a price measure that puts greater weight on the important export commodities, such as an index of export prices or producer prices, as the target in place of the standard CPI,

6. Emulate Chile: avoid excessive spending in boom times and allow deviations from a target surplus only in response to output gaps and long-lasting commodity price increases, as judged by independent panels of experts rather than politicians.

7. Run commodity funds transparently and professionally, with rules to govern the payout rate and with insulation for the managers from political pressure in their pursuit of the financial well-being of the country.

8. When spending oil wealth, consider lump-sum distribution on an equal per capita basis, as occurs in Alaska.

9. Mandate an external agent, for example a financial institution that houses a commodity fund, to provide transparency and to freeze accounts in the event of a coup.

Needless to say, policies and institutions have to be tailored to local circumstances, country by country. But with good intentions and innovative thinking, there is no reason why resource-rich countries need fall prey to the curse.

2

Sometimes the Grass Is Indeed Greener: The Successful Use of Energy Revenues

Patrick Clawson

Juan Pablo Pérez Alfonzo, Venezuela's oil minister in the early 1960s and a father of OPEC, referred to oil not as "black gold" but as the "devil's excrement." In recent decades, the natural resource curse argument has often been presented as either a universal or near-universal rule.[1]

The rule nature of the argument is not plausible, however, because the exceptions are so glaring. The most important countercase is historical. Edward Barbier convincingly demonstrated that "throughout history abundant natural resources and favorable conditions in the world economy have combined often to generate successful resource-based development in many economies," particularly during the "Golden Era of resource-based development" from 1870 to 1913.[2] Indeed, over the millennia of recorded history, ample natural resource endowments have more often than not been associated with sustained development.

Another important countercase to the natural resource curse argument is provided by the six oil-rich monarchies of the Persian Gulf: Bahrain, Kuwait, Oman, Qatar, Saudi Arabia, and the United Arab Emirates (UAE).[3] As these six states constitute the members of the Gulf Cooperation Council (GCC), they are sometimes referred to collectively as the GCC. This chapter shows that without oil, the Gulf monarchies would be desperately poor, but with oil they have become spectacularly well-off. The chapter then asks what accounts for the success of oil-driven growth in the Gulf monarchies and looks at three classes of possible explanations: favorable circumstances, good policies, and vast resources.

Gulf Monarchies Without Oil

Before the discovery of oil, the Gulf monarchies were weak and desperately poor. It is hard for Westerners to appreciate how underdeveloped Gulf societies were only a few short decades ago. Consider the following description of Saudi Arabia:

> In 1940 the wheel was not in general use in most areas of the nation. Saudi Arabia had a pastoral economy based on the raising of goats, sheep, and camels. The majority of the urban population lived in small villages built of mudbrick and earned a living from subsistence agriculture. The nomads drove their herds of animals across the desert in search of forage, carrying their meager belongings on camel back.[4]

Karl Twitchell used data from the UN Food and Agriculture Organization (FAO) to estimate that in 1956, 66 percent of Saudis were nomads and semi-nomads, 12 percent were settled peasants, and 22 percent were urban dwellers.[5] The oil firm Aramco was already operating in Saudi Arabia by that time, and Twitchell notes, "Initially Aramco even employed slaves, whose masters took part of their salary. Some tribal shaikhs, merchants, and money-lenders acted as intermediaries in supplying the workers and received part of their salaries."[6]

Thanks to oil income, the kingdom was able to buy slaves from their owners in 1963 and abolish slavery.[7] After a series of strikes and unrest by workers in the 1950s, Aramco improved laborers' conditions. Still, a 1962 survey found that among Aramco workers—the elite of ordinary Saudis—16 percent of homes had neither running water nor electricity, 48 percent had running water but no electricity, and 36 percent had both running water and electricity.[8] Having both running water and electricity is what constituted well-to-do in Saudi Arabia fifty years ago—that is, when the current Saudi elite was young.

Education and health conditions in Saudi Arabia were dreadful during this period. In 1954, when the kingdom's Ministry of Education was established, only 8 percent of school-age children attended school. The curriculum centered on religious education, which was 57 percent of the second-grade school day, 53 percent of the third grade, and 35 percent of the fourth grade.[9] In short, "education consisted primarily of the teaching of Moslem doctrine and memorization of the Koran to boys; education of girls was practically nonexistent."[10] In 1956, the literacy rate in the kingdom was slightly above 5 percent. As late as the 1971–72 school year, in a country with at least three million citizens, only 27,109 Saudis graduated from elementary school and 3,279 from secondary school. In 2009, these secondary-school graduates were fifty-six years old and at the height of their careers in business or politics, so the impact of this legacy of educational underdevelopment remains relevant.

Saudi Arabia's economic situation before the development of the oil industry was no worse than that of other Gulf monarchies. Indeed, thanks to the pilgrimage trade and some agricultural and livestock prospects, Saudi Arabia was better placed economically than Kuwait, Qatar, and the UAE. (Bahrain and Oman also had some agricultural potential.) Pre-oil, those three regions depended on the sea to a considerable extent, especially on pearl diving. In his definitive 1915 *Gazetteer of the Persian Gulf*, J. G. Lorimer wrote, "Were the supply of pearls to fail . . . the ports of Trucial Oman [the future UAE], which have no other resources, would practically cease to exist; in other words, the purchasing power of the eastern coast of Arabia depends very largely upon the pearl fisheries."[11] Unfortunately for the locals, the 1930s combination of the global depression and Japanese development of cultured pearls was catastrophic for the Gulf pearl diving industry. The Gulf economic situation was becoming desperate just as oil income started flowing into the Arabian Peninsula.

After her detailed and well-researched description of life in the pre-oil Trucial States—including the region's efforts toward developing via pearling and entrepôt trade—Frauke Heard-Bey sums up the area's limited potential for change:

> Before the export of oil from Abu Dhabi began, even the most industrious of the people in the Trucial States could not dramatically increase their wealth or improve upon the overall economic situation in these shaikhdoms. . . . Whether pearls were in fashion in Europe, whether entrepôt trade with neighbouring countries shifted to the Trucial States, whether there were a few years of good rains or whether

the locust swarms destroyed the date crop, the economic base remained the same: pearls, dates, boats, camels, domestic animals, fish, agriculture, and trade.[12]

Bahrain, Kuwait, and Qatar began their economic development much earlier than the UAE, given that these three regions' oil output began in1934, 1946, and 1947, respectively. But their pre-oil standard of living was also extremely low. During the 1936–37 academic year, Kuwaiti schools had 600 students, all boys.[13] The British political resident described Qatar's capital, Doha, at the end of the 1940s as "little more than a miserable fishing village straggling along the coast for several miles and half in ruins. The *suq* [market] consisted of mean fly-infested hovels, the roads were dusty tracks, there was no electricity, and the people had to fetch their water in skins and cans from wells two or three miles outside the town."[14] With the collapse of the pearling industry, Qatar's population in 1949 was estimated at less than 60 percent of its level at the beginning of the century.

The last Gulf monarchies to begin to develop were the UAE and Oman, where oil production only began in the late 1950s and 1960s, respectively. "In May 1962, two British engineering firms submitted [to Abu Dhabi's ruler Sheikh Shakhbut] a joint Development Plan [for Abu Dhabi]. . . . It provided for a hospital, water distillation, and electric power plants, four residential areas [for the anticipated growth to 25,000 residents], drainage and sanitation plants, public parks, and a public transportation system. . . . Sheikh Shakhbut refused to approve this plan . . . stating that it was too grandiose for Abu Dhabi's needs."[15] To be sure, Sheikh Shakhbut was cautious and suspicious about modernization, but it was also the case that in 1962 Abu Dhabi's government revenue was only $150,000 (by 1966, it was $42 million). Yet Abu Dhabi was arguably more advanced than Oman. When Qaboos became Oman's sultan by overthrowing his father Said in 1970, the capital, Muscat, had no central electricity, and the city gates were still locked at night.[16]

In 1966, as the oil era started, Abu Dhabi had exactly six primary schools with 587 students—students who in 2009 would be aged 49 to 55.[17] To be sure, there were additional schools in some of the other emirates of what would in 1971 become the UAE though it is worth noting that most were financed by other Gulf monarchies (mostly Kuwait), where oil exports had started earlier. It was only with the inflow of oil income and with the ascendancy of the more development-minded Sheikh Zayed (who replaced

Sheikh Shakhbut in 1966) that schooling developed in Abu Dhabi. In 1968, Abu Dhabi had seven new primary schools and enrollment was up to 4,937 students. That put it far ahead of Oman, which, despite a population at least ten times larger than Abu Dhabi in 1970, had only 900 students in the state-run schools. (There were also some students enrolled in schools run by the Petroleum Development [Oman] oil company.)[18] After coming to power that year, Sultan Qaboos sent 700 Omanis to elementary school in what was soon to become the UAE. This is well within the memory of many in the contemporary Omani elite.

In their survey of Middle East economies, Roger Owen and Şevket Pamuk summarize the many ways the pre-oil Gulf monarchies were the least developed parts of the Middle East.[19] Indeed, as the evidence above suggests, these monarchies were arguably the least developed places on earth, with social indicators and infrastructure that were on the whole no better than, and often behind that of, the poorest parts of sub-Saharan Africa or South Asia.

Not only were the economy and social infrastructure underdeveloped, but also so was the state. In the pre- and early oil days, the Gulf monarchies were fragile states often on the brink of becoming failed states. The governments were extremely weak. Monarchs were dependent on the powerful merchants who paid the taxes that sustained them. The region was often on the brink of war over boundary disputes, most notably between Saudi Arabia and Abu Dhabi and between the historical enemies Bahrain and Qatar. Oman had a series of civil wars, including one fought off and on for decades until the 1960s between the sultan and the imamate—the religious leadership of the main Ibadi sect. Another war was fought from 1963 to 1975 against communist rebels in Oman's southern region of Dhofar, a war put down by British special forces and, later, thousands of Iranian troops. Bahrain's majority Shi'a population regarded the ruling al-Khalifa family as foreigners, even though they had been in power for more than two centuries. Saudi Arabia has deep regional and tribal divisions, and these are not only among the Shi'a, who are a large portion of the population along the oil-rich Gulf coast. There are also divisions among the more cosmopolitan residents of the Red Sea coast (known as the Hejaz), which was ruled for most of a millennium by the Hashemite family that is now on the Jordanian throne. Lastly, there are divisions among the more traditionalist tribal elements in the kingdom (including the royal family) from the Nejd region around Riyadh. Without oil, the Gulf monarchies could easily have experienced devastating unrest from a combination of interstate wars, ethno-religious unrest, and civil strife.

Sharing the Arabian Peninsula with the oil-rich monarchies is the populous and desperately poor country of Yemen. Yemen shows what could have happened to the Gulf monarchies had they not found oil—they could have remained weak and underdeveloped. Until reunification in 1990, Yemen was split into two countries: the more populous and always independent North Yemen and the ex-British colony South Yemen. South Yemen was more formally known as the People's Democratic Republic of Yemen, for it was indeed a communist-run country. Both North and South Yemen depended upon foreign aid—Saudi and Soviet aid, respectively—and most especially on remittances from Yemeni workers in Saudi Arabia. In the 1970s, one-fifth of North Yemen's labor force and one-third of South Yemen's were employed abroad, and for both countries, remittances made up the vast majority of foreign exchange earnings; they were 40 percent of the South Yemen GDP.

After reunification, Yemen began producing modest amounts of oil. Even with that income, which provides about three-fourths of the country's GDP, the country remains desperately poor, with a per capita income of below $1,000 at purchasing power parity. The 2009 UN Development Programme (UNDP) Human Development Report ranks Yemen 138th of 179 countries, by far the lowest UNDP Human Development Index ranking of any Arab country.[20] And this is in a country with much more favorable natural conditions for non-oil development than that of the Gulf monarchies, because large areas of Yemen have sufficient rainfall to support agriculture. If the Gulf monarchies did not have oil, they would be hard-pressed to do better than Yemen—which is on the edge of being a failed state.[21]

Development Thanks to Oil

With oil, the Gulf monarchies have developed a standard of living comparable with Central Europe or the most advanced parts of Latin America. All six Gulf monarchies are in the top third of the 179 countries ranked in the UNDP's Human Development Index, with Saudi Arabia the lowest of the group at 55th and Kuwait at the top at 29th. That puts Kuwait ahead of eleven members of the EU and Saudi Arabia ahead of two EU members. In the lowest-ranked state, Saudi Arabia, life expectancy at birth is 72.7 years, higher than in some EU countries, such as Latvia and Lithuania. To be sure, Saudi adult literacy rate at 84.3 percent is lower than anywhere in Europe, but the figure is still quite respectable. And if one looks solely at GDP per capita, then the Gulf monarchies rise sharply in their relative rankings. With high oil income in 2008, the Gulf monarchies as a group had a GDP per capita higher than EU countries as a group. In short, the Gulf monarchies have a standard of development that is much closer to that of the world's most advanced nations than that of most developing nations.

The Gulf monarchies have undertaken tremendous physical infrastructure investments to support social development and higher consumption.[22] In such hot and dry countries, increased income has translated into vastly higher consumption of electricity and desalinated water, which political realities required delivering at subsidized prices. The hot temperatures have also contributed to the automobile culture; neither walking nor public transportation is particularly comfortable when the temperature is 50 degrees Centigrade (122 degrees Fahrenheit), especially since along the Gulf relative humidity can be above 80 percent. That has required constant expansion of roads, often in dense urban surroundings. The reliance on imports, rather than local production, has meant frequent expansion of port and airport infrastructure. The Gulf monarchies started the oil era with an almost complete lack of public services—hospitals, schools, universities, and so on. And these states have experienced rapid population growth, which has slowed only in the last decade. (Birth rates began dropping after female literacy rose, as has happened in so many places around the globe.) In short, demands for public investment have been enormous, yet the Gulf monarchies have been able to keep up.

It was not inevitable that the Gulf monarchies would economically develop to this extent. They have faced many challenges on the path to their current prosperity. In particular, over the last forty years, oil income has been extremely volatile, with peak years seeing the Gulf monarchies' oil export earnings grow to more than four times the trough years' earnings.[23] The cycles have been unpredictable. Who could have predicted that oil prices in 2008 would not only burst through the $100 per barrel level but also reach $147 and then crash to $28—all in the same year? Perhaps one could say that on the whole, the oil revenue peaks and troughs have each lasted for three to five years, but that may overstate the regularity of the fluctuations. Furthermore, neither analysts nor investors have accurately predicted the timing of inflections (turns up or down), the magnitude of price changes, or the duration of peaks and troughs.

As a side note, it is not plausible to blame this volatility on price manipulation by the Gulf monarchies. For partisans of market mechanisms, it is sobering that oil prices have if anything become more volatile in the years since most oil sold in the world has had a price based on trading at commodity exchanges. Indeed, the actions of the Gulf monarchies—such as their willingness to hold millions of barrels a day of excess capacity off the markets when oil prices weaken and then restore them when markets tighten— seem to have been major factors in tamping down price swings.

Oil price volatility was particularly marked in the period between 1972 and 1987. Gulf monarchies' nominal oil export earnings rose about fivefold between 1972 and 1974. That increase is all the more impressive since oil revenue in 1972 was already 60 to 80 percent of GDP in these countries (except for Kuwait, where in 1972 oil revenue was "only" half of GDP). Earnings then fell by half by 1977–78, rose to record levels in 1981–82, and then collapsed to about 1972 levels in 1985–86.

Extreme volatility in export earnings can pose many different challenges to economic development. For instance, some commodity exporters have ramped up their public spending during peak years but then have attempted to sustain the peak public spending levels during trough years by incurring external debts. This borrowing strategy can lead to a debt crisis, which forces disruptive adjustments such as suspending partially completed projects. This pattern has been an important part of the resource curse. By contrast, Gulf monarchies have had remarkably little disruptive yo-yoing on account of export price fluctuations. There have been very few cases in any of the oil-exporting Gulf monarchies in the last thirty-five years of development projects cancelled in mid-construction, even during periods of low oil export earnings. Although government capital expenditures were trimmed during the lean years, there are few if any cases in which maintenance and repair of existing infrastructure were deferred. To be sure, there have been times when infrastructure had difficulty keeping up with growing demands. For instance, Riyadh and other Saudi cities have not always been able to provide continuous piped water to every neighborhood. But those have been exceptional circumstances. In fact, infrastructure shortfalls—especially with regard to electricity and roads—have been more significant during periods of rapid growth than during periods of low income.

The Gulf has experienced unsustainable bubbles, but most of those bubbles have been driven as much by private sector behavior as by government action. Some of the worst cases have been stock market bubbles, such as those of the early- and mid-2000s. The sums involved were huge, as the capitalization of the GCC stock markets went from $129 billion in early 2002 to $499 billion at the end of 2004. Then in 2006 came the crash, which badly hit many small investors who entered the market late. The Saudi market started 2006 at a $645 billion valuation before losing 52 percent of its value during the year. The drop in 2006 affected markets across the region: a 43 percent loss in Abu Dhabi, 44 percent in Dubai, and 47 percent in Qatar. (The Kuwaiti stock market index is calculated in a unique way, which makes it a poor indicator of what is happening to the value of stocks.)

There is no definitive account of the government role (if any) in these stock market bubbles though available information does not suggest a large government role in any of these cases. It does not seem, for instance, that governments' monetary and credit policies were particular drivers of the stock market bubbles. Perhaps investors were influenced by expectations that governments would bail them out if markets crashed. If so, they must have been disappointed. When investors loudly demanded public bailouts in the face of the 2006 market crashes, governments generally resisted and provided only limited relief. After all, even after the 2006 crash, markets in Gulf states were still up between 55 and 91 percent over the three-year period from 2004 to 2006.

Perhaps the worst case of an unsustainable bubble in the Gulf since the 1973 oil price boom has been in Dubai during the last decade.[24] Right after the turn of the millennium, the Dubai economy became red-hot. Local boosters claimed that a substantial chunk—some said one-fourth—of the world's construction cranes were at work in Dubai.[25] Private investors, usually with quiet quasi-government participation, launched a wide array of ambitious projects, such as construction of the world's tallest building, an indoor ski slope, and an artificial island in the shape of a palm tree with more than 4,000 luxury villas. Other than tourism and leisure, Dubai positioned itself as a commercial entrepôt, an air transport and shipping hub and a home to a variety of free zones for light industry and services. Many of these projects have excellent prospects for being profitable over the long run, and Dubai has a long track record of opening up the country to attract foreign merchants, investors, and tourists.

However, the timing for the Dubai property boom was terrible, with large numbers of apartments, villas, and office buildings coming on the market in 2008 after the global financial crisis hit. With potential buyers unable to secure financing, property prices began to fall and cause a drop-off in construction, which led to a further contraction in the market. By late 2009, property prices had fallen by about half from their 2008 peak—which still left them at least twice what they had been at the beginning of the decade. The Dubai bubble was arguably as much the fault of the Dubai government as of the private sector, in that Dubai's ruling family was heavily involved in many nominally private real estate developments. With prices dropping and demand falling, several major government-linked developers were unable to repay their debts as originally scheduled. In November 2009, Dubai World, a major government-linked firm, announced it was seeking a six-month "standstill" on $26 billion of its debt. World financial markets reacted with great concern, not only regarding Dubai government-linked firms' approximately $100 billion in debt, but also regarding the possibility that other semi-official borrowers in emerging markets around the world would not pay their debts on time. In December 2009, the government of Abu Dhabi stepped forward to make a $4 billion debt payment on behalf of Nakheel, a Dubai World subsidiary. At the same time, Abu Dhabi extended an additional $6 billion to be used for an orderly workout for the debt of firms linked to the Dubai government with the implication that debt holders would have to agree to some concessions.[26] In March 2010, the Dubai government proposed a restructuring of Dubai World and Nakheel debts.

But the episode differs from the stereotype of resource export volatility in at least three ways. First, Dubai was not a major oil exporter, and its borrowing binge was arguably based more on loose international lending standards than on expectations of future oil income. Indeed, the "Dubai Model" was one of an entrepôt leveraging foreign funding to create commercial and leisure opportunities, rather than depending on oil for development.

Second, Dubai's problems were on a par with those simultaneously occurring in major non-resource-based economies, such as the United States. In many cases, investors in Dubai may not make the extraordinary returns on which they were counting but will still do better from their Dubai holdings than from investments on the New York Stock Exchange or other major international markets. Dubai real estate prices hit bottom in 2010 and drop to about one-third of their summer 2008 peak—but still at about double the 2000 price level.[27] So while investors who came into the market late lost a great deal, those who bought early and held on for the long-term have earned a strong return. And the prospects going forward are quite good. Helped by a recovering world economy and business diverted from other Arab countries experiencing turmoil, Dubai bounced back from the 2009 crisis with GDP growing 4 percent in 2010 and a projected 6 percent in 2011.[28]

Third, the Dubai crisis is primarily about the profitability of private investments, without many repercussions on government spending. Concerned that major defaults would hurt the reputation of both the emirate and the ruling family (which was, one way or another, a partner in most developments), the Dubai authorities took responsibility for working out debt refinancing for both the government and also major real estate and commercial development projects. After initial hesitation the Abu Dhabi authorities provided the financing Dubai needed to weather its financial problems, though at a political price for Dubai, symbolized by the renaming of the world's tallest building—of which Dubai is immensely proud—as the Burj Khalifa (Khalifa being the name of the Abu Dhabi ruling family) instead of Burj Dubai. Dubai appears on track to finance the $20 billion in debt repayments due in 2011. On this assumption, it appears that the main impact of the crisis in Dubai will be delayed development plans and trimmed government spending. That is nothing like the destructive impact of crises in other oil-exporting states, where governments have had to make dramatic cuts in such basic services as elementary education and infrastructure maintenance—cuts with long-lasting costs to national development.

Why Oil Helped the Gulf Monarchies

Explanations for why oil has helped the Gulf monarchies develop economically fall into three major classes: favorable circumstances, good policies, and vast resources. Let us examine each in turn.

Favorable Circumstances

No one seems to have argued that, aside from their oil and natural gas endowments, Gulf monarchies enjoy circumstances favorable to economic development. So we have to start from scratch in constructing a list of potentially favorable characteristics. The only ones that come to this author's limited imagination are: institutional continuity, monarchy, unified societies, and Islam. None of them is in the least bit credible as an explanation for the successful use of oil income by the Gulf monarchies.

INSTITUTIONAL CONTINUITY

Some economists have argued that the economic development of Africa— or even of Latin America—has been held back by the colonial experience, which destroyed preexisting social structures to such an extent that the postcolonial societies have had difficulty sustaining stable and effective governing institutions. Perhaps. But the Gulf monarchies have hardly been free of imperial interference. Kuwait, Bahrain, Oman, Qatar, and the Trucial Coast (which became the UAE after independence) were all British colonies, achieving independence only in 1961 (Kuwait) or 1971 (the other four). And Saudi Arabia existed as a country for only twenty years before the discovery of oil; the kingdom was the forcible merger of several quite distinct regions, at least one of which (the Hejaz along the Red Sea coast) has a long history of hostility toward societies from the Arabian Peninsula's interior, such as the Saudi royal family.

MONARCHY

Monarchy as a system of governance is not likely to promote inclusiveness, transparency, and accountability, which are often said to be important parts of the good governance that promotes economic development. It would be hard to suggest that the Gulf monarchies rank well on these indicators. Indeed, World Bank rankings of public accountability show the Gulf monarchies doing poorer than the rest of the Middle East, which is not a high standard to meet.[29]

Vigorous disputes rage about the connection between democracy and economic development. Although participants in this debate agree on few points, I suspect there would be broad agreement that monarchy is not a positive factor for economic development. The argument has been made, however, that monarchy in the Middle East has been good for political openness and stability because monarchies are more secure and stable than revolutionary republics, having preserved links to valued traditions.[30]

CHARACTER OF SOCIETY

It could be argued that more unified societies, without deep ethno-religious or regional splits, enjoy better development prospects. Perhaps. The Gulf monarchies are characterized by deep divisions along those lines. The most obvious case is Bahrain, where many in the majority Shiʿa population consider the Sunni ruling family to be foreigners (even though they have been in Bahrain for two centuries) and certainly illegitimate. Both Saudi Arabia and Kuwait have large Shiʿa populations that are not fully integrated into national life. In addition, three of the six Gulf monarchies have deep regional divisions: (1) the UAE, in which seven emirates jealously guard their prerogatives and are often unwilling to work together; (2) Oman, which experienced more than a century of intermittent civil wars until the mid-1970s; and (3) Saudi Arabia, which the ruling family cobbled together in the 1920s and 1930s from three regions with very separate histories and peoples who did not particularly like each other.

ISLAM

Some have argued that particular religions are better than others for economic development, most famously Max Weber in his *The Protestant Ethic and the Spirit of Capitalism*. Perhaps this is so, though it is humbling to realize how wrong Weber was in his argument in *The Religion of China: Confucianism and Taoism* in which he argued that China was poorly placed to develop a capitalist economy. It is not clear that Islam is particularly conducive to capitalist growth, although as Maxime Rodinson has shown, Islam is highly compatible with capitalism.[31] Indeed, the way in which Islam has been implemented in the Gulf monarchies has at times posed problems for economic development. For instance, it has had an impact on the administration of justice, the enforceability of contracts, and the leveling of interest charges. In addition, violent radicals inspired by their interpretation of Islam have in Saudi Arabia—by far the largest of the Gulf monarchies—been a major source of internal instability, imposing heavy security costs on economies, discouraging foreign investors, and leading to complications in foreign trade and travel.

Even if someone were to come up with some circumstances that made the Gulf particularly suitable for economic development, they would still have to be balanced against other circumstances that have made the Gulf a poor location for economic growth. Two such obvious examples are water and wars. The Gulf is arguably the least water-endowed populated region in the world. In addition, the Gulf monarchies have some neighbors who pose severe security challenges. Six prominent examples include (1) Gulf states had reason to worry about being drawn into the eight-year Iran-Iraq war

during the 1980s; (2) Iran has targeted Kuwait on several occasions, including the attacks on oil tankers that led to the U.S. Navy tanker convoys in the
Gulf during 1988 and 1989; (3) the 1990 Iraqi conquest of Kuwait was followed by a twelve-year standoff with a U.S.-led coalition and a complex war
and insurgency thereafter; (4) Iran continues to occupy islands that had been
part of the UAE; (5) Bahrain, Kuwait, and Saudi Arabia have accused Iran
of organizing terrorist attacks in their countries; and (6) the impasse over
Iran's nuclear programs has been a major factor behind more than $50 bil-
lion in Gulf monarchy arms orders in the last five years.

Good Policies

Those who emphasize resource endowments' negative impact acknowledge
considerable variation in that impact, depending on the state's policies. Extending that thesis, could one argue that the reason Gulf monarchies have
done well is that they have followed especially good policies? The evidence
for such an argument is slim. The Gulf monarchies have adopted some policies
supportive of growth, especially an embrace of globalization, macroeconomic stability, and a reliance on the private sector to the extent practicable.
But the Gulf monarchies have also implemented policies that have contributed to corruption, waste, policy paralysis, and excessive reliance on foreign
labor—all of which have hindered sustainable development.

GLOBALIZATION

The Gulf monarchies have been extraordinarily open to interaction with the
world. Obviously, they were major exporters. But they have not gone down
the route of being mercantilists or import-substituting industrialists that
have tried to meet domestic needs through local production. One could be
cynical about these countries' openness to foreign labor, which could
be read as reflecting a weak local work ethic, but Gulf societies' willingness to
tolerate large numbers of foreigners living in their midst has benefited both
the Gulf economies and the labor-exporting countries, such as Jordan and
Lebanon, enriched by remittances. And societies as capital-rich as the Gulf
monarchies did not have to be as open to foreign investment as they have
been. Furthermore, the Gulf monarchies have been open to foreign brands
and foreign service industries in ways that have transformed conservative
local cultures. Obviously, Gulf monarchies, most especially Saudi Arabia,

have limits that Westerners find grating, but any Westerner will find much to recognize in Saudi Arabia's numerous shopping malls.

To be sure, there have been limits to the openness of Gulf monarchies, even beyond those related to religion. The long-imposed requirements that foreign firms operate through local agents were little more than a tax on the foreign firms, in that local agents rarely did much to merit their substantial share of profits. Most Gulf monarchies have subsidized local agriculture and imposed various barriers to imports in order to protect local producers—some traditional (dates) but many newly established (poultry, eggs, and vegetables). To a much larger extent than other Gulf monarchies, Saudi Arabia had relatively high tariffs on industrial products that were competing with local industry. However, the Saudi case is a good example of how the trend over time has been toward greater openness. In the course of its 2005 accession to the World Trade Organization, Saudi Arabia eliminated the requirement that foreign firms operate through local agents and reduced tariffs from 12 percent to 5 percent on three-fourths of Saudi imports. It also simplified a wide range of trade procedures.[32]

As an example of the much more closed-to-the-world policies that the Gulf monarchies could have pursued, consider the policy mix adopted by Libya or Algeria. Their focus on self-sufficiency and their hostility to foreign influences—for instance, to Western brand-name services—was driven largely by leftist ideology, which has served as a greater barrier to globalization than the Gulf's conservative Islam. Libya and Algeria have societies with a very different feel than those of the Gulf monarchies—without the same ubiquitous presence of Western brands and Western lifestyle. Furthermore, the most charitable interpretation would be that Libya and Algeria have had considerably worse growth outcomes than the Gulf monarchies, despite ample resource endowments.[33]

MACROECONOMIC STABILITY

An important aspect of the resource curse has typically been an asymmetrical response to income shocks. Namely, government spending has risen quickly when income soars but also stays high when income plummets, with foreign borrowing being used to postpone the inevitable adjustment. The adjustment becomes all the more harsh due to the country's taking on substantial foreign debt. This pattern has not been seen in the Gulf monarchies. As a rule, though arguably with a few exceptions, Gulf states' adjustment to lower income has been timely, and windfalls have not led to unsustainable increases in government spending. The most significant exception—the Dubai bubble of recent years—was discussed above.

The acid test of commitment to macroeconomic stability has come when revenue fell sharply and reserves ran out. There have been few such cases in the Gulf in the last quarter century; reserves have generally been sufficient to cover deficits. A unique case of the importance of building reserves for unexpected contingencies is Kuwait prior to the 1990 Iraqi invasion. Kuwait faced massive spending, equal to several times GDP, for both the war costs (including grants to states providing troops to repel the Iraqi invaders) and the postwar reconstruction bill. Retreating Iraqi troops destroyed many buildings and set fire to all Kuwaiti oil wells, causing spectacular environmental damage that required tens of billions of dollars to reverse. Although the Kuwaiti government has not provided a clear accounting of the crisis's costs or the country's financial situation prior to the war, it appears that Kuwait exhausted nearly all its reserve fund of about $100 billion.

In the last quarter century, Saudi Arabia has twice faced serious budgetary problems.[34] The first was in the aftermath of the spectacular 1986 oil price crash. Government revenue, which had already plummeted from $100 billion in 1981 to $36 billion in 1985, dropped to $21 billion in 1986 and then averaged $27 billion from 1987 to 1989. An embarrassing run-up in unpaid bills to contractors squeezed local businesses hard, because local banks were reducing lending to Saudi firms. Banks did this partly because of increasing defaults and partly because they were increasingly financing the government's deficit. The Saudi government did not, however, try to sustain its previous spending plans through foreign borrowing. Instead, it responded by drastically curtailing investment expenditure while using scarce resources to complete all projects underway and to sustain repairs and maintenance on existing infrastructure.

By contrast, the Saudi government did turn to foreign borrowing, as well as to pressure on local financial institutions, on the second occasion when it faced serious budget problems, during the aftermath of the 1990–91 Kuwait crisis. That was hardly surprising: few countries go through a major war without incurring a national debt. The spending went both for war costs and for the substantial postwar arms purchases meant to guard against the perceived continuing Iraqi threat. But Saudi Arabia kept a tight lid on spending during the 1990s, even though that meant that civil servants' standard of living fell noticeably, unemployment became a serious social problem, and water, electricity, and roads did not keep up with demand.[35]

The last decade in Saudi Arabia has seen dramatic increases in oil revenues accompanied by largely modest increases in government spending. Beginning in 1999, the combination of rapid Asian economic growth and OPEC solidarity at restraining oil production resulted in steadily increasing oil export revenues for Gulf monarchies. This income increase, coming after fifteen years of more modest export earnings, could have fueled another unsustainable spending boom. It did nothing of the sort. Instead of immediately funding massive new projects, the Gulf states, if anything, accelerated their economic reform efforts and used the additional income sparingly, only launching new projects when the funds to pay for them were already in the bank. For instance, Saudi Arabia paid down much of its debt to the local banking system, which allowed banks to vigorously lend to private businesses. Particularly striking was that military budgets and arms purchases throughout the Gulf monarchies significantly fell despite the higher oil income.[36] It would appear that Gulf states' high levels of military spending in the 1980s and 1990s were based on the perception of real threat from first Iran and then Iraq. As those threats faded, so did the Gulf states' spending. And now as the Iranian nuclear impasse worsens, military spending in the Gulf has trended sharply upward in the last few years. Furthermore, Gulf monarchies have spent more wisely on their militaries in recent years, acquiring real capabilities well in line with the conventional threats they face.

A substantial but measured increase in oil export earnings turned into another oil boom in 2005. The income windfall was stunning, but still the Gulf governments did not rush to spend it all. For instance, Saudi oil exports tripled from 2002 to 2006, and most of that windfall went into turning a 2002 budget deficit into a $60 billion surplus four years later. Spending initiatives were modest: a 15 percent government salary increase (the first in almost twenty years), an $8 billion program for basic infrastructure, and a $19 billion purchase of seventy-two Eurofighter Typhoon jets to replace an aging force and counter a growing perceived Iranian threat. By the end of 2008, the Saudi government had wiped out the national debt, which in 2002 had been $250 billion, slightly more than the annual GDP at the time.

However, the path of economic reform and cautious spending changed sharply in early 2011 when the royal family became concerned that the protests in many other Arab countries might spread to Saudi Arabia (indeed, there were some modest protests in the kingdom). In forty-one royal decrees in February and March 2011, King Abdullah announced $129 billion in spending designed to address social discontent.[37] Government workers got an extra two months' salary; unemployment benefits of $533 a month were instituted; the Ministry of Interior created 60,000 new law enforcement jobs; $67 billion was allocated to build 500,000 housing units; and a minimum wage for citizens was introduced. These benefits do little if anything to add to economic growth; indeed, they could further erode the Saudi work ethic, as the benefits suggest that government largesse, rather than work effort, is what will raise personal income. Furthermore, the spending on these benefits may exhaust the government budget surplus if oil prices stabilize at $100 a barrel, leaving the government with little room for the increased spending on education and infrastructure which would contribute to economic growth.

For Kuwait and the UAE, combined oil exports rose more than threefold from 2002 to 2006, from $35 billion to $120 billion, and then rose another 50 percent by 2008 to $180 billion.[38] Although government spending certainly rose in the two countries, much of the extra revenue was saved and yielded budget surpluses of more than 25 percent of GDP. So much has been added to Kuwait's Reserve Fund for Future Generations that the International Monetary Fund estimates that by 2010, interest from government funds invested abroad will be $14 billion, which is more than $10,000 per Kuwaiti. But it is unclear if these economically sound policies will be sustained in face of the worries about protests similar to those in many other Arab countries. In early 2011, Kuwait and the UAE both announced generous benefits for citizens, though not as over-the-top as those in Saudi Arabia.

RELIANCE ON THE PRIVATE SECTOR

The vast sums of oil revenues flowing into Gulf monarchies' government coffers, combined with the meager resources (managerial, technical, and financial) of these countries' private firms, would seem to push them toward state-run development. And of course the state has been the principal funder of industry, commercial real estate, housing, and all manner of infrastructure in the Gulf. That said, the Gulf monarchies have done a remarkable job at encouraging the private sector. Consider Saudi Arabia. A census of establishments in 1962 showed how small and undercapitalized Saudi firms were. Over the next four decades, the Saudi state used its resources to encourage private wealth. Giacomo Luciani describes a typical case, namely, electricity:

> The state did not nationalize the originally private electricity companies, but underwrote increases in their equity capital so that they could expand their generation capacity in line with demand; in this

way it acquired the vast majority of the equity. Furthermore, because electricity was for several years sold below cost to check increases in the cost of living, the private equity holders were guaranteed a minimum return on their equity notwithstanding the fact that the companies may have been operating at a loss. Overall, it was a sweet deal for the original owners.[39]

Luciani goes on to document the development of substantial Saudi private entrepreneurs, some of whom have made billion-dollar investments in industrial projects. He also shows how these entrepreneurs have become quite independent of the Saudi state. One indication is that they increasingly turn to the Saudi stock market and to privately owned Saudi banks to raise funding for projects, which has led to increasing transparency in business practices. Another sign is that they are investing billions of dollars in major international banks, hotels, retail store chains, and real estate projects. Perhaps most surprisingly, given the closed character of the political system, the Saudi state has been quite comfortable with Saudi entrepreneurs who act quite independently of the government, including a few who are open critics of the political system.

Saudi policy has been good not only to the ultrarich but also to businessmen in general. Perhaps one of the best ways to illustrate this is to turn to the World Bank's *Doing Business* series, which ranks 183 economies on a wide range of policies, including enforcing contracts, protecting investors, registering property, getting credit, and procedures for starting or closing a business. In the 2010 edition, Saudi Arabia ranks 13 out of 183.[40] In short, Saudi Arabia is hardly a model of crony capitalism, much less of state capitalism. Nor has reliance on the private sector in the Gulf been confined to Saudi Arabia. Writing in the mid-1990s, one eminent economist of the Middle East ranked the UAE as by far the most market-oriented and friendly to the private sector of the four OPEC-member Gulf monarchies.[41] All the Gulf monarchies rank in the top half of countries in the World Bank's 2010 *Doing Business* index: Saudi Arabia at thirteen, Bahrain at twenty, UAE at thirty-three, Qatar at thirty-nine, Kuwait at sixty-one, and Oman at sixty-five. By contrast, three EU members, including Italy, rank below all of the Gulf monarchies in this index.

Intriguingly, although the Gulf states all adopted similar policies of relying on the private sector to the extent practicable, their development strategies differed considerably. The 1970s oil boom accentuated the preexisting differences in the development strategies that various Gulf monarchies had already chosen by the late 1960s (if not earlier). To develop in the face of ample cash but limited human capital and small local markets, the different monarchies followed four general development strategies: industrial, natural gas, financial, and trading. Bahrain and Saudi Arabia have been the states most focused on industrial development. Industrialization in these two countries was at first thought of as primarily producing for the local market, in line with the economic development theory popular in the 1960s known as import-substituting industrialization. But it later shifted to energy-intense products for world markets in line with the economic development theory of the 1980s known as export-led industrialization. Natural gas was the route chosen by Qatar, with its limited oil but massive natural gas reserves, which it has developed for use both in industry and as liquefied natural gas for export. Investing wealth abroad has been a major activity for Kuwait, which early on established a formal reserve fund, but the domestic economy was dominated by commerce and services for the local population. Being a trading center has been Dubai's ambition for decades, at least since Sheikh Rashid came to power in 1958. Dubai developed as a regional trade entrepôt, with extensive port and airport facilities and a welcoming attitude toward foreign investors.

CORRUPTION, WASTE, AND PARALYSIS

The Gulf monarchies have certainly suffered from corruption, particularly Bahrain and Saudi Arabia. Saudi ambassador to the United States Prince Bandar bin Sultan responded to criticisms of corruption by saying "So what?" if the royal family had siphoned off $50 billion over the years, arguing that they had spent $350 to $400 billion modernizing Saudi Arabia.[42] In a lengthy interview with a prominent American journalist, the prince argued that much of the criticism of corruption was either a misunderstanding of the Saudi system of personal patronage or an example of hypocrisy, because the West also tolerates the dispensing of favors to prominent politicians and excessive charges by suppliers to the government. Prince Bandar may have overstated the case, but he is quite correct that Saudi practice is not as different from Western experience as is often suggested. In this context, it is worth noting that in the 1990s the direct financial payments from the state to Saudi royals were relatively modest, with most of the 6,000 to 10,000 princes receiving less than $1,000 a month. That is a remarkably different situation from 1959, when the king's "private treasury" took up 20 percent of the budget and all economic projects were only 9 percent. Even that was probably an improvement on previous years, given that 1959 was the year financial reforms along the IMF lines were introduced in Saudi Arabia.[43] In contrast to the 9 percent for economic projects in 1959, a much larger percentage of the budget was devoted to capital investment projects in the 2010 budget.[44]

Waste has been a much greater drain than corruption on the Gulf monarchies' resources. Through the 1980s, governments often felt compelled to cushion locals from losses. Kuwait, for instance, spent $90 billion to offset losses from the bursting of a 1981 stock market bubble; those payments were equal to $180,000 per citizen. More common were generous subsidies that had perverse effects. Scared by rising world wheat prices, Saudi Arabia so generously promoted wheat raising, which entailed production of highly subsidized water, that the land under cultivation rose twentyfold, and the kingdom became the world's sixth-largest wheat exporter. The subsidized purchase price was finally cut in 1988; output then stabilized. A similar case of waste occurred in the UAE, where the competition among the different emirates led to spectacular duplication. There were, for instance, six international airports in a small area at a time when demand could have been met by any one of them.

In four of the six Gulf monarchies—Bahrain, Kuwait, Oman, and Saudi Arabia—arguably the most serious policy shortcoming has been policy paralysis. Kuwait has had great difficulty resolving standoffs between the popularly elected parliament and the executive branch—that is, the royal family. The result was years of delay in implementing investments of potentially great benefit, especially in the oil industry, though that the logjam was broken in 2010 when consensus was reached on a number of contentious issues.[45] In Saudi Arabia, decision making has been similarly slow. Part of the problem has been a succession of elderly unhealthy kings. Another issue has been what Steffen Hertog refers to as segmented clientalism, in which "juxtaposed groups of stakeholders tend to have different patrons within the state and the political elite . . . The system has created a number of institutional, regulative, and distributive 'fiefdoms,' sometimes with strongly overlapping areas of jurisdiction."[46]

THE EMPLOYMENT MESS

The Gulf monarchies' most troubling economic policy may be their heavy reliance on foreign laborers. Although data about employment in the Gulf monarchies are notoriously unreliable, it appears that approximately three-fourths of those employed in the Gulf monarchies are foreigners and that the great majority of employed locals work for the government.[47] According to the 1995 UAE census, 12,000 nationals worked outside the public sector compared to 102,000 working in the public sector; that made UAE nationals 27 percent of the public sector workforce but only 1.3 percent of the non-public workforce.

The heavy reliance on foreign labor creates two profound socioeconomic problems. The first is unemployment, a subject so sensitive that there are no reliable figures in these countries. For instance, serious estimates for unemployment among Saudi males in 2002 range from 10 percent to 30 percent. And unemployment is getting worse because the rapid population growth rate in past decades is translating into a rapidly growing pool of young people, many of them university graduates, joining the labor market. From 1999 to 2004, the UAE's national labor force grew at 10 percent a year. To be sure, in all the Gulf monarchies, extended family networks cushion the social impact of unemployment, which generally takes the form of young men having to stay in their parents' home for years until they finally land a government job. But those idle young men are both an economic waste and a potential political problem. A problem set to mushroom in the next decade is unemployment among women, who now make up a majority of university students in every Gulf country but whose participation in the labor force has been only about 10 percent of the working-age population. That participation rate has risen in Kuwait in recent years, and so has female unemployment.

The second problem related to the heavy reliance on foreign labor is the social tension from foreigners predominating the local population. The situation is most extreme in the UAE, where many businesses cater to the foreign residents and foreign tourists rather than to UAE citizens. Furthermore, the overwhelmingly male foreign labor force means that 67 percent of the UAE population is male, with the proportion being even higher among young adults—a socially explosive situation, particularly in a society so conservative about sexual mores. The heavy dependence on foreigners also creates security concerns of many sorts, from conflicts among foreigners of different nationalities (for example, Pakistani and Indian) to infiltration by foreign subversives (for example, radical Islamists). And in Bahrain, the local population's Shi'a majority is deeply embittered by what it perceives as a concerted government campaign to give citizenship to Sunni foreigners and change the country's religious mix.

Gulf governments have had at best limited success at addressing the problem of heavy reliance on foreign labor. Programs requiring private firms to hire locals have been marked by failure; the typical response of private firms is to treat the program as, in effect, a tax, with the hired locals not expected to be seriously competitive with their foreign coworkers. Some small reforms have been made in schooling to make education more responsive to labor market needs, but the emphasis should be placed on the word *small*. Locals' expectations about how much effort they must make at work and how much income they should expect to make have only changed incrementally. On the whole, the response of Gulf societies to the employment problem has been to continue with the old model—foreign labor for private-sector work, nationals working for the government—and hope for the best. After all, it would only take modest adjustment in the proportion of new jobs going to nationals rather than foreigners to absorb the growth in the national labor force. Consider that between 1999 and 2004, employment in the UAE rose by 929,000 yet the national labor force rose by only 96,000. Had the share of nationals among those being hired been only 11 percent, national unemployment would have been eliminated; instead, it more than doubled to a total of 29,000.

THE BALANCE SHEET ON THE POLICY MIX

In sum, can it be argued that good policies explain the Gulf monarchies' escape from the resource curse? To be sure, many of their policy choices have been admirable, especially the embrace of globalization, macroeconomic stability, and the private sector to the extent practicable. But the Gulf monarchies have also implemented many policies that held back sustainable development. Waste, corruption, and policy paralysis, with the partial exceptions of Qatar and the UAE, have too often been the norm. The heavy reliance on foreign labor also undercuts the local work ethic and creates serious social problems. On balance, government policies in the Gulf states have been modestly supportive of sustainable growth.

It is not clear that the policies modestly supportive of growth have been enough to account for the spectacular growth of the Gulf monarchies. That said, perhaps other oil exporters have had such bad policies that the Gulf's modestly growth-supportive policies account for the better outcome in the Gulf compared to many other oil exporters. Further research would be necessary to address the question of whether the combination of modestly pro-growth policies plus oil exports is sufficient to avoid the resource curse.

Vast Resources

It would be comforting to think that good policies account for the Gulf monarchies' successes at using resource wealth for development. That explanation would suggest that if other resource exporters adopted similar policies, they, too, would avoid the natural resource curse. However, at least as plausible an explanation for the Gulf monarchies' growth is the simple fact that they have had so much oil income that even if they wasted much of it, they would still be immensely rich. Consider the extreme case of Qatar. Qatar's 2008 oil and gas exports were $66 billion.[48] There are perhaps 200,000 Qatari nationals, meaning that these exports came to $330,000 per national. Even if we take as the denominator the entire population of 900,000—including foreigners, most of whom are simple laborers—Qatar's per capita oil and natural gas exports were $73,000. It is hard to argue that $73,000 per person per year is a curse. And there is little reason to think that this income is a flash in the pan: Qatar's presently proven oil reserves are sufficient to sustain current production levels for 54 years, and its proven gas reserves (and gas products account for more exports from Qatar than oil) are sufficient for 335 years.[49]

With such an extraordinary income stream from an industry that requires so few inputs other than the natural resource endowment, Qataris are well positioned to enjoy a high standard of living even if much of the income is wasted or appropriated by a small part of the population. Indeed, much money has gone into luxury and prestige projects. In 2008 and 2009, Qatar built too many buildings of all types, feeding a real estate asset bubble similar to that which affected much of the world, but building prices recovered thereafter. In 2011, Qatar announced plans for $140 billion in infrastructure construction over four years, even before it committed to $64 billion in additional spending for the 2022 World Cup.[50] On top of that are multibillion plans for art museums, educational facilities, housing, and showcase commercial developments. The program is extraordinarily ambitious, but it is arguably appropriate for a country with Qatar's income level and accumulated financial reserves.

Perhaps the natural resource curse theory needs to be rephrased as "Lots of natural resources are a curse, but incredibly huge amounts of natural resources are a blessing." We are used to thinking of correlations that are either positive or negative, but perhaps in the case of the correlation between natural resource endowments and economic development, there is a tipping point at which the correlation shifts from negative to positive. If so, that would be an interesting converse to Thad Dunning's argument that modest oil wealth can be good for democracy but that vast wealth is bad.[51]

However, more research into the situation of other countries with very large resource endowments is needed before we conclude that the natural resource curse theory needs any such coda. In particular, the experience of Libya and Brunei would seem to suggest that some extremely well-endowed countries have social indicators and economic development below what would seem achievable with their readily exploitable resource wealth. It could be argued that Equatorial Guinea is on the same path: its 2008 oil exports were $30,000 per capita but its life expectancy, at fifty-one years, was 159th in the world.[52]

Words of Caution

The evidence is clear that the Gulf monarchies are economically better off due to their oil and gas resource endowments. The standard of living in the Gulf monarchies is certainly higher than it would have been in the absence of oil and gas. However, it would be premature to conclude that we know why these countries have avoided the natural resource curse. There are no obvious factors in the Gulf monarchies' historical and cultural circumstances that would account for this success. It seems that decent government policies were a considerable factor. However, it is also plausible that the vast size of the Gulf monarchies' natural resource endowment was at least as important. Certainly that latter explanation fits the popular image—that is, that the Gulf monarchies are so rich because they are swimming in oil.

The counterintuitive argument that oil is a curse was never going to be easy to make. Selling that theory becomes all the more difficult when there are counterexamples. The Gulf monarchies' spectacular success at raising their standard of living through oil income has arguably shaped popular and policy maker views about the impact of oil on economies. Who would not want one's country to be as wealthy as Qatar? And if vast amounts of oil and gas have been good for Qatar, then it would seem to make sense to hope that one's country has substantial oil and gas reserves. Plus, it is a natural human failing to be optimistic. So it would not be surprising if policy makers and publics feel that their countries could imitate the Gulf monarchies' success. They may think they can implement policies that are at least as good for development as those in the Gulf monarchies, and they may hope their countries turn out to have vast natural resource endowments on the scale of Qatar's. I suspect that this optimism is generally misplaced. But I doubt that policy makers and publics will abandon their hopes for oil until we economists and political scientists can provide a fuller explanation of why oil and gas helped the Gulf monarchies.

3

Is There a Policy Learning Curve? Trinidad and Tobago and the 2004–8 Hydrocarbon Boom

Richard M. Auty

Since gaining independence in 1962, Trinidad and Tobago has experienced three hydrocarbon booms (1974–78, 1979–81, and 2004–8). The first two booms each conferred an additional 35 to 39 percent of non-energy GDP in revenue annually, and the most recent windfall conferred an average extra 59 percent of non-energy GDP annually. The over-rapid domestic absorption of the first two booms through increased consumer subsidies and state-led resource-based industrialization triggered a protracted growth collapse through 1982–93 that cut incomes by one-third and destabilized politics.

Some lessons have been learned from the 1974–81 booms, and the deployment of Trinidad and Tobago's 2004–8 hydrocarbon windfall revenue was more cautious. Two-thirds of the 2004–8 windfall was saved by both the private sector and the public sector. Even so, the third of the windfall that was absorbed domestically expanded the non-energy public sector deficit to three times the IMF estimate of a sustainable deficit level. The scale of absorption also intensified "Dutch disease" effects (that is, the relative contraction of nonhydrocarbon tradable activity, notably agriculture and manufacturing, relative to service activity) and sustained rent-seeking interests. Consequently, despite the welcome gain in policy-making caution, Trinidad and Tobago has yet to nurture an effective pro-reform political coalition that can neutralize rent-seeking interests and promote competitive diversification of the economy.

Fashionable statist policies encouraged government intervention in many developing countries through the 1960s and 1970s, and these policies cumulatively distorted these countries' economies and triggered growth collapses during the 1974–85 period of commodity price vulnerability. This was notable among the resource-rich countries.[1] The growth collapses proved protracted because the interventionist policies established powerful rent-seeking constituencies that resist International Financial Institutions (IFI) efforts at economic reform. Nevertheless, evidence of a policy learning curve emerged among the rent-distorted developing economies through the late 1990s and early 2000s. However, high-rent, hydrocarbon-driven economies have struggled through the 2004–8 commodity boom. Three hydrocarbon-dependent economies in South America (Bolivia, Ecuador, and Venezuela) appear to have learned little, but this chapter finds patchy evidence of policy learning in Trinidad and Tobago.

The chapter is structured as follows: The first section briefly summarizes the literature pertaining to the political economy of rent deployment in Trinidad and Tobago and identifies five features of the country's political economy that create the risk of maladroit rent deployment. It also compares the scale of the hydrocarbon windfall rents of 1974–78 and 1979–81 with those of the 2004–8 windfall and establishes the legacy of the 1974–81 deployment. The next section analyzes the political economy of the 2004–8 rent deployment in Trinidad and Tobago. Briefly, the chapter finds that although recent rent deployment has improved compared with 1974–81, the rent-seeking interests established during the earlier booms persist and channel revenue in ways that retard the long-term competitive diversification of the economy.

The Legacy of Past Hydrocarbon Rent Deployment

Implications of the Rent Cycling Literature for Trinidad and Tobago

The emerging theory of rent cycling suggests that the scale of rent relative to GDP impacts both elite incentives and the development trajectory.[2] Whereas low rent incentivizes elites to grow the economy (because that increases the level of taxation, which is the principal source of discretionary expenditure and one that the elite frequently benefit from disproportionately), high rent encourages rent distribution at the expense of investment efficiency and sustained long-term growth.

More specifically, low rent motivates governments to provide public goods and efficiency incentives that align the economy with its comparative advantage, which in low-rent economies for the most part initially lies in early competitive labor-intensive manufactured exports. The low-rent development trajectory rapidly absorbs surplus rural labor so that rising wages automatically drive diversification into productivity-boosting, skill-intensive, and capital-intensive sectors. In addition, early industrialization drives early urbanization that accelerates the demographic cycle to reduce the dependent/worker ratio, which raises the share of investment in GDP and accelerates per capita GDP growth.[3] Finally, the rapid structural change engendered by competitive industrialization drives a virtuous sociopolitical circle as it proliferates social groups that restrict policy capture by one group and also strengthen sanctions against antisocial governance as: (1) firms protect their investment by lobbying for property rights and the rule of law;[4] (2) unsubsidized urbanization strengthens civic voice;[5] and (3) early government reliance on taxing income, profits, and expenditure (forced by the absence of rent from trade) spurs demand for accountable public finances.[6]

In contrast, high rent creates contests for its capture that deflect elite incentives toward cycling rent to boost patronage and personal enrichment that offer more immediate (often personal) rewards than the long haul of wealth creation. Consequently, more rent flows through patronage networks at the expense of markets than in low-rent economies, and this shifts the high-rent economy away from its comparative advantage. In the absence of competitive industrialization, surplus labor persists and encourages governments to deploy some rent to expand employment that markets would not support in protected industry and an expanded bureaucracy. The demand for transfers from the subsidized sector eventually outstrips the rent due to structural change or falling commodity prices, so the high-rent economy becomes locked into a staple trap trajectory of increasing reliance on a weakening primary sector. But rent recipients resist market reform because it shrinks their rent. In the absence of reform, investment efficiency declines. GDP growth decelerates and causes the economic growth rate to collapse, and recovery from this is protracted. Rent cycling theory also recognizes that the adverse impacts of high rent are exacerbated (and therefore more intractable) in the presence of (1) statist policies,[7] (2) high ethnicity,[8] (3) concentrated commodity linkages,[9] and (4) parliamentary democracies[10] that are young.[11]

Rent cycling theory therefore suggests that hydrocarbon rents risk feeding rent-seeking activity at the expense of sustained economic growth in Trinidad and Tobago. First, the country's rent has been both high and concentrated on the government. In addition, the country gained independence from Great Britain in 1962 as a parliamentary democracy that was racially divided. Around 40 percent of the population is descended from Indian indentured plantation workers who succeeded the slave labor force and remained largely rural and strongly dependent on the sugar industry at independence.[12] Around 39.5 percent of the population is black, comprising mostly freed slave immigrants to Trinidad and Tobago who reside mainly in the northern urban region that extends east from Port of Spain. Finally, some 17 percent of the population is mixed and includes Syrians, Europeans (who dominate finance), and Chinese.[13] Each of the two largest ethnic groups (Indians and blacks) formed a political party, but neither commanded a majority and both relied on co-opting smaller groups in order to govern.

The Scale of the Three Hydrocarbon Booms

Trinidad and Tobago lies at the eastern edge of a set of hydrocarbon fields that extends from northern Venezuela. Most of the fields are offshore, and these require elaborate technology for the extraction of the resources and impose technical demands that require capital and expertise that have rendered the tiny country reliant on leading international oil companies (IOCs). After oil output peaked in Trinidad and Tobago during the 1970s, natural gas extraction rose to dominate hydrocarbon production. Reserves were constantly expanded and by 2004, the total reserves of oil and gas were estimated at 4.5 billion barrels of oil equivalent (just 17 percent of which comprised oil) and double that if probable and possible reserves are included.[14] The IMF projects that oil production will stabilize at around 125,000 barrels per day and then abruptly cease in 2042.[15] Natural gas production will flatten around 4.3 billion cubic meters per day (bm^3pd) and cease around 2022. These projections are likely to prove underestimates, however, given the scale of the existing probable and possible reserves together with remaining exploration prospects. However, the government of Trinidad and Tobago has targeted 2020 for the country to achieve "developed" status when it will no longer rely heavily on hydrocarbon extraction.

Trinidad and Tobago experienced three hydrocarbon booms that each conferred sizeable rents. More specifically, the 1973–74 price shock quadrupled oil prices and coincided with a two-thirds expansion in hydrocarbon production in Trinidad and Tobago to render the 1974–78 windfall there large relative to GDP compared to those of countries examined by Alan Gelb and his associates—namely, Algeria, Ecuador, Indonesia, Nigeria, and Venezuela.[16] In total, the hydrocarbon revenue of Trinidad and Tobago rose by an extra 39 percent of non-energy GDP annually through the 1974–78 boom. The shorter 1979–81 boom conferred another windfall equivalent to 35 percent of non-energy GDP annually on top of the earlier one after oil prices doubled to confer an overall eightfold gain from the early 1970s.

The 2004–8 boom exceeded the two earlier booms, and it owed more to price effects (three-fifths) than volume effects (two-fifths). Natural gas production quadrupled from 1998 to 2007 to reach 39 bm^3, yet oil production briefly reversed its long-term decline to average 166,000 barrels per day in 2005–07 compared with 134,000 in 1998.[17] Table 3.1 shows that from 2005 to 2007, the combined effect of the expansion in oil and gas production plus the sharp rise in energy prices almost doubled the share of energy rent in GDP compared with 2000–04 and tripled it compared with the cyclical low point of 1995–99. Taking 1999–2003 as the pre-boom benchmark, the 2004–8 windfall amounted to an additional $6.1 billion (TT$38.2 billion) annually, which is equivalent to an extra 32.1 percent of GDP annually and an extra 59.3 percent of non-energy GDP annually. The 2004–8 windfall was therefore significantly larger than the earlier booms, which each conferred windfalls of 35 to 39 percent of non-energy GDP during 1974–78 and 1979–81.[18]

The Legacy of Hydrocarbon Revenue Deployment
from the 1974–81 Booms

In 1970, extraparliamentary protests in Trinidad and Tobago, mainly by black youth protesting unemployment, shook a seemingly strong government into pursuing populist policies. Through the 1970s, the government espoused a nationalistic strategy for deploying the hydrocarbon rent. After a promising start that saved around 70 percent of the 1974–78 windfall abroad and pushed international reserves to $1.8 billion by 1978, the rate of domestic absorption became overly rapid. The 1974–78 deployment increased both

Table 3.1 Rent, Domestic Absorption, Structural Change, and GNP Growth, Trinidad and Tobago, 1970–2007[1]

	1970–74	1975–79	1980–84	1985–89	1990–94	1995–99	2000–2004	2005–7
Rent proxies								
Energy depletion (percent GNI)	12.7	32.5	26.8	17.1	17.1	13.6	22.8	42.6
Terms of trade	n.a.	n.a.	155.6	97.4	n.a.	n.a.	101.8	129.9
Aid (percent GNI)	0.2	0.1	0.2	0.2	0.2	0.1	0.1	0.1
Arable land/hd (ha)	0.1	0.1	0.1	0.1	0.1	0.1	0.1	0.1
Absorption (percent GNP)								
Fixed capital	24.3	24.1	26.1	17.9	15.4	25.9	22.3	13.9
Final govt. consumption	14.1	12.9	17.8	19.3	12.3	11.8	12.2	11.6
Private consumption	54.2	48.3	54.4	60.1	62.0	58.0	53.7	48.6
Exports (percent GDP)	45.2	49.5	38.8	36.3	43.6	51.5	54.3	64.3
Real exchange rate[2]	n.a.	95.7	126.8	118.9	107.8	95.1	105.0	129.9
Structural change								
Agriculture (percent GDP)	n.a.	n.a	n.a.	2.9	2.5	2.2	1.2	0.4
Industry	n.a.	n.a.	n.a.	41.7	46.0	44.4	50.0	60.2

(continued)

Table 3.1 (continued)

	1970–74	1975–79	1980–84	1985–89	1990–94	1995–99	2000–2004	2005–7
Manufacturing	n.a.	n.a	n.a.	10.8	10.1	8.4	7.5	5.9
Services	n.a.	n.a	n.a.	55.4	51.5	53.4	48.7	39.5
Growth								
Population (percent/yr)	0.9	1.2	1.8	0.9	0.7	0.5	0.4	0.3
GDP (percent/yr)	3.2	6.1	0.8	−3.3	1.0	4.6	8.1	7.9
PCGDP (percent/yr)	2.2	4.9	−1.0	−4.2	0.2	4.0	7.7	7.5
PCGDP (US$2,000)	4,800	5,755	6,755	5,196	4,866	5,440	7,265	9,954
Crop output index[3]	184.5	160.3	110.9	99.6	116.8	108.2	92.8	79.3

Source: World Bank, *Development Indicators 2008* (Washington, D.C.: World Bank, 2008).
1. 2008 data still not available
2. 2000 = 100
3. 1999–2001 = 100.

domestic investment (12 percent of the windfall) and consumption (18 percent) and boosted inflation so that investment efficiency fell. Half the domestic investment went into infrastructure and just under one-third went into state-led gas-based industry.[19] The expansion of state ownership included the nationalization of some hydrocarbon operations such as the Shell oil refinery and the labor-intensive sugar industry, which was dominated by Indian supporters of the leading opposition party and was subsidized to maintain employment rather than being competitively restructured.

The nationalistic strategy sought to maximize domestic rent retention by investing in state-led resource-based industrialization (RBI). Unfortunately, the government invested in those options offering the lowest potential rent per unit of heat value. Estimates made from feasibility studies in the early 1980s indicate that direct-reduced iron (steel made by this process uses scrap and is cheaper than blast furnace [DRI] steel, the principal choice of the government of Trinidad and Tobago) offered considerably lower potential rent per unit of gas applied than chemicals, which in turn generated less rent than liquefied natural gas.[20]

Moreover, the new state enterprises struggled to implement and operate the RBI projects. The wholly state-owned $500 million ISCOTT steel plant experienced a 30 percent cost overrun and then lost $108 million annually through 1982–85 before the management was contracted to private European firms. The plant was eventually sold in 1988 to Mittal as a viable concern but for a nominal sum. The methanol and fertilizer plants were implemented as joint ventures with multinational firms and proved more profitable. However, the proposed LNG project offered the highest potential netback per unit of gas, but the government rejected it because its domestic multiplier seemed limited.[21]

Control of public expenditure lapsed toward the end of the 1974–78 boom and then broke down through the 1979–81 boom. The domestic rent deployment became more expansionary so that barely half the 1979–81 windfall was saved overseas and the rest was split evenly between investment and consumption. Far from expanding the relative size of the non-energy tradable sector, the ambitious industrialization strategy was associated with a further contraction. On the eve of the oil boom, in 1972, the share of non-energy tradables in non-energy GDP had been only two-thirds the size expected for an economy of Trinidad and Tobago's size and per capita income and through 1981 the ratio shrank by another 10 percent of non-energy GDP.[22] The rent-seeking public sector propagated pay raises throughout the economy, but, as Dudley Seers had warned,[23] without offsetting gains in productivity.[24] Inflation intensified and strengthened the real exchange rate by two-thirds during 1980–85, exacerbating Dutch disease effects.

Meanwhile, the efficiency of domestic public investment deteriorated as inflation quadrupled the cost of capital projects such as schools and hospitals, indicating leakage of rent into the overstretched domestic construction industry. Instead of seeking to boost productivity in the non-energy tradables sectors, the government protected agriculture and manufacturing—simultaneously removing their incentive to be efficient and expanding their reliance on subsidies that further drained the rent, as rent cycling theory predicts. In addition, the RBI cost overruns combined with deteriorating global markets to render their contribution to public finances negative rather than positive, as planned.

When energy prices sagged in the mid-1980s and rent recipients resisted cutbacks, the subsidies to the public sector and also to mainly middle-income consumers eroded the accumulated reserves. This tardy economic adjustment ran down the foreign exchange reserves to only $200 million by 1992 compared with $3.4 billion a decade earlier.[25] The windfall consumption expansion mainly benefited the urban middle class by lowering non-energy taxation (income tax and value-added tax) and expanding energy subsidies, which through 1981–83 absorbed one-quarter of the hydrocarbon revenue. Moreover, public sector employment became the largest source of jobs, though many jobs were uneconomic. The perpetual fiscal deficits impeded stabilization and economic recovery. Trinidad and Tobago experienced a painful growth collapse through 1982–93, which cut per capita income by one-third and almost doubled unemployment to 22 percent by 1989.[26] The long-serving Afro Caribbean government was swept from office in 1986, and this ushered in a period of political instability and eventually a constitutional crisis that further impeded economic stabilization.

Table 3.1 shows that economic recovery belatedly commenced in 1993 after a 25 percent depreciation of the real exchange rate. It was, however, propelled by a sustained expansion of investment in natural gas rather than non-energy activity. In 1998, the economy was again destabilized when low oil prices abruptly cut government revenue from hydrocarbons by 6 percent of GDP. The trade gap ballooned, albeit mainly due to the surge in imports to construct gas-based plants, and debt reached 40 percent of GDP. In 1998, hydrocarbons and petrochemicals still generated 46 percent of exports, 21 percent of GDP, and 7 percent of government revenue, and the IMF encouraged the government to prioritize non-oil diversification.[27] However, the unexpected hydrocarbon windfall of 2004–8 eased reform pressure and tested how much governments like that of Trinidad and Tobago had learned from previous windfalls.

Trinidad and Tobago's Response to the 2004–8 Hydrocarbon Windfall

The Deteriorating Quality of Governance

The quality of governance declined during the 1998–2007 period, so although Trinidad and Tobago retains superior governance indices compared with some other middle-income, oil-driven economies such as Mexico and Russia (see Table 3.2), it lags best practice for mineral economies as set by Chile and Botswana. Moreover, the indices for Trinidad and Tobago declined during this period despite the fact that per capita income doubled and that rising income is expected to improve governance. The memo item in Table 3.2 benchmarks the extent of the deterioration, which was especially marked in respect to the control of graft, the rule of law, and political stability. It is more modest with regard to government regulation and voice and accountability.

The decline in governance was initially associated with heightened political uncertainty. The Indian-dominated government that came to power in 1995 was weakened by allegations of electoral irregularities that surfaced in 2000. Three elections occurred in as many years during 2000–2002 as accusations of corruption undermined the government and returned to power the Afro Caribbean-dominated opposition party that had governed from 1962 to 1986. The business of government was virtually paralyzed for almost one year by noncooperation between the parties after a tied election result until fresh elections in 2002 returned the Afro Caribbean party to power with a slim majority of four seats. The opposition (Indian party) leader was subsequently arrested and briefly detained on charges of having an undeclared overseas savings account. The incoming Afro Caribbean government benefited from the 2004–8 hydrocarbon boom and won re-election in 2007 with almost two-thirds of the seats in parliament, but it too experienced accusations of corruption.

Despite the deterioration in governance, the underlying direction of economic policy remained nominally consistent and continued to prioritize

Table 3.2 Per Capita GDP and Institutional Quality 2007: Trinidad and Tobago and Comparator Economies

Country	PCGDP (US$ PPP 2007)	Voice + accountability	Political stability	Effective governance	Regulation burden	Rule of law	Control of graft	Aggregate index
Bolivia	4,206	0.02	-0.99	-0.83	-1.18	-0.98	-0.49	-4.45
Ecuador	7,449	-0.23	-0.91	-1.04	-1.09	-1.04	-0.87	-5.18
Azerbaijan	7,851	-1.13	-0.69	-0.66	-0.50	-0.83	-1.04	-4.85
Venezuela	12,156	-0.58	-1.23	-0.87	-1.56	-1.47	-1.04	-6.75
Botswana	13,604	0.49	0.84	0.70	0.48	0.67	0.90	4.08
Chile	13,880	0.98	0.55	1.22	1.45	1.17	1.35	6.72
Mexico	14,104	-0.02	-0.57	0.13	0.39	-0.58	-0.35	-1.00
Russia	14,690	-1.01	-0.75	-0.40	-0.44	-0.97	-0.72	-4.29
Trinidad + Tobago	23,507	0.61	0.08	0.37	0.68	-0.22	-0.19	1.33
Oman	22,225[1]	-1.03	0.76	0.38	0.63	0.73	0.82	2.29
Norway	53,433	1.53	1.28	2.12	1.44	2.00	2.09	10.46
Memo Item								
Trinidad + Tobago 1998	10,145	0.83	0.44	0.01	0.79	0.36	0.15	2.58

Source: World Bank, *Development Indicators 2007* (Washington, D.C.: World Bank, 2007).

1. Oman PCGDP 2006

Note: Index range from 2.5 to −2.5, based on several surveys in each country.

a more competitive and diversified economy but with limited commitment and even less success. The IFIs became the main advocates of economic reform to sustain growth over the long term, whereas domestic governments focused on electoral arithmetic.

Efficient Hydrocarbon Production and Revenue Extraction

Hydrocarbon production and revenue extraction are both efficient in Trinidad and Tobago. The government owns the hydrocarbon resources, but the fact that the reserves are almost entirely offshore has boosted the total capital and expertise required so that governments have had little choice but to rely heavily on foreign corporations for capital, technology, and marketing. State-owned Petrotrin handles government partnerships with international oil companies. Other state-owned companies further downstream include the National Gas Corporation, which distributes gas, and the National Energy Corporation, which manages resource-processing activity through joint ventures with multinational partners. The joint ventures with reputable foreign companies that take a sizeable equity commitment are prudent because the private partners ensure the joint ventures are run commercially.[28]

The government allocates state-owned hydrocarbon fields for exploration through competitive bidding. However, the principal incumbents, BP (via its acquisition of Amoco) and British Gas (BG) benefit from some inertia. BP and state-owned Petrotrin produce 95 percent of the oil in the country and contribute roughly equal shares, and this provides most of the oil processed in the domestic refinery. BP also produces 70 percent of the gas, BG produces 23 percent, and four small companies produce the rest. By 2005, LNG production had expanded to 15 million tons, with the state owning up to 11 percent of the equity in the five LNG trains. The National Gas Corporation distributes the two-fifths of the gas production that is not exported to power generators (9 percent), DRI steel (1 percent), and petrochemical plants: fertilizer (22 percent) and methanol (9 percent). Although domestic industrial gas prices fluctuate with product prices, the low cost of delivery confers a competitive edge to local industrial users, and Trinidad and Tobago captured 3 percent and 5 percent, respectively, of global fertilizer and methanol sales.[29] By the eve of the 2004–8 hydrocarbon boom, the production of oil and petrochemicals in Trinidad and Tobago generated almost 40 percent of GDP, 41 percent of government revenues, and 83 percent of exports. Admittedly, it generated barely 3 percent of total employment, some 20,000 jobs.[30]

The revenue extraction in Trinidad and Tobago is also efficient though unfortunate timing of lifting agreements has rendered the gas revenue low. The tax regime is profit-sensitive and also moderate in scale, so investors are encouraged to exploit the resources efficiently. The government charges a royalty of one-tenth of the wellhead cost, which is treated as a cost for tax purposes. In addition, the government raises a levy that is less than 3 percent of revenue plus a small fee to cover the Ministry of Energy costs and a 0.1 percent green levy. After taking account of the fixed government imposts, corporate profits are taxed at a rate of 50 percent in the case of oil, plus another 5 percent employment tax. In addition, there is a supplementary windfall tax that is linked to the price of oil and calibrated at 0 percent when oil is $13 a barrel and 25 percent when the price reaches $50 a barrel or more. The total tax take is 80 to 85 percent, within the top quartile of global government takes according to the work of Daniel Johnstone and Emil Sunley.[31] Gas is more lightly taxed than oil, with a negligible royalty, a 35 percent income tax, and no supplementary or windfall taxation.

Consequently, during the initial investor tax holiday, most of any price windfall accrues to the (overwhelmingly foreign) investor while, absent contract renegotiations, almost two-thirds of any windfall will accrue to those investors when the tax break expires. The gas contracts imply that government revenues from the new LNG plants have been negligible during the 2004–8 boom, so the gas revenue the government received during that boom emanated overwhelmingly from previously established fields that were producing around 150,000 barrels of oil equivalent per day, barely one-fifth the projected rate of LNG production. Although total revenue from gas production is three times that of oil, the *aggregate* government revenue from natural gas is less than one-third that of oil. Part of the discrepancy in gas and oil revenue reflects the fact that gas costs more to ship per unit of heat value than oil, and the rapid recoupment of the vast sums invested, mainly by the international oil companies, dominates the initial cash flow. Gas extraction also tends to have a longer and flatter production curve than oil, and this lowers returns and taxable revenue by shrinking the net present value of the gas revenue stream relative to oil.[32] It may have been providential that the gas windfall was muted, given the impact of domestic windfall absorption.

Hydrocarbon Revenue Deployment 2004–8: Saving

Limited as it was by unfortunate timing of the LNG contracts, the 2004–8 hydrocarbon windfall still exceeded earlier booms. Taking 1999–2003 as the pre-boom base period and 2004–8 as the boom years, the energy windfall conferred an extra $6.2 billion (TT$38.9 billion) annually when averaged across those years. Increased hydrocarbon prices augmented the gas sector growth effect to double the share of government revenue from energy. Rising prices first doubled the share to 11.5 percent of GDP, when comparing 2003–5 with 1998–2002, and then almost double it again to average 19.6 percent of GDP through 2006–8.[33] Compared with countries that have similar per capita income and population size, Trinidad and Tobago's share of *non-energy* GDP was almost one-third higher. This amounted to an extra 4.7 percent of GDP, even before adding revenue from energy taxation.[34]

Trinidad and Tobago's government needed to allocate its windfall revenue between saving and consumption as well as between the public sector and private sector. The final column of Table 3.3 provides a crude estimate of the allocation of the annual energy windfall of TT$38.9 billion (in current prices) (the approximate exchange rate is TT$6.30/US$1). Table 3.3 uses a simplified version of the methodology devised by Alan Gelb and his research associates, which assumes that the windfall was responsible for any deviations in the allocation of GDP during the boom compared with the pre-boom allocation.[35] This approach first calculates the actual gain in GDP during the windfall (column 4) and then re-estimates absorption in the absence of extra energy output (column 5). This amount is then subtracted from the actual gain in GDP to yield the increase attributable to the windfall (column 6). The resulting windfall allocations are then calculated as ratios for their shares of the total windfall (column 7) and non-energy GDP (column 8).

Table 3.3 estimates that more than two-thirds of Trinidad and Tobago's hydrocarbon windfall was saved. The rate of saving jumped through 2004–8 and was associated with a sharp rise in government saving that lifted the foreign currency reserves by 16 percent of GDP and the Heritage Saving Fund (HSF) by 8 percent of GDP. The government had already established an Interim Saving Fund (ISF) in 2000 as a cushion against an unexpected negative price shock. The HSF replaced the ISF in 2004 with a mandate to save part of the energy revenue for stabilization, achieve intergenerational wealth transfers, and make strategic investments.[36] The fund automatically

Table 3.3 Estimated Absorption of Trinidad and Tobago's 2004–8 Windfall (TT$b, except columns 7 and 8)

Absorption category	Base absorption rate 1999–2003	Actual absorption 2004–8	Absorption rise 2004–8 >1999–2003	Predicted gain without energy windfall[1]	Absorption gain attributed to energy windfall[2]	Estimated share of windfall (percent total)[3]	Estimated windfall gain (percent NEGDP)
Total GDP	55.3	118.9	63.6	24.4	39.2	100	
Non-energy GDP	39.0	64.4	25.4	17.2	8.2		59.3
Energy GDP	16.3	54.5	38.2	7.2	31.0		
Consumption	36.8	59.0	22.7	16.0	6.7	17.0	10.4
Public	6.7	13.1	6.4	2.9	3.5	8.9	5.4
Private	29.6	45.7	16.1	13.0	3.1	7.9	4.8
Investment	12.6	24.8	12.2	5.5	6.7	17.0	10.4
Public	3.0	12.1	9.1	1.3	7.8	19.8	12.1
Private	9.6	12.7	3.1	4.2	–1.1	–2.8	–1.7
Net saving (net exports)	6.5	35.3	28.8	2.9	25.9	66.0	40.4
Unaccounted absorption	n.a.	1.1	0.1	0.3	–0.2	0.0	1.9
Memo Item							
GDP growth rate (percent/yr)	7.6	6.9	–0.7	n.a.	n.a.	n.a.	n.a.

Source: IMF, "Trinidad and Tobago: Article IV Consultation—Staff Report," *IMF Staff Country Report 09/78* (Washington, D.C.: IMF, 2009).
1. Based on constant level of energy GDP and assuming (i) no real growth in energy GDP and (ii) the composition of absorption remains the same in 2004–8 as in 1999–2003
2. Column 4 minus column 5
3. Percentage share of total energy windfall from column 6

receives revenue in excess of 10 percent of budget projections, and by 2008 the HSF had accumulated $2.9 billion, equivalent by then to 11.6 percent of GDP. The fund's average annual rate of accumulation during the boom was almost 2 percent of GDP.

The HSF allocates 60 percent of its revenue to a financial investment portfolio to acquire more liquid assets that are managed by the Central Bank. The remaining 40 percent is allocated to secure strategic assets that are supervised by the HSF board, chaired by the Minister of Finance, which publishes quarterly accounts. In addition to the HSF, the government oversaw an expansion of the official reserves from TT$12.3 billion in 1999–2003 to TT$34.0 billion through 2004–8, a rise equivalent to an extra 5 percent of GDP annually (see Table 3.3). Finally, the saving effort was associated with a contraction in the ratio of public sector debt to GDP from 53 percent at the start of the energy boom to 16 percent by 2008.[37] However, this decline was achieved almost entirely by holding the debt level constant rather than by retiring debt. Worse, the overall saving effort during the windfall *decreased* as the boom persisted, impairing the HSF stabilization role and boosting the procyclical nature of public expenditure.[38]

Despite the government saving effort in Trinidad and Tobago through the 2004–8 boom, IMF projections suggest it has been insufficient. The IMF provided two fiscal projections for assessing the level of public expenditure in Trinidad and Tobago through the mid-2000s.[39] The first approach converts the expected revenue from hydrocarbon extraction into a fund that can sustain non-energy deficits but at a rate that shrinks as the size of both the population and the non-energy sector grow. The second method targets a constant non-energy fiscal deficit ratio that can be maintained indefinitely as population grows and the non-energy economy expands.[40]

The first of the two projections accumulates a fund equivalent to 135 percent of non-energy GDP, which after 2042 (when hydrocarbon production is projected to cease) continues to generate an income at a rate that matches the non-energy deficit. The IMF projects that in order to maintain a non-energy fiscal deficit constant in absolute terms (albeit shrinking in relative terms), Trinidad and Tobago's fiscal deficit should not exceed 10.7 percent of non-energy GDP in the mid-2000s.[41] In fact, the country's non-energy deficit for 2004–8 was around 28 percent of non-energy GDP (and 15 percent of total GDP) as a consequence of sustained public expenditure.[42]

The second projection is even more stringent. It keeps the deficit constant indefinitely as a *ratio* of non-energy GDP (that is, taking account of growth in population and income), which requires the accumulated sum saved to reach 430 percent of non-energy GDP by the time hydrocarbon production ceases. To meet this condition, the non-energy fiscal deficit must shrink to 4.5 percent, which is the level that the accumulated sum can sustain indefinitely. If the IMF assumptions are broadly correct and Trinidad and Tobago's government persists with the current higher non-energy deficits, an adjustment in the balance of public finances totaling 30 percent of non-energy GDP must be compressed into the period 2008–20 in order to achieve a sustainable position.

Delia Velculescu and Saqib Rizavi suggest the HSF can be improved by initially transferring all energy revenues into the fund and drawing upon it to cover budget deficits only as the permanent income hypothesis (PIH) rule prescribes.[43] They also recommend that HSF assets should comprise bonds and equity (perhaps in the ratio of 60/40) in diverse currencies to earn the target return while limiting risk. A statute should also be enacted to ensure that the assets are not loaned for projects or used as collateral. Finally, any boost to "normal" expenditure from running a sustainable non-energy deficit should take the form of capital rather than consumption. These recommendations are consistent with the principles of the environmental accounting approach to sustainability. For example, investment in both infrastructure and education is preferable to raising public sector wages or expanding consumer subsidies, which came to dominate the deployment of the 1979–81 Trinidad and Tobago windfall and resurfaced during the 2004–8 boom.

Hydrocarbon Revenue Deployment, 2004–8: Domestic Absorption

Adherence to the PIH rule has limited appeal to politicians who must manage coalitions to remain in office. It is too rigid to deal with a situation in which no single political party has a built-in majority, which allows sectional interests to play the largest parties against each other in order to extract concessions for their own groups. In contrast to conditions in Trinidad and Tobago, the longevity of both the Augusto Pinochet regime and its center-left democratic successor in Chile appears to have helped confer a more long-term perspective on politicians regarding rent allocation. At the other extreme, the singular instability of Ecuador's factional politics nudges the government in that country toward short-run allocations that jeopardize future investment and therefore revenue. Trinidad and Tobago lies somewhere between these two cases because its windfall allocation rules confer higher immediate revenue than the PIH would and that revenue can be invested in government survival. The flexibility also confers scope to boost revenues in the event of strongly deteriorating political fortunes. In addition, these flexible revenues allow the government to target interest groups through an expansion of public sector projects and subsidized consumption of "essentials" that all too often benefit the well off in the name of helping the poor.

Such political considerations have driven the economically suboptimal deployment of the 2004–8 rent windfall in Trinidad and Tobago. One-third of Trinidad and Tobago's energy windfall was absorbed domestically (see Table 3.3, column 7). The extra absorption was shared equally between consumption and investment, but the ratios of the shares of the public and private sectors changed markedly. At the start of the 2004–8 boom, public expenditure targeted reducing poverty and improving health and education rather than, as had been the case in the 1970s, expanding construction and subsidizing loss-making state enterprises. The increased domestic absorption by the public sector during 2004–8 lifted consumption via higher civil service remuneration and an expansion of subsidies on fuel[44] and state-run firms, along with a boost to social expenditure. Public sector wages grew by just under 1.5 percent of GDP during 2004–8, and the rise in public sector transfers (subsidies) totaled 4.7 percent of GDP, pushing them to 8 percent of GDP. The transfers included a 1.4 percent increase in energy subsidies[45] along with a 1.1 percent rise in transfers to state-owned enterprises and utilities, a 1.2 percent of GDP rise in transfers to education and health, and a doubling in unspecified transfers.

After an initial delay, the rate of public investment in Trinidad and Tobago rose very sharply as the boom persisted. The 2004–8 boom was associated with a more than fourfold expansion in public investment that absorbed almost one-tenth of the windfall (see Table 3.4). It lifted public sector investment to parity with private sector investment, but this does not augur well for the economy-wide efficiency of investment because the rapid rate of public investment expansion increased the likelihood of encountering capacity constraints both within the public sector and from private sector suppliers. The principal government justification for the expanded investment was the developmental one of reducing the backlog in transport infrastructure and utilities. But the Inter-American Development Bank (IADB) deplores the inefficiency of public investment in Trinidad and Tobago.[46] It

Table 3.4 Public and Private Investment, Trinidad and Tobago, 1999–2008 (% GDP)

	1999	2000	2001	2002	2003	2004	2005	2006	2007	2008
Gross domestc investment	21.1	17.1	19.5	19.2	25.2	16.6	14.6	21.0	24.0	24.2
Public	6.9	5.8	6.0	4.6	4.3	6.3	8.1	10.5	11.8	12.0
Private	14.2	11.3	13.5	14.6	20.9	10.3	6.5	10.5	12.2	12.2
Oil price (US$/b)	18.0	28.2	24.3	25.0	28.9	37.8	53.4	64.3	71.1	97.5

Source: IMF, "Trinidad and Tobago: Article IV Consultation—Staff Report," *IMF Staff Country Report 09/78* (Washington, D.C.: IMF, 2009), 21.

also sharply questions a trend toward increasing recourse to off-budget expenditures that further reduces transparency, which would improve efficiency. Whatever its economic merits, increased government expenditure on consumption (via public sector wage hikes and subsidies) and sharply higher public investment projects carry political dividends that helped the Afro Caribbean government win the 2007 election.

Private consumption also rose because non-energy taxation became a smaller share of the country's GDP. Although non-energy taxes rose, in absolute terms they were surpassed by an even faster expansion in energy tax revenue. Non-energy taxation grew slower than GDP, so its share fell by 5 percent of GDP in 2004–8 compared to its share in 1999–2003, and this intensified a trend that had preceded the boom. The private sector also experienced a marked surge in saving during the 2004–8 boom, but this did little to boost private investment, which fell short of the predicted outcome in the absence of the windfall (see Table 3.3, column 5). The gap between private saving and private investment is partly attributable to the energy sector's dominance of private investment in Trinidad and Tobago. The private sector ended a period of rapid construction just as the boom took off and began to recoup the massive front-loaded funds invested in the LNG project. The gap is also partly due to the continued perception by the private sector of disappointing returns in the non-energy economy. One result of this singular pattern of absorption was a marked fall in the share of total investment in GDP during 2004–5, after which a modest recovery set in that was for the most part due to the sharp expansion in public investment that dominated total investment.

Consistent with the rent cycling theory, inflation accelerated as the labor market tightened and unemployment was cut in half to 5 percent of the workforce, lowering investment efficiency. The incoming government in 2003 stoked inflation with a 15 percent increase in public sector wages (to reward a key political constituency), and inflation reached double figures by 2008. The rise had demonstration effects throughout the private sector so that economy-wide wage inflation outstripped gains in productivity. Meanwhile labor shortages emerged in energy and finance even as surplus labor persisted elsewhere, indicating that overall the workforce is underskilled. Total employment expanded by around 10 percent during 2000–2008, but the structure of employment shifted away from tradable activity, which points to Dutch disease effects, an outcome consistent with the 30 percent strengthening of the real exchange rate during the boom (see Table 3.1, line 12). Although employment in oil and gas grew by one-third, its modest total (20,000 workers) could not prevent the overall contraction in the tradables sector workforce caused by the net fall of employment in agriculture and manufacturing (see Table 3.5). Employment in agriculture shrank by one-third, which was linked to the demise of Caroni sugar, and manufacturing employment stagnated. Meanwhile, the cyclical construction sector doubled its employment to one-fifth of the total, an amount almost equivalent to the economy-wide increase in employment. A similar number of jobs were created by government make-work programs. Table 3.6 confirms the manifestations of "Dutch disease" by tracing structural change in terms of value added.

The impact of the 2004–8 boom proved timely for economic growth: the investment in gas production from 1999 to 2004 had created its own boom that drove the economy at a rate of 7.6 percent per annum, and the windfall sustained a similar growth momentum until the end of 2008. When the major energy investment in LNG ceased, increased domestic revenue absorption sustained GDP growth of 6.9 percent annually in 2004–8. Growth in the energy sector decelerated abruptly in 2008, however, due to the softness of oil prices and to capacity constraints on petrochemicals. GDP growth slowed to 0.5 percent.

Overall, despite a high rate of saving through the 2004–8 boom, insufficient windfall revenue was saved to prevent the deployment from being procyclical. Trinidad and Tobago's economy experiences the highest volatility within its region, an outcome that fiscal policy has accentuated rather than muted.[47] This trend continued into the 2008–9 downswing, albeit in

Table 3.5 Employment Trends, Trinidad and Tobago, 1999–2008 (1,000s)

	Unemployed	Total employed	Construction	Oil and gas	Agriculture	Manufacturing	Transport + communication	Other employment	Total workforce
1999	74.0	489.4	67.1	15.1	39.6	53.6	35.8	269.4	563.4
2000	69.6	503.3	69.7	15.9	36.4	55.6	39.2	285.9	572.9
2001	62.4	514.1	78.8	15.5	40.1	53.9	38.9	285.3	576.5
2002	61.2	525.1	75.6	17.2	36.1	56.6	41.8	296.4	586.2
2003	62.4	534.2	80.0	16.1	31.4	55.8	41.6	307.3	596.6
2004	51.2	562.4	91.1	18.6	26.0	60.3	41.6	322.9	613.5
2005	49.7	574.8	101.8	19.3	25.0	56.6	41.8	327.1	623.7
2006	39.0	586.6	104.6	19.7	25.8	56.2	42.7	335.6	625.2
2007	34.5	587.9	110.2	21.5	22.4	55.4	41.5	336.5	622.4
2008	30.4	594.0	117.7	19.8	25.2	56.0	42.2	332.3	624.3

Source: Central Bank (2009).

Table 3.6 Structural Change by GDP/NEGDP Ratio, Trinidad and Tobago, 1999–2008

	1999	2000	2001	2002	2003	2004	2005	2006	2007	2008
GDP (percent GDP)	42.89	51.37	55.00	56.29	71.17	82.65	100.39	122.11	137.43	151.36
Non-energy	76.0	69.1	71.6	73.4	64.2	61.9	53.9	50.6	53.7	52.8
Energy	22.5	31.3	28.3	26.2	35.9	39.1	46.0	49.2	45.1	46.5
Non-energy GDP (percent NEGDP)										
Agriculture	2.5	2.0	1.8	1.9	1.5	1.2	0.9	1.0	0.7	0.6
Manufacturing	10.4	10.2	10.3	10.9	10.8	12.2	9.8	10.1	10.9	9.2
Construction	10.5	10.8	11.1	9.9	11.4	11.6	13.8	13.9	15.6	17.9

Source: IMF, "Trinidad and Tobago: Article IV Consultation—Staff Report," *IMF Staff Country Report 09/78* (Washington, D.C.: IMF, 2009).

reverse as cutbacks deepened the growth deceleration. In 2009, the government responded to a projected deceleration in the rate of economic growth to 2 percent by reducing public expenditure by 2 percent of GDP and permitting a modest increase in the overall fiscal deficit projected at 1 percent of GDP. The IMF recommended a further cut in public spending of 4 percent of GDP through the medium term in order to trim the non-energy deficit to at least 8.5 percent of GDP as an *interim* step toward a more sustainable balance.[48] Wary of its declining popularity ahead of elections, however, the government preferred to trim public sector investment, embracing public/private partnerships in an effort to minimize the impact of the cuts while still maintaining higher social spending.[49]

The imperative to maintain political support in Trinidad and Tobago has deflected public windfall expenditure from efficient wealth creation, which rent cycling theory warns against. Unfortunately, data regarding public spending on programs such as health, education, and social security are incomplete and cannot be used to measure changes linked to windfall expenditure.[50] However, the levels of such expenditure on the eve of the boom appeared to lag behind the mean for upper-middle-income economies even though Trinidad and Tobago is one of the wealthiest in this group and might be expected to have ratios above the mean. Yet despite being one of the region's richest countries, education enrollment lagged, yet the share of GDP allocated to subsidies doubled in real terms through the boom.[51] By far the biggest increase in windfall expenditure was in public investment projects, which garner more political support for the ruling regime than national programs do because the latter tend to benefit all voters alike rather than just potential supporters.

The prime domestic constituencies that benefited from the increased windfall expenditure have been middle-class consumers, the urban unions, and businesses. Consumers benefited from the reduced ratio of non-energy taxation that the increase in energy revenue made available and from fuel prices subsidized below global levels, both of which benefit the urban middle class disproportionately, as discussed earlier. Traditionally, each main party favored a specific set of unions based on differences in the ethnic composition of the union membership. The Indian party favored rural workers and the Afro Caribbean party favored the predominantly urban civil service. Although restructuring of the sugar industry during the boom severely weakened the agricultural unions, the civil service unions remain a political force to be reckoned with.[52] Public sector workers tend to be well remunerated compared with the national average, and their importance within the economy confers strong capacity to trigger wage inflation. Whereas the economy-wide real unit cost of labor had been falling prior to the 2003 public sector wage hike, it subsequently began to rise at a rate that outstripped inflation. Higher wage costs, falling unemployment, and supply bottlenecks from boom-driven growth in public expenditure combined to strengthen the real exchange rate and neutralize the beneficial competitive effect of the 25 percent real depreciation in 1993.

Public investment has also proved a double-edged sword. Despite relatively high levels of public spending for a country of its per capita income, Trinidad and Tobago had until the 2004–8 windfall experienced a low rate of public investment that, worse still, had earned relatively poor returns in education, health, and economic infrastructure services.[53] In this context, the sharp rise in public investment through the boom does not augur well for the efficiency of resource use. Nor does the political emphasis on investment projects in order to woo business support and create employment in construction appear to have translated into improving the competitiveness of the business environment. Rather, as rent cycling theory predicts, it has bestowed favors on specific firms at the expense of efficient wealth creation. Trinidad and Tobago performs poorly as a business environment, notably in terms of registering property, enforcing contracts, closing businesses, and firing labor.

Far from boosting competitive diversification, economic growth during the 2004–8 boom was dominated by the energy sector and mainly by domestic expenditure of government energy revenue rather than the multiplier from directly linked oil supply activity. The energy sector has developed only low-end linkages to the domestic economy, such as manufacturing simple plastic products such as garden furniture, rather than more sophisticated activity such as geological modeling, deep-sea drilling, and energy equipment manufacturing.[54] Aside from energy, an IADB study of revealed comparative advantage found few prospects for Trinidad and Tobago, which performed worse than any other economy in the Latin American and Caribbean region.[55] Public expenditure grew to account for almost 50 percent of non-energy GDP and crowded out private investment, which is also constrained by apprehension over rising crime, underinvestment in infrastructure and human capital, the appreciating real exchange rate, inadequate bank regulation, and the ballooning non-energy fiscal deficit.[56] Competitive diversification of the economy remains an aspiration rather than a priority.

Conclusions

Rent cycling theory suggests that Trinidad and Tobago has faced high risk of deploying its hydrocarbon windfalls maladroitly due to a combination of high point source rent, ethnic diversity, statist policy, and a young, ethnically diverse parliamentary democracy. Certainly, the deployment of the 1974–78 and 1979–81 windfall revenues left a disappointing legacy. Extraparliamentary protests in 1970 rattled a cautious government into pursuing statist and populist policies from 1974 to 1981 that caused over-rapid domestic absorption of the rent through expanded consumer subsidies and (loss-making) state enterprises, many in resource-based industries. The strategy entrenched rent-seeking interests and intensified Dutch disease effects, which triggered a protracted growth collapse from 1982 to 1993 that cut incomes by one-third. It also destabilized the polity as the two main political parties, each rooted in a major ethnic group, vied to co-opt one or more rent-seeking political factions. Growth finally resumed after an IFI-backed depreciation of the real exchange rate in 1993 and, perhaps more significantly, as natural gas exports expanded.

The response of Trinidad and Tobago to the 2004–8 boom was more circumspect than the reaction to the 1970s boom. In this respect, Trinidad and Tobago was unlike regional comparators Bolivia, Ecuador, and Venezuela. Trinidad and Tobago hydrocarbon *extraction* relied heavily on international oil company investment and has been efficient while the tax regime secured a share of hydrocarbon revenue that is near the global average.[5/] Although the unfortunate timing of recent natural gas projects diminished the scale of the rent, the rent *deployment* has been unsatisfactory because an effective pro-growth political coalition has yet to emerge. Although two-thirds of this rent was saved, public expenditure was still excessive and procyclical, lifting the non-energy fiscal deficit to three times what the hydrocarbon resource can *constantly* maintain (4 percent of non-energy GDP). The reason lies in a political economy that prioritizes coalition maintenance at the expense of long-term development. Concerns about political survival prompted governments to maintain support by accommodating rent-seeking groups, notably the unions, important private businesses, middle-class consumers, and smaller political parties that represented special-interest groups. The doubling in per capita income through the 2004–8 oil boom was associated with a decline in governance indices and may yet prove ephemeral, like that of the earlier booms. Dutch disease effects perpetuate the country's disappointing progress with the competitive diversification of the non-energy economy.

Trinidad and Tobago's experience underlines the need to expressly complement economic reform with a political strategy to manage rent-seeking recipients. The country requires a dual-track strategy that can grow a dynamic market economy and build a pro-growth political constituency that eventually neutralizes rent-seeking interests. Countries as diverse as China, Mauritius, and Malaysia achieved this through a dual-track strategy that grew a dynamic market economy in special economic zones and postponed confrontation with rent-seeking interests in the rent-distorted economy until the dynamic sector grew a strong political constituency. One of Trinidad and Tobago's main parties should espouse such a dual-track strategy.

4

The Illusion of Unlimited Supply:
Iran and Energy Subsidies

Ahmad Mojtahed

Iran, one of the world's largest energy producers, also has some of the world's lowest domestic energy prices. This would seem to be an economic advantage, but the Iranian government has kept energy prices artificially low through a series of subsidies. These subsidies have created significant distortions in Iran's economy, including an inflation rate that reached 25.4 percent in 2009.

The Central Bank of Iran in 2008 estimated the annual amount of energy subsidies in Iran from 2001 to 2007 (see Table 4.1). Energy subsidies increased from $15.2 billion in 2001 to $87.6 billion in 2007. These figures mean subsidies increased from 7.6 percent of Iran's GDP to 26.2 percent of its GDP during this period. By any economic standard, this amount is too large and indicates inefficiencies and a waste of resources in the Iranian economy.

The costs of these subsidies are profound. The Iranian Oil Ministry estimates that the Iranian government as recently as 2005 spent more than a third of its budget on energy subsidies—an astronomical sum that amounts to almost a quarter of Iran's GDP.[1] In addition, Iranians have become accustomed to low energy prices and use more energy than they would if domestic prices were more in line with prices on the international market. Iran's total domestic energy consumption growth rate was 6 percent from 2000 to 2006, which is very high with respect to other countries. Even though it has some of the world's largest energy reserves, Iran's largest im-

Table 4.1 Energy Consumption, Prices, and Subsidies in Iran (2001–7)

Year	Total final consumption (barrel of oil equivalent)	Domestic energy price (rials/liter)	International energy price (rials/liter)	Energy subsidies ($ billion)	Subsidy as percent of GDP*
2001	149.9	230	687	15.2	7.6%
2002	165.7	259	1,281	21.1	13.2%
2003	174.4	318	1,391	22.6	12.2%
2004	189.3	360	1,966	24.8	15.8%
2005	201.2	356	3,003	59	23.5%
2006	208.4	352	3,449	70.1	25.9%
2007	214.7	382	4,206	87.8	26.7%
Average growth rate	6.2%	9.3%	37.6%	35.6	26.2%

Source: Central Bank of Iran, Energy Subsidies Report, Tehran, 2008.
*Iran's cumulative total energy subsidy from 2001 to 2007 was $446.1 billion.

port in terms of value is petroleum products. Iran has oil and natural gas that remains to be developed, but the state will not meet increasing domestic demand through drilling alone.

Several members of the Iranian political and economic elite have identified the problems that energy subsidies have created for Iranian society and want to eliminate them. During President Ahmadinejad's second presidential term, the Iranian Parliament began to consider a bill that would increase the price of gasoline to $0.43 a liter—still well below the price in most countries, but a 396 percent increase for Iranian consumers. Some projections suggest this type of change could cause a short-term contraction in Iran's GDP, but some economists disagree and stated "an increase in energy prices decreases its consumption and causes increase in efficiency and production."[2]

This kind of dramatic economic change presents significant political obstacles. The Iranian government will need to offset these changes through other economic and transportation policies, including the expansion of public transportation in cities and the development of energy conservation policy in industry and housing.

This chapter examines Iran's recent history of energy subsidies, proposals to reduce these subsidies, and attempts to bring Iran's energy prices more in line with international norms.

Iran's Energy Background

With a population of 71.5 million and area of 1.64 million square kilometers, Iran is among the world's twenty largest countries in both population and size. Iran is also a resource-abundant country with vast energy reserves and minerals such as iron, copper, zinc, and chromium. Iran's proven natural gas reserves in 2006 totaled 28.1 trillion cubic meters, which is 17 percent of the world's total reserves and ranks second only to Russia.

In addition, Iran's oil reserves of 137.5 billion barrels are the fifth largest in the world. Iran is currently the fifth-largest oil producer and the fourth-largest oil-exporter in the world.[3] With its fast population growth, industrialization, and electrification of rural areas, Iran faces a high rate of domestic energy consumption. With the depletion of Iran's existing oil fields, there are increasing demands for investment in new oil fields and for maintaining the production of existing fields with new technology such as gas injection. Iran faces real challenges in sustaining its current level of oil exports and meeting domestic demand at the same time. Iran's oil income increased dramatically during the first decade of this century and reached $82 billion in 2007 thanks to higher oil prices. Due to high domestic consumption in Iran, however, most new oil production went to meet domestic demand and compensate for depleted oil wells.

The Iranian government's policy of setting energy prices has had an important impact on energy consumption in the country. Iran's fuel prices are among the lowest in the world. Tehran's policy of keeping oil product prices constant or making only small price increases has kept gasoline and gas oil (diesel oil) prices low in Iran despite significant increases in oil prices worldwide. This policy has also dramatically increased demand for all types of energy in Iran compared to demand in other countries. Iran's "energy consumption intensive"—a measure of the use of energy for producing one unit of goods and services—was one of the world's highest in 2006.

To combat the hyperinflation that has plagued Iran during the last twenty years, Tehran has controlled energy prices—regardless of the impact this policy has had on domestic energy consumption or world market prices. These energy subsidies were popular among Iranian government officials and lawmakers until recently. But with dramatic changes in world oil prices and Iran's domestic energy consumption rates, attitudes have changed. In the government's Third Economic Development Plan (2000–2004) and Fourth

Economic Development Plan (2005–9), reducing energy subsidies has been a priority.

Energy Production

Among Middle Eastern countries, Iran ranks second among oil producers and first among natural gas producers. Iran's vast resources in oil and natural gas have not been fully explored, and every year a new discovery adds to previous reserves. In addition to oil production activities onshore, Iran is actively involved in offshore oil exploration in Persian Gulf areas belonging to Iran or close to maritime borders.

But Iran is behind the other Caspian countries in oil development due to a number of problems. (The northern part of Iran borders the Caspian Sea.) The legal status of Caspian seabed resources remains unclear. In addition to Iran, there are four other states—Azerbaijan, Kazakhstan, Russia, and Turkmenistan—that have claims on the Caspian's undersea resources. Access to known resources located in disputed border areas has not been resolved.

The second problem is a technical one. Iran's oil and gas resources in the Caspian Sea are located in deeper water than hydrocarbon deposits in other parts of the sea. Therefore, Iran needs special drilling equipment, which only recently became operational after a more than five-year delay. Because most of Iran's oil and gas activities have been concentrated in the southern part of the county, Tehran still needs to develop new facilities—including ports, pipelines, and refineries—for oil and gas development in the north.

With new oil-extraction technology and more investment in secondary recovery by gas injection and other methods, Iran could increase the oil recovery rate in its fields from around 16 percent to 30 percent. This would mean a considerable increase in production, but there are several obstacles to this goal. Most notably, U.S. sanctions on Iran have prevented international oil companies from investing in Iran, and Iran's constitution bars the government from granting concessions to foreign oil companies, as had happened prior to the 1979 Iranian Revolution.

In the last decade, Iran has invested heavily in natural gas exploration. This strategy is intended to increase the amount of natural gas available for domestic energy consumption and keep oil exports at a high level. Furthermore,

Table 4.2 Oil and Gas Production and Consumption in Iran (oil in 1,000 barrels per day; gas in billion cubic feet)

Year	2000	2001	2002	2003	2004	2005	2006	2007	2008
Total oil production	3,765.39	3,799.99	3,523.97	3,833.03	4,104.21	4,238.58	4,148.69	4,033.85	4,174.44
Oil exports	2,517	2,515	2,174	2,407	2,616	2,682	2,494	2,326	2,419
Natural gas production (dry natural gas)	2,127.4	2,330.8	2,648.6	2,860.5	2,962.9	3,563.3	3,835.2	3,951.7	NA*
Natural gas consumption (dry natural gas)	2,221	2,478.4	2,798	2,910	3,020.8	3,615.5	3,839.1	3948.2	NA

Source: Energy Information Administration (EIA) (2009); International Energy Outlook 2009, EIA.
*NA=Not Available

developing Iran's petrochemical industry, which is thought to add more value to the economy than oil and natural gas exports, is an industrial development policy priority. A new technology that substitutes natural gas for naphtha as a main input for petrochemical products gives Iran, which has the world's second-largest natural gas reserves, a potential cost advantage over many petrochemical producers in Europe and elswhere.

Iran's most important gas reserves are located in South Pars, a Persian Gulf gas field it shares with Qatar. Tehran has prioritized exploration of this field and declared twenty-five phases for production,[4] with more than 500 million cubic meters of production per day. Iran succeeded in developing ten phases and is negotiating with other countries to develop the remaining ones.

There are many other onshore and offshore gas fields in Iran that require new technology and heavy investment in exploration, pipelines, refineries, and other facilities to reach their final stage of development. Table 4.2 shows Iran's oil production, oil exports, natural gas production, and natural gas consumption from 2000 to 2008. Note that Iran imports slightly more natural gas than it exports.

Energy Consumption

Iran's total domestic energy consumption growth rate from 2000 to 2006 was 6 percent, which is very high in comparison to other countries. In 2007, the world's primary energy consumption grew by 2.4 percent to 11.1 billion tons of oil equivalent. During that year, Iran's primary energy consumption amounted to 182.9 million tons of oil equivalent, up by about 1.8 percent from the previous year. The annual growth rate has varied between 2000 and 2006. Some years it exceeded 10 percent, but in 2003 it was less than 1 percent, according to Iranian Energy Ministry reports (see Table 4.3).

Iran's refined petroleum product consumption grew by 3 percent between 2000 and 2007. The growth rate of these products—which include gasoline, diesel oil, liquid gas, heavy oil, and kerosene—varied. In some years it was negative, but in most years it was positive and even reached 7.7 percent in 2005. In addition to low prices, the growth rate for these products can be attributed to urbanization and the lack of adequate public transportation in Iran's big cities.

Promoting natural gas production and consumption is the core of Iran's energy policy, both domestically and internationally.[5] Iran—with vast

Table 4.3 Annual Growth Rate of Energy Consumption in Iran (%)

Year	2000	2001	2002	2003	2004	2005	2006	2007	Average growth
Refinery products	6.30	−2.77	3.75	1.71	3.13	7.68	5.13	−1.00	3.0
Natural gas	15.42	3.55	12.72	9.39	15.41	7.40	15.93	17.79	12.21
Electricity	6.17	9.72	6.10	3.41	8.71	5.28	4.98	8.79	6.65
Total energy consumption	12.97	1.94	10.79	0.84	8.97	5.52	1.48	5.38	5.99

Source: Iranian Energy Ministry, Annual Energy Balance Sheet, Tehran, 2008.

natural gas reserves and a strategic location between seven countries and several seas—can play an important role in the region. Iran exports natural gas to Turkey, Azerbaijan, and Armenia, and at the same time imports natural gas from Turkmenistan and Azerbaijan. Iran is also negotiating to export natural gas to Pakistan, India, Bahrain, the United Arab Emirates, Kuwait, and Oman. Iran, Turkey, and Turkmenistan are planning to transport Iran's and Turkmenistan's natural gas to Europe.

Iran's natural gas consumption grew by an average annual rate of 12.2 percent from 2000 to 2007, the highest among all energy sources in Iran. The natural gas consumption growth rate reached 17.8 percent in 2007, the highest in last eight years, due to very cold weather. This growth in natural gas use resulted from the government policy of promoting natural gas consumption by building networks of pipelines to substitute natural gas for refined petroleum products in household consumption, power plants, industry, petrochemical production, and public transportation (substituting compressed natural gas for gasoline and diesel oil in buses and taxies in cities). It is expected that Iran's natural gas consumption rate will continue to grow by more than 10 percent in some years if supply is sufficient.

From 2001 to 2007, Iran's annual electricity consumption grew by an average of 6.6 percent, the nineteenth-fastest rate in the world. The high rate of population growth since the Iranian Revolution, low electricity prices, electrification of rural areas, and the substitution of electricity for diesel oil in the agricultural sector are the most significant factors causing Iran's high rate of electricity consumption growth. Iran faces electricity shortages in peak hours, even though it has made large investments in power plants, exports electricity to neighboring countries (particularly Iraq and Pakistan), and exchanges electricity with other counties (notably Turkey and Azerbaijan).

Iranian Studies on Energy Production, Consumption, and Subsidies

Iranian government institutions regularly commission and publish studies related to the state's energy consumption and production patterns. Iran's Ministry of Oil, the National Iranian Oil Company (NIOC), and other affiliated companies have conducted several studies about the high demand for fuel in Iran and the impact a price hike on refinery products would have. In one 2005 study[6] about gasoline price adjustment using an econometric method (ARDL), researchers estimated that price elasticity for gasoline in the short run is inelastic (0.12), which means a price increase does not affect consumption much, but in the long run it increases to 0.22. The income elasticity for gasoline in the short run and long run is 0.48 and 0.88, respectively, indicating that gasoline is an inelastic commodity and is considered a necessity good. What this means is that in the short run, any increase in gasoline prices does not decrease consumption. An increase in income, on the other hand, has a more significant affect on demand for gasoline.

Another factor in this study is the number of vehicles using gasoline as fuel. If the stock of vehicles in Iran increases 1 percent, per capita demand for gasoline will increase 0.35 percent in the short run and 0.66 percent in the long run. Therefore, any policy that expands public transportation or substitutes old cars with new and more efficient ones will help reduce the demand for gasoline.

Using different methods, the study's authors showed that the price adjustment effect in this model is 0.54, meaning that 54 percent of disequilibrium resulting from the quantity of petrol consumption in each period would be eliminated in the long run. Thus, they argued that the effect of real price adjustment on the consumption of gasoline and other refinery products would occur quickly and be completed in less than two years. In contrast to other studies that suggest that price increases would not have an effect on consumption, this study suggested that if Iran increased real gasoline prices gradually from 800 rials to 6,000 rials per liter in five years, per capita consumption would decrease from 2,170 liters to 1,732 liters, a 20 percent reduction. But if these increases happen all at once, the per

Table 4.4 Results of Different Energy Price Increases (%)

Different scenarios	Household inflation	Intermediate inflation	Total inflation
Energy price increases based on Third Development Plan	1.21	1.32	2.53
Gasoline and diesel oil price increases in five steps	4.65	5.56	10.21
Gasoline, diesel oil, kerosene, and heavy oil price increases in five steps	7.10	8.53	15.63
Gasoline price increases in five steps	2.46	3.13	5.59
Gasoline price increases in one step	5.22	7.51	12.73
All energy prices increase to Persian Gulf FOB* price in one step	72.40	58.60	131.00
Gasoline, diesel oil, kerosene, and heavy oil price increases in one step	40.50	41.00	81.50

Source: Iranian Oil Ministry, "The Study of Energy Carriers' Price Increase on Inflation and Budget Expenditures of the Urban and Rural Families," Tehran, 2005, 94–95.
*FOB (Free on Board) is used in conjunction with a port of loading, under the International Chamber of Commerce standard. Indicating an FOB port means the seller pays for transport of the goods to port of shipment plus loading costs, and the buyer pays costs of marine freight transport, insurance, unloading, and transport from arrival port to final destination. Passing of risks occurs when the goods pass the ship's rail at the port of shipment.

capita consumption of gasoline will decrease even further—28 percent in five years.

In a study conducted by the Iranian Oil Ministry in 2005, researchers showed that if there were a 20 percent price increase for all refinery products, the average inflation rate would increase by 1.32 percent for intermediate sectors and 1.21 percent for households.[7] Among all economic sectors, the transportation and construction sectors would be affected most by price changes (see Table 4.4). Inflation is already a significant problem in Iran, as it reached 25.4 percent in 2009.

The total inflation under different scenarios of energy price increases ranged from 2.5 percent to 131 percent. The highest inflation would occur if all energy prices increased immediately to Persian Gulf FOB prices. But Iran's Oil Ministry researchers realized that a price increase alone will not decrease energy consumption, and it would not be a good policy unless accompanied by the expansion of public transportation in cities, railroad expansion, the optimization of energy consumption, and energy efficiency in industry and housing. In addition, the Iranian government must implement some protective measures to help low-income groups in order to prevent price increases from having undesirable effects.

Finally, the Oil Ministry report suggested the creation of a special fund or account for revenues generated by energy price adjustments. A board of trustees would supervise the account and spend the money in five areas:

1. The development and improvement of public transportation systems in all metropolitan areas
2. Direct energy subsidies to low-income families
3. Improvement of the environment and institution of pollution controls
4. Investment in new refineries and new technologies for old refineries
5. Investment in new energy-conserving technologies

An Iranian National Oil Company study titled "The Importance of Energy in National Economy" estimated the revenues that would be generated if Iran raised all refinery products' domestic prices to their 2006 global market prices. Table 4.5 shows the domestic and international (Persian Gulf FOB) prices for refinery products in 2006. Iran's Central Bank estimated the country spent $87.8 billion dollars in energy subsidies in 2007 alone. A separate 2005 Iranian Oil Ministry study reviewed all types of government subsidies during the government's Second and Third Development Plans. The share of energy subsidies out of total subsidies in the Second Development Plan continuously increased from 85.4 percent in 1996 to 92.4 percent in 1999. In the Third Development Plan (2000–2004), the share of energy subsidies decreased, but it was always above 90 percent of total subsidies. In the first year of the Fourth Development Plan, it reached an unprecedented 95 percent, which was due to higher oil prices in international markets. It is important to note that because Iran's exchange rate was fixed until 2000, energy subsidies were hidden. These subsidies became transparent when they were based on the market exchange rate. Also, this oil ministry study did not account for the opportunity cost of oil used in refineries.

Moreover, the share of Iran's GDP that went to energy subsidies increased substantially, from 5.54 percent of GDP in 1992 to 13.93 percent of GDP in 1993. It decreased during the period from 1993 to 2001 but remained above 10 percent on average. It then increased again and reached 16.9 percent in

Table 4.5 Prices of Refinery Products in Iran and International Prices, 2006

Refinery products	Iran domestic price per liter (rials)	International price per liter (rials)	Percentage difference in prices
Gasoline	800	3,510	339
Diesel oil	165	3,816	2,213
Heavy oil	95	2,213	2,242
Kerosene	145	4,016	2,343
Liquid gas	258	2,039	690

Source: Iranian National Oil Company, "Importance of Energy in the National Economy," Tehran, 2006.

2004. Based on Iranian Oil Ministry calculations, energy subsidies increased from 24 trillion rials in 2001 to 184 trillion rials in 2004, which was 36.2 percent of all general budget expenditures.[8] Meanwhile, the amount of budget expenditures on capital investment increased from 24 trillion rials to 99 trillion rials in the same period, and this constituted less than 20 percent of total budget. So during this period, the Iranian government spent more on energy subsidies than on capital investments.

The Central Bank of Iran also developed a computable general equilibrium (CGE) model in parallel with input-output tables to study and compare the results of the energy price changes on inflation. In 2008, the bank consolidated the results of those models with another model of financial programming and policy (FPP) to estimate the demand-side effect of price changes. It concluded that inflation would increase as a result of energy price changes, but the extent of the increase would depend on energy prices and many other variables, including the feedback of the demand for energy.

Energy Subsidies

Iran has spent a large amount of its oil wealth on direct and indirect subsidies. Many economists consider this policy to be a waste of money and an inefficient means of promoting economic growth and income distribution.[9] In the long run, these subsidies cause budget deficits and chronic inflation. Iran's budget depends heavily on oil revenues, which means price fluctuations in oil markets bring instability to government expenditures and hamper economic growth. This economic policy, based on a model of promoting income distribution above economic growth, cannot continue in the long run, and Iran will be obliged to change it sooner or later. This is not an easy decision. And even if the Iranian government reaches this decision, there are many controversies over how to change the policy.

On one side, economists argue in favor of reducing energy subsidies, which account for more than 85 percent of the country's total subsidies— more than the government spends on subsidies for bread, drugs, fertilizer, edible oil, and other products. These economists argue that energy subsidy reduction would increase government revenues and reduce energy consumption, which has caused environmental problems in the country and forced Iran to import large amounts of oil products from abroad. Even with Iran's large petroleum reserves, oil products are now the country's top import in terms of value.

Higher oil prices on the international market in 2007 and the first quarter of 2008 raised Iranian energy subsidies considerably. Iran's Ministry of Oil estimated that these subsidies reached $100 billion in 2008, which accounted for almost 25 percent of GDP. However, lower oil prices in 2009 reduced Iran's energy subsidies to an estimated $35 billion in that year.

Due to the relative low price of all types of energy in Iran, reducing subsidies cannot be accomplished solely by encouraging people to conserve energy. In particular, Iranians need to change their habit of using energy-intensive equipment and appliances in households and industry. Also, most of the energy used in Iran is nonrenewable energy.

Those who favor continuing energy subsidies at the current level in Iran argue that price increases would cause hyperinflation and that low-income families would suffer most. These supporters of subsidies have suggested that any energy price adjustment must be gradual and carefully planned to take into account social welfare considerations and avoid pressure on the poor. In particular, they argue public transportation must be developed adequately before any changes happen and that industry must be compensated for making changes from old technologies to new ones (in order to preserve their comparative advantage over imports). Despite these reservations, recent developments in international oil markets and studies showing problems with energy subsidies have generated strong support among Iranian politicians and economists for the elimination or reduction of these subsidies.

However, people have different views on how—and how quickly—to implement these changes.

The consequences of Iran continuing its current energy pricing policy of subsidizing artificially low prices can be outlined as follows:

- A high rate of domestic energy demand would continue, and scarce energy resources would be overutilized.
- Nonrenewable energy resources could be exhausted in the near future.
- Pollution from use of fossil fuels could increase health problems and other external costs. In 2005, the World Bank and Iran's Environmental Protection Agency estimated the cost of gas emissions in Iran to be $7.1 billion. Based on U.S. Environmental Protection Agency coefficients, these costs were estimated to reach $18 billion in 2007.
- A fair income distribution policy would not be achieved. High-income groups use more energy and benefit more from some subsidies than low-income groups.
- Smuggling of all refinery products, especially gasoline and diesel oil, to neighboring countries, would occur. Significant differences between domestic and international energy prices tend to increase this.
- Energy-intensive industries crowd out labor- and capital-intensive industries and discourage conservation.
- Subsidies produce budget deficits in the short term and hindered economic growth and employment in the long run.
- Iran would not be motivated to develop new types of energy or renewable energy (such as solar, wind, etc.).
- Large energy subsidies would hinder domestic investment in energy industries (such as oil, gas, and petrochemicals) and cause a slow rate of growth in this sector due to low domestic prices.

Iran's continuation of energy subsidies during recent years of increasing international oil and gas prices has increased the gap between domestic and international prices. This causes price distortions, which decrease relative energy prices compared to other domestically produced commodities. Accordingly, continuing this energy subsidization policy has become a heavy economic and political burden. The costs of changing the policy increase every year and force the government to postpone an important decision in order to avoid undesirable social and economic consequences.

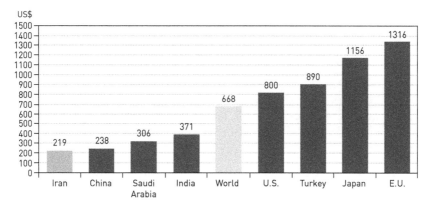

Figure 4.1 Energy productivity based on GDP in selected countries, 2007. BP Statistic, June 2008 in World Economic Outlook.

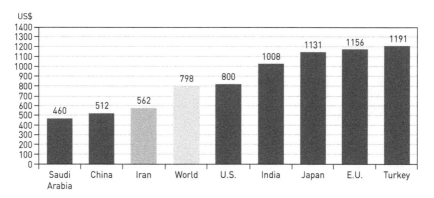

Figure 4.2 Energy productivity based on GDP calculated on PPP in selected countries, 2007. BP Statistic, June 2008 in World Economic Outlook.

Energy Efficiency in Iran

A 2007 review of energy consumption in Iran shows that energy productivity in Iran was only $219.[10] That means for every barrel of oil equivalent of energy consumption in Iran, the country produces $219 in GDP. Iran's energy productivity is less than that of India, Saudi Arabia, and China. The world average is $668, and the EU's average was $1,316 (see Figure 4.1). However, in terms of purchasing price parity (PPP), Iran's energy productivity is better (see Figure 4.2).

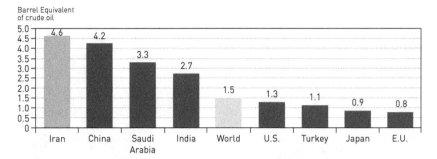

Figure 4.3 Energy consumption intensive based on GDP in 2007 (barrel of crude oil equivalent per $1,000 GDP). BP Statistic, June 2008 in World Economic Outlook.

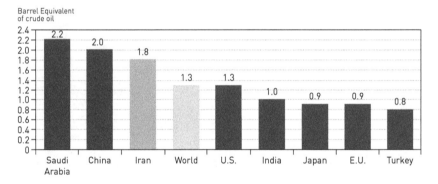

Figure 4.4 Energy consumption intensive based on GDP calculated on PPP in 2007. BP Statistic, June 2008 in World Economic Outlook.

The use of energy for producing one unit of goods and services is called "energy consumption intensive." There are several ways to measure it. One method is the amount of energy use (in barrels of crude oil equivalent) needed to produce $1,000 of GDP. In 2007, the figure for Iran was 4.6. The comparable figure for India was 2.7, the world average was 1.5, and Japan and the EU were at 0.9 and 0.8, respectively (see Figure 4.3). In terms of GDP in PPP, Turkey with 0.8 is in better position than the EU, Japan, India, and the rest of the world's average. Iran, at 1.8, is above the world average but requires less energy than China and Saudi Arabia to produce $1,000 of GDP (see Figure 4.4).

Energy consumption intensive in Iran, which is among the lowest in the world, hasn't improved much in recent years. Between 1980 and 2000, it decreased, but since then it has increased. The reason for this improvement

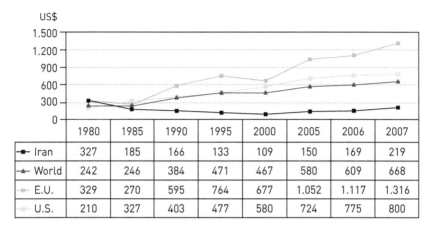

US$	1980	1985	1990	1995	2000	2005	2006	2007
Iran	327	185	166	133	109	150	169	219
World	242	246	384	471	467	580	609	668
E.U.	329	270	595	764	677	1.052	1.117	1.316
U.S.	210	327	403	477	580	724	775	800

Figure 4.5 Productivity trends in energy consumption in selected countries, 1980–2007 (GDP per barrel of crude oil equivalent). BP Statistic, June 2008 in World Economic Outlook.

is not an increase in efficiency but an increase in international oil prices,[11] which were 250 percent higher in 2007 than in 2000. Hence, due to lower oil prices in 2008 and 2009, we expect lower energy consumption intensive in Iran during these years (see Figure 4.5).

Moreover, the same situation is true for energy consumption intensive based on GDP in PPP. The figure for Iran increases from 399 in 1980 to 500 in 1985 and decreases in 1990 and 1995 to 476. However, it went up to 562 in 2007, an increase of 17 percent. Between 1980 and 2007, the world, the EU, and the United States increased their energy consumption intensive by 312, 350, and 380 percent respectively (see Figure 4.6).

We can see the same scenario in terms of trends in energy consumption intensive in Iran and other countries. Iran's energy consumption intensive (per barrel of oil for $1,000 of GDP) increased from 3.1 to 9.2 between 1980 and 2000, decreased after that, and then improved to 4.6 in 2007, still above the figure for 1980. The same figures for the world, the EU, and the United States show that productivity improved considerably in all these contexts. The global average improved from 4.1 to 1.3, the EU improved from 3.0 to 0.8, and the United States improved from 4.8 to 1.3 (see Figure 4.7).

In terms of GDP in PPP, Iran fairs better in terms of energy productivity. Iran's energy consumption intensive improved from 2.5 to 1.8 between 1980 and 2007, but Iran's energy consumption is still less productive than most

US$

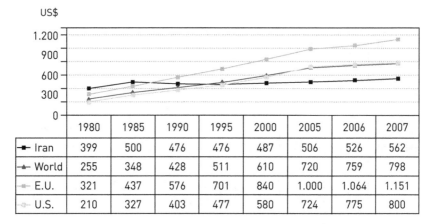

	1980	1985	1990	1995	2000	2005	2006	2007
Iran	399	500	476	476	487	506	526	562
World	255	348	428	511	610	720	759	798
E.U.	321	437	576	701	840	1.000	1.064	1.151
U.S.	210	327	403	477	580	724	775	800

Figure 4.6 Productivity trends in energy consumption in selected countries, 1980–2007 (GDP based on PPP calculation per barrel of crude oil equivalent). BP Statistic, June 2008 in World Economic Outlook.

Barrel Equivalent
of crude oil

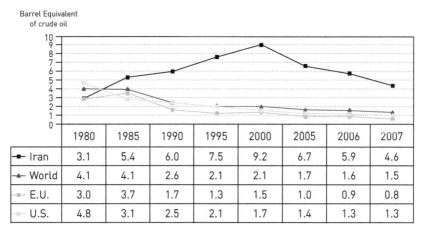

	1980	1985	1990	1995	2000	2005	2006	2007
Iran	3.1	5.4	6.0	7.5	9.2	6.7	5.9	4.6
World	4.1	4.1	2.6	2.1	2.1	1.7	1.6	1.5
E.U.	3.0	3.7	1.7	1.3	1.5	1.0	0.9	0.8
U.S.	4.8	3.1	2.5	2.1	1.7	1.4	1.3	1.3

Figure 4.7 Trends in energy consumption intensive in selected countries (barrel per $1,000 GDP). BP Statistic, June 2008 in World Economic Outlook.

other countries. The same figures for the world, the EU, and the United States were 1.3, 0.9, and 1.3, respectively, in 2007 (see Figure 4.8).

Figure 4.9 shows energy efficiency as the relationship between the price of gas oil and energy productivity based on GDP produced per barrel of crude oil equivalent. With an increase in gas oil prices, energy productivity in Iran has increased substantially, but efficiency has slowed. This trend

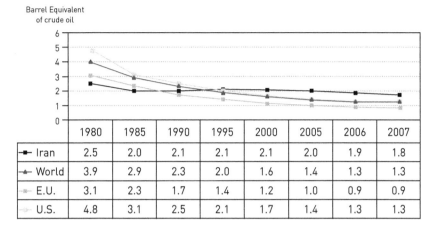

Figure 4.8 Trends of energy consumption intensive in selected countries, 1980–2007 based on PPP. BP Statistic, June 2008 in World Economic Outlook.

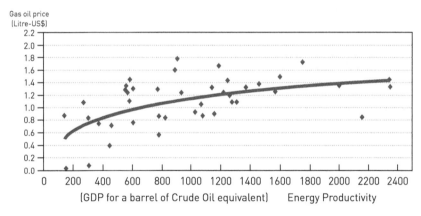

Figure 4.9 Relationship between price of gas oil and energy efficiency. BP Statistic, June 2008 in World Economic Outlook.

shows that we cannot expect energy price increases to translate into productivity increases indefinitely.

The gap between Iran's domestic energy prices and international prices has increased considerably. Figure 4.10 shows the trends of energy prices domestically and internationally between 2001 and 2007. Due to Iran's energy pricing policies and rapid increases in international energy prices, the

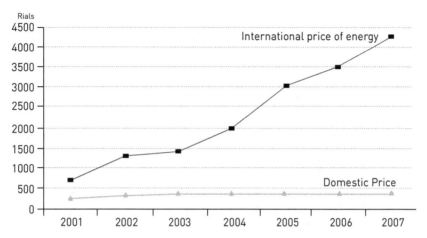

Figure 4.10 Comparison of Iran and international energy prices. Central Bank of Iran.

gap has widened. This trend shows that price adjustment is very important for the health of the Iranian economy and that government inaction has had a high opportunity cost.

With respect to the present (unfortunate) situation of energy efficiency in Iran, any delay in the decision to change the country's energy subsidization policy would result in high costs to the Iranian economy in terms of wasted energy, inefficiency in production and consumption, and lost opportunities.

However, if Iran is going to adjust energy prices, it needs to take a few important items into consideration:

- Due to Iran's long delay in adjusting its energy prices, any increase in prices will require social and political support for economic restructuring.
- The indirect effect of energy price adjustments on households depends on macroeconomic policy. Therefore, Iran needs to introduce a comprehensive package that includes new fiscal and monetary policies.
- The government must protect low-income groups that would suffer the most in the short run.

In many developed and developing countries, there is a substantial tax on fuel consumption. Governments impose taxes on fuel consumption for several reasons, including to generate income for the government; to conserve energy; to address environmental and health considerations; to increase investment in highways and transportation; and to encourage the development of alternative sources of energy. Because there is an inverse relationship between energy intensity and prices, higher prices decrease energy intensity. Accordingly, Iran is obliged to adjust energy prices to decrease energy intensity.

Development Plans and Energy Subsidies Laws

Under Iran's Third and Fourth Development Plans (2000–2004 and 2005–9, respectively), lawmakers required the government to adjust energy prices. The Third Development Plan, required the government, until the second year of the plan, to study the subsidies targeted to basic commodities, including wheat, sugar, dairy products, drugs, fertilizer, pesticides, and energy. After completion of the third year of the plan, the subsidies system was supposed to change according to the following goals:

- Rationalizing subsidized commodities prices to prevent smuggling to neighboring countries
- Encouraging the production of domestically subsidized commodities
- Reducing upper-income groups' share of subsidies and increasing lower-income groups' share
- Gradually replacing subsidies with welfare projects
- Financing infrastructural investment and employment
- Developing production and employment by way of soft loan facilities from revenues generated by the elimination of subsidies

In practice, the Iranian government decreased subsidies by gradually increasing the price of some refinery products and other commodities, but it was short of a total elimination of energy subsidies. In Iran's 2000 parliamentary election, fundamentalists won a majority in the Seventh Parliament and passed a bill to freeze the prices of all refinery products, electricity, natural gas, water, communications, and some government services, and this reversed changes in prices anticipated in the Fourth Development Plan (2005–9). In addition, Article 95 Section B of Iran's Fourth Development Plan ordered the government to establish justice and social stability and to reduce the income distribution gap. The government was required to allocate funds generated from subsidies reduction and other social funds toward achieving these goals.

In the past ten years, Iranian governments and lawmakers have showed their intention to reduce energy subsidies and allocate the funds directly to needy people to reduce income inequality. But due to differences between the parliament and the executive branch on how to implement the laws, energy subsidies have continued.

In 2008, Iran's government decided to eliminate energy subsidies after one year of research. It put together "The Economic Transformation Law," a package of reforms on monetary issues, customs, labor rules, taxes, productivity, and energy subsidies. This bill was presented to Parliament in January 2009 as a top priority.

Parliament approved the energy subsidy bill on January 22, 2010, and it was supposed to be implemented on March 21, 2010. But the government decided to postpone it until December 2010. It is a multidimensional piece of legislation that will have a very important impact not only on Iran's economy, but also on social and political developments in the country. If it fails to achieve its goals or faces difficulties, the government might stop or postpone the implementation of part of the law as has happened in similar previous cases (for example, the value-added tax law). If this happens, the energy subsidy problem will continue to waste resources and hinder the Iranian economy.

The Iranian Government's Plan for Energy Subsidies

In January 2009, the Iranian president introduced a bill to Parliament to provide "targeted subsidies" (cash payments) to low-income groups that would suffer the most from energy price adjustments. The Parliament nominated an ad hoc committee to review the bill, and after some changes it became a law at the beginning of 2010. The law includes the following features:

- Over the next five years, the prices of gasoline, diesel, heavy oil, liquid gas, and kerosene must gradually increase to reach 90 percent of the Persian Gulf FOB price, taking into consideration economic circumstances.
- The price of crude oil to Iranian refineries must be 95 percent of the Persian Gulf FOB price.

- The domestic price of natural gas must equal 75 percent of the export price.
- After five years, the domestic price of electricity and water must equal the costs of production. Also, for different geographic regions, different electricity and water prices can be charged.
- In order to encourage investment, Iran's domestic natural gas price for manufacturing industries, refineries, and petrochemical industries must be 65 percent of the Persian Gulf FOB natural gas export price (without transportation costs).

Revenues generated by these price adjustments would be distributed according to the following categories:

- Up to 50 percent of revenues would be paid directly to low-income families in cash or in kind or would be spent on a comprehensive social welfare system, health insurance coverage, housing assistance, and employment.
- The government would be permitted to spend 30 percent of revenues on energy optimization and conservation, including technology improvement, renewable energy development, and compensation of utility companies' losses. In addition, the government is authorized to spend funds on public transportation, agricultural and industrial production, industrial bread producers, and electronic services to reduce the use of vehicles.
- Under Article 11 of the "targeted subsidies" law, the government can spend 20 percent of the generated revenues for general budget expenditures.

The law is a part of the Fifth Development Plan, which was approved by Parliament in 2010, but its implementation was delayed until March 21, 2011.

Different economists have different projections regarding the impact these energy price adjustments would have on the Iranian economy. Economic growth would be reduced between 3.4 and 3.7 percent. Inflation would increase 15 to 24 percent in a country where the inflation rate was already 25.4 percent in 2009. Anticipated revenues generated by the scheme would be around $40 billion, with 50 percent distributed to households, 20 percent to the government, and 30 percent to industries affected by the price adjustment.

The consequences of the energy price adjustment on consumption, production, employment, and other economic factors are not yet clear, and predictions are only speculative. Complex interactions between economic variables and the current world economic crisis introduce additional uncertainties. The Iranian population's reaction to the implementation of the law also remains to be seen. However, most Iranian politicians and economists agree that reform is necessary and that any delay imposes a heavy burden on the Iranian economy and future generations.

The Ministry of Economic Affairs and Finance is the principal authority for implementing the law, with cooperation from other government ministries. Implementing the law may not be an easy job. Even if the government implements it properly, the potential impact of undesirable potential outcomes—such as inflation and unemployment—are not clear. The law's timetable, the sequence of implementation, and the payment system for people in the bottom half of the economy are very important concerns and must the scrutinized at every stage of implementation. The Iranian government can build on the similar experiences of other countries and international institutions to increase the plan's efficiency.

Determining Energy Prices in Iran

The formula Iran uses to calculate energy subsidies is based on the opportunity cost of energy—that is, the difference between the domestic price of oil products and FOB prices in the Persian Gulf. Also, natural gas prices are calculated based on 80 percent of export prices, and electricity prices are determined by the costs of production. Due to the high rate of inflation in Iran, any price changes must take inflation into account. Therefore, an increase in energy prices must be real (taking into consideration the consumer price index) and not merely nominal.

The exchange rate also plays an important role in determining prices. Even price increases based on Persian Gulf FOB energy prices are not sufficient for adjustment. Despite wide differences between world inflation rates and Iran's domestic inflation rate, the Central Bank in Tehran has kept the rial exchange rate almost constant in the last five years (it has devaluated only 15 percent). This policy causes Iran's exchange rate, which is supposed to be a floating rate, to become overvalued and not reflect the real value of the rial.

Table 4.6 January 2010 and Projected Energy Prices

Energy carriers		Present		Suggested price		Percent change
		Rials	US$*	Rials	US$	
Gasoline (1 l)		1,000	0.11	4,000	0.43	396
Diesel (1 l)	Non-power plant	165	0.02	3,500	0.37	2,122
Heavy oil (1 l)	Non-power plant	945	0.10	2,000	0.21	212
	Power plant	945	0.10	2,000	0.21	212
Kerosene (1 l)		165	0.02	3,500	0.57	2,122
Liquid gas (1 l)		288	0.03	2,000	0.21	695
Natural gas (1 m³)	Non-power plant	110	0.02	1,300	0.14	1,182
	Power plant	110	0.02	1,300	0.14	1,182
Electricity (1 kw)		165	0.02	1,000	0.11	606

Source: Iranian Ministry of Economic Affairs and Finance, A Report on Energy Subsidies, Tehran, 2008, and author's calculations
*US$1=9,500 rials

The annual amount of Iran's energy subsidies has gone from $100 billion in February 2008, when international oil prices were at their highest level, to around $40 billion in 2009. Because oil prices fluctuate, any estimate of future subsidies is a rough approximation and could vary up to 50 percent with oil price changes.

Table 4.6 shows January 2010 energy prices in Iran and the prices projected by some experts during the first year of the proposed energy subsidy reduction law. According to the Iranian government's Fourth Development Plan, Iran's domestic energy prices were supposed to gradually increase every year and reach Persian Gulf FOB prices by the end of the plan. However, the Seventh Parliament introduced a bill in 2003 that changed the previous law on energy price reforms. This law froze the price of seven items including refinery products, natural gas, electricity, and water in 2004. Members of Parliament argued that annual price increases raise people's inflationary expectations and cause accelerated inflation. In 2005, the first year that the law was implemented, inflation decreased to the lowest level in five years (11.9 percent). But due to government fiscal and monetary expansionary policy, inflation increased in subsequent years. Many economists argue that the first-year decrease was the result of previous monetary and fiscal policy and cannot be solely attributed to the law.

The energy price freezes halted the projected plan for investment in infrastructure, public transportation, and energy conservation. Shortages of electricity in 2008 were attributed to the delay in finishing power plants under construction due to lack of adequate financing. In 2007, the government introduced rationing coupons—for the first time since the end of the Iran-Iraq war in 1989—for gasoline and then diesel oil, with a small increase in prices compared to the high rate of inflation in the previous five years. (Inflation rates were 13.5, 18.4, 25.4, 10.8, and 12.4 percent, respectively, in 2006–2011.) However, the government increased gasoline prices by only 25 percent in June 2007 and has kept them at that level until the implementation of the targeted subsidy law on December 21, 2010, despite the more dramatic increase in oil prices worldwide. With introduction of the subsidy law, the gasoline prices have more than quadrupled. The price of gasoline was approximately $0.7 per liter ($2.50 per gallon) in May 2011, when it was just $0.1 before 2009 and about $0.3 in late 2010.

In November 2008, the Iranian government introduced the nonrationed gasoline price, which was four times the coupon price. The ration system has created a black market for petrol. But by introducing nonrationed gasoline, prices have decreased on the black market. Black market prices are still above subsidized prices but are below the nonrationed price. In fact, the amount of gasoline rationed per month (80 liters per car) increased to 100 liters after nine months. Later, the government allowed an additional 100 liters of gasoline to each car for New Year's trips and another 100 liters for summer trips. The result of this rationing system was a 20 percent reduction in gasoline consumption, which can mainly be attributed to a reduction in smuggling to neighboring countries and not a decrease in consumption.

A week before the targeted subsidies were introduced, the government ordered the banks to pay any individual who had been pre-registered and opened a bank account a two months cash subsidy in the amount of 820,000 rials, which is the equivalent of $82.

The government also introduced two different prices for gasoline and diesel oil. The ration price was 4,000 rials for gasoline and 1,500 rials for diesel, which were 4 and 9 times more than the previous prices. In addition, the non-ration prices were 7,000 and 3,500 rials, which were respectively 7 and 21 times more than the previous ration prices. The prices of electricity and natural gas for home and industrial consumption have increased substantially under a complicated formula. All refinery products prices have increased significantly. The reforms went further than energy carriers, and the subsidy cuts also included bread and water. To help low-income families the government added an additional 40,000 rials into the previously set level of cash handout per person.

According to the official data, since the implementation of the subsidy law in December 2010, the daily gasoline consumption has declined by 12 percent to 54 million liters in April 2011 from 61 million liters a year earlier. The government has saved $1.8 billion just on fuel consumption as a result this policy.[12] This was accompanied by increased inflation, though the level of inflation was below the anticipated mark due to to the price control by the government.

Conclusions

Energy subsidies in Iran have increased substantially in recent years—from $15.2 billion in 2001 to $87.8 billion in 2007—due to increases in consumption and oil prices.

The Iranian government's Third and Fourth Development Plans laid out policy changes for domestic energy prices. First, these prices were supposed to increase gradually along with international prices. However, members of Iran's Seventh Parliament overwhelmingly approved a bill in 2003 to freeze the price of energy and some other public goods in order to curb inflation. At that time, the annual rate of inflation was around 13 percent.

As a result, the gap between Iran's domestic energy prices and international prices became wider, and domestic consumption increased substantially. Due to the limits in Iranian oil refineries' capacity and the delay in constructing new oil and gas refineries, Iran became an importer of refinery products, particularly gasoline and diesel. But the rationing program introduced in 2007 for gasoline and in 2009 for diesel reduced domestic consumption by 20 percent.

Finally, in response to several studies by Iranian government agencies, the president decided to overhaul the government's energy pricing policy by introducing comprehensive legislation on "economic transformation." Parliament approved it on January 5, 2010, and the Council of Guardians ratified it one week later. The law included the energy subsidy plan that has been implemented since December 2010. It changes universal energy subsidies to targeted subsidies in order to compensate low-income families and increase energy productivity in Iran. The government postponed the implementation of the law for nine months in order to pay direct cash handouts first and then increase the prices. It was a wise policy and did not cause social disturbances. In 2011, the implementation of subsidy cuts was in full swing, which is a move in the right direction from an economic point of view but it might be politically difficult to sustain the speed of subsidy reform due to the social and economic consequences.

Therefore, the execution of this law to eliminate or reduce energy subsidies completely must take into account the reaction of consumers, producers, and investors (domestic and foreign) into consideration. In spite of many studies on this subject, we cannot predict with certainty the outcome of the law. In practice, even a comprehensive, carefully designed, and properly implemented law may require adjustment. The timing and the speed of price adjustments are of the utmost importance. The evaluation of the results of the subsidy law implementation needs more time but it seems that the government is cautious about price changes and price adjustment taking into account views of customers and producers. At this time, the gradual approach to subsidy cuts seems to be the most balanced option for continuing the started process.

5

Challenges Facing Central Banks in Oil-Exporting Countries: The Case of Azerbaijan

Elkin Nurmammadov

Central banks have evolved over time. Whereas the Swedish Riksbank and the Bank of England of the late-seventeenth century were established to finance war expenditures of their governments, modern central banks function as regulators of a nation's money supply and as monopoly providers of legal tender. They pursue a variety of goals, such as price stability, output growth, and the stability of the financial sector. Moreover, central banks today exhibit much higher degrees of independence and transparency than even twenty years ago, when many of them practically functioned as departments of ministries of finance.

The economic structures of different countries vary considerably today, and so do the practices and challenges of central banks. Many consider the practice of central banking an art, albeit one benefiting from scientific foundations. In the words of Sir Ralph Hawtrey:

> it is a special characteristic of the art of central banking that it deals specifically with the task of an authority directly entrusted with the promotion of human welfare. Human welfare, human motives, human behavior supply material so baffling and elusive that many people are skeptical of the possibility of building a scientific edifice on so shifting a foundation. But however complex the material, and however imperfect the data, there is always an advantage to be gained from systematic thought.[1]

Arguably, central banking in emerging market countries is much more of an art than elsewhere. These countries usually suffer from political instability, are "small open" economies (relying on exports of a single major agricultural or mineral commodity), and, in the case of transition economies, have taken on the difficult task of institution building from scratch. The focus of this chapter is the practice of central banking in yet another type of economy—namely, the economies of oil-exporting countries.

Oil-exporting countries often suffer from important problems that stem from oil-price volatility. Oil prices are twice as volatile as prices for other commodities.[2] Moreover, changes in oil prices have historically been poorly forecast.[3] Oil prices collapsed with the onset of the global financial crisis and hit a price of less than $40 a barrel in January 2009. Just half a year earlier, oil prices were at an all-time high of $147 a barrel, the culmination of the unprecedented 2003–8 oil boom.

Oil price booms lead to strong fiscal and external positions in oil-exporting countries. Higher international oil prices are associated with higher revenues for these countries' public sectors, and lower international oil prices are associated with lower revenues. The same logic applies to government spending in oil-exporting countries: it rises when oil prices are high and falls when they are low. Recent estimates show that the overall fiscal balance in a subsample of oil-producing countries would on average decrease by 3.5 percent of GDP in response to a $10 per barrel reduction in the price of oil.[4] Because the public sector plays a major role in oil-exporting countries, oil price shocks pose a number of serious challenges to a central bank's goals of macroeconomic and financial stability.

Oil-price volatility makes the choice of an exchange rate regime a critical and difficult policy choice for oil exporters. As oil-exporting economies depend heavily on revenues from transactions carried out on international markets in foreign currencies, the exchange rate can have a significant impact on the health of these economies. On one hand, the exchange rate regime must account for the vagaries of international oil prices, the need to anchor inflationary expectations, and the potential risk of currency and banking crises. On the other hand, the exchange rate regime must accommodate other priorities, such as economic diversification and reduction of unemployment. In practice, it seems very problematic for oil exporters to find a single exchange rate regime that is compatible with all these considerations. Most oil-exporting countries fix their currencies to the U.S. dollar (see Table 5.1). Some countries announce the fixed exchange rate formally;

Table 5.1 Selected Oil-Producing Countries

Country	Oil revenue (% fiscal revenue)[1]	Oil GDP (% total GDP)[1]	Oil production (billion boe, 2008)	R/P (2008)[2]	Exchange rate regime
Algeria	77.8	45	1.298	32	Managed float
Azerbaijan	54.3	52	0.431	35	Fixed to U.S. dollar
Bahrain	80.1	26	0.422	−772	Fixed to U.S. dollar
Indonesia	28.3	10	0.826	30	Floating
Iran	69.0	26	2.346	142	Managed float
Kazakhstan	38.0	32	0.767	68	Managed float
Kuwait	73.2	58	1.101	103	Fixed to basket
Libya	92.2	79	0.779	69	Fixed to SDR
Mexico	39.5	7	1.515	10	Floating
Nigeria	82.3	37	1.023	69	Managed float
Norway	29.0	26	1.551	17	Floating
Oman	83.5	49	0.424	28	Fixed to U.S. dollar
Qatar	61.8	59	1.009	194	Fixed to U.S. dollar
Russia	30.7	23	7.578	48	Managed float (euro-U.S. dollar basket)
Saudi Arabia	88.7	55	4.474	70	Fixed to U.S. dollar
Trinidad & Tobago	57.2	46	0.314	13	Managed float
UAE	75.9	37	1.419	99	Fixed to U.S. dollar
Venezuela	48.9	34	1.144	115	Fixed to U.S. dollar
Vietnam	26.0	34	0.168	50	Medium
Yemen	73.4	33	0.111	53	Medium

Source: Pablo Lopez-Murphy and Mauricio Villafuerte, "Fiscal Policy in Oil Producing Countries During the Recent Oil Price Cycle," IMF Working Paper 10/28 (2010); national central banks.
1. Average 2005–8.
2. Proved reserves to production ratio. Source: British Petroleum Statistical Review of World Energy, June 2009.

others pursue foreign exchange market interventions without making explicit announcements. This substantially limits the scope of independent monetary policy to address domestic problems and exposes oil exporters to the risk of speculative attacks on their currency. There are strong arguments in favor of oil-exporting countries adopting more flexible exchange rate regimes, which will be discussed later in this chapter.

Negative oil price shocks may lead to banking crises in oil-exporting countries. The banking sector, which is the major component of the financial system in most oil-exporting countries, is vulnerable to oil-price volatility. The profitability of commercial banks exhibits cyclical behavior with respect to oil booms and busts: positive oil price shocks are associated with lending booms and higher bank profits, and negative shocks are associated with reduced profitability of commercial banks.

As part of their mandate for maintaining financial stability, central banks are responsible for regulating and supervising a country's banking sector. As the history of global financial crises indicates, the lack of regulation or misguided regulation may lead to severe bank failures culminating in a crisis such as the Great Depression.[5] Hence, central bankers in oil-exporting countries need to design and implement policies to buttress banking sector stability in the face of volatile oil prices.[6] The 2008–9 financial crisis, which ended the 2003–8 oil price boom, provides a unique natural experiment to test the performance of central banks in oil-exporting countries.

Central banks in oil-exporting countries are not immune to problems even in the absence of oil-price volatility. Reliance on a constant flow of oil revenues often leads these central banks to adopt an overly expansionary fiscal policy, which in turn causes inflation in an economic environment characterized by accommodative monetary policy. A lack of central bank independence and exchange rate flexibility exacerbates inflationary pressures. This phenomenon is referred to as fiscal (or oil) dominance of monetary policy, whereby monetary policy accommodates fiscal policy objectives (for several reasons). Oil dominance may significantly undermine a central bank's goal of achieving price stability. Ultimately, central bank independence may prove an important tool to tackle the oil dominance of monetary policy.

To summarize, choosing the optimal exchange rate regime, maintaining the stability of the banking sector, and overcoming the oil sector's dominance over monetary policy are major challenges that central banks in oil-exporting countries face. The main goal of this chapter is to discuss these challenges and oil-exporting countries' potential policy responses, and, more specifically, to analyze how the central bank has handled these challenges in the case of Azerbaijan. Azerbaijan, in addition to being an oil-exporting country, is a transition economy that has experienced a radical transformation from a centrally planned economy to a market economy. Establishment of a two-tier banking system, consisting of a central bank and a number of commercial banks the central bank supervises and regulates, is an important step in building institutions that make the market economy work. An independent, Western-type central bank has become a "stamp of economic respectability" for transition economies.[7] By analyzing how Azerbaijan has dealt with the aforementioned challenges facing central banks in oil-exporting countries, this chapter will also shed light on how successful the country has been along the perilous path of building a Western-type central bank.

The analysis in this chapter suggests that the Central Bank of Azerbaijan has achieved success in maintaining the stability of the banking sector, especially during the challenging period from 2007 to 2009. The Central Bank's record on exchange rate policy, however, is controversial. Azerbaijan's exchange rate regime (which essentially fixed the local currency to the U.S. dollar) may have helped the country weather the recent global financial crisis, but it did not anchor inflationary expectations in the face of sustained oil price increases of the last decade and contributed to the oil sector's dominance over monetary policy. It seems that the high level of legal independence, which the government granted to the Central Bank of Azerbaijan through the 2004 law, has not translated into high levels of actual independence.

Oil-Price Volatility and Financial Stability

Price stability is listed as the primary objective in most central bank laws. Yet there are more imminent challenges for central bankers today, such as maintaining financial stability.[8] Central banks, especially in major developed countries, have done quite well fighting inflation in the past couple of decades, and their recipes for fighting inflation may be applied to developing and emerging market economies with adjustments for local circumstances. Central banks do not, however, have a clear-cut record of maintaining financial stability in economic environments characterized by volatile asset and commodity prices. This section describes how oil-price volatility jeopardizes banking sector stability in oil-exporting countries.

As emphasized in Walter Bagehot's classic doctrine of "the lender of last resort," a central bank should lend to "illiquid but solvent" institutions to help them meet their short-term obligations.[9] Moreover, central banks must lend whenever the act of not lending could trigger a systemic crisis. Indeed, central bank lending throughout history has been a prominent part of regulatory assistance to troubled financial institutions. The global financial crisis of 2008–9 is a case in point: central banks worldwide mobilized resources to restore the stability of the financial system, although the extent and direction of the loans these banks made have been subject to severe criticism.

Other than proactive measures taken by central banks, it is important to understand to what extent these institutions manage to stabilize the economy once an adverse oil price shock hits. There is evidence that oil price shocks do not influence an economy per se; rather, the monetary policy response that follows an oil price shock is what influences the economy.[10]

How do oil prices affect the stability of the banking sector in oil-exporting economies? The story is simple. During oil booms, there is a massive inflow of foreign currency into oil-exporting countries. In practice, only part of the inflow is sterilized by the central bank. This raises the level of money supply—that is, banks have more liquidity and can lend more. The surge in credit is also fueled indirectly by overly expansionary fiscal policy and the rise in "animal spirits" among both firms and households. Under these circumstances, it is not surprising that banks engage in excessive lending to reap higher profits and pay less attention to their customers' credit risk. Bank profits increase with their activity. When oil prices fall, the opposite happens: economic activity falls, government spending decreases, liquidity problems arise, asset quality worsens, nonperforming loans increase, and lending falls along with bank profits. There is evidence supporting the systemic importance of oil price shocks for bank performance in oil-exporting countries.[11]

Choosing the Exchange Rate Regime

The choice of exchange rate regime is a crucial decision for policy makers in any country. With rare exceptions, oil-exporting countries peg their currency to the U.S. dollar, whether through a de jure or de facto arrangement (see Table 5.1). As will be argued below, these countries have strong reasons to peg. It is important for oil-exporting countries to consider the oil sector's role in their country's GDP, exports, and government revenue when they choose an exchange rate regime. However, oil-price volatility may lead to severe external shocks, possibly resulting in banking and currency crises. Floating exchange rate regimes can automatically accommodate these shocks. Overall, oil-exporting countries confront both political and economic tradeoffs when choosing exchange rate regimes.

Exchange rate regimes are broadly categorized into fixed, intermediate, and floating regimes. There is no universal rule for choosing an exchange rate regime: the choice should reflect the domestic economy's structural characteristics, the country's openness to trade and capital inflows, and political considerations.

Official exchange rate regimes do not necessarily reflect a country's actual exchange-rate policy. One should be cautious as to whether de jure and de facto exchange rate regimes of a country match. There is a larger number of de facto pegs than de jure pegs in the world: central banks often intervene in the foreign exchange market without prior announcement of a fixed exchange rate regime.[12]

A fixed exchange rate regime implies that a country pegs its currency to that of another country. This arrangement essentially allows a less developed country to import the monetary policy of a more developed and stable country. If the exchange-rate peg is credible, it anchors inflation expectations in the less developed country to those in the more developed country. Moreover, fixed exchange rate regimes are associated with increased international trade and an influx of foreign capital into a country due to reduced transaction costs and exchange rate risk. Another advantage of exchange rate peg is that it helps alleviate the "time-inconsistency problem" of monetary policy—that is, political pressure on central banks to pursue an overly expansionary monetary policy in the short run at the expense of containing inflation in the long run.

Oil-exporting countries tend to fix their exchange rates mainly because real appreciation of their currencies may undermine their goal of diversifying their economies and developing non-oil sectors. Another rationale is to avoid the "currency mismatch problem," or volatility and inconvenience arising when major public revenues are invoiced in foreign currency yet government expenditures are made in domestic currency. Finally, most state-owned oil companies and other businesses incur large valuation losses when exchange-rate appreciation occurs.

Fixed exchange rate regimes have drawbacks, as a series of currency crises in Europe (1992), Mexico (1994), East Asia (1997), Russia (1998), Turkey (2001), and Argentina (2002), among others, has shown. First and foremost, under fixed exchange rates a country loses the ability to pursue an independent monetary policy that allows for the handling of asymmetric shocks. Second, shocks in the anchor country tend to be easily transmitted to the domestic economies of countries that have pegged to that anchor country's currency. As a result, there is an increased likelihood of speculative attacks on the local currency and increased potential for financial crises. Moreover, under a fixed exchange rate regime, a central bank loses seigniorage revenue—that is, the gains from printing money.

Floating regimes essentially imply exchange rate appreciation during good times and depreciation during bad times. For oil-exporting countries, good times are when the international price of oil goes up, and bad times are when the international price of oil goes down.

Some studies argue that oil-exporting countries should adopt floating exchange rate regimes.[13] One straightforward argument is that, as opposed to the fixed exchange rate regime, a floating exchange rate leaves room for independent monetary policy to address domestic and external shocks to the economy. A second argument is that imported inflation, stemming from currency depreciation in the anchor currency, could be avoided by abandoning the peg.

Other studies, however, question the merit of these arguments.[14] Oil-exporting countries with shallow capital markets often experience distortions in the monetary transmission mechanisms that constrain the scope of independent monetary policy even in the presence of a floating exchange rate regime. Also, imported inflation fears are overstated due to low exchange rate pass-through effects and administrative price controls.

Apart from "corner solutions," there are intermediate ones. A "basket peg"—pegging to a basket of several different foreign currencies—could introduce more flexibility to oil-exporting countries and retain certain advantages of a fixed exchange rate. Pegging to a basket of currencies reduces the risk of exposure to volatility in any one specific currency. However, the basket peg does not help if different currencies in the basket move in the same direction. Moreover, it is not as good as a pure peg, in terms of credibility and transparency, in anchoring inflationary expectations of economic agents.

Jeffrey Frankel proposed a "Peg the Export Price" (PEP) arrangement that would simultaneously deliver the main advantages of both a simple exchange rate peg and a floating regime—namely, a nominal anchor against inflation and automatic adjustment in the face of commodity price volatility.[15] The narrow form of the PEP proposal implies pegging the currency to the price of oil. A less extreme version implies pegging to a basket of currencies that also includes the price of oil. See Chapter 1.

Oil Dominance of Monetary Policy

Until the late twentieth century, central banks were frequently under pressure by the fiscal authorities to finance government debt. The majority of central banks de facto functioned as "departments of ministries of finance" and suffered from the government's fiscal dominance over monetary policy, which basically refers to the central bank monetizing the government's debt at the expense of higher long-term prices. The situation is much different today: central bank independence and transparency have become the norm. In oil-exporting countries, the fiscal dominance of monetary policy is still present, albeit in a different form, referred to as oil dominance of monetary policy.

To understand how fiscal policy may dominate monetary policy, consider two opposite cases. In the first, a country's fiscal authority fully finances government debt with future taxes. The fiscal authority raises taxes to finance the principal and interest payments on the newly issued debt, but the central bank does not accommodate. The second case describes the fiscal dominance of monetary policy. Under this scenario, the central bank fully finances the government's debt. If a budget deficit is financed with new debt, the central bank responds by printing money to finance principal and interest payments on the new debt. If monetary policy is dominant, as in the first case, fiscal policy will be forced to reduce the deficit. Thus the fiscal authority also commits to price stability. Under the second scenario, there is a better alignment between fiscal and monetary policies. Otherwise, financing the government debt through printing money leads to a vicious cycle, which has been termed "unpleasant monetary arithmetic."[16]

The view above ignores the role fiscal plays policy in determining price levels. The fiscal theory of the price level claims that inflation is not solely a monetary phenomenon and thus that an independent central bank is not sufficient to ensure price stability without appropriate fiscal policy.[17] This theory denies the argument that if the central bank is "dominant," the fiscal authority will be left with no other choice than to pursue appropriate fiscal policy. Quite the contrary, it says that in the absence of appropriate fiscal policy, the goal of price stability is unattainable regardless of how strong and independent a country's central bank is.

Fiscal dominance of monetary policy appears in a different form in oil economies: these countries' central banks do not buy government bonds by printing money, as traditional fiscal dominance literature suggests.[18] Instead, the monetary base expands as a result of an increase in net international reserves. To illustrate the point, consider the identity

$$MB = NIR + NDA,$$

where MB is monetary base, NIR is net international reserves, and NDA is net domestic assets.

According to this equation, an oil-export transaction leaves the monetary base unchanged, as the increase in NIR (due to the oil company selling foreign exchange to the central bank) is precisely offset by the decline in NDA (due to a rise in government deposits at the central bank) by the same amount. The monetary base expands only when the government finances its expenditures with its deposits at the central bank. In essence, oil dominance of monetary policy means the central bank is forced to undertake unsterilized purchases of foreign exchange coming from the oil export proceeds, which ultimately leads to the expansion of the monetary base.

Central bank independence may be a strong shield against both fiscal and oil dominance of monetary policy. The concept of central bank independence broadly refers to the pursuit of policies that give absolute priority to price stability. Central bank independence implies the existence of a legal and institutional framework that allows the bank to withstand pressures from a country's fiscal authority as well as pressures from the financial system and other lobbies. In oil-exporting countries, central bank independence implies that the bank resists government demands to undertake large unsterilized purchases of foreign exchange revenues earned from oil exports.

The Case of Azerbaijan: Banking Sector Stability

Azerbaijan's financial system is underdeveloped as its capital markets are very shallow. Yet the banking sector, which dominates the financial sector in Azerbaijan, has grown rapidly since 2005. The main force driving this growth was the surge in credit that resulted from improved macroeconomic conditions associated with the 2003–8 oil price boom. Yet the surge in credit has not led to higher financial intermediation: in 2008, the ratio of total lending to GDP in Azerbaijan was approximately 17 percent, compared to 50 percent for EU-accession countries.[19]

From 2005 through 2008, Azerbaijani banks enjoyed high profits and low levels of nonperforming loans. In the first nine months of 2008, the average return on assets was 2.2 percent, indicating high profits by international standards. Moreover, in September 2008, nonperforming loans in Azerbaijan were at 2.2 percent, compared to 29 percent in 2001.[20]

As global economic conditions tightened in 2007, Azerbaijani banks—just like their counterparts in the rest of the world—started experiencing liquidity problems. The 2008–9 crisis allows us to evaluate the effectiveness of the measures the Central Bank of Azerbaijan (CBA) took before and during the crisis to maintain banking sector stability.

Outside of the developed world, the global financial crisis hit the former Soviet countries harder than anywhere else.[21] The crisis did not hit Azerbaijan directly, however. Indirect spillovers—such as lower availability of foreign financing and FDI for the non-oil sector, a drop in global GDP growth, and, most importantly, a significant decline in international oil prices and revenues in the second half of 2008—have slowed the country's previous double-digit economic growth. Nevertheless, Azerbaijan withstood the crisis much better than other former Soviet countries. Although all energy importers and some energy exporters (Russia and Kazakhstan) in the region recorded negative growth rates in 2009, Azerbaijan faced only moderate problems, and its real GDP growth remained as high as 9.3 percent. This partly stems from the nature of Azerbaijan's economy, with its underdeveloped financial sector and limited openness to foreign financial markets. But it also reflects timely and effective policy measures taken by the CBA and other authorities.

In 2010, the International Monetary Fund released a report about how Azerbaijan's economy has performed since the crisis hit in October 2008:

> The Azerbaijani economy has withstood the impact of the global financial crisis well but has not been immune to it. The most direct impact of the crisis was through a large drop in the price of oil and lower external demand, which caused fiscal and export revenues to fall by nearly 30 percent. In addition, commercial banks cut back their loans to the private sector because of lower access to foreign financing, and a number of state-owned enterprises experienced refinancing difficulties. As international commodity prices fell, average annual inflation dropped dramatically from more than 20 percent in 2008 to 1.4 percent in 2009.[22]

Indeed, the CBA took timely and appropriate policy measures prior to and during the global financial crisis. The CBA tightened prudential regulations in the face of rapidly increasing risk taking by banks. The domestic credit surge of the period between the inflow of oil money and the global financial crisis of 2007–9 in Azerbaijan was accompanied by domestic banks' rising foreign liabilities, which increased by 138 percent in 2007. But Azerbaijani financial authorities quickly changed course, limiting the country's exposure to debt in foreign currencies. Most probably, a devastating banking crisis in neighboring Kazakhstan in 2007 convinced Azerbaijani policymakers to take preemptive measures against excessive foreign borrowing by domestic banks. The banks' prudential indicators generally improved in 2007, and the banking sector has become more resilient to shocks.

When the global financial crisis entered its critical phase in October 2008, the Central Bank of Azerbaijan decided to keep the U.S. dollar/Azerbaijani manat exchange rate stable even thought it meant reducing foreign exchange reserves. The stability of this exchange rate contributed to lower inflation in Azerbaijan and prevented the return of dollarization so widespread in the early 1990s in post-Soviet countries. Stable exchange rates— accompanied by the expansionary monetary policy measures listed in Table 5.2—moderated the effect of the crisis on households' and banks' balance sheets. The CBA's foreign exchange reserves declined but remained relatively high at approximately $5.4 billion by the end of 2009. Some experts criticized the CBA for drawing down foreign exchange reserves in its effort to maintain exchange rate stability. In retrospect, the benefits of this course of action outweighed the costs.[23]

Important amendments to the Law on the Central Bank of Azerbaijan were signed into force in June 2009, strengthening the CBA's lender-of-last-resort role. With these amendments, the CBA was given the right to purchase government bonds in the primary market if necessary, provided that those bonds are issued with the CBA's consent. Moreover, the CBA was authorized to extend loans to commercial banks for the purpose of financing socially important projects. In practice, these changes to legislation allowed the CBA to extend credits to a few struggling commercial banks and to help the State Oil Company of Azerbaijan roll over its debts to foreign lenders.

Table 5.2 Chronology of Implemented Preventive Measures for Azerbaijani Banking System, 2008

Period of anti-inflationary policy	Liquidity management
Monetary policy measures	Monetary policy measures
03.11.2008 Exchange rate moved from peg to dollar to two-currency (U.S.$ and EUR) basket regime.	10.14.2008 1. Discount rate reduced from 15% to 12%. 2. RR norm reduced from 12% to 9%. 3. RR on foreign liabilities of banks eliminated.
04.10.2008 Discount rate raised from 13% to 14%.	
06.09.2008 Discount rate raised from 14% to 15%.	10.31. 2008 Discount rate cut from 12% to 10%.
08.01.2008 1. Required reserves (RR) norm raised from 10% to 12%. 2. Set 5% RR norm for foreign liabilities of banks.	11.26.2008 RR norm cut from 9% to 6% (liquidity effect 130 mln. manats) 12.01.2008 Discount rate cut from 10% to 8%.

09.27.2008
Capital outflows absolutely liberalized (valid from 10.16.2008)
	Prudential regulation measures
	Increase provisions in banking sector:
	1. Classification degrees of assets in terms of risks have been tightened. As a result provisioning norms have been raised for:
	  - Substandard assets from 6% to 10% (04.30.08)
	  - Nonperformed assets 25% to 30% (04.30.08)
	  - Loss assets from 50% to 60% (04.30.08)
	2. Required minimum for loan to value (LTV) ratio increased from 120% to 150% (04.30.08).
	3. Share of subordinated debts in total capital was limited (02.18.08):
	  - Maximum quantity of subordinated debt limited at extent 50% of tier 1 capital.
	4. LTV for mortgage loans raised from 50% to 100% (02.18.08).

(continued)

Table 5.2 (*continued*)

Period of anti-inflation policy	Liquidity management
	5. Profits of banks and insurance companies used for recapitalization were exempted from taxes (Stipulated in amendments to the 2004 law on the Central Bank of Azerbaijan, effective from 01.01.09). **Strengthen risk management in banks:** **1.** The risk management system has been improved. *To this aim, new methodology of assessment on the risk management performance of banks has been prepared. Systems have been ranked according to this methodology and given ratings. The weakness elimination measures plan has been prepared, and banks have started to fulfill it.* **2.** The development strategy of each bank has been evaluated in the context of management capacity. *Strategic development plans of banks have been reviewed with bank managers and mutual memorandums on their future action framework have been signed.*

Source: Central Bank of Azerbaijan, Annual Report 2008, available at http://cbar.az/assets/793/report_2008.pdf. Accessed May 8, 2011.

The Case of Azerbaijan: Exchange Rate Policy

The Central Bank of Azerbaijan has mostly pegged the manat to the U.S. dollar throughout its history. As noted previously, oil prices rose considerably from 2003 to 2008, which led to real appreciation pressures in Azerbaijan from the exceptionally large terms-of-trade gains. Terms-of-trade pressures may materialize through nominal exchange rate appreciation, inflation, or both. Under a fixed exchange rate regime, the only option is higher inflation. Moreover, it is important to distinguish between temporary and permanent improvements in the terms of trade. Many believed that terms-of-trade improvements for Azerbaijan were permanent and that the exchange rate was undervalued; thus, a nominal appreciation would be preferable vis-à-vis adjustment through inflation.[24]

One can make a strong case in favor of a fixed exchange rate regime in Azerbaijan. It could be argued that the interest rate channel of the monetary transmission mechanism in Azerbaijan is not effective anyway, due to the country's underdeveloped financial markets. Government spending seems to exert a major influence on corporate and household spending, especially in an economic environment characterized by the limited financial markets. Apart from that, the fear of a fixed exchange rate regime leading to imported inflation is exaggerated due to low exchange rate pass-through effects and the presence of Azerbaijan's Tariff Council, a regulatory agency that oversees price controls.

Political-economy considerations also play an important role in choosing the exchange rate regime. A fixed exchange rate regime is believed to help an oil-exporting country diversify its economy. For Azerbaijan, whose primary purpose is to diversify its economy by developing tourism, agriculture, and other sectors, real (currency/exchange rate) appreciation would impede these efforts substantially.[25] Moreover, the two largest players in Azerbaijan's foreign exchange market—the International Bank of Azerbaijan (IBA) and the State Oil Company—would incur large valuation and income losses from nominal appreciation.

The costs of not adopting a floating exchange rate are low in Azerbaijan. Substantial foreign exchange rate reserves, accumulated during the oil price boom, underpin the credibility of Azerbaijan's peg to a foreign currency and largely eliminate the threat of speculative attacks on the manat. Yet it is not clear which single currency Azerbaijan should choose as a nominal anchor. Pegging to the U.S. dollar today implies volatility vis-à-vis the Euro, and vice versa. Moreover, neither the United States nor the European Union are among Azerbaijan's major trade partners; Turkey and Russia are. However, one cannot possibly choose the Russian ruble or the Turkish lira for a single-currency peg; they do not qualify as credible nominal anchors for the time being.

More flexible exchange rate arrangements could serve Azerbaijan well if the country is able to diversify away from the oil sector. As Azerbaijan completes its negotiations to enter the WTO, the costs of sustaining an exchange rate peg increase. In the meantime, Azerbaijan must impose timely regulatory preconditions for exchange rate flexibility and strengthen the monetary transmission mechanism so that monetary policy becomes a more effective means for economic stabilization.

In fact, the CBA has sometimes deviated from its de facto pure fixed exchange rate policy. For instance, Azerbaijan adopted a basket peg for some periods of time in 2005 and 2008. Together with fiscal prudence, this policy change in 2005 helped control inflation: the rate declined from 15.4 percent in April to about 10.5 percent in September. However, yielding to public opinion against nominal appreciation and exchange rate volatility, the government publicly announced a return to the peg in September 2005.[26] The CBA complied with this decision, despite adverse consequences for inflation. Potential downward revaluation of Azerbaijan's official foreign exchange reserves and a reduction of the international competitiveness of the country's non-oil export sector played a major role in this decision. The reason for abandoning the basket peg policy was different in 2008: the authorities thought a pure peg would provide a stronger anchor for domestic monetary policy during the crisis.

The Case of Azerbaijan: Oil Dominance of Monetary Policy

This section explores the legal and regulatory response to the oil dominance of Azerbaijan's monetary policy in two steps. First, I assess the CBA's degree of legal independence. Second, I analyze the actual data from CBA accounts as well as anecdotal evidence.

To assess the CBA's degree of legal independence, we must ask: what degree of independence did policy makers *mean* to grant the CBA? To answer this question, I calculate the Legal Variables Weighted (LVAW) index score of central bank independence based on Azerbaijan's central bank laws. From 1991 to 2008, spanning the period from Azerbaijan's independence to the onset of the global financial crisis, three central bank laws were adopted in Azerbaijan, in 1992, 1996, and 2004. Examining these laws provides insights on how the CBA's independence has evolved over time.

Table 5.3 reports LVAW index scores used to judge these laws. The values range from 0 to 1, with higher values indicating a stronger degree of independence. It is worth looking at the index scores comparatively (see Table 5.4). In an earlier study, the LVAW index score based on Azerbaijan's 1992 Law on the National Bank is 0.22, whereas the LVAW index based on the 1996 law is 0.24, which ranks lowest among the 26 former socialist countries in their sample.[27] These index scores indicate that the CBA's legal independence was rather limited in the early post-Soviet period and that there was no noteworthy improvement between 1992 and 1996. This is despite the fact

Table 5.3 Structure of Legal Variables Weighted (LVAW) Index

Criteria	Values
I. Central Bank CEO (0.20)	
1. Term of office of CEO (0.25)	
Equal to or more than 8 years	1.00
Equal to 6 years or more but less than 8 years	0.75
Equal to 5 years	0.50
Equal to 4 years	0.25
Less than 4 years	0.00
2. Who appoints the CEO (0.25)	
The Central Bank Board	1.00
Executive and legislative branch and Central Bank Board	0.75
Legislative branch	0.50
Executive branch	0.25
One or two members of executive branch	0.00
3. Provisions for dismissal of CEO (0.25)	
No provision	1.00
Only for nonpolicy reasons (e.g., incapability or violation of law)	0.83
At a discretion of Central Bank Board	0.67
For policy reasons at legislative branch's discretion	0.50
At legislative branch's discretion	0.33
For policy reasons at executive branch's discretion	0.17
At executive branch's discretion	0.00
4. CEO allowed to hold another office in government (0.25)	
Prohibited by law	1.00
Not allowed unless authorized by executive branch	0.50
No prohibition for holding another office	0.00
II. Central Bank objectives (0.15)	
5. Central Bank objectives (0.15)	
Price stability is the only major goal, and in case of conflict with government, the Central Bank has final authority	1.00
Price stability is the only goal that does not seem to conflict with the government's other goals	0.80
Price stability along with other objectives	0.60
Price stability along with other objectives with potentially conflicting goals (e.g., full employment)	0.40
Central Bank charter does not contain any objective	0.20
Some goals appear in the charter but price stability is not one of them	0.00
III. Policy formulation (0.15)	
6. Who formulates monetary policy (0.25)	
Central Bank has the legal authority	1.00
Central Bank participates together with government	0.67
Central Bank in an advisory capacity	0.33
Government alone formulates monetary policy	0.00

(continued)

Table 5.3 (*continued*)

Criteria	Values
7. Government directives and resolution of conflicts (0.50)	
Central Bank given final authority over issues defined in the law as objectives	1.00
Government has final authority over issues not clearly defined as CB goals	0.80
Final decision up to a council with members from the CB, executive branch, and legislative branch	0.60
Legislative branch has final authority	0.40
Executive branch has final authority, but subject to due process and possible protest by CB	0.20
Executive branch has unconditional authority over policy	0.00
8. Central Bank given active role in formulation of government's budget (0.25)	
Yes	1.00
No	0.00
IV. Central Bank lending (0.50)	
9. Limitations on advances (0.30)	
Advances to government prohibited	1.00
Advances permitted but subject to limits in terms of absolute cash amounts or relative limits (government revenues)	0.67
Advances permitted subject to relatively accommodative limits (more than 15 percent of government revenues)	0.33
No legal limitations on advances. Subject to negotiations with government.	0.00
10. Limitations on securitized lending (0.20)	
Advances to government prohibited	1.00
Permitted but subject to limits in terms of absolute cash amounts or relative limits (government revenues)	0.67
Permitted subject to relatively accommodative limits (more than 15 percent of government revenues)	0.33
No legal limitations on advances. Subject to negotiations with government.	0.00
11. Who decides control of terms of lending to government (0.20)	
Central bank controls terms and conditions	1.00
Terms of lending specified in law, or Central Bank given legal authority to set conditions	0.67
Law leaves decision to negotiations between the Central Bank and government	0.33
Executive branch alone decides and dictates to the Central Bank	0.00
12. Beneficiaries of Central Bank lending (0.10)	
Only central government	1.00
Central and state governments as well as further political subdivisions	0.67
Government divisions as well as public enterprises	0.33
Central Bank can lend to all of the above and to the private sector	0.00

Table 5.3 (*continued*)

Criteria	Values
13. Type of limits when they exist (0.05)	
As an absolute cash amount	1.00
As a percentage of Central Bank capital or other liabilities	0.67
As a percentage of government revenues	0.33
As a percentage of government expenditure	0.00
14. Maturity of loans (0.05)	
Limited to a maximum of six months	1.00
Limited to a maximum of one year	0.66
Limited to a maximum of more than one year	0.33
No legal upper bounds	0.00
15. Restrictions on interest rates (0.05)	
Interest rate must be at market rate	1.00
Interest rate on loans to government cannot be lower than a certain floor	0.75
Interest rate on Central Bank loans cannot exceed a certain ceiling	0.50
No explicit legal provisions regarding interest rate in Central Bank loans	0.25
No interest rate charge on government's borrowing from Central Bank	0.00
16. Prohibition on Central Bank lending in primary market to government (0.05)	
Prohibition from buying government securities in primary market	1.00
No prohibition	0.00

CB=Central Bank

Due to problems of availability of the large number of the postulated variables, Cukierman initially regroups them to form eight more comprehensive legal variables. The four CEO items are combined into a single item, calculated by computing their arithmetic mean. The three items of the Policy Formulation sub-index are combined using a weighted average with weights given above. Finally, the last four variables for the Limitations on Lending sub-index are combined using an arithmetic mean. Finally, the LVAW score is calculated using a weighted average of the resulting eight variables, with weights shown below:

Aggregated variable	Assigned weight
CEO	0.20
Policy formulation	0.15
Objectives	0.15
Limitations on lending – advances	0.15
Limitations on securitized lending	0.10
Limitations on lending – who decides	0.10
Limitations on lending – width	0.05
Limitations on lending – miscellaneous	0.10

Source: A. Cukierman, *Central Bank Strategy, Credibility, and Autonomy* (Cambridge, Massachusetts, MIT Press: 1992).

Table 5.4 Legal Independence (LVAW) Index, Central Bank of Azerbaijan

Criteria	1992–96 (weighted)	1996–2004 (weighted)	2004–8 (weighted)
Central Bank CEO	**0.05**	**0.08**	**0.13**
1. Term of office of CEO	NA*	0.50	0.50
2. Who appoints the CEO	0.50	0.00	0.25
3. Provisions for dismissal of CEO	0.33	0.17	0.83
4. CEO allowed to hold another office in government	0.00	1.00	1.00
Central Bank objectives	**0.09**	**0.06**	**0.09**
5. Central Bank objectives	0.60	0.40	0.60
Policy formulation	**0.02**	**0.05**	**0.08**
6. Who formulates monetary policy	0.33	0.67	1.00
7. Government directives and resolution of conflicts	NA	NA	NA
8. Central Bank given active role in formulation of government budget	0.00	0.00	0.00
Central Bank lending	**0.06**	**0.07**	**0.31**
9. Limitation on advances	0.00	0.00	0.66
10. Limitation on securitized lending	NA	NA	NA
11. Who decides control of terms of lending to government	0.00	0.33	0.66
12. Beneficiaries of Central Bank lending	NA	0.33	0.33
13. Types of limits when they exist	NA	NA	0.66
14. Maturity of loans	1.00	0.00	1.00
15. Restrictions on interest rates	0.25	0.25	0.25
16. Prohibition on Central Bank lending in primary market to government	0.00	0.00	1.00
Total	**0.22**	**0.26**	**0.61**

*NA = No record of this item in the law

that latecomers to the circle of central bank reformers generally tend to enact laws with higher levels of independence.[28]

In contrast, the 2004 law yields a significantly higher LVAW score compared to the previous laws. According to my calculations, the LVAW index based on this law is 0.61, a substantial improvement over the 1996 score.[29] Numerically, the LVAW value more than doubles from 1996 to 2004; it increases by 134 percent, as shown in Table 5.4. This is clear evidence for the argument that lawmakers *meant* to grant higher legal independence to the central bank. Azerbaijani policy makers are now well aware of the importance of having a credible monetary authority.

The progress on central bank independence has occurred in four categories: central bank governor, central bank objectives, policy formulation, and central bank lending, as shown in Table 5.4. Nevertheless, the greatest advance in the CBA's legal independence index stems from the 2004 law's strict prohibition of loans to the government. With the new law, the LVAW's weighted central bank lending subindex improved from 0.07 in 1996 to 0.31 in 2004. Under the 2004 law, the CBA can only purchase government securities in the secondary market when there is a short-run liquidity gap in the state budget. Article 16 of the law clearly defines the maximum amount and the repayment conditions for the loan.[30]

The 2004 law does not specify provisions for the resolution of potential conflicts between the CBA and the government. Moreover, in practice, one can hardly recall a single public policy conflict between the CBA and the government. Such a conflict would provide a real test of central bank independence. Even though the CBA is prohibited from extending direct credit to the government, there may still be a need for a conflict-resolution mechanism because fiscal dominance may significantly complicate the central bank's primary goal of maintaining price stability.

The position of the governor of the Central Bank of Azerbaijan is not sufficiently independent. The five-year tenure is equal to that of Azerbaijan's president, who appoints the governor. The 2004 law requires the governor to report only to the president, which makes the former heavily dependent on the latter. Of course, accountability is an important issue in a democracy, but I believe the solution that would best promote accountability—full central bank independence—is not possible under democratic regimes; the second-best solution is making the governor report both to the president and to parliament. On the upside, the long tenure of the current CBA governor (sixteen years) might be a sign of the central bank's independence. On the downside, this may also reflect the governor's willingness to pursue accommodative monetary policies even at the expense of higher inflation.

There are also concerns regarding the management board of the CBA, which is the decision-making body of the bank and, according to the 2004 law, must consist of seven members: the governor, four internal members, and two external members. Individual members are not held responsible for the board's decisions. The weak position of the board in this sense leaves all

Table 5.5 Selected Economic Indicators, Azerbaijan, 2004–9 (annual % changes, unless otherwise specified)

Years	2004	2005	2006	2007	2008	2009
Real GDP	10.4	26.4	34.5	25.0	10.8	9.3
Oil sector	2.5	65.4	62	37.3	6.9	14.8
Non-oil sector	13.8	8.2	12.1	11.3	15.7	3.0
Consumer Price Index (period average)		9.7	8.4	16.6	20.8	1.4
Nominal GDP per capita (US$)	1040	1538	2415	3759	5213	4807
Overall fiscal balance (% of GDP)	1	2.6	−0.2	2.6	20.8	6.8
Non-oil primary fiscal balance (% of non-oil GDP)	−12.9	−12.6	−31.1	−28.3	−38.2	−38.5
Manat base money	38.2	7.5	132.6	101.4	48.5	1.7

Source: IMF, *Azerbaijan Article IV Consultation Discussions* (Washington, D.C.: IMF, 2010).

the burden of responsibility on the governor, who may not be able to carry out his duties effectively all the time. Moreover, to my knowledge, two external members of the board have not been appointed yet.

Important amendments to the 2004 law were signed into force during the recent global financial crisis. The crisis has generally undermined the case for central bank independence worldwide, as resources were mobilized to bail out struggling financial institutions. Similarly, the new articles in the Law on the Central Bank of Azerbaijan stipulate that the CBA may extend government-backed credits to commercial banks to finance socially important projects and support the real economy. Under special circumstances, the CBA is now allowed to purchase government bonds in the primary market.

Indices of central bank legal independence such as the LVAW have their drawbacks and do not necessarily imply the same level of actual independence. There are two weaknesses associated with the central bank independence indices based on the law. First, laws cannot precisely specify the limits of authority between the central bank and the government. This results in voids that are filled by tradition at best and by power politics at worst. Second, actual practices can always differ from the law, regardless of how explicit the latter is.[31] Indeed, as shown in Table 5.5, the rate of inflation in Azerbaijan, which picked up in 2005 and hit double digits in 2007, raises the

Table 5.6 Central Bank of Azerbaijan Summary Accounts, 2005–9 (millions of manats)

	2005	2006	2007	2008	2009
Net foreign assets	1,033	1,954	2,872	4,036	3,336
Net international reserves	931	2,061	3,524	5,115	4,257
Net foreign assets of commercial banks	109	−103	−468	−869	−659
Other	−7	−3	−185	−210	−263
Net domestic assets	802	1,466	3,026	4,458	5,133
Net claims on consolidated central government	−69	36	48	−804	−754
Credit to economy	1,445	2,364	4,644	7,225	8,556
Other items, net	−574	−935	−1,667	−1,962	−2,669
Broad money	1,835	3,420	5,897	8,494	8,469
Manat broad money	791	2,123	4,402	6,081	6,169
Cash outside banks	547	1,311	2,714	4,146	4,175
Manat deposits	244	812	1,688	1,935	1,994
Foreign currency deposits	1,043	1,297	1,496	2,413	2,300

Source: IMF, *Azerbaijan Article IV Consultation Discussions* (Washington, D.C.: IMF, 2010).

question of how successful the CBA has been at translating legal independence into actual independence.

To answer this question, it is useful to analyze data from Central Bank accounts coupled with anecdotal evidence. The CBA's summary accounts for the 2005–9 period, shown in Table 5.6, help assess the level of oil dominance of monetary policy in Azerbaijan. Since 2003, one can note a gradual decrease in the "net claims on government" item. From January 31, 2004 on, there is no evidence of direct loans to the government or purchases of government obligations. However, as argued above, fiscal dominance—actually, oil dominance—of monetary policy may appear in oil economies in a different form, without being reflected as a direct loan to the government in central bank accounts. More precisely, fiscal dominance of monetary policy is more likely to manifest itself as an increase in net international currency reserves accompanied by an increase in the country's monetary base. Indeed, this is what has been happening in Azerbaijan since 2004. Large unsterilized conversion operations by the CBA, presumably under government pressure, have led to sustained increases in net international currency reserves, money supply, and inflation. For instance, in 2006 the CBA bought about US$2 billion from the State Oil Company and sterilized only a fraction of that amount, which led to an approximately 133 percent increase in Azerbaijan's monetary base (see Table 5.5).

Let us return to the central bank accounts shown in Table 5.6. There is hardly a change of equal proportions in net international reserves and net domestic assets: whereas net international reserves increase by huge amounts, net domestic assets do not decrease at the same pace. Moreover, in some years net domestic assets even increase, reflecting the fact that let alone keeping its oil receipts in the CBA, the government actually borrows money from the CBA to finance its expenditures. Even though these loans to the government do not exceed legally permissible amounts, this analysis leads to the conclusion that Azerbaijan's budget deficit might be partly financed through increases in the monetary base. This indicates that the CBA is not as independent as it might seem.

Conclusions

This chapter discussed the challenges facing central banking in oil-exporting countries. Specifically, it analyzed how fiscal dominance of monetary policy, banking sector stability, and the choice of exchange rate regime may become challenges for central banks in oil-exporting countries. In Azerbaijan, the Central Bank of Azerbaijan has done quite well in maintaining the stability of the banking sector in the face of tightening global liquidity conditions and the sudden end of the 2003–8 oil price boom. Notwithstanding Azerbaijan's underdeveloped financial markets and limited economic openness, the bank's bold and swift policy actions prior to and during the crisis safeguarded the economy from a banking crisis similar to the one that occurred in Kazakhstan.

The CBA's record on exchange rate policy is ambiguous. On one hand, pegging Azerbaijan's currency to the U.S. dollar served the economy well in stabilizing prices and providing a credible and transparent nominal anchor for monetary policy after the Soviet Union collapsed in the 1990s. Yet the oil price boom of the 2000s and the increased influx of petrodollars into the Azerbaijani economy resulted in a substantially higher price level in the presence of the country's accommodative monetary policy stance. It seems as though political priorities outweighed the concern for price stability.

6

Power to the Producers:
The Challenges of Electricity Provision
in Major Energy-Exporting States

Theresa Sabonis-Helf

The Problem

It may seem intuitive that petrostates, whose economies and federal revenues are based on oil and natural gas, would have energy to spare at home.
In fact, many petrostates have persistent trouble keeping the lights on. Their
electricity sectors are plagued by low reliability, poor quality power, and
high transmission and distribution losses. This phenomenon is limited neither to times when the price of oil is low (meaning times when petrostates'
budgets are tight), nor to times when the price of oil and natural gas is high
(causing higher opportunity costs to using energy at home). Petrostate problems in electricity provision are persistent. They are technical, political, and
economic in nature—and all three aspects of this problem overlap.

Technologically, electricity choices—in terms of creating and supplying
power, building and maintaining grids, and distributing and charging for
electricity—are choices that have to be sustained over time if an electricity
system is to continue to function. Electricity is one of the largest, most
capital-intensive sectors of a developed economy,[1] and it requires sustained
commitment. The World Bank notes that a population's access to electricity
and a self-sustaining electricity sector are two hallmarks of developed economies.[2] In petrostates, people's access to electricity tends to be high, but the

electricity sector tends not to be self-sustaining and therefore requires constant intervention from the government.

Economically, electricity is best rationed by pricing: amount and time of usage can be influenced by price signals. But if the price to consumers is very low, it becomes difficult to ration the quantity of electricity. Cutting off groups of customers, brownouts (periods of persistent, lower-than-optimal voltage), and blackouts are the only tools available. This tends to cause governments to get locked in a losing race to stay ahead of demand. If an electricity system allows for most or all households to be connected to the grid, underpricing electricity becomes very expensive for a government, because demand continually rises as populations and standards of living grow. If a system is to continue functioning under these conditions and deliver predictable electricity with reliable quality, the supplier has to keep pace with growing demand. Uneven power quality—with surges, spikes, or sags in voltage—will damage commercial, industrial, and residential equipment. If power supply cannot meet the demands on the system, brownouts or blackouts will result.

Fundamentally, electricity is a highly politicized good in both democratic and authoritarian states. In their research on electricity and regime type, David Brown and Ahmed Mobarak find a strong correlation between democratization and electricity distribution. In their study, low-income democracies favor provision of residential electricity over industrial electricity (even though industrial energy is less expensive to supply and more productive in terms of national wealth). Voters tend to prefer home electrification over industrialization.[3] This trend, which may be considered a "constituent service" effect, is not confined to democracies. Citizens, regardless of their form of government, desire electricity. Moreover, the pervasive rhetoric in oil-rich nations—"Our oil wealth belongs to our citizens"—makes it difficult for petrostates to be stingy in their provision of energy to residential users. The energy goods citizens tend to desire most are electricity and gasoline, and in petrostates both of these are often highly subsidized.

As other chapters in this volume have illustrated, oil-producing states extend generous subsidies, and these subsidies make it difficult to efficiently allocate the goods and services that a nation needs most. Subsidies also tend to encourage overconsumption of the subsidized products and lead to underinvestment in the sector producing the subsidized goods.[4] Part of petrostates' problems with electricity is indeed related to this question of subsidies, but that only tells part of the story. Much of the opportunity cost of underpriced electricity is hidden, allowing governments to underestimate and even ignore its long-term impact on the government budget and overall economy.

Electricity is, in some sense, a measure of governance, because planning within the sector is a long-term activity and requires responsiveness to changing conditions. The electricity sector requires frequent recapitalization and maintenance, and receipts in the sector are vulnerable to corruption at the local level and demagoguery at the highest governmental levels. Population growth, urbanization, and changes in standards of living have strong impacts on the sector's ability to supply the necessary amount of electricity. Opportunity costs to states that subsidize electricity are often hidden and misunderstood, even though they tend to grow over time. The ever-present political component of electricity supply and pricing means states are unwilling to make difficult and unpopular choices unless absolutely necessary, which usually only happens in response to a crisis.

To some extent, petrostates' electricity problems are similar to all developing states' electricity problems. Based on decades of experience with electricity sectors in developing and transition economies, World Bank economists Venkataraman Krishnaswamy and Gary Stuggins recommend six key requirements for states seeking a durable supply-demand balance in electricity: 1) rule of law and enforcement of property rights extend to the electricity sector; 2) the sector must generate some surplus cash in order to keep the system properly maintained and capable of expanding to meet rising demand; 3) good governance and transparency are critical components to cooperation between industry and private companies; 4) third parties—particularly international financial institutions—play an important role in promoting, assisting, and evaluating reform; 5) electricity can only be delivered reliably if demand management, optimal generation planning, and electricity trading are all allowed to play their roles; and 6) the private sector plays a key role in the electricity sector, and the state must be ready to meet the increased demands that regulation and working with the private sector will make on the state's capacity.[5] States that import the raw materials necessary for their power generation typically cannot afford to meet demand without meeting these six requirements. They cannot afford the inputs and so must limit access to electricity within their country, thereby limiting development along with it. In contrast, petrostates, which do not have to worry as much about raw inputs, are able to extend electricity to their population and provide initial supply even if they have problems in all six categories listed above. But they do so at a great cost, which grows over time.

To illustrate petrostates' electricity provision challenges, this chapter lays out some general problems and then goes into more depth on four cases: Venezuela, Iran, Russia, and Azerbaijan. These states have some things in common. One is that all four are in the bottom 20 percent of states in terms of corruption. Of the 180 states ranked by Transparency International in 2009, Azerbaijan ranked 143rd, Russia 146th, Venezuela 162nd, and Iran 168th.[6] This provides some evidence that all four states can be expected to have problems with Krishnaswamy and Stuggins's requirement for rule of law in the electricity sector. None of the four states' electricity sectors have surplus cash or large roles for the private sector. The countries differ significantly in their electricity sector crises. Each has a persistent crisis born of a distinct combination of political, economic, and technological challenges that make efficient, cost-effective provision of electricity difficult. In addition, each of these states has pursued a distinctive response to the crises they face; these responses, however, differ significantly from the Krishnaswamy and Stuggins's recommendations and have had limited, if any, success.

For Venezuela, the populist imperative is leading to renationalization of electricity provision and prioritization of residential over industrial customers. The result as of 2011 remained chaotic. For Iran, the rising population and rising standard of living increased the cost to the government of subsidized electricity to almost unbearable levels. In spite of its commitment to a planned economy, the Iranian government responded by creating space for competitive private energy suppliers and by institutionalizing very limited energy efficiency measures. The Iranian government's 2009 annual power sector report said that the following policies and activities have been a priority for the preceding decade and will remain priority for the future: "Deployment of privatization, development of the qualities and quantities of the industry related to the electricity market, utilizing renewable energy sources, efficiency improvement, development of demand side management, and loss reduction."[7] Iran has also begun reducing subsidies, despite difficult political consequences. For Russia, the combined effects of Soviet-era infrastructure, harsh climate, and popular expectations of a "right" to electricity caused the government itself to note that it expends "the world's largest energy subsidy," which it estimated at $40 billion in 2005.[8] In response, the government began moving forward with difficult and unpopular measures, starting in earnest in 2007. Like Iran, the Russian government concluded that reductions in energy subsidies are essential and began pursuing significant rate increases. For Azerbaijan, a failed effort at partial privatization in 2006 led the government to abandon many aspects of reform and concentrate instead on increasing electricity generation and, with it, government subsidies. The government is only now beginning to re-approach the problems that caused the earlier effort at privatization to fail.

Basics of the Electricity Sector

It is very difficult to store electricity after it is generated, so generation (the process of producing electricity at power plants) is constantly adjusted to match demand. This can be difficult because demand for electricity fluctuates across seasons—and even during a single day. Demand can fluctuate more than 100 percent in a twenty-four-hour period. The operation of electricity systems must be closely coordinated with the electricity needs of the industrial and residential users. In order to manage these shifts in demand, many states price off-peak power for industry at low prices to encourage industry to shift its higher demands to times when residents are using less power in their homes. Another component of managing these demand fluctuations is in the infrastructure itself: a stable grid has baseload generation (which runs all the time), peaking capacity (which runs only at maximum demand times), and intermediate generation (which is somewhere in between). An economically efficient grid uses its least-cost generation as baseload and uses peaking and intermediate only when demand is higher than the baseload can meet. Managers of an efficient grid would then pass the higher cost of peaking capacity on to the customer. Generation must be carefully managed to ensure that the amount of electricity going into the grid is sufficient to meet demand. If that does not happen, the quality of the electricity is degraded, and equipment in households and industries can be damaged.

As electricity is generated from different power plants, it is pooled into the transmission system. Larger transmission grids use a mix of alternating current (AC) and direct current (DC). Direct-current, high-voltage lines are used because they minimize electrical loss when moving electricity from one point to another. Facilities at the end of each high-voltage (DC) line then convert that power back into alternating current before it is delivered to distribution systems. The power is "stepped down" yet again before it enters households for use. Most transmission systems include substations that contain circuit breakers and other equipment to protect the transmission system from failures on the distribution lines. A well-designed transmission system can reroute power if one line fails, but transmission systems under stress lose electricity that is generated but never reaches the customer.

After generation and transmission, the third component of electricity is distribution. Thousands of distribution systems branch from the central transmission lines and branch again as they reach buildings and individual homes. Distribution includes delivery to residential, commercial, and industrial facilities. In a system with no cross-subsidies, residential customers usually pay higher rates than commercial or industrial customers because household electricity is more expensive to supply and maintain.

Because electricity systems are large, complex, and integrated and the cost of production is lower if the scale is greater, electricity is considered a "natural monopoly." In most countries, electricity is managed as a regulated monopoly. The prices producers are allowed to charge depend on their expenses. Prices can vary by basic fuel source and by difficulty of delivery. A regulated monopoly is given the opportunity to serve the market because popular demands and economic productivity require electricity that is reliable, affordable, and capable of adjusting to changes in demand.

To get a sense of the electricity industry's capitalization and labor intensity, it may be useful to use the U.S. electricity system as a basis of comparison. In the United States, the cost of electricity generation represents 65 percent of the bill received by the consumer. The generation process employs around 120,000 people nationwide to service approximately 10,000 U.S. power plants. Transmission accounts for only 5 percent of the total bill and employs less than a tenth of those involved in generation, or about 15,000 people. Distribution accounts for the remaining 30 percent of the bill and employs the largest number, about 400,000.[9] The U.S. system is highly ranked among Western nations in terms of its extent and quality of power; however it still suffers from inefficiencies. These inefficiencies, described below, are often magnified in poorly managed states and result in disruptive imbalances between supply and demand.

Generation, as the most costly (and perhaps most visible) component of electricity provision, is an obvious place for states to focus their efforts. Construction of new power plants is a highly visible way for a country to demonstrate their efforts to solve problems of scarcity. Critics also note that "megaprojects" such as large power plants make it possible to collect bribes and hide payoffs.[10] As such, generation is attractive to government officials both because it is visible and because it can be an opportunity for elites to enrich themselves. Even if generation is built honestly, high losses and inefficiencies in transmission and distribution can degrade a grid substantially.

The four states examined in this chapter have, for the most part, focused on improving generation rather than on other components of the electricity sector. Each of these states continues to experience high rates of electricity loss. Electricity losses are usually a reflection of poor practices in both transmission and distribution. These take the form of either technical failures or an inability to meter and bill electricity at the distribution level. These problems complicate an electricity company's ability to determine how much supply the customers are receiving and collect revenue. Theft of electricity—which can be achieved by illegally tapping into transmission lines or by making illegal agreements with local power plants—is very common in many states and also contributes to losses.

Prior to the 1990s, electricity grids were exclusively in government hands. The trend toward privatization and "unbundling" the sector began in the early 1990s. The World Bank advocates electricity market reform that includes unbundling the sector (into generation, transmission, and distribution) to maximize transparency and competition. It also advocates privatization of at least part of the sector to promote efficiency that comes with the commercialization of management practices. Government-owned electricity often performs poorly (especially in developing states) unless the state finds ways to reduce politicians' willingness and ability to use utilities for political purposes and finds ways to subject the utilities to political and economic pressure to perform well.[11] The World Bank recognizes, however, that power sector reform often involves more political complexity than technical complexity and that electricity is an important part of the state-citizen social compact in developing states.[12] According to the World Bank, approximately 70 of the world's 150 developing and transition economies have worked to reform and to some extent restructure their power markets since 1990. The power markets of most petrostates remain in the category of "vertically integrated monopolies," a category that includes Azerbaijan, Iran, Venezuela, and seventy-six other developing and transition economies, most of which have engaged in little or no electricity sector reform. Russia belongs to a smaller group of states that has developed what is known as "single-buyer transit companies with third-party access," a complex approach to reform followed by only six states, all of which (except Ecuador) are transition economies.[13]

How Much Should Electricity Cost,
and How Is This Determined?

Electricity in energy-rich states enjoys explicit and implicit subsidies. Explicit subsidies, which are relatively easy to estimate if a federal budget is available, are funds a government transfers to the electricity provider to make up for the difference between the price charged and the economic cost of producing electricity. Such subsidies are usually for a category of customers, such as the subsidy Azerbaijan extends to internally displaced persons. Explicit subsidies can also take the form of encouraging new energy technologies (such as renewable energy) to enter the electricity market.[14]

Implicit subsidies are usually more extensive. They can be cross-subsidies in which one class of users (such as industrial consumers) are charged more in order to help bear part of the cost of another class of users (such as residential consumers). This type of cross-subsidy was quite common in post-Soviet states in the early years of independence, because leaving residents to "freeze in the dark" was politically impractical. Other types of implicit subsidies can include state guarantees to producers, or, most commonly, simply selling electricity domestically at far below its market value and then putting state money into the state electricity company as necessary.

Many energy-rich states price residential electricity lower than industrial due to people's political expectations of energy provision. Because of the structure of their economies, many petrostates supply most of their overall electricity to residential consumers. From an electricity provision perspective, this means that petrostates' electricity systems are more expensive, harder to manage, and more prone to fluctuations in demand (industrial users are more likely than residential users to be persuaded to shift their energy use to off-peak hours). The cost to supply residential and industrial users with electricity is quite different. The unit cost of supplying a residential consumer is quite high, and the unit cost of supplying an industrial consumer is quite low. Residential users require low-voltage electricity in small quantities, usually during the peak demand to the power system, yet industrial users require medium or high voltage in large quantities and have a more consistent demand pattern—one that will use the electricity system during low-load periods as well as during peak and intermediate times.[15]

The opportunity costs to a state of supplying electricity at below cost are many and will be examined in some detail for each of the cases included in this chapter. One reason why the economics of subsidized electricity are so problematic is that the decision to extend or increase subsidies leads to higher consumption, and these expanding costs leave the government unwilling or unable to make investments in the electricity sector to improve the quality of service. Over time, the reliability of electricity suffers, and this places strain on societies—particularly in urban areas where people rely on electricity for a wide range of everyday needs. Efforts to charge higher rates for products such as electricity, which the populace sees as essential and is accustomed to receiving free (or very cheaply), have high political costs. Some goods, such as gasoline, can be rationed even though they are provided cheaply. Electricity, by contrast, is difficult to allocate in controlled quantities without cutting off entire communities or significantly degrading the quality of power.

Costs of generation fluctuate with global prices for each power-generating commodity: coal, oil, natural gas, and nuclear fuel. Of these, the price for oil is the most volatile, followed by natural gas. In states that import the fuels used for electricity generation, changes in fuel cost are passed on to the customer, even if not immediately. For petrostates, what a customer pays for electricity typically does not change, but the state's opportunity cost of using its own oil or natural gas in the domestic market instead of selling it on the world market rises and falls with the global price of that commodity. In other words, precisely at the time when oil prices are high and there is pressure from the public to give the population more goods and subsidies, it is more expensive for the government to comply with providing more electricity. When possible, petrostates have shown a preference for using hydroelectricity because its cost does not fluctuate with global market prices for oil and gas. Petrostates, at a minimum, have shifted away from use of oil to the use of natural gas in their electricity sectors over the past few decades. In justifying their pursuit of nuclear power, Russia and Iran make an argument similar to the argument in favor of hydroelectricity: the cost of nuclear fuel does not fluctuate with global oil and gas prices, and the price is more predictable because it is possible to store an entire year's supply of fuel on site at the plant. One assumption that petrostates can make about their energy sectors is that overall energy consumption per capita will increase as standards of living rise (see Figure 6.1), even though developed states improve the energy efficiency of their economies over time. Electricity is no exception to this trend of higher per capita energy consumption; in fact, the global trend is for electricity to take up an increasing percentage of total

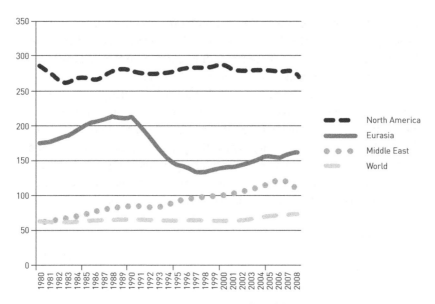

Figure 6.1 Per capita energy consumption. EIA, "World per Capita Total Primary Energy Consumption," *International Energy Annual 2006*, http://www.eia.doe.gov.

energy demand as nations develop. In the United States, for example, electricity constituted 10 percent of total energy consumption in 1940, grew to 25 percent by 1970, and reached 40 percent in the 2000–2009 period.[16] This is a reflection of the fact that, as standards of living rise, citizens tend to use more electricity as they acquire more appliances and home equipment.

Electricity: Does It Matter?

Petrostates have persistent problems providing many public goods to their citizens, so it is reasonable to inquire why electricity is different and what significance it might have for international relations. After all, the international electricity trade is relatively limited. Only eight nations exported more than ten terawatt hours (trillion watt hours) of electricity in 2007. In overall terms, petrostates have the raw materials to produce large quantities of electricity and tend to consume large quantities of it as well.

The world's highest concentration of petrostates is in the Middle East, and it is notable that only in the Middle East has energy consumption risen

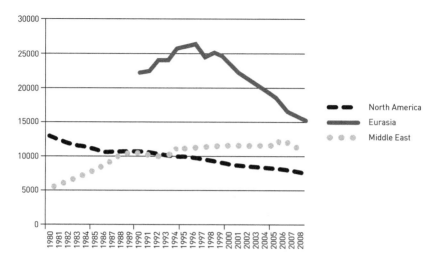

Figure 6.2 Energy intensity of economies. EIA, "Energy Intensity of Economies: Total Primary Energy Consumption per Dollar of GDP (BTU per year 2005 U.S. Dollars at Market Exchange Rates)," http://www.eia.doe.gov.

faster than GDP since 1980, with energy intensity (the amount of energy consumed per unit of GDP) actually growing from 1980 through 2001. Energy consumption per unit of GDP reflects the structure of an economy as well as its overall efficiency, so it is not a perfect measure of efficient use of energy. For instance, a state with extensive manufacturing will have a higher energy intensity than a state that is largely supported by tourism, even if both states use energy inefficiently. Economies tend to be responsive to price, however.

Price signals have caused the oil-importing part of the world (North America) to use energy more efficiently as it became more expensive in world markets (see Figure 6.2). Concerns about greenhouse gas emissions have driven other states (particularly in the European Union) to become more energy efficient. Oil exporters (represented by OPEC in Figure 6.2), however, have neither experienced nor responded to many of the price signals that have shaped the energy behavior of importing states nor have they engaged in greenhouse gas abatement for environmental reasons. According to a World Bank study of electricity in the Middle East and North Africa, the most energy-intensive states—the states that use energy least efficiently—in this high-consuming region are oil states. States with "extremely low" prices (known in the electricity industry as tariffs) for electricity include Bahrain,

Egypt, Iraq, Kuwait, Libya, Oman, Qatar, and Saudi Arabia. States with "below-cost" tariffs include Algeria, Yemen, Iran, and Syria.[17]

Azerbaijan, Iran, Russia, and Venezuela—the four states discussed in this chapter—all had below-cost tariffs and high levels of energy intensity at the start of 2010. High per-capita energy consumption combined with low efficiency of that energy use has clear opportunity costs for states though those costs differ across states and across time. That said, all four states have seen the cost to the state of providing subsidized electricity increase over time. All four states failed to maintain their grids and experienced high losses and degraded quality of power. In especially difficult times, each of the states has experienced blackouts and brownouts in key urban areas. Iran, Venezuela, and Azerbaijan have all been compelled at various times to import supplemental fuels for their electricity sectors. Russia and Iran have reduced commitments in their exports in order to meet domestic electricity needs.

These are among the clearest opportunity costs of energy subsidies. At a minimum, the opportunity cost of the government's provision of electricity must be compared to the potential export price of the resources consumed to supply that electricity. This amount is an important component of implicit energy subsidies. Because most resources used to supply electricity are internationally tradable, many experts recommend that the opportunity cost in most cases should be calculated as the world market price of the goods.[18] This simple calculation may require modification in cases where states use large amounts of domestic natural gas—because the costs of transporting gas (particularly in relatively small quantities) exceed the costs of extraction—but in any event, resources spent at home are not available for international sale.[19] Other opportunity costs include the negative impact on industry when it bears the cross-subsidy cost of providing cheaper electricity to residents and damage to industrial and residential equipment when electricity services become degraded.

High domestic opportunity costs can have international effects. Persistent underinvestment in the natural gas sector in Azerbaijan, Russia, and Iran can be linked to domestic electricity policies. Because natural gas and gas-fired electricity are highly subsidized at home, these states have failed to develop the natural gas sector fully, despite international demand for their natural gas and their proximity to markets that wish to buy. European Union insistence that Russia raise its electricity prices to cost-recovery levels as a prerequisite for acceptance to the World Trade Organization is based in

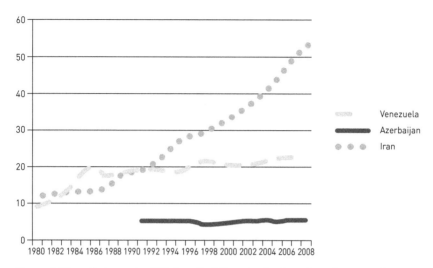

Figure 6.3 Installed capacity. EIA, Installed Capacity database, http://www.eia.doe.gov.

part on European fears that Russia will fail to develop the natural gas sector sufficiently to ensure long-term provision of gas to Europe.

Petrostate Examples

Petrostates' electricity sectors tend toward the grandiose in their design. In terms of gigawatts of electricity generated or numbers of customers served by the national grid, such states are usually leaders in their regions. In the period from 1985 to 2005, two of the case states from this chapter continuously expanded their installed capacity (see Figure 6.3). Two did not: Russia did not expand capacity significantly because it inherited capacity from the Soviet Union that exceeded its need for most of the period, especially because it experienced population decline. Azerbaijan, which is the only one of the case states with clearly inadequate electricity supply, did not begin expanding capacity until 2007, when revenues from oil significantly increased.

All four states shown in Figure 6.3 have experienced problems with electricity provision, because demand continually expands (with population size and the standard of living) and the costs of supply continue to grow as these states persist in charging less than cost to supply their nations. The four case studies that follow have a lot in common. Although the mix of

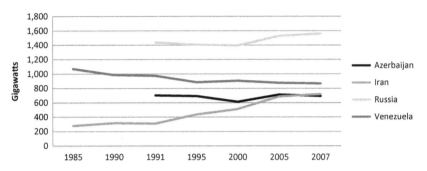

Figure 6.4 Installed capacity per capita. Installed capacity data from EIA, Installed Capacity database, http://www.eia.doe.gov. Population data from U.S. Census Bureau, International database, http://www.census.gov/ipc/www/idb/informationGateway.php.

political, economic, and technological challenges differs across states, the electricity sectors in each of these countries have struggled to maintain service. Increases in capacity, where made, were quickly absorbed by increases in population and per capita demand for electricity, as Figure 6.4 illustrates.

Petrostates, then, are not underachievers in building power generation, but they struggle to maintain the electricity commitments they have made to their populations, particularly as those populations, and their consumption per capita, grow. The following case studies illustrate the political, economic, and technical reasons why the challenges of electricity provision are seldom resolved simply, even when states possesses an abundance of exportable energy resources.

Case Studies in Petrostate Electricity

Venezuela

In October 2009, Venezuela was in the midst of a severe electricity crisis. Drought had brought the water tables too low for hydroelectric dams, which provide approximately 70 percent of Venezuela's electricity. The water level at the Guri Dam, the largest in Venezuela, was said to be about 30 percent below the previous record low.[20] A consumer advocacy group reported that blackouts had hit all twenty-four states in Venezuela, eight of which were experiencing three to five outages a week for up to twelve hours at a time.[21]

These outages imposed high costs on residential and industrial customers; as the quality of electricity deteriorated, appliances and industrial equipment were destroyed by power surges. Many demonstrators during October and November left damaged appliances on the steps of state electricity companies as a new form of protest.[22] The government of Hugo Chavez blamed the weather and implied that members of the Federation of Electrical Sector Workers were sabotaging the system, an accusation that sparked an angry response from the workers.[23]

The real responsibility lay with the Venezuelan government's years of petrostate energy policies. The Venezuelan electricity system had already been in need of repair more than twelve years earlier, when Chavez's predecessor Rafael Caldera considered privatizing regional power companies because they required significant capitalization, which Venezuela could not afford in an era of low oil prices. With growing demand for electricity and declining generation capacity, the network was becoming increasingly brittle. In the twelve years of Chavez's presidency, the situation has worsened. No new large power plants were constructed in the country, but access to power was extended to more people. And prices for both industrial and residential power customers were reduced significantly. The political decision to cut prices has had a measurable impact on the electricity system: Venezuela has been inadvertently destroying what had been an impressive set of electricity accomplishments. Some 90 percent of its population is on the national grid, which means Venezuelans have enjoyed the highest rate of electricity provision in Latin America. They also consume the highest level of electricity per capita in South America.[24] Instead of seeing improvements or even steady service, recent years have brought a significant degrading of the system.

Venezuela has enjoyed installed capacity of more than nineteen gigawatts since 1985 (although that number has decreased several times in the intervening years).[25] In recent years, there have been repeated warning signs that the Venezuelan system was under great strain. The system relies heavily on hydropower and is therefore vulnerable to fluctuations in rainfall. The system has also not been well maintained. Crises in the system have prompted the government to make changes in management and ownership, but unfortunately continuous reorganization with very limited recapitalization has been the approach. In the first six months of 2008, 391 unplanned power outages in the main power lines were reported. The 2008 power outages caused the Venezuelan government to announce that it was moving away from hydroelectricity and installing new decentralized capacity in the form of small power plants purchased from Cuba.[26] This decentralization approach was announced a year after the electricity sector had been recentralized: The fragile state of the electricity sector in 2007, combined with the populist drive to renationalize, had led to the renationalization of fourteen regional power companies into a new state-owned electricity company called CORPOELEC.[27]

CORPOELEC came into being together with a law mandating significant changes, many of which have still not been implemented as of 2011. In an effort to help CORPOELEC achieve its promise, the Inter-American Development Bank (IADB) approved a $200 million loan (with an additional $50 million to be provided by the government of Venezuela) to improve the organization of CORPOELEC.[28] The IADB loan is perplexing because CORPOELEC is attempting to conduct a set of reforms that contradict internationally supported electricity sector reforms. Namely, CORPOELEC is attempting to absorb all public power companies and take over all generation, transmission, and distribution. Advocates of CORPOELEC's reforms argue that the sector became inefficient when it was broken into separate subsectors for generation, transmission, and distribution. Critics note that reintegration is unlikely to improve transparency or accountability in the electricity sector.

The decline of Venezuela's electricity sector is evident in many trends. The international standard for acceptable distributional losses—that is, losses of electricity somewhere between generation and consumption—is around 10 percent for developing countries.[29] Venezuela's grid, which had operated within normal parameters before 1996, has shown a steady decline since 1997, as Figure 6.5 demonstrates. By 2005, before discussion began about significant renovation of the system, distributional losses had risen to almost 18 percent. These distributional losses are attributed to both technical losses (aging equipment and faulty transmission) and commercial losses (an inability to properly track and collect tariffs).

Patterns of electricity pricing in Venezuela before 2001 are not readily available, but the recent trend is clear: average residential tariffs came down dramatically in Venezuela from 2001 to 2005, beginning at 97.06 cents per megawatt hour and ending at 55.12. Industrial tariffs also declined during this period, though less dramatically, beginning at 44.45 cents per megawatt hour and ending at 40.59.[30] As noted above, Venezuela's 18 percent distributional loss rate is higher than an "acceptable loss" level for developing coun-

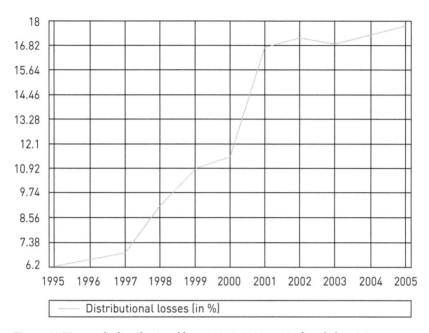

Figure 6.5 Venezuela distributional losses 1995–2005, as % of total electricity generated. Chart generated from World Bank, "Benchmarking Data of the Electricity Distribution Sector in the Latin America and Caribbean Region 1995–2005," World Bank Group, http://info.worldbank.org/etools/lacelectricity/home.htm.

tries, but about half of the Latin American nations for which data is available have losses above that international standard. Notably, however, Venezuela has fared worse than most of the rest of South America in electricity provision during the past fifteen years. During this period, available electricity per capita has declined, electricity losses have increased, and length of power outages has become higher than any other state in the region except Colombia. Venezuela has the lowest average residential tariff among Latin American states providing data. It also has the lowest industrial tariff. This means it is very cheap to use electricity for any purpose.

It is reasonable to ask how electricity should be priced in Venezuela. As a nation that relies heavily on hydroelectricity (supplemented by natural gas), Should Venezuela's cost per kilowatt-hour be lower than that of other states? Is Venezuela's opportunity cost of providing the electricity lower? To a certain extent, using hydroelectricity does reduce the opportunity cost to Venezuela of providing subsidized electricity and therefore the benchmark price for hydroelectricity should be lower than for a state that imports energy resources for its power plants. By relying on the Guri Dam complex, Venezuela saves nearly half a million barrels of oil a day that it would otherwise need to meet demand for electricity.[31] However, it is clear that the current prices for electricity in Venezuela remain below the costs of maintaining even a hydroelectricity-based system and that the system is dangerously reliant on a single, variable power source. Venezuela is subsidizing electricity at a level that is detrimental to the sector and the economy overall. It cannot be said that Venezuela is engaging in cross-subsidies (because industrial and residential customers are all paying less than cost), but it should be noted that the current system favors residential electricity use to the detriment of the overall grid. To date, the government has not put into place any strategies that pressure industry to use more power at times when residential demand is lower. Such strategies, pursued in places such as Iran, reduce the strain to the grid.

Subsidizing electricity presents another substantial opportunity cost to the government of Venezuela—the cost of natural gas. Curiously, Venezuela has periodically imported natural gas from Colombia to supply its electricity sector, in spite of the fact that Venezuela has the second- largest natural gas reserves in the Western Hemisphere. According to recent official counts, Venezuela imported some 151 trillion cubic feet of natural gas from Colombia in 2009, in addition to the purchase of limited amounts of electricity from Colombia.[32] What was Venezuela doing with its own natural gas? Much of Venezuelan natural gas occurs in association with its oil, meaning it is found together with the oil, and must be somehow managed to maintain safe access to the oil. In 2004, Venezuela used 26 percent of its associated gas in its domestic energy market, used 43 percent of it to help extract oil by reinjecting it into the ground, and deliberately vented (released into the atmosphere) or flared (burned on location) 8 percent of the gas that rose to the surface in association with oil. Venting and flaring are done when a state lacks the capacity to trap and use the gas but must get the gas out of the way of the oil it wishes to exploit. In spite of the fact that Venezuela could use the natural gas in its electricity mix, the government has chosen instead to continue treating natural gas as a waste product. According to World Bank reports, Venezuela flared 2.8 billion cubic meters of gas in 2010, an increase from the 2.1 billion cubic meters flared in 2006. Emissions in 2010 accounted for 2 percent of all global gas flaring, placing Venezuela tenth in global gas flaring.[33] Flaring has high environmental costs and health costs. It can release caustic agents, such as sulfur dioxide, carcinogens including benzene, and nitrogen oxides (NOx gases) that cause smog, and greenhouse gases.[34] Vented gas is often high in methane, an especially potent greenhouse gas. The World Bank is very optimistic about the prospects for using the natural gas in a cost-effective manner and leads a Global Gas Flaring Reduction Partnership (GGFR) program to assist countries in reducing flaring. The government of Venezuela, however, has not joined the GGFR and has not made notable progress on flaring reductions in recent years.[35]

The Venezuelan experience demonstrates that a political decision (to cut the price of electricity to residents in half) can have a fairly rapid impact on a system's technological capabilities and cause the quality and reliability of power to degrade rapidly. Hydroelectricity is the cheapest source of electricity, so as Venezuela moves to diversify (which it must do for the system to become more reliable), it will incur a higher cost per kilowatt-hour. The state will not be able to keep pace with increased demand for power, and it will face substantial political consequences if customers—especially urban customers, for whom electricity is an hourly necessity—experience service disruptions. Internationally, Venezuela's short-term solution, to import natural gas and electricity from Colombia, may begin to shift relations between those two countries and limit Venezuela's freedom to maneuver in other sectors. Venezuela has not developed its own natural gas sector to better serve the electricity needs of the state or to export to regional markets. The government's most visible response to the 2009 crisis has been to embrace the idea of nuclear energy, but little development has occurred in that arena or in other electricity related realms. It is evident that few if any of Krishnaswamy and Stuggins' six key requirements for success in balancing supply and demand can be met in the current environment.

Iran

Iran's electricity transmission, distribution, and most of its generation are managed by Tavanir, a specialized state-owned holding company. Subsidiary companies of Tavanir include sixteen regional electric companies, forty-two distribution companies, and twenty-seven generation management companies. The company also owns a power plant project management company (MAPNA), the Iranian Organization for New Energies (SANA), the Iran Organization for Energy Productivity (SABA), and the Iran Power Plant

Repairs Company.[36] Although the state owns most aspects of electricity, it is possible for private producers to sell electricity to the grid, and the sector has been disaggregated into self-managed companies for generation, transmission, and distribution. The sector has also been "corporatized" in the sense that the legal identity of the state-owned enterprise is separate from the government itself. The World Bank views these steps as inferior to privatization but still likely to lead to marginal improvement in governance in state-owned power companies.[37]

Iran is ahead of Venezuela in addressing its power generation problems, if only because its grid began experiencing significant instabilities more than a decade earlier than Venezuela's. In the early 1990s, blackouts plagued the country's main cities and led to an ambitious program to expand the electricity system.[38] A drought in the winter of 1990–91 caused acute electricity shortages in Tehran, leading to three-hour blackouts each day.[39] As late as March 1991, the citizens of Iran were still experiencing daily blackouts, and the government called for resumption of work on the Bushehr nuclear plant to help the nation diversify its electricity sources. The plant had been abandoned during the 1980–88 war with Iraq and had been a target of repeated Iraqi bombings.[40] In addition to renewing its nuclear power ambitions, the Iranian government pursued conventional electrical generation as well. From 1995 through 2008, the government invested substantially in new generation and more than doubled the government-owned installed capacity, from 21,914 megawatts in 1995[41] to 52,944 megawatts in 2008. According to Iran's Ministry of Energy, the country had extended electricity to 100 percent of its urban population and 99 percent of its rural population by the end of 2008.[42]

Demand for electricity, however, rose as fast as new generation. Electricity consumption in Iran annually rose 7.5 percent from 1995 to 2005, increasing 1.5 percent faster than the Third Five-Year Economic Development Plan's target.[43] According to the Economist Intelligence Unit, Iran's current configuration of electricity generation is enough to meet current demand. But demand is forecast to expand at approximately 8 percent per year, driven by growth of the adult population, an emphasis on industrialization, and the heavily subsidized cost of supply.[44] Iran's Ministry of Energy has planned that generation capacity will reach 60,000 megawatts by 2015. (Installed capacity was 52,944 megawatts in 2008.)[45] Critics anticipate that even this expansion will be insufficient to meet the increase in demand unless the price of electricity changes markedly.

In an effort to ensure that this goal is reached, Iran has engaged the private sector. As early as 2005, the government had begun a program to attract independent power producers in addition to expanding government power plants. The nongovernment share of power production climbed from 4 percent in 2000 to 7 percent in 2005 and continued to increase in 2006 and 2007, to 9 percent and 11 percent, respectively.[46] The government noted that the shortfall in electricity investment was around $2.34 billion in January 2007, in spite of this progress.

The program of encouraging independent electricity generation is expected to continue. New generation projects are planned, many of which will grant foreign companies the chance to supply power to the Iranian national grid. Some foreign companies will even be allowed to own the supply.[47] Under these terms, the government is working with Quest Energy of Dubai to build a 1,000-megawatt power plant that is open cycle and gas fired in the city of Shiraz[48] Iran, then, has made a substantial ongoing investment in its electricity sector and has taken the step of making room for nongovernment production. But it is still unable to keep pace with demand. Pricing is partly to blame, but the sector is also challenged by urbanization, population growth, and increases in the standard of living. (Population increased dramatically through the 1980s, and GDP per capita improved dramatically in the 1994–2004 period.)

Iran's main challenges on the energy front are political, however. The Iranian government bears a high and growing cost for subsidizing the population's electricity consumption. According to the World Bank, Iran continues to sell its electricity to customers at below the cost to produce it, so the impact of electricity subsidies on the total federal budget is increasing together with consumption. The World Bank estimates that total energy subsidies in 2006 amounted to 17.5 percent of Iran's GDP—the highest in the Middle East, where the average was 7.1 percent of GDP.[49] This subsidy total includes gasoline and natural gas as well as electricity. In fact, Iran does not have the highest electricity subsidies in the region; Saudi Arabia, Iraq, Kuwait, Oman, and Qatar all have extremely low tariffs.[50] But because of Iran's high population density and because its electricity tariffs are below cost, the expense to the government is considerable and harder to keep under control.

Strategies of rationing, which the government has applied to the gasoline sector, are much more difficult to apply to electricity (short of brownouts and rolling blackouts). Consequently, the government is locked in a losing race to stay ahead of demand. In terms of pricing, Iran uses domestic natural gas for much of its generation but still remains "clearly far below even the lower benchmark values"[51] recommended by the World Bank for states that use domestic natural gas. Such low prices reinforce Iran's energy intensity, which is well above the average in the Middle East (which is, in turn, above the world average).

As the Iranian government tries to keep up with growing demand for electricity, there are signs of increasing strain. Like Venezuela, Iran's electricity transmission and distribution losses are well above the international industry standard of 10 percent. With a loss rate of 16.7 percent in 2007, Iran was losing more electricity in transit than any other Middle Eastern country except Yemen (26.0 percent) and Syria (23.7 percent). The World Bank estimates that reducing the losses to 10 percent would provide Iran the equivalent of adding 2,800 megawatts to the state's generating capacity.[52] It is evident that the distribution networks in Iran need renovations, and Iranian trade unions have emphasized that regional electricity companies face substantial financial problems that threaten the steady provision of service.[53]

But the emphasis in the energy sector, so far, has remained on new generation. In 2007, 78.5 percent of Iran's electricity supply came from natural gas,[54] but the Iranian government has recognized the advantages of diversifying supply. Regardless of international concerns about nuclear proliferation, the government of Iran intends to pursue nuclear energy, which it regards as technology enhancing (while also providing high-tech jobs) and countercyclical (the cost to provide electricity from nuclear power does not vary with volatile changes in world oil and natural gas prices). According to the Iranian government, Bushehr will provide the first 1,000 megawatts of electricity of a total of 7,000 megawatts of nuclear power expected to be online by 2020.[55] The government notes that development of 7,000 megawatts of nuclear power will free up the oil equivalent of 13 percent of the country's current production.[56] In addition, installed hydroelectric capacity has risen from 804 megawatts in 1974 to 7,422.5 megawatts in 2007, and plans continue for further expansions.[57] The desire to engage more in hydroelectric provision is evident: as of late 2007 there were eighty-five dams under construction. This effort, however, has been called into question by a severe drought in 2007–8, which led hydroelectric generation to drop by nearly 70 percent.[58] Economically, energy efficiency becomes very attractive to a country in Iran's position. The Iranian Efficient Energy Organization was established in 1994, one of the first efficiency organizations in the region.[59] It remains a relatively weak organization, but it has given priority to large industrial and commercial consumers and offers financial incentives for use of technologies such as compact fluorescent light bulbs.[60] The public, however, remains skeptical about energy efficiency. In 2007 when President Mahmoud Ahmadinejad called for citizens to consume less electricity, the public responded with panicked rumors.[61] Because of the experience of 1991 and the fact that the government had made announcements about rationing of gasoline that same summer, the president's call for conservation was interpreted as a sign that electricity, too, was about to be rationed. The opposition newspaper *Ham-Mihan* was shut down on July 3, 2007, the day it ran an article titled "The Energy Ministry Can Ration Electricity."[62] The reformist press was later officially reprimanded for publishing "false stories" that accused the president of considering electricity rationing.[63]

The government has made one choice that has had both economic and technological effects: Iran has chosen to begin pricing in a manner that should help smooth demand in the grid. Tariffs for industrial users—which made up some 33 percent of demand in 2007[64]—now depend on time of use (TOU) pricing, which creates an incentive for industrial customers to use electricity at nonpeak times. Residential users have tiered prices, depending on their total household demand, so that poor households' first 100 kilowatt-hours of electricity each month are subsidized by households that use over 700 kilowatt-hours. See Table 6.1. Although the rates as they currently exist remain below the economic cost of supplying electricity to both categories of customers, these pricing strategies do follow the structure that is usually recommended for improving the viability of an electricity sector.

The move toward more efficient pricing grew out of political considerations. Concerns about constituent services are not merely the province of Western democracies. Iran has a well-developed political culture in the sense that citizens make public demands on their government. Presidential and parliamentary elections are held on a predictable timeline, and people turn out to vote in large numbers.[65] When the Iranian people are dissatisfied, as the events of 2007 and 2009 showed, they demonstrate, even if the consequences for demonstrating are severe. This makes constituent service an important component of governance in Iran.

Iran began pursuing substantial electricity reforms in 2005, when the fiscal cost of subsidies in energy was estimated to have reached 11 percent of the overall government budget. The government expressed concern with the cost but also with the regressive distribution of benefits, because wealthy homes used more electricity than poor homes.[66]

Theresa Sabonis-Helf

Table 6.1 Iran's Pricing Reform: 2007 4th Quarter Prices ($US)

Residential	Price	Industrial	Price
First 100 kWh[1]	$0.90	TOU[2] peak	$5.40
300 kWh	$1.20	TOU medium	$1.60
500 kWh	$3.20	TOU low	$0.40
700 kWh	$6.30		
900 kWh and more	$8.40		

Source: World Bank ESMAP, *Tapping a Hidden Resource (2009)*, 79.
1. kWh = kilowatt-hour
2. TOU = time of use

The Iranian experience demonstrates the considerable challenge faced by even a highly organized government in trying to keep ahead of demand in a society where both the population and the standard of living are growing rapidly. Iran's efforts to reform the electricity sector, though not yet ambitious, may stand a greater chance of success because of the strength of Iran's institutions. In a comparison of power sector reforms across many developing states, the World Bank notes that strong institutions and commitment to reform—even if it is modest reform—tend to fare better than states with weak institutions.[67] Of the six key requirements offered by Krishnaswamy and Stuggins for balancing supply and demand in electricity, Iran is making progress on at least one aspect of each of them, including reinforcing rule of law in the sector, moving toward self-sufficiency in cash flow, improving transparency, allowing foreign investment, allowing review of progress in the sector focusing on demand management, and making room for private companies.

The policy decisions Iran has made suggest that the government believes that efforts to make the sector more economically feasible can be managed in a politically acceptable manner. While keeping a public emphasis on provision of more electricity (and creating the economic space for private providers), the government has also implemented strategies that will likely level off and ultimately reduce demand. Internationally, Iran seeks to become a leader in regional electricity, and this necessitates a higher level of success in the sector.

Iran already exports modest levels of electricity to Armenia, Pakistan, Turkey, Iraq, and Afghanistan, and it imports modest levels from Armenia and Azerbaijan. In 2007, Iran exported some 2,520 gigawatt-hours and imported 1,842.[68] The exchange patterns for electricity vary from year to year, depending on hydroelectricity levels and Armenia's nuclear power plant output. Iran's simultaneous importing to and exporting energy from Armenia is a result of the need to balance Armenia's electricity grid: Armenia's reliance on one large nuclear power plant means that the country has surplus electricity at night and insufficient electricity during peak demand. Although it is the most prominent example, Armenia is not the only country in the region that manages its own grid by linking to larger grids. The World Bank, regional governments, and businesses are all interested in establishing a circular power grid connecting Russia, Azerbaijan, Iran, Turkey, and Georgia.[69] This issue will be examined in more detail in the Azerbaijan case.

Russia

Russia's accomplishments in electricity are impressive. It operates the largest parallel, integrated grid in the world; it spans eleven time zones and incorporates fifteen countries.[70] Russia is an electricity exporter on a large scale: it sold thirteen terawatt hours internationally in 2007—one of only six countries that exported more than ten terawatt hours.[71] Russia exports significant amounts of electricity to states of the former Soviet Union[72] as well as to China, Poland, and Turkey. It is also seeking to integrate its grid with the Western European electricity grid. Russia's installed capacity of 217 gigawatts[73] dwarfs the capacity in most other countries (including all the other cases in this chapter). By way of comparison, Pakistan, Bangladesh, and Russia all have populations that are about the same size. But Pakistan's installed capacity is 10 percent of Russia's, and Bangladesh's is a mere 3 percent of Russia's.[74] Russia's electricity comes from diverse sources but relies most heavily on natural gas. In 2006, natural gas constituted 46 percent of Russia's energy supply, coal and hydropower each constituted 18 percent, nuclear provided 16 percent, and oil provided 2 percent.[75]

In spite of its substantial natural resource endowments, Russia faces significant challenges on the electricity front. The Russian government has acknowledged that electricity consumption has been increasing faster than supply. It began importing electricity from Ukraine in 2006, and Finland—which historically imported electricity from Russia—retooled its system to begin exporting to Russia in 2009.[76] Meeting domestic customers' needs has become problematic. The Moscow electricity grid collapsed in May 2005, leading to government investigations. Electricity shortages in 2007 caused RAO-UES (at that time the electricity monopoly in Russia) to approve only 36 percent of new connection requests. In 2006, the figure was 16 percent.[77] The problem of electricity provision is complicated by aging infrastructure, the Soviet legacy of high subsidies (and the public expectation that such subsidies will continue), the size of the country, and extreme temperatures.[78] These forces have combined to make Russia astonishingly energy intensive: it is the third-largest consumer of energy in the world and consumes more energy per unit of GDP than any large-scale global energy consumer.[79] The Russian government itself acknowledges that it extends "the world's largest energy subsidy," which it estimated as $40 billion in 2005.[80]

In spite of the daunting nature of the task, Russia is committed to reducing this subsidy and energy intensity. In 2008, President Dmitry Medvedev publicly called for an action plan to cut Russia's energy intensity in half by 2020. In his speech, Medvedev noted that other former Soviet republics had managed to achieve 6–7 percent annual reductions in energy intensity since the end of the Soviet era, but Russia had managed reductions of only about 3.4 percent per year since 1990.[81]

Medvedev's goal may be achievable, in no small measure because restructuring of the electricity sector began in earnest in 2007. By 2009, the sector was transformed by unbundling generation, transmission, and distribution, by partial privatization, and by tariff increases. RAO-UES, once the huge electricity monopoly in the Russian Federation, was dissolved in July 2008. Since that time Russia has operated on a system in which the state retains control of the transmission grid (under the state company FGC-UES), but generation and distribution are partially privatized. Some foreign companies have invested in generation, including Germany's E.ON and RWE, Italy's Enel, and Finland's Fortum.[82] The system Russia has chosen, a single-buyer transit system owned by the state, offers competitive access. Originally, the new system was supposed to account for real costs, but prices continued to reflect political considerations as late as 2011. Tariffs, for example, have been the same for the whole country rather than being based on the cost of supplying energy to particular regions. This constitutes a regional subsidy. In addition, the World Bank has criticized Russia's single-buyer transit system as a system that lends itself to abuse:

> When supply is less than demand in the market, the wholesale market entity can be pressured by government to allocate power to favored

large users and distributors, instead of following the agreed algorithm. Likewise, when the demand is below available supply, the wholesale market entity can be pressured to allocate demand to favored generators, such as the coal-fired plants (to appease the strong mining lobby). It can also be pressured to allocate demand among all generators to ensure that every plant is kept working and employment in the plants is sustained, so that uncompetitive plants are not faced with bankruptcy. These practices distort least-cost dispatch by partial loading of the thermal plants that reduces efficiency and increases fuel consumption.[83]

Russia's restructuring of its electricity sector is, therefore, a controversial approach and one that may allow corruption to remain entrenched. It should be noted, however, that this reform is extensive, has broken up a powerful monopoly, and has been coupled with dramatic reform of electricity prices. Russia's response to reforming the sector differs so dramatically from other petrostates that it is worth examining more closely. On its face, the reforms are particularly perplexing because the disbanded monopoly—RAO-UES—had a superb reputation and was internationally regarded as the best of the Russian parastatal energy companies. The answer lies in Russia's shifting sense of opportunity cost, Russia's role as a natural gas exporter, and the close relationship between the state and the state-owned company Gazprom.

Although the relationship between domestic consumption of electricity and potential exports has been difficult to extrapolate in some other cases, the link in Russia's case is explicit. In fact, there is significant evidence that the push to reform the electricity sector in Russia was driven by Gazprom and its concerns about the future of Russian natural gas exports. Gazprom's historic close ties with the Russian government came at a price to the corporation. The government perceived tight price control of domestic gas as essential to the Russian economy. In its role as a "national champion," Gazprom has historically sold the majority of its natural gas within the Russian Federation at highly subsidized rates (for use in electricity and in heating), and those rates rose very slowly for an extended time in the post-Soviet era. Natural gas fuels almost half of the electrical generators in Russia, so keeping consumer electricity prices below the cost of production was having an impact on natural gas availability.[84] As late as 2005, the domestic price for gas remained between 36 and 46 percent of the world price.[85] By January 2007, domestic sales accounted for only 30 percent of Gazprom's revenues though they constituted 70 percent of Gazprom's sales.[86] Gazprom's own *2006 Annual Report* acknowledged

> in the beginning of the current decade . . . Gazprom's sales of natural gas to Europe at free market prices provided for over 60 percent of its total revenues although they only accounted for one third of the total gas supply. Thus, the losses from selling natural gas in the domestic market . . . were covered by export revenues.[87]

In 2006, Gazprom expressed optimism about price reform within Russia, but that optimism seemed misplaced to most observers. The Russian government had indicated its intention to keep some subsidies in place for at least the next five years.[88] President Vladimir Putin, eager to strengthen the sector but loath to raise prices, put off many price reforms. In the end, Gazprom proved more prescient than optimistic. Liberalization of all domestic energy prices began in earnest in 2007, due to concerns over looming energy shortages and the realization that the sector would become more attractive to investment if it were to be unbundled into separate subsectors.[89] In electricity, the price increases were dramatic. Between 2002 and 2009, prices rose from \$0.02 to \$0.06 per kilowatt-hour, and President Putin announced in May 2008 that Russia would complete the transition to long-run marginal cost tariffs (a rate of approximately \$0.08) in all the country's regions by 2011[90] (see Figure 6.6). The timeline was adjusted to accommodate the global economic downturn. Russia now expects to complete the transition on a slightly extended timeline.

This transformation of the electricity sector toward cost recovery attracted the direct participation of Gazprom. Gazprom is now participating in the Russian electricity business with a controlling share (53.5 percent) of Mosenergo (the largest fossil-fuel-electricity-generating company in Russia) and significant stakes in what remains of RAO-UES, the former electricity monopoly.[91] Clearly, the corporation is a multiple beneficiary, both of price reform and regulatory reform. This new role for Gazprom represents a significant transformation. Energy investors had long assumed that provision of gas to the Russian population was weakening Gazprom and publicly wondered if the company was approaching a moment when it would have to choose between its domestic commitments and its international obligations, especially because domestic demand had grown approximately 2.5 percent per year while energy production remained stagnant or declined.[92]

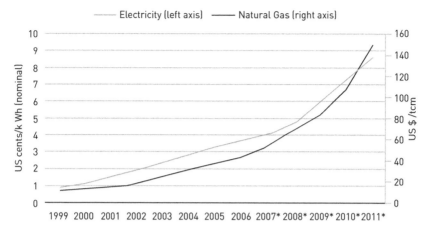

Figure 6.6 Russian electricity and natural gas prices, 1999–2011 (projected). World Bank, *Energy Efficiency in Russia*, 2008, 21. FEC, FTS, Minpromenergo, and MEDIT projections for 2007–2010.

In 2004, the World Bank estimated that Gazprom would need to invest $80 to $100 billion over the next ten years just to maintain energy production at current levels and recommended investment requirements of $10 billion a year.[93] With prices once again rising in Russia and Gazprom absorbing less of a loss in the extensive domestic market, the company is now freer to serve the more lucrative export markets and more willing to capitalize its infrastructure in Russia.

Critics of Gazprom have long feared that the company was not investing enough in new gas fields to ensure that Europe's demand—expected to double by 2030—could continue to be met. In fact, Russia's gas exports did not grow significantly from the early 1990s through the end of 2006.[94] As Gazprom stops losing money in the domestic market, Europe may find the gas company's investment patterns shifting. The European Union has long hoped that appropriate domestic energy pricing would help Gazprom make investments for the future.

The European Union has also insisted for many years that Russia needs to raise its electricity prices to cost-recovery levels in order to gain acceptance into the World Trade Organization. This reflects European fears that Russia will fail to capitalize its natural gas sector sufficiently to ensure long-term provision of gas to Europe. Russia's interest in the organization has shifted in recent years, but as demand and price for natural gas in the European market have risen in recent years, the opportunity costs of highly subsidized, gas-powered electricity in the domestic market became more apparent. Once the Russian government recognized this opportunity cost, it was willing to take on the difficult political task of changing electricity expectations and tariff levels. Of course, it was also helpful that Gazprom's former president, Dmitri Medvedev, had become president of Russia.

In his 1989 book on the Soviet Union, *Crisis amid Plenty*, Thane Gustafson provided evidence that the USSR had, for many years, been selling oil to Europe for a price less than the cost it took to get the oil out of the ground in Siberia and to the European market.[95] Soviet planners were unaware of these losses because budgets for construction and maintenance were organized separately from accounts for sale of oil. In recent times, Russia had more help in recognizing the costs of an electricity policy that did not use pricing to control consumption. The powerful forces of Gazprom leadership and European pressure combined to make the Kremlin aware of the opportunity costs to the state of continuing to pursue heavy subsidies in electricity. As we have seen in previous cases, the evidence was most compelling when it included natural gas, a commodity for which the international market was clear and growing.

After many years of not examining the opportunity costs of subsidizing electricity, the overwhelming evidence that they were much higher than the government had suspected and the potentially crippling impact on future exports convinced the Russian government to change prices and thereby begin to shift its citizens' electricity consumption patterns. If Russia's approach is compared to the six requirements posed by Krishnaswamy and Stuggins, there is cause for skepticism. The rule of law in Russia—even that governing just the energy sector—remains problematic, transparency remains low, international financial institutions are largely left out of the equation, and the future of the private sector's role remains unclear. This suggests that Russia has made progress on only two of the six Krishnaswamy and Stuggins requirements: the sector is closer to generating its own surplus revenues, and demand management, optimal generation planning, and electricity trade devices are being allowed to shape behavior.

Azerbaijan

Among the four case study countries in this chapter, Azerbaijan is the only one that, as late as 2004, was classified as a country with a per capita income of less than $900. Azerbaijan is now considered a lower middle-income country, with a Gross National Income (GNI) per capita of $3,600 in 2008.[96] The average annual GDP growth rate in Azerbaijan was 20 percent from 2003 to 2008, buoyed by the country's ability to export oil more freely and the production and exportation of natural gas. Azerbaijan's net oil exports were around 754,000 barrels per day in 2008, a stark rise from 90,870 barrels per day in 1998.[97] Natural gas production has risen with even more dramatic speed: the 345 billion cubic feet produced in 2007 represented a 70 percent increase from the previous year.[98] As the Azerbaijani government found itself awash in oil money, it declared electricity, utilities, education, and transportation to be priority sectors.[99]

The electricity sector was long overdue to receive priority attention. With the collapse of the Soviet Union, Azerbaijan had inherited less generating capacity (relative to its population size) than neighboring Armenia or Georgia. Azerbaijan's generation capacity was designed to work in coordination with Georgia and Armenia, which became impossible in the chaos of the 1990s. During that period, Azerbaijan's conflict with Armenia resulted in closed borders between the states, and civil war in Georgia and a resultant collapsing Georgian electricity grid made connections in that direction useless to Azerbaijan. Further complicating matters, the existing aging generation capacity in Azerbaijan was concentrated in the north, yet demand was centered in Baku and the west. Natural gas that was retrieved in association with Azerbaijan's oil was flared, yet Azerbaijan imported natural gas from Russia for domestic consumption. Although Azerbaijan was energy rich, it had been functioning for many years in constant electricity crisis. The following excerpt from a newscast in January 2000 gives a sense of the magnitude of the crisis:

Muslim Imanov, chairman of Azerbaijan's state power generating company Azerenerji, announced on January 25 that effective immediately, electricity supplies will be cut daily between the hours of 7 and 9 a.m. and from 7 p.m. to midnight . . . The cuts will apply nationwide except for Baku, where they will be timed from noon to 5 p.m. and from 1 to 6 a.m. Hospitals, schools, kindergartens, and TV and radio companies will not be affected. The rationing has been made necessary by the failure of up to 70 percent of all customers to pay their electricity bills. The resulting shortage of funds, in turn, had precluded badly needed repairs to transmission lines and transformer stations. Many rural areas of Azerbaijan have already received only sporadic power supplies for months, leading to repeated popular protests.[100]

Azerbaijan limped through many cold, dark winters and received—but largely ignored—extensive advice from USAID, the World Bank, and other international assistance organizations on how to improve its electrical system.[101] Aware that consumption would increase if service improved, the government was unwilling and unable to make substantial investments in the sector. The usual remedies were recommended: unbundling parts of the industry, metering, privatizing, and increasing tariffs. After stalling on electricity sector reforms for a decade, the government made the difficult decision in 2002 to privatize management of electricity distribution in Baku, the capital city. Suspicious of Russia's expansion into nearby states' electricity sectors, Azerbaijan blocked Russia from participating in bids to purchase any portion of its electricity sector and awarded a twenty-five-year contract to operate Baku's electricity networks to a Turkish energy company, Barmek. Industry experts credit Barmek with making some significant improvements in the system, especially better revenue collections systems, but less than four years after it signed the contract, Barmek shut down operations in an acrimonious dispute with the Azerbaijani government. This dispute was submitted for international arbitration under the European Energy Charter in October 2006 and was resolved in September 2009 in favor of Barmek. Details of the settlement are not publicly available,[102] but the situation caused strain in relations with Turkey, ordinarily regarded as one of Azerbaijan's greatest allies in the international community.

Barmek and the government of Azerbaijan each accused the other of failure to honor contract obligations. The contract had specified that Barmek would pay 50 percent of its energy costs in the first year, and this would rise incrementally to 100 percent after the fifth year of its operations.[103] But energy prices remained low and collection rates, although they rose somewhat, also remained below recovery of cost in each year. Within the first quarter of its operation, Barmek was already in arrears. Barmek argued that it did not have a free hand to act, that the government did not follow through on promised rate increases, that there were political motivations behind the accusations made, and that the government was looking for an excuse to renationalize the industry.[104] The Azerbaijani government countered that Barmek committed to equipment upgrades but invested only 10 percent of what its contract specified. It also accused Barmek of embezzlement and misappropriation of funds.[105] During the years of arbitration, details of the case were far less clear than two domestic results of the case: the court case itself discredited privatization in the popular eye, and the company became wholly owned by the government of Azerbaijan and is likely to remain that way for some time.

Barmek's experience echoes the experience of other Western companies that have been involved in the Caucasus region's electricity sectors (Armenia and Georgia each had similar scandals) and offers a reminder that privatization does not necessarily resolve problems in the electricity sector. Even if electricity is outsourced, the government must still play a critical role.

Part of the problem of making the sector viable in private or in public hands is what the World Bank identifies as a Cash Recovery Index (CRI). Because it is so difficult to separate technical from commercial losses in the electricity sector, the CRI combines them. It is a product of the collection ratio and the ratio of billing to electricity input into the system. If the CRI is persistently low, private investment will fail.[106] For a corporation's CRI to improve, the government needs to support the company's efforts to improve collections. This is very difficult, especially in a case where the quality of service does not visibly improve. This leads to a second common problem of privatization of troubled electricity sectors: governments that lack the capacity to run the electricity sector also often lack the capacity to cooperate with or effectively regulate private industry.

Although Azerbaijan had support from outside third parties such as the World Bank, one of the criteria recommended by Krishnaswamy and Stuggins for successful supply-demand balance, it lacked other critical components needed for the private sector to succeed. The government was faced with a private company (Barmek) enforcing disconnections for the first time, the government was expected to raise tariffs, and improvements in service could only come after some difficult problems had been resolved. Given the weakness of the overall electricity sector in Azerbaijan, it is not surprising that Barmek failed and that the relationship between the government and Barmek became acrimonious.

Azerbaijan's tariffs have remained below recovery costs and lower than tariffs paid by other states in the region since independence. At the time Barmek took over portions of Azerbaijan's electricity sector, the price of electricity was below the cost of supply, and collection rates were quite low. Table 6.2 shows a comparison of collection rates in capital cities in the region,

Table 6.2 Regional Tariffs and Collection Rates

Capital cities	Tariff (US$/kWh)	Collection rate (payment/billing)	Mean household consumption (kWh/month)
Baku, Azerbaijan (2002)	0.0196	71%	198
Chisinau, Moldova (2003)	0.0529	98%	58
Tbilisi, Georgia (2002)	0.0564	90%	158
Yerevan, Armenia (1999)	0.0475	82%	169

Source: World Bank ESMAP, *Tapping a Hidden Resource (2009)*, 4.

but it should be noted that Baku's collection rate of 71 percent was not indicative of the country overall.[107] In this same period, collections for urban areas outside Baku averaged 50 percent, and collections for rural areas averaged a meager 30 percent, even though most rural homes did not have meters and customers were charged a fixed price based on the square footage of their homes.[108] Winter supply of electricity outside Baku remained between 8 and 16 hours a day, depending on the location.

As Barmek was settling in to run its portions of Azerbaijan's grid, the World Bank expressed optimism that improving service could help generate popular support for price increases. It also noted, however, that there would be a problematic mismatch in timing between improvements in service and higher costs to the customers.[109] Barmek was familiar with international practices and capable of implementing significant changes in the sector. It was confident that it was possible.

In 2006, in an effort to help Barmek meet its goals and provide more reliable service, international advisors began recommending shifting toward a sophisticated two-part tariff pricing structure for electricity sales in which distribution companies would pay (and charge) different rates depending on time of day and peaking capacity needed to meet the demand.[110] Azerbaijan never took the opportunity to try this approach, and Barmek had been run out of the country before improvements in services were evident. The government now claims credit for long-term improvements put into place by Barmek, such as increased revenue collections and provision of meters to most households (meters were made mandatory in 2007).

The government of Azerbaijan revoked Barmek's contract in July 2006. Rates increased only once from 2006 through 2009, from 0.041 Azerbaijani manat per kilowatt-hour to 0.06. BakiElectricSebeke (the state-owned company that took over distribution from Barmek) maintains that there must be improvements in quality before the people can be charged more. The company admitted that in 2009 consumption declined slightly, technical losses went up dramatically, and revenue collections improved slowly. BakiElectricSebeke estimated collections in its area (Baku only) were at 81 percent for the first six months of 2009 and noted that—given the low cost of electricity—they were still not recovering costs.[111] The average collections for 2009 for all of Azerbaijan was even lower, at 72 percent. [112]

The situation did begin improving in 2010. As the government focused on increasing metering and collecting payments owed, cash recovery improved even without the price increasing. In May 2010, the national energy company, Azerenerji, reported a 6 percent growth in overall (residential and industrial) payments, with total national payments increasing to 88 percent. Most of the gains came from rural areas, which had been the lowest payers in the past. This growth was coupled with a significant decline (almost 10 percent) in overall demand for electricity concentrated in the industrial sectors.[113]

Simultaneous changes in metering, billing, and payments cause changes in consumption patterns at the same time they improve accounts. For example, in its January 2010 report, Sumgaiyit Executive Power reported an increase in demand in its region and success in providing meters to 95 percent of its clientele.[114] In the same period, other news sources reported Sumgaiyit as the region in which payments for electricity increased the most dramatically: up 174 percent from the previous year.[115] Sumgaiyit's increase in demand was caused by a mix of many factors: decline in corruption (it became harder to hide illegal electricity sales and theft), an improvement in quality of service, a willingness to make improvements in distribution, and an increase in the service sectors (Sumgaiyit contains the resort areas of Azerbaijan). It most likely also indicates that much of the power Sumgaiyit received previously had not been included in official accounts.

Since the government took back management of the grid, expansion of generation was identified as the top priority, and this proceeded rather rapidly. In 2009, Azerbaijan generated approximately four gigawatts from ten thermal plants and six hydroelectric stations. The government had planned to generate seven gigawatts by the end of 2009, but had not met that goal by 2011, and remains at approximately 6 gigawatts.[116] Since 2002, there has been a significant retirement of old power generation equipment and a shift

Table 6.3 Azerbaijan Electricity Imports and Exports

Year	Electricity imports (million kWh)	Electricity exports (million kWh)
2007	773.7	443.3
2008	266.5	808.8
2009	133.9	710.4

Source: Alena Salaeva, "Azerbaijan snizil import elektroenergii,"
18 May 2010, 1 News.Az, http://www.1news.az/economy/
20100518025137049.html, translation from Russian by author.

away from oil to natural gas as the base fuel for electricity generation. Azerbaijan, which relied on oil for over 90 percent of its power generation in 1991, produced less than 20 percent of its electricity from oil by 2009.[117]

After consistent expansion for several years, Azerbaijan's production of electricity declined in the first half of 2010. This suggests that the system is saturated with generation. Azerbaijan continued to both import and export electricity within the region. A substantial shift has occurred in the direction of electricity trade, as Table 6.3 demonstrates.

As in Iran, the electricity sector is state-owned but has been disaggregated. Separation of the grid into production, transmission, and distribution in Azerbaijan has led to acrimony between the three types of state companies but has not yet led to transparency or the resolution of key problems in the sector. Transmission losses, which are estimated between 12 percent and 20 percent annually—and may be as high as 38 percent in Baku—have caused Azerbaijan to lose much of what it gained before the consumer could enjoy it.[118] The government currently makes direct transfers to the energy companies to make up for the fact that that these companies' CRIs still remain negative, but a decline in oil revenues in 2009 led to a decline in money available to make system improvements. When money becomes available, the electricity sector in Azerbaijan has ambitious plans to improve transmission. In the 2007–2015 plan for the electricity sector, Azerbaijan proposes to construct the Muxrani line, a lengthy 550-kilowatt (high voltage) line with three connectors. This will be the longest (and only the second) 550-kilowatt line in the system. In addition, plans are in place to add a significant number of 330- and 220-kilowatt lines and connectors.[119] These improvements in transmission will help ensure that Azerbaijan can move electricity more rapidly and with less loss across its own country and can participate in the emerging regional electricity markets.

Clear cost signals have caused the government of Azerbaijan to shift several strategies in energy. The promise of being able to export electricity at a profit has helped shift the government approach to electricity. In a complementary way, the rising cost of natural gas caused the government to re-examine that issue as well. In the wake of Russia's dramatic raising of the price of natural gas, in 2007 Azerbaijan ceased flaring gas in its oil exploration, began using its own gas from the Shah Deniz gas field, and began exporting natural gas to Georgia. The rise in production of natural gas was dramatic. From January to April 2010, the state oil and gas company, SO-CAR, produced 4.5 billion cubic meters of gas, of which 90 percent went to Azerbaijani domestic consumption (including consumption in the enclave of Nakhchivan, which is usually provided by swaps with Iran). The remaining 10 percent was exported to Russia (5.81 percent) and Georgia (4.09 percent).[120] This represents a significant change in resources available for the electricity sector, and it enabled Azerbaijan to move away from use of oil as a fuel to generate electricity. However, if the shift to natural gas is made without improvements in efficiency, Azerbaijan will be substantially slowed in its plans to export natural gas to Turkey and beyond due to dramatically rising consumption in its own territory.

There are clear opportunity costs to Azerbaijan allowing its electricity system to remain in disrepair. Some of these costs are not immediately visible but have a significant impact on Azerbaijan's economy and its citizens' quality of life. In rural areas, for example, the limited hours that electricity is supposed to be available are posted, but the postings are unreliable. This means that water filtration systems—essential for healthy drinking water in the rural areas where many rivers are contaminated—cannot function properly. Unstable electricity supply damages the equipment, and outages are frequent and unpredictable.[121] Municipalities are asked to pay for the electricity they use in official buildings, but municipalities do not have budgets or authority to spend money. So power to sewage treatment is often cut off even in tourist areas.[122]

It is difficult for the state to maintain an arms-length relationship with state-owned companies that provide a commodity so valued by the citizenry. As the World Bank notes about state-owned electricity companies worldwide, governments face a "conflict of interest that undermines the quality of policy."[123] It is also, apparently, difficult to resist transfers of resources and bribes. The relationships between the Azerbaijani government and the state-owned companies have poor reputations: in a country with both oil and gas, electricity is reputed to be the most corrupt of the energy sectors. Critics note that fuel continues to disappear, and accountability is low in spite of the hope that dividing into sectors would increase transparency.[124]

But the incentives for the government to manage electricity differently are growing. As was the case in the Russian electricity sector, change in Azerbaijan is driven by a heightened sense of the opportunities available for Azerbaijan in natural gas and in regional electricity provision. In early 2010, the European Bank for Reconstruction and Development began a project to raise the quality of electricity in the Caucasus region by linking the Georgian grid to the Turkish grid with a goal of eventually connecting Azerbaijan to Turkey via the Georgian grid. Azerbaijan will not become the focus of the project until 2012,[125] but the project, which has corporate and multilateral organization support, has begun and is the topic of much discussion in Azerbaijan.

Conclusions

Establishment and maintenance of a national electricity grid is a complex task that requires sustained commitment in any state. All governments, regardless of their natural resource endowments, face pressure to provide their citizens with opportunities, and electricity is a critical component of urbanization and the "good life" in general. The petrostates' challenge in electricity (as illustrated by the four case studies in this chapter) differs from the challenge faced by non-oil-rich developing states in several ways. First, petrostates tend to build ambitious grids as demonstrations of state strength and as a way to share energy wealth with the nation. Subsequently, they face difficulties in maintaining the grids, because an effective electricity sector requires rational pricing and good governance. In the absence of appropriate price signals, demand will grow indefinitely, and rationing cannot be implemented effectively without a high cost to society and the government's credibility. Third, because most petrostates (Russia is an exception) do not have much industry (due to "Dutch disease" and other factors), the grids serve more residential than industrial demand, which makes them difficult to keep balanced and functioning efficiently as demand fluctuates in the course of a day or year. Finally, opportunity costs are not immediately obvious to the state, so the combined costs of subsidy and opportunity costs of lost revenues tend to grow substantially before they receive government attention.

The case studies in this chapter have demonstrated the importance of mastering the technical challenges of large-scale electricity provision. Each of the four countries discussed here has a share in the difficulties of providing quality of service, collecting tariffs, and the reducing losses in both transmission and distribution. Politically, not every state is able to address its internal problems. Russia appears to have gathered the political will to send strong price signals in spite of the popularity of low-cost electricity. Iran has made a similar choice though the demonstrations and violence associated with rising gasoline prices (and rationing) may compel the government to slow its progress in this area. Azerbaijan and Venezuela both suffer from a lack of political will on this issue though political will is apparently beginning to grow in Azerbaijan. The benefit of centralized power is realized in nations where there is limited political risk to making unpopular choices as well as the ability to collect tariffs from customers; however, even in the most centralized of the nations, it is often not possible to raise electricity prices until the opportunity costs become too much to bear.

The opportunity costs to states of subsidizing their electricity sectors depend on the structure and generosity of the subsidies, the export options available to the state, the size of the population, the source used to generate the electricity, and the losses that occur in the electricity system. Evidence in this chapter suggests that although states will avoid politically expensive changes to the sector if possible, the opportunity costs grow over time and may eventually compel state actions—as they did in the Iranian and Russian cases. By 2011, all four states have noted increasing costs of electricity subsidies. Iran and Russia have explicitly recognized the opportunity costs of existing patterns of electricity subsidy and are attempting to change tariff structures and public expectations. Venezuela has not yet taken the dramatic steps necessary to change course, and Azerbaijan has only recently begun its course change.

PART II

Energy Exports, Society, and Politics

7

The Impact of Energy Resources on Nation- and State-Building: The Contrasting Cases of Azerbaijan and Georgia

Murad Ismayilov

The demise of the Soviet Union gave birth to fifteen new states, all with a similar set of basic interests to pursue. Given the diverse material conditions these states were born into, however, the combination of resources and the mechanisms they could choose to utilize to address their interests was particular to each newborn republic. The latter reality, in turn, has worked to inform the diversity of pathways through which these nations' postcolonial identities have emerged and evolved and to shape the channels through which their postcolonial polities have developed. This chapter will analyze the ways in which the forces that came with pipeline politics and energy resources worked to bear upon, and conditioned, the evolving dynamics of national identity formation in the region of post-Soviet Central Eurasia. In doing so, the chapter draws on the contrasting examples of energy-rich Azerbaijan and energy-poor Georgia.

The chapter proceeds as follows. First, it contextualizes the evolution of state identities in post-Soviet Central Eurasia in a postcolonial setting and theorizes that process within a constructivist (largely Wendtian) conceptual framework. It then provides a brief analysis of the domestic and foreign policy challenges Azerbaijan and Georgia faced in the aftermath of the collapse of the Soviet Union and the two states' national interests those challenges worked to shape. The chapter goes on to demonstrate how a complex interplay of the pressure of Baku's and Tbilisi's dire internal and external security challenges (military and economic) and their inability to deal with those problems in an autonomous mode shaped a common postcolonial agenda for Azerbaijan and Georgia—one shared by all post-Soviet states—by pushing them to engage in the struggle for "thick" Western recognition. Finally, the chapter concludes with an analysis of the mechanisms by which pipeline/energy politics introduced significant variation in the way Azerbaijan's and Georgia's struggle for recognition was effected and the way their post-Soviet political identities evolved.

A Theoretical Framework and a Conceptual Road Map

Mainstream constructivists conceptualize a state's "national interests" as objective interests rooted in a state's corporate identity and, as such, common to all states and relatively exogenous to the international system.[1] Drawing largely on Alexander L. George and Robert O. Keohane,[2] Alexander Wendt identifies four basic (objective) national interests that any state must satisfy if it is to exist and function, and, by virtue of its stable existence, lay the groundwork for pursuing its subjective interests, those rooted in its type, role, and/or social identity. Those objective interests are physical survival, autonomy, economic well-being, and collective self-esteem.[3] These interests, directly related to states' material survival and ability to function, featured strongly on the agendas of the newly established states in post-Soviet Central Eurasia in the early stages of their postcolonial state-building. The states would have to satisfy all four interests, if they were to stabilize their statehoods and acquire long-term sustainability for their independence.

A primary mechanism through which new states seek to satisfy their objective interests and thereby stabilize their postcolonial statehoods is what could be referred to as the quest, or struggle, for recognition. Indeed, it is through "recognition" from other states that a particular state can "engage . . . in legal relations with other States" and, in virtue of those relations, "can lawfully request military support from other States; can lawfully refuse entry to foreign military forces; can lawfully negotiate and conclude international agreements; can avail itself of other rights accorded sovereigns under international law and vindicate those rights before available international forums; and can demand respect by other States for sovereign acts exercised within its territory."[4]

In his seminal article "Why a World State Is Inevitable," Wendt intro-duces the concept of "the struggle for recognition" among states and indi-viduals as the micro-level driving force behind structural change and collective identity formation.[5] Picking up from Georg W. F. Hegel's *Phenom-enology of Spirit*,[6] Wendt defines recognition as "a social act that invests dif-ference with a particular meaning [in which] another actor ('the Other') is constituted as a subject with a legitimate social standing in relation to the Self."[7] Elaborating further on the concept, Wendt differentiates between "thin" forms of recognition, which he defines as recognition of a state "as an independent subject within a community of law," and "thick" recognition, which "is about being respected for what makes [a state] special or unique."[8]

The notion of the struggle for recognition is more than relevant for under-standing the evolving dynamics of security relations and postcolonial politi-cal identities in post-Soviet Eurasia, for international recognition of their newly acquired statehood was a number one priority for all states in the re-gion. Importantly, although those states attained legal—thin—recognition rather easily in the immediate aftermath of their newly acquired indepen-dence, it was their continuous struggle for thick recognition that deter-mined the dynamics of the security landscape in Central Eurasia for decades that followed.

One of the principal mechanisms through which a state's struggle for thick recognition is most likely to proceed—particularly in a postcolonial setting—is one by which a state "tries to conform as closely as ever possible to the rules [and norms] which govern life" in the temporal and social context in which it has emerged.[9] Wendt terms the process "imitation" and concep-tualizes it as an evolutionary mechanism of "cultural selection" through which state identities evolve at the micro level of interaction.[10] Under this conceptualization, imitation presents itself as a process in which "actors adopt the self-understandings of those whom they perceive as 'successful.'"[11]

Wendt fails to establish any workable connection between imitation as a mechanism of socialization and collective identity formation on one hand, and the struggle for recognition as the main driving force behind imitation, on the other. The two, however—if treated as an integrated conceptual whole—are well suited to explain the evolution of the security dynamics and postcolonial identities in post-Soviet Central Eurasia. Indeed, the analysis of the workings of the struggle for recognition-imitation nexus, and their effects on regional units and their interactions (both with each other and the outside world) does much to shed light on the evolution of the nation- and state-building processes that unfolded in young postcolonial polities of the region and in all other postcolonial societies for that matter.[12] As is the case with basically all postcolonial polities, the struggle for recognition, and imitation through which that struggle was effected, set in motion an evolutionary mechanism through which the "international" has borne its effects on the evolving identities and behavior of post-Soviet states. Consequently, the direction the regional states took to construct their new—post-Soviet—political identities was inextricably linked to the notion of international legitimacy as widely understood at the time. In this context, the nation- and state-building processes the post-Soviet Central Eurasia states have gone through have been significantly shaped and constituted, at least in the early stage of the postindependence period, by internationally accepted norms of state legitimacy, which involved liberal democratic governance, rule of law, and human rights.[13] With the regional states effectively emulating Western knowledge[14] in organizing their domestic and foreign policies, an overall result of the process that the workings of the struggle for recognition-imitation nexus unleashed was the "homogenization of state forms,"[15] however temporary and rough, in the region.

As important as the role of ideational factors (in which the struggle for recognition and imitation are mostly, if not exclusively, rooted)[16] in the evolution of state identities in post-Soviet Central Eurasia may be, there are also some "brute material forces" on which this process has been contingent.[17] This chapter, therefore, seeks to analyze the mechanisms through which and the ways in which energy resources and energy pipelines (one such brute material force) interfered with the post-Soviet collective identity formation processes by providing an alternative means through which a resource-rich state's struggle for recognition could occur.

National Interests, State Weakness, and the Struggle for Recognition in Post-Soviet Georgia and Azerbaijan

Post-Soviet Georgia and Azerbaijan found all four of what Wendt described as "objective" national interests severely challenged by both external threats they were facing and internal vulnerabilities intrinsic to these states' young polities: two problems associated with the early stage of postcolonial state-building that the Baku and Tbilisi governments stepped into following independence and two that formed the core of their domestic and foreign policy agendas.

Indeed, the very physical survival of these two states was challenged from both the outside and the inside. To start, for both Azerbaijan and Georgia, independence from Moscow was simultaneously the biggest value to attain and the biggest challenge to retain.[18] One of the first moves Azerbaijan and Georgia made in asserting their independence and sovereignty was demanding the withdrawal of Russian (that is, former Soviet) troops from their territories. Azerbaijan, in fact, became the first among the former Soviet countries to secure the full withdrawal of these forces as the last Russian troops left its soil in May 1993 during the tenure of Abulfaz Elchibey, the second president of newly independent Azerbaijan.[19] And despite the expectations for the converse, Heydar Aliyev, who succeeded Elchibey, did not allow Russian forces back in Azerbaijan. Furthermore, the position of Baku has since been that no foreign troops—Russian or Western—must ever be allowed in Azerbaijan.[20] Georgia, on the other hand, signed a 1995 agreement with Russia on the withdrawal of the latter's troops from its territory. With Russia reluctant to give up its hold on what it considers its "near abroad," however, that agreement has never been fully implemented.[21]

One way or the other, Russia, the former imperial core, has never ceased to be perceived either in Baku or Tbilisi as an imperialist and potentially revisionist power willing and able to terminate their young statehood should international and domestic configurations be permissive. The two nations remembered (and still do) the tragic experience of their first statehood earlier that century when both, following a short-lived independence period, were forcibly incorporated into the Soviet Union in 1920–21.[22] Apart from that, people in the two states also had a more recent history to remember. Both Baku and Tbilisi had experienced a bloody assault from Soviet troops in the final years of Soviet rule that massacred tens of civilians in the two capitals in brutal attempts to quell anti-Soviet nationalist movements there: 20 Georgians were killed as a result of the Soviet crackdown in Tbilisi on April 9, 1989, and 137 people were shot and killed during the Soviet-ordered massacre in Baku on January 20, 1990.[23]

In addition to Russia on its north, Azerbaijan has another potentially revisionist neighbor to the south, Iran, with whom it has never managed to establish truly cordial relations during its post-Soviet independence despite, and to a significant extent due to, the fact that some 30 percent of the Iranian population is Azerbaijani and that the two states—as we know them now—used to form one country.[24] Elchibey's open criticism toward Iran's human rights performance and his active efforts to advocate the creation of Great Azerbaijan through the unification of the post-Soviet Azerbaijan and the Iranian Azerbaijan provinces[25] only worked to exacerbate these relations. Despite the efforts Azerbaijani President Heydar Aliyev made to ease relations between the two countries, they could only improve up to a certain level. Indeed, Iran has occasionally displayed aggressive behavior toward Baku, thus reminding it how potentially threatening its southern neighbor may become.[26]

The second challenge, which was no less threatening to the physical survival of their statehood, lied in that both governments had their territorial integrity challenged by secessionist movements from the very onset of their independence, and both failed to adequately tackle them on their own. As a result of the war with Armenia (1988–1994) over Azerbaijan's Nagorno-Karabakh Autonomous Region (NKAR), Azerbaijan was left with some 16 percent of its territory occupied and with Nagorno-Karabakh enjoying de facto independence.[27] Georgia, on the other hand, fought two wars with its two autonomous administrative units, the Abkhaz Autonomous Republic (August 1992–September 1993) and the South Ossetian Autonomous Oblast (1990–June 1992), that resulted in de facto, if unrecognized, independence for both from Georgian control.[28]

Third, it was not only *physical* independence that Azerbaijan and Georgia sought from Moscow. After decades of colonial existence, the two countries cherished hopes for *actual* autonomy from Moscow—and any other country for that matter—in pursuit of their domestic and foreign policies. Looked at from this perspective, "assertiveness in selecting domestic and foreign policies . . . for these countries was . . . a matter of growing up and walking on their feet rather than being held by the hand by 'big brother' Russia," it has been a means of "shaking off political dependencies and establishing full sovereignty, a long-held dream for these countries."[29] This quest for autonomy prompted some states in the post-Soviet region to adopt what the Baku government hailed as a "balanced" foreign policy, Kazakhstan termed as a "multi-vectored" foreign policy, and Turkmenistan simply defined as "neutrality": tired of being guided by a single "boss," these states now sought greater leeway both in pursuit of their foreign policy and domestically.

And fourth, both Azerbaijan and Georgia experienced severe economic disruption in the early postindependence years, as did all other post-Soviet states.[30] With its output fallen by 70 percent and exports by 90 percent,

Georgia, in fact, suffered the worst decline among the post-Soviet transition economies.[31] Consequently, the two states' ability to exercise full sovereignty has been intimately linked to their progress in addressing the challenge of post-Soviet economic reforms and the transition from the command system to a more successful model of organizing the state economy. Foreign investment and the hard currency that was to come with it were key prerequisites to the success of these efforts. Indeed, along with the problem of Nagorno-Karabakh, the issue of economic investment in Azerbaijan was one of the major problems raised by President Heydar Aliyev in all his foreign visits, especially at earlier stages of his presidency.[32]

As vital and pressing as all these challenges were, they could hardly be addressed by either state in an autonomous mode. With independence, the two—and all other former Soviet states for that matter—became constituent parts of a broader (international) social context. And because they found the latter organized around principles rooted in what Wendt conceptualized as the Lockean culture,[33] with the institution of sovereignty being by far the most important, the states' ability to pursue and realize their basic interests was primarily contingent on their success in having the organizing principles of the Lockean culture extended to post-Soviet Eurasia, that is, having their sovereignty recognized by the system.

Thin, or juridical, recognition of independent statehood of the post-Soviet states came within the first years of their independence. Apart from individual recognitions extended within different bilateral frameworks, at least two developments in a multilateral context were crucial in extending international legal (thin) recognition to the newly established states in Central Eurasia: their admission to the Conference on Security and Cooperation in Europe (CSCE) / Organization for Security and Cooperation in Europe (OSCE)[34] and their accession to the United Nations.

By April 1992, all post-Soviet states had been admitted as members of the CSCE/OSCE, a fact that came to confirm *Western* recognition of their statehood.[35] This was followed by the extension of United Nations membership to these states. By August 1992, all former Soviet republics had officially become UN members,[36] an important fact in that it reflected *international* recognition of these states' "empirical sovereignty" and—in virtue of that recognition—symbolized their *formal* entrance into the international society of states.

Of even greater importance, though, were developments that came to reflect the formation of a Lockean culture at the regional level, that is, the regional states' formal acknowledgment of Lockean norms and rules in their relations *with each other*. Apart from the states' acquired membership in the CSCE/OSCE, two developments deserve special mention in this respect: those states' signing of the OSCE's Helsinki Final Act of 1975[37] and their signing of agreements that led to the formal disintegration of the Soviet Union and the establishment of the Commonwealth of Independent States (CIS).[38] Both the Helsinki Act and the two agreements that formalized the establishment of the CIS proclaimed the Lockean principles of respect for sovereignty, territorial integrity, and the inviolability of the existing borders among the major principles guiding the relations among member-states. Consequently, acceptance of those principles by the regional states and Turkey and Iran's extension of official recognition to the states, effectively established, if formally, the Lockean culture in the *regional* context of Central Eurasia. That is, the states in the region became formally bound by the organizing principles that Lockean culture rests upon, those of mutual recognition of sovereignty and, as an extension of it, renunciation of "war for conquest."[39]

This was an important, if quick, achievement in that it partly addressed the regional states' quest for material security by "validat[ing] their statehood"[40] and, as an extension, providing a *legal* shield to guarantee against aggressive moves by potentially revisionist neighbors (for example, Russia and Iran).

This easily secured thin recognition yet did not and could not serve to stabilize either Azerbaijan's or Georgia's statehood—and hence the Lockean culture in which they were embedded—in that it was inadequate to fully address either external or internal challenges with which they were confronted in their early postindependence period. Put differently, although international recognition through UN membership worked to secure the "juridical independence" of the post-Soviet states, "their sociological 'stateness' [was yet] to be established" and "even the fact of their durable statehood [was] not yet settled" making them in a sense "states-in-the-making."[41] Most importantly, legal recognition could not in and of itself provide for either economic prosperity or physical security of the two states in that it could not serve either to generate the flow of foreign investment into their economies or alleviate the possibility of a Russian (or indeed Iranian) move to reincorporate these states back into its imperial borders. Indeed, with thin recognition in place, there were still no viable guarantees that Russia—still viewed as a potentially revisionist state—would abide by international law and would not end up launching a war of conquest to restore the borders of its historical empire, or—if it indeed chose to do so—that international community would opt to react to eliminate the consequences of Moscow's aggressive moves. Therefore, legal, or thin, recognition, did not satisfy Azerbaijan's or Georgia's quest for physical security and economic prosperity and hence could not mean an end to their struggle for recognition. And due to the inherent weakness of their postcolonial statehood, the states could not address those challenges by means of their domestic resources only. Consequently, these two factors, the failure of either international thin recognition or domestic resources to satisfy the two states' quest for physical security and economic prosperity—which in effect was a quest to have the Lockean culture stabilized in the region—prompted them to seek additional (thick) recognition from an external actor or group of actors capable of supporting them in addressing their basic objective interests.[42]

It was at this juncture that the West came into play; the perceived prevalence of its economic and compulsory power [43] in the post-Cold War era made the West a natural pole to ally with and seek thick recognition from.[44] Indeed, the two states' desire for physical security logically positioned a power constellation capable of satisfying that interest and providing viable security guarantees, whether formal or informal, against potential Russian (or Iranian) assault as a party whose recognition would be worth seeking. A winner in the half-century-long Cold War with the Soviet Union, the West was viewed as an obvious candidate for this role.[45] Furthermore, with the collapse of the Soviet model of the command economy and with the West apparently enjoying a period of economic prosperity, the West was seen by all post-Soviet states as the best partner to seek investments from, and its model of market economy was naturally viewed as the best model to emulate. Indeed, Russia itself has been highly dependent on Western economic support for its post-Soviet stable existence and development and was therefore in no position to meet the economic needs of its former colonies.[46]

Furthermore, compulsory and economic power of the West worked in tight conjunction with undisputed institutional power,[47] which the West exercised in the post-Cold War international system, for given that the West dominated most, if not all, international and regional security and economic institutions, legitimation by which (whatever form that would take—membership or partnership) actually implied legitimation in the international realm, for many of the newly born Eurasian states, membership in those organizations was perceived as ultimate recognition of their legitimacy and hence an ultimate guarantor of their sovereignty and security. The struggle for membership in, or close partnership with, those organizations then was a perceived extension of their struggle for Western, and international, recognition; success in the latter was deemed to be a function of success in the former.[48]

Indeed, similar considerations that were driving Azerbaijan and Georgia's struggle for thick recognition pushed Central European and Baltic countries to apply for NATO and EU membership shortly after acquiring independence. Unlike the former, however, the latter could comparatively quickly succeed in their bids and in that way fulfill their quests for external recognition. However, for Azerbaijan and Georgia the struggle, and hence the process, has taken far longer and in that way has come to define to a considerable extent the foreign and domestic policy dynamics of these states, far more so than it did for the former Warsaw Pact members.

In sum, Western economic, compulsory, and institutional power worked in tandem with the objective interests of Azerbaijan and Georgia—their quest for physical security and economic prosperity being by far the most important—and their inability to deal with those on their own to lay out the context, normative and strategic, in which their decisions for the struggle for Western recognition was taken and the choice for Euro-Atlantic integration was made.

Imitation and Pipeline Politics: Toward Effecting the Struggle for Recognition

Imitation of Western (democratic) practices emerged as a cornerstone in the regional states' struggle for Western recognition, which itself was derivative of their quest for "full" sovereignty and independence. Indeed, in their struggle for what could count as "full" recognition,[49] the post-Soviet elites in the region—guided not so much by the logic of appropriateness as by that of consequentiality—moved to rewrite their constitutions toward incorporating the principles of democratic governance, human rights, and free markets. Azerbaijan and Georgia proved no exception: both the Azerbaijani Constitution, adopted November 12, 1995,[50] and that of Georgia, adopted August 24, 1995[51] were deeply rooted in, and inspired by, Western liberal democratic discourse. It is in this way that the struggle for recognition that Azerbaijan and Georgia engaged in during the early days of their independence and the imitation mechanism through which that struggle was effected started to shape the very identities of those states and to condition the nature of their statehood.

However, pipeline/energy politics introduced a significant variation in the way Azerbaijan's and Georgia's post-Soviet political identities evolved. There are at least two ways that pipeline/energy politics interfered significantly with the evolution of political identities of the states in the region, and both are associated with their effect on the breadth and depth of intra- and interstate socialization in the region. The first way has to do with a dubious role energy politics played in the region. On one hand, it served as one of the mechanisms through which the regional states' struggle for western recognition was effected, and on the other hand, it worked to boost the regional states' domestic capacities to realize their objective interests on their own and hence diminish the rationale behind that struggle. In its former effect, energy politics worked to strengthen the role the "international" played in the evolution of state identities; in its latter effect, energy politics served to undermine it. The second way energy politics interfered with the evolution of state identities in the region concerns its relation to imitation as an alternative mechanism through which these states' struggle for recognition could be exercised.

A Dual Role for Pipeline/Energy Politics in the Struggle for Recognition

From the onset of independence, pipeline politics served as a major mechanism through which both Azerbaijan and Georgia sought to establish solid links to the West and display their strategic importance for it, thereby ensuring sustainability of their newly acquired statehood and, indeed, independence. As Steve LeVine, author of *The Oil and the Glory*, narrates it, the birth of the very concept of a westward pipeline route for Azerbaijani oil was a result of deliberations among Georgian policymakers seeking to find a way to "establish [their country] as important to the West." And a pipeline linking Caspian energy resources to the West through Georgian territory was found to be the best way to "make Georgia interesting to the West."[52]

Reflecting on the significance of the signing of the 1994 Contract of the Century, Hafiz Pashayev, Azerbaijan's first ambassador to the United States, admits that

In many respects, we had managed to not only get the commitment of these major oil companies to invest billions of dollars in Azerbaijan, but their presence would be an insurance policy for our new-found independence. The Consortium of Companies was deliberately designed as a mini-United Nations in terms of the number of participating countries.[53]

Each of those countries, it was hoped, "would have a stake in ensuring Azerbaijan's territorial integrity. The more nations [there were], the more international support Azerbaijan would enjoy against Russia, and Armenia as well."[54]

This link between pipeline/energy politics and independence has been recurrently reiterated and emphasized by the leaders in both states. For example, speaking at the Summit of OSCE Heads of State in Istanbul, Eduard Shevardnadze, then the president of Georgia, stated: "The 18th of November, 1999, is a historic day in the realization of the most important projects that lay the foundation for independence of the states participating in these global projects."[55] This was the day when a set of agreements to provide the legal framework for the construction of the Baku-Tbilisi-Ceyhan (BTC) pipeline, as well as a declaration of support were concluded. Echoing that statement, Shevardnadze's successor, President Saakashvili, hailed the BTC at its inauguration ceremony in July 2006 as a "symbol of independence,"[56] specifying that it "concerns not only power and economical independence; it is generally independence."[57]

Politicians actively used symbolism in efforts to emphasize the connection between pipeline politics and independence. For example, of such symbolic significance was the date when the agreement between the Azerbaijani government, the State Oil Company (SOCAR), and the British Petroleum-led BTC Sponsor Group was signed on the development of the BTC project—17 October 2000—a day before the ninth anniversary of the adoption of the Constitutional Act on National Independence of Azerbaijan was to be celebrated. No less significant was the date on which Azerbaijani oil first reached the Ceyhan terminal, May 28, 2006, the day when Azerbaijan's first independent republic was established in 1918 and the one now commemorated as the Republic Day.

Furthermore, in its early postindependence period, the Baku government always sought to link the West's exploitation of Azerbaijan's energy deposits to the West's support in the resolution of the outstanding problems the country faced at the time. During his first official visit to the United Kingdom in early 1994, for example, President Heydar Aliyev, when pushed by the British politicians to urgently complete the draft of what was to become the Contract of the Century, responded by impelling them to provide greater support in the resolution of the Nagorno-Karabakh conflict, in what was an attempt to establish an explicit linkage between the two.[58] A year earlier, in August 1993, during his meeting with the representatives of the oil companies in Baku, Heydar Aliyev put it bluntly: "if the oil companies of great powers are interested in Azerbaijan's oil deposits, the governments of those powers must show interest in the current social-political situation in the republic."[59] Reflecting on his first years in Washington and his search for ways to gain U.S. "sympathy" for Azerbaijan's "cause," Ambassador Pashayev recalls that, "It became apparent to me that I had a major card to play: Azerbaijan's vast energy resources and potential as a transport hub for the export of millions of barrels of oil from the Caspian Sea to international markets."[60]

Apart from using it as a tool/mechanism in its struggle for Western recognition and its quest for Western support, the Baku government viewed energy politics, and the rents it was to fuel, as an *independent* way to advance and sustain the state's post-Soviet independence. Lack of financial resources, however, prevented Azerbaijan from stepping up the development of its oil deposits on its own and, therefore, determined the need to turn to Western investors. As Natiq Aliyev, the president of SOCAR, recalls when analyzing the factors that led to the signing of the Contract of the Century, Azerbaijan, back in those years, "had the foundation, highly qualified experts . . . national technology, the Soviet standards and oil deposits that were exploited in the old way. We had all that, but we lacked the essential—the finances."[61]

In both cases, once the regional states turned to pipeline/energy politics—either as the primary or supportive (meant to ensure Western support) element in their quest to advance their independence and autonomy—it proved an essential, indeed crucial, mechanism that worked to establish important links, material and social, between the region and the West, thus solidly tying the two together.

In parallel, however, pipeline/energy politics has also served as a powerful driving force behind the rapid economic development of Azerbaijan as an energy producing state during the past ten to fifteen years. This, in turn, worked to strengthen internal capacity of Azerbaijan and boost its self-confidence and self-reliance, thus gradually undermining the rationale behind, and the need for, the state's struggle for Western recognition.

Indeed, with billions in oil revenues flooding the Azerbaijani economy, the country has gone through what was in fact exceptionally strong GDP growth with an average annual growth rate over the last five years of 21 percent (as opposed to −6.3 percent average annual growth from 1990–2000);[62] this immeasurably boosted the economy and made Baku increasingly self-confident in its relations with Russia and the West and allowed it to take actions independently from and against the stated interests of both.

At least three developments have come to reflect this growing, energy-fueled self-sufficiency that Azerbaijan has been increasingly enjoying in addressing its objective national interests: a dramatic increase in military spending paralleled by active steps toward the creation of the national military-industrial complex; Baku's move to finance the Kars-Akhalkalaki-Tbilisi-Baku railway project (KATB) in light of U.S. and EU refusal to do so; and the country's refusal to buy Russian gas following Gazprom's decision to double the price for it.

In what was indicative of Azerbaijan's growing desire to reach self-sufficiency in the military-security sector, or at least its desire to get to that level, in 2003 the country began consistently increasing its military expenses, with its military budget reaching US$2 billion in 2008. Furthermore, in what signaled the country's desire to ease its overdependence on external support for its physical survival, Azerbaijan announced in 2005 its intention to build up its defense capabilities and a national military-industrial complex. If successful, the move—also reflected in the country's *National Security Concept*[63]—will make the country self-sufficient in meeting its needs in the military-security sector. To that effect, the new Ministry of Defense Industry[64] was established in December 2005, and several military plants have since been created.[65] The latter's planned products include unmanned reconnaissance aircraft, armored equipment and machinery, military helicopters, aircraft bombs, and other military equipment.[66] In what was meant to demonstrate the achievements made in building the country's military might (to both a domestic and external audience), Azerbaijan staged a truly grand military parade—the first in 16 years— when marking the ninetieth anniversary of its armed forces on June 26, 2008. Apart from troops, the parade featured some 210 units of military hardware, including multiple rocket launch systems; 19 attack helicopters; 25

planes including bombers, fighter jets, and unmanned reconnaissance aircraft; and 31 ships.[67] It has since become an annual event.

Azerbaijan's second move refers to the leadership Baku provided in moving the KATB forward following over a decade of deferral due to the lack of funding and U.S. and EU reluctance to provide it. Indeed, as important as the railroad is claimed to be, one with "the strong power to change history," according to Turkish President Abdullah Gul,[68] the European Commission had long refused funding and opposed the project arguing that it was unnecessary and inefficient due to the existing Kars-Gyumri (Armenia)-Tbilisi railroad connection, which Turkey had closed in 1993 in response to the war between Azerbaijan and Armenia.[69] On this account, the EU did not include the Kars-Baku railway project in its Transit Corridor Europe-Caucasus-Asia (TRACECA) program or the European Neighborhood Policy (ENP) Action Plans signed individually with Azerbaijan and Georgia. Likewise, the U.S. House of Representatives Financial Services Committee, pressured by the Armenian American lobby, voted on June 14, 2006, to support a bill that banned the U.S. government's Export-Import Bank from financing the construction of the railroad on grounds that it would isolate Armenia. Resolved to keep Armenia outside the regional projects and, consequently, unwilling to use the existing Kars-Gyumri-Tbilisi railroad until its conflict with the country is settled, Azerbaijan moved to assume the entire burden of financing the Georgian and Azerbaijani sections of the KATB and effectively solved the finance problem that had stalled the project for so long.[70] A credit agreement to that effect was reached between Azerbaijan and Georgia on January 13, 2007. According to the agreement, to cover the construction and rehabilitation of the Georgian section, the Baku government was to provide a US$200 million loan to the Tbilisi government, repayable over twenty-five years with an annual interest rate of only 1 percent. Georgia, in turn, was to repay the loan by using transit revenues from the operation of the railway.[71] Shortly after the financial issues were resolved, on February 7, 2007, Azerbaijan, Turkey, and Georgia finally moved to sign a framework agreement to launch construction work on the railroad.

The way the West dealt with the project and the way Azerbaijan responded had a twofold effect on the dynamics of Azerbaijan's, and by extension other regional states', struggle for Western recognition; in both cases, it worked effectively to undermine the struggle. On one hand, that both the

EU and the United States declined to fund the project—and did so for political reasons—called attention to a reality that the West would not always act in Azerbaijan's (or other regional states') best interests and hence full reliance on the West might not be the best strategy for Azerbaijan to employ in pursuit of its national interests. On the other hand, Azerbaijan's move to cover a significant portion of project costs on its own effectively served to demonstrate Azerbaijan's energy-fueled capacity to promote its national interests without the support of, and even against the will of, the West. Indeed, as Rovshan Ismayilov aptly notes, "in many ways, the project [was] a case study in regional self-reliance."[72]

And finally, in what signaled the country's rising capacity to exercise full sovereignty vis-à-vis Russia, the Baku government ceased buying natural gas from Russia as of January 1, 2007, following Gazprom's decision late in 2006 to double the price of its natural gas exports to Azerbaijan.[73] Furthermore, Baku suspended oil exports via the Russia-controlled Baku-Novorossiysk pipeline for three months in what could be seen as a response to what Azerbaijan's President Ilham Aliyev defined as "commercial blackmail"[74] and its Foreign Minister Elmar Mammadyarov referred to as "more than just a market message."[75] The government justified the move by identifying the need to redirect significant volumes of crude oil from exports toward meeting the country's domestic energy needs.[76] In what reflected Baku's growing confidence in its relations with external powers, President Ilham Aliyev, in an explanation for his country's decision to stop buying Russian natural gas, made it clear that "Azerbaijan is no longer the kind of state that can be forced into anything" and added, "We are a self-sufficient state. We do not depend on anyone."[77] Echoing that statement, Elin Suleymanov, Azerbaijan's consul general in Los Angeles, stated: "We base our relations with our neighbors on our interests. Attempts by other states to impose their will on Azerbaijan will be rejected."[78]

Azerbaijan's actions described above clearly demonstrate the ways in which, and the extent to which, pipeline politics served to equip the Baku government with the resources it needed to be able to work toward addressing its objective needs (military security and physical survival as well as economic well-being) through its own internally generated means, thereby decreasing the rationale behind the country's struggle for Western (or any other) recognition. The latter reality, in turn, has served to gradually undermine the role "the international" played in informing the ways in which the state's postcolonial identity and behavior evolved, working instead to strengthen the role intrastate, indigenous, channels of socialization have come to play in this respect.

Not an energy producer but merely a transit country, Georgia, despite also associating sustainability of its post-Soviet independence with pipeline/energy politics, did not *directly* benefit from it as much as its neighbor to the east did. Although the ambitious reforms the Tbilisi government embarked on following the revolution in 2003 did generate sustainable economic growth, with an annual growth rate averaging 10.5 percent between 2004 and 2008, the country still remains strongly dependent—for satisfying its objective interests—on external support, economic and other, that the West and, increasingly, two of its neighbors, Azerbaijan[79] and Turkey, have to render. This dependency became especially salient following a number of important disruptions as a result of the August 2008 war with Russia and the effects that the global economic crisis had to bear upon the Georgian economy.[80]

In sum, although pipeline politics as an independent variable (operating within the "pipeline politics-domestic capacity" nexus) has been an important factor in defining the evolving dynamics of Azerbaijan's struggle for recognition and has worked to significantly undermine the latter, in Georgia's case pipeline politics has continued to work largely, if not exclusively, as a dependent variable serving as a mere tool behind the country's struggle for Western recognition. In its latter effect, pipeline politics worked to reinforce the mechanism of imitation of Western knowledge, through which the regional states' (namely, Georgia's) political identities evolved. In its former effect, pipeline politics worked to broaden the range of cognitive choices the energy-rich states, such as Azerbaijan, had in building their post-Soviet statehood and crafting their postcolonial political identities and in doing so served to strengthen intrastate modalities of socialization informing those choices.

Pipeline Politics Versus Imitation: Competing Modalities of the Struggle for Recognition

The second way in which energy politics interfered with the evolution of state identities in the region has to do with the relationship that energy politics and imitation have with each other. In fact, pipeline/energy politics provided for an alternative mechanism (in addition to imitation) through which Azerbaijan, an energy-rich country, could struggle for Western recognition. Consequently, there has been clear tension between imitation and pipeline politics in that the two are inversely proportional to each other; success in the latter decreases the importance of the former. Indeed, the success of a number of pipeline projects realized within the East-West corridor so far and a key part Azerbaijan has played in, and the way it benefited from, those have made the role imitation came to play as part of the country's struggle for recognition rather negligible. Consequently, in its struggle for Western recognition, Azerbaijan, albeit falling short of denouncing imitation altogether, came to count on pipeline/energy politics primarily. On the other hand, for Georgia, still weak in both economic and political terms, imitation has remained the most important mechanism through which Western attention is gained and its "protection" ensured.

The temporal and spatial context in which the two countries found themselves embedded was also crucial in defining the dynamics and nature of the struggle for recognition they ended up pursuing. A Christian, if orthodox, nation, Georgia is culturally far closer to Europe than Azerbaijan. The latter—a Muslim, if secular, nation—has been mindful of how little Western attention Moscow's brutal actions in Baku in January 1990 attracted, especially compared with far greater European attention to much "lesser levels of [Russian] intimidation in the Baltic states"[81] and has been continuously resentful of what it refers to as "the double standards" the West allegedly employs in dealing with its Christian and non-Christian partners.

This difference in the effects that pipeline politics—placed in temporal and spatial context—has had on Azerbaijan's and Georgia's struggle for recognition directly bears on the regional policies the two states have been pursuing. Highly dependent on a cognitive element in its struggle for recognition, Georgia (on par with Viktor Yushchenko's Ukraine) has been left compelled—and was indeed encouraged—to follow, and indeed actively promote, Western knowledge as the cognitive basis for the future security structure in the region. Two major outcomes of this policy have so far been the transformation of GUAM—a regional grouping established in October 1997 and bringing together four post-Soviet states: Georgia, Ukraine, Azerbaijan, and Moldova—from "the alliance of necessity" of the 1990s into a full-fledged regional Organization for Democracy and Economic Development in May 2006 and the establishment of the Community of Democratic Choice (CDC) in December 2005. The latter includes Georgia, Ukraine, Moldova, the Baltic countries, Romania, Slovenia, and the Republic of Macedonia, and it seeks to promote "political, security, and economic rapprochement between the Western and the Eastern part of the European continent."[82]

Far less dependent on, and less encouraged to pursue, the cognitive element in its quest to satisfy its objective interests, Baku, on the other hand, has enjoyed greater flexibility in terms of choosing, or indeed creating, a cognitive structure on which it would wish to rest its (and the region's) evolving political identity. Consequently, Azerbaijan has been increasingly keen to emphasize the multivector nature of its foreign policy, one which is neither exclusively pro-American, as that of neighboring Georgia, nor exclusively pro-Russian, as that of neighboring Armenia, with national interests as the only source in which it is rooted. As Elkhan Nuriyev, the former director of the Centre of Strategic Research under the administration of Azerbaijan's president established in November 2007, put it, Azerbaijan "goes its own way."[83]

Indeed, disappointed in the West's ability and desire to help it address its objective interests and, consequently, drifting away from unidirectional imitation of Western knowledge, Azerbaijan has now been aspiring to draw on several cognitive/political elements, Islamic and Turkic probably being the most salient (apart from, and in addition to, Western) and—more often than not—to utilize pipeline politics and the products it bears (material resources) to facilitate the appropriation/internalization of each of those elements among its own population and in the broader region. Furthermore, Azerbaijan now seeks to position itself as an emerging leader in those indigenously regional cognitive/political frameworks it seeks to draw upon in its efforts to diversify cognitive/political sources upon which to rest the state's—and the broader region's—emerging collective identity and upon which to capitalize in its quest to address the state's objective interests.

In many respects, Azerbaijan's ongoing relations with the Islamic world could best be described as a struggle for Islamic recognition that Azerbaijan now seems to have stepped up in parallel to its struggle for Western recognition. In what is indicative of this effort, the country came up with an initiative to have Baku (the capital of Azerbaijan) as the capital of Islamic culture in 2009 during the Fifth Conference of Culture Ministers of the Organization of the Islamic Conference in November 2007 in Tripoli (Libya), and this proposal was approved and acted upon.[84] Furthermore, capitalizing on its energy-boosted economic capacity, Azerbaijan has been getting increasingly active in providing "material and humanitarian support to the Islamic states in zones of conflict." As part of those efforts, Azerbaijan, for example,

committed to reconstruct one of the sites in Gaza destroyed as a result of the
Israel-Hamas war from December 2008 to January 2009. In addition, the
Baku government has been closely working with the Iraqi government to
provide financial and humanitarian aid, and the Heydar Aliyev Foundation,
a Baku-based NGO headed by the country's first lady, has worked to construct several schools in Pakistan.[85]

On the other hand, Azerbaijan—capitalizing on the politicization of
energy security and the possibilities for energy-related regional cooperation
this suggests[86]—has lately come to embrace Turkey's efforts in, and has
grown increasingly more active in, promoting integration among Turkic-
speaking states in post-Soviet Central Eurasia. For example, on November
17, 2006, the leaders of Azerbaijan, Turkey, Kazakhstan, and Kyrgyzstan as
well as a representative from Turkmenistan gathered in Antalya (Turkey)
for what came to be the first Turkic summit since 2001.[87] Underlining the
significant role cooperation in the energy sector played in the revival of the
Turkic integration process, the Antalya Declaration stated that "increasing
energy cooperation would positively and directly contribute to economic
and political stability" in Eurasia.[88] Unlike earlier attempts in this direction,
the regional states' post-Antalya efforts bore significant fruits, and the process of institutionalization of what increasingly looks like a "Turkic Commonwealth" has gathered momentum. Among the remarkable achievements
so far are the launch of the Turkic world TV channel TRT Avaz on March
21, 2009;[89] the summoning on November 21, 2008, of the Conference of
Turkic-Speaking Countries' Parliamentary Speakers in Istanbul where the
participating representatives of Azerbaijan, Turkey, Kazakhstan, and Kyrgyzstan signed a declaration for the establishment of a Parliamentary Assembly of Turkic-Speaking Countries (TURKPA), which was set to meet on
an annual basis and which was to have its general secretariat based in
Baku;[90] and the establishment—at the ninth Turkic summit held in Nakhchivan (Azerbaijan) in October 2009—of what came to be named the Turkic-
Speaking Countries Cooperation Council with its permanent secretariat
based in Istanbul.[91]

Conclusions

As the analysis evinced, although the two regional states—Azerbaijan and
Georgia—displayed behavioral patterns that fit well under the explanatory

notion of the struggle for recognition, what recognition is, how its end-state is understood, and what its dynamics and ultimate effects on collective identity formation have been is different in each of the two cases; variation conditioned by, and contingent upon, brute material influences that pipeline/energy politics had to bear upon the states in the region.

There are at least two ways in which pipeline/energy politics affected evolution of state identities in the region. First, pipeline/energy politics provided an alternative mechanism (in addition to imitation) that energy-rich and—to an extent—transit states in the region could employ in their struggle for Western recognition. Second, energy politics worked to enhance domestic capacities of the energy exporting states in the region, which enabled these states to realize their objective interests on their own and hence diminished the rationale behind their struggle for recognition. In both cases, energy politics worked to expand the range of cognitive choices available to an energy-rich (and to an extent transit) postcolonial nation in constructing its new political identity.

Although in both cases, energy politics seem to have had an exclusively positive effect on the evolution of the postcolonial polities of resource-rich states in post-Soviet Central Eurasia, it becomes clear upon closer scrutiny that the influences the politics brought to bear also entail some perils. Indeed, the influences pipeline politics have had on the evolving polities and identities of the energy-rich states also worked to open up the possibilities for, and indeed unleash tendencies toward, the heterogenization of identities within a state and in the broader region, processes that worked to set the ground for intra- and interstate conflicts in the region. Consequently, on the one hand, by working to boost state support for a divergent set of indigenous—sub- and transnational—identities, ones rooted in ethnic kinship and/or religious affinity and, as such, exclusive to many members within the state, energy politics served, if indirectly, to plant the seeds for potentially profound conflicts of interest among the various domestic groups within an energy-rich state.

On the other hand, the interlocking tensions within and between the two mechanisms (imitation and pipeline politics) energy-rich Azerbaijan's and energy-poor Georgia's struggle for recognition rested on worked to prompt the two states to promote different regional institutional frameworks, with divergent cognitive foundations they came to be rooted in and divergent memberships they came to be based upon, the process that shaped and promoted divergent modalities for regional socialization.

In the first effect, energy politics has come to interfere negatively—states' expectations for the converse notwithstanding—with the nation- and state-building efforts the energy-rich states were going through in the post-colonial period of their evolution, and it is not improbable that the processes the politics unleashed may eventually cause the intrastate "political conflict over the determination of national identity."[92] In the second effect on the evolution of polities of the resource-rich states, pipeline politics has worked to undermine the chances for regional integration and raise the likelihood of regional conflict.

8

Education Reform in Energy-Exporting States:
The Post-Soviet Experience
in Comparative Perspective

Regine A. Spector

A significant literature has emerged that seeks to explain the economic, political, and institutional underpinnings of the resource curse—that is, why
countries that export natural resources such as oil tend to grow more slowly
and underperform economically over time compared with those that do
not. This chapter investigates the challenges that energy-rich countries face
in their attempt to build human capital as a way to promote economic development.[1] As opposed to other forms of capital such as land and natural resources, human capital refers to the education and health of the people that
constitute a community.[2]

This chapter focuses on human capital's educational component, which
relates to a population's knowledge, skills, and capabilities. Although energy-
exporting countries often face challenges in reforming education systems
and building human capital similar to those of other developing countries,
the former face two additional obstacles. First, governments of energy-rich
countries often struggle to mitigate the tendency for labor and human capital to support the energy-exporting sector to the exclusion of other sectors
and industries. Second, although rents from the export of energy provide
the financial opportunity to invest in education and human capital, political
and bureaucratic structures mediate the amount of money spent and the
ways in which it is spent. Some energy exporters invest relatively little in

education, and others that invest more significantly do not necessarily emerge with quality education systems relevant to the labor market. In a world in which high energy prices continue and demand for fossil fuel energy increases, such outcomes may not be so perilous. Yet energy prices have been volatile historically, leading to cycles of boom and bust,[3] and concerns about the negative impacts of fossil fuel use for the climate and the environment may invigorate attempts to shift transportation systems away from oil and reduce fossil fuel consumption in other sectors. When prices drop or mineral flows taper, portions of the population in energy-exporting countries may be unemployed or without the skills and knowledge to compete in a globalized, non-mineral economy.

After a review of the literature on education, human capital, and development, the first part of the chapter identifies particular challenges of education reform in long-standing energy exporters in the developing world such as Nigeria and Saudi Arabia. The second part examines trends in education reform in two more recent energy exporters, Azerbaijan and Kazakhstan. Although the new post-Soviet energy-exporting countries differ in certain ways from traditional energy exporters with regard to their education systems and human capital reform efforts and it is too early to make definitive claims about outcomes in these new countries given the relatively recent inflows of energy rents, initial trajectories suggest that that Azerbaijan and Kazakhstan face certain similar challenges to those of long-standing energy exporters.

Human Capital and Economic Development

Studies by economists have shown a positive correlation between a country's human capital base and that country's development and economic potential.[4] A better-educated and well-trained population can increase productivity as well as innovate and/or adopt new technologies that—if accompanied by favorable macroeconomic conditions and opportunities to engage in relevant work—will allow the country to gain a competitive edge in the global economy. Educational expansion may also increase growth indirectly by reducing inequality.[5] Quality higher education is a particularly important component of a country's human capital outlook because it is at that level (as opposed to primary education) that innovation, new knowledge, and specialized skills training take place, whether at research universities, professional schools, or vocational programs.[6] World statistics on education and innovation confirm this relationship: the top twenty countries for higher education and training in the 2006 World Economic Forum Global Competitiveness Index 2006 were all among the top twenty-five in innovation.[7]

With the postwar success of the newly industrial East Asian countries and the heightened interest of international organizations and financial institutions in promoting education reform in the 1990s, governments have understood education as an investment in human capital necessary for development and integration in the global economy.[8] Early policy making to improve education focused on providing greater access and higher quality at the primary and secondary levels; more recently, education reform has included tertiary or higher education at university level as well as vocational training at the secondary and tertiary levels.[9] Access to primary education became universal in most countries by the 1980s, and over the past thirty years, access to education at the secondary and tertiary levels has expanded across the world: secondary gross enrollment ratios in the world expanded from 41 percent in 1985 to 66 percent in 2007, and tertiary ratios increased from 9 percent to 26 percent in the same period.[10] Education quality, though more difficult to define and measure across countries, entails a focus on critical thinking, problem solving, and studying the latest information and knowledge in a range of disciplines that allows students to promote research and innovations in public and private sectors.[11] Indicators that evaluate education quality of a population include international test scores in math, science, and reading comprehension, literacy rates, and the range in fields of study taught at various levels.[12] Other important factors that are important but more difficult to measure cross-nationally include teacher quality, labor market relevance of education, and effectiveness of education governance.

Social scientists have studied the politics of education policy together with health and pension policy as part of social welfare regimes. Much of the literature on variation and trends in social policy has focused on the experience of democratic Organisation for Economic Co-operation and Development (OECD) countries.[13] One recent study on education in OECD countries, for example, attributes postwar national variation in higher education outcomes to differences in political partisanship within these countries.[14] In contrast, our understanding of social policy in the developing world has been described as "sketchy and preliminary" to date,[15] but this is a rapidly growing research area. One recent comparative study of social policies in middle-income developing countries reveals varying models in Latin America, Eastern Europe, and East Asia that are attributed to factors such as differences in political coalitions, political institutions, government development strategies, and economic performance.[16]

A handful of studies have focused specifically on the human capital and education component of social policy in the developing world.[17] Javier Corrales reviews and synthesizes the multiple reasons for variations in educational access and quality since the 1960s and focuses on three incentives or pressures for education reform: international pressures, state-led initiatives, and societal demands.[18] Ben W. Ansell identifies variations in government spending as a percent of GDP on education across countries and regions of the world as well as within countries over time and concludes that these differences are explained first by whether a country is a democracy and second by the extent to which it is open to the global economy.[19] Specifically, he finds that democratization and integration with the international economy lead to higher levels of public education spending, which supports a body of literature that points to these variables in explaining variations in social policy outcomes more broadly.[20] Changes in spending levels in the Philippines (which changed both regime type and levels of economic openness over the past five decades) bolster the importance of these two explanatory factors, and a case study of relatively high spending levels on education by the authoritarian government of Malaysia underscores the importance of economic openness in creating incentives for education levels to meet the demands of export-oriented industries.[21]

Nancy Birdsall and colleagues find that successful governments in East Asia after World War II played two important roles in building human capital.[22] First, governments supplied education to the poor, focusing not only on building infrastructure such as schools and hiring teachers, but also on ensuring that the quality of education was high and relevant to the labor market. Second, governments also connected education policy with a broader development strategy to ensure that jobs and opportunities were available for people by focusing on "increasing demand for labor and demand for skills in an internationally competitive economy."[23] To the extent that poorer parts of the population experienced the benefits of greater education in a relatively short period, people continued to save and invest in human capital; over time, inequality decreased, and national growth occurred, leading to a virtuous circle.[24]

Although there have been successes in quality of education and impact on growth and development outcomes—notably in certain East Asian countries—the results across developing countries on average have been sobering. The World Bank attributes the disappointing results of developing countries in the sphere of higher education to multiple factors, including the systemic challenges in escaping the low-level education trap that many developing countries face, the absence of vision by the leadership, and the lack of political and financial resources.[25] Corrales expands upon the political challenges confronting developing countries in implementing education reform and argues that quality reforms often produce concentrated costs and distributed benefits. This often results in highly organized veto groups such as teachers unions, bureaucrats, and university students who stymie reform efforts and disbursed and fragmented beneficiaries who are not powerful enough to demand reform. Education policy entrepreneurs can attempt to push through reforms incrementally by linking education reform with integration in the global economy and by politically compensating the losers of reform, but the success rate across the developing world is not encouraging.[26] Finally, global trends toward decentralization of education decision making and financing often coincide with weak local institutions that lack effective monitoring and enforcement mechanisms, and this compounds an already challenging reform environment.[27] Even if enrollment numbers are increased, quality of education may suffer and negatively impact productivity and labor market benefits more generally.[28] Therefore, measures such as years of schooling and spending on education are "not sufficient indicators of human capital accumulation," and measures of education quality and labor market relevance must also be included.[29]

Human Capital and Economic Development in Energy-Exporting Countries

The study of social policy in a subset of developing countries—energy-exporting countries—has only recently gained the attention of social scientists. In 2007, the United Nations Research Institute for Social Development (UNRISD) elevated this topic to the top of its research agenda through a project entitled "Financing Social Policy in Mineral-Rich Countries." Through thematic papers and case studies, the project's goal is to fill a gap in the literature on the relationship between social policy and mineral rents in countries around the world.[30]

During the past decade, a handful of studies by economists have investigated the relationship between mineral wealth and education indicators.

One subset of studies finds that resource-rich countries fare worse than non-resource-rich countries across multiple education-related indicators. According to Thorvaldur Gylfason, resource-rich countries have lower public expenditures on education as a percent of GNP, and students in these countries have on average less schooling measured in number of years.[31] Birdsall and colleagues also find that resource-rich developing countries on average invest less in education than other developing countries.[32] Thus, resource-rich countries often have a relatively sudden and large windfall to invest in sectors such as education, yet, on average, this does not necessarily translate to better education-related spending and access outcomes.

Two reasons account for this outcome: the first having to do with the broader economic and development response to a booming mineral export sector and the second to do with institutions and the politics of education spending. Regarding the former, the effects of Dutch disease (whereby increased revenues from energy exports lead to local currency appreciation thus resulting in the atrophy of manufacturing and agricultural sectors) lower the rate of return to agricultural and other human capital-intensive sectors. As a result, investments flow into energy-related sectors, which even if they employ specialized and educated people, often constitute a very small percentage of the labor pool in the country. Moreover, appreciated exchange rates can lead to inefficient import substitution-based industrialization strategies and government protection for local producers competing with cheaper imported goods. Government policies can thus exacerbate the concentration of highly skilled workers in the resource-based sector or in the protected, import-competing manufacturing sector and disincentivize poor or rural populations from investing in skills in the atrophying agricultural and manufacturing sectors.[33] This is potentially problematic because of the importance of education in moving away from mineral production for sustainable long-term growth. As Gylfason states: "More and better education tends to shift comparative advantage away from primary production toward manufacturing and services, and thus to accelerate learning by doing and growth."[34]

In addition to economic policy response, political institutions and politics shape education spending and quality. There are cases in which energy rents have been channeled more successfully toward improving educational access, quality, and employment opportunities, for example in Indonesia and Malaysia in the 1970s and 1980s,[35] but in other cases, rents can be a source of personal enrichment and patronage for the ruling elite. They can

Table 8.1 Variations in Education Spending and Quality Among Select Energy-Exporting Developing Countries

		Domestic education quality and labor market ties	
		Lower	*Higher*
Domestic education spending	Lower	Nigeria	—
	Higher	Saudi Arabia	Indonesia/Malaysia

Source: The Author

be used to improve access to education but in a way that does not significantly improve education quality. In short, education spending does not necessarily lead to education quality, and education spending and quality are mediated by political institutions and politics more generally (see Table 8.1).[36] The next two sections elaborate on the education spending and reform patterns of Nigeria (which spends relatively little on education and has lower quality education) and Saudi Arabia (which spends relatively significant amounts on education but also with lower quality outcomes) over the past 40 years.

Nigeria

Low commitments to education reform can be measured by government spending on education as a percent of a country's GDP. A number of energy-rich countries spend less than world and regional averages on education; Nigeria, the United Arab Emirates, and Qatar are three examples. As of 2005, UAE spent 1 percent of GDP on education;[37] as of 1998, Nigeria spent 2.3 percent;[38] and Qatar spent 2 percent in 2003 and 3 percent in 2004. World averages have hovered around 4 percent over the past decade, sub-Saharan African averages were at 3 percent in 2000, and Middle East/North African averages were at 5 percent in 1999. The experience of Nigeria serves as an instructive case of education spending and development outcomes in this type of state.[39] Because rents are taken in by the central government and controlled by a small number of individuals or companies, "owners of the firms or the government officials concerned can capture the rents."[40] Instead of making long-term investment commitments, including in education, these countries "are confident that their natural resources are their most important asset [and] may inadvertently—and perhaps even deliberately!— neglect the development of their human resources, by devoting inadequate attention and expenditure to education."[41]

Before proceeding, a caveat is in order: reliable data on Nigeria are in "short supply" as one scholar recently wrote.[42] The World Bank began a series of reports aimed at uncovering the reasons for poor education data in Nigeria, and made estimates based on elaborate designs of local and regional cases and field research. Because data are not collected systematically at the national level and thus are not available in databases, the material from this section was amassed from such reports as well as other secondary literature.[43]

Oil revenues coincided with statehood in Nigeria in the 1960s. Upon independence in 1960, Nigerian policy making was fragmented and based on regionalism and patronage politics; within its first two decades after independence, the country experienced multiple leadership changes and civil war. Oil revenues increased dramatically in the 1970s under the country's military leadership, and among the main priorities of the government were expanding education and physical infrastructure throughout the country. At this time, public expenditures on education jumped considerably to 6 percent of GDP by 1981, and the state established universal, free primary education and opened seven new universities. Gross enrollment ratios from 1970 to 2005 increased from 44 percent to nearly 100 percent at the primary level, from 5 percent to 35 percent at the secondary level, and from 0 to 10 percent at the tertiary level.

Although these indicators point to some improvements in access, quality education was not prioritized and diversification of the economy faltered. Energy rents were distributed in the education sector as a way to consolidate power and coopt various regional and solidarity groups; by 1976, the number of governing units in the country had expanded from four to nineteen. The goal was to even out regional inequalities in services such as education rather than redistribute funds to rural areas or the agricultural sector,[44] and the creation of new states and corresponding infrastructure helped the country achieve this goal: "Not only was statehood an element in the formula for distributing revenues to population groups, but creating new state capitals meant investment in services and infrastructure."[45] Importantly, government spending did not consider the quality of education or the capacity of government to implement these goals sustainably over the long term: "the higher up one went on the education ladder, the less impressive were the gains."[46] Despite initially high education expenditures, by

1982, education spending had fallen to 1 or 2 percent of GDP and remained low in subsequent years.

As the number of local and state bureaucracies increased, oil revenues targeted state employee salaries and benefits, leading to an expansion in the number of civil service employees from the leadership's home region.[47] Federal employment grew from 65,000 in 1965 to 300,000 in 1984, and by 1986 there were over two million people in the public sector at all levels of government. Estimates in the late 1990s suggest that the government may have been absorbing 70 percent of the oil income via employment in state-sector jobs.[48] Moreover, "Unfortunately this bureaucratic growth did not enhance the quality of the civil service."[49] These expenditures and state-led industrialization attempts that resulted in inefficient white elephant projects reflected the disastrous management of oil rents: "the Nigerian state was thus a very poor entrepreneur, wasting resources and appropriating others for personal use."[50] Although these trends were due initially to a neopatrimonial state that lacked long-term vision and organizational capacity—in part a legacy of the nature of British colonial rule[51]—the "increased reliance on petrodollars to purchase loyalties and fuel patronage" combined with continual political instability led to an "acute form of political rent seeking."[52] In sum, although access to education has increased, enrollment levels at the secondary and tertiary level remain relatively low in Nigeria compared to world averages, and except for a few brief years in the 1970s, spending on education has been relatively low. Moreover, unemployment in Nigeria had risen to almost 20 percent by 2010,[53] and the population is growing at over 3 percent a year.

Saudi Arabia

Although Nigeria is an example of a country at the low end of the spectrum of education spending as a percent of GDP, other energy exporters spend significant amounts of GDP on education. Countries in this category include Kuwait, Saudi Arabia, Venezuela, and Iran, which all spent more than 4 percent of GDP as of 2006. Figure 8.1 puts these percentages in comparison with other energy exporters and OECD countries. These data confirm recent studies that have challenged findings that education spending on average is less in natural-resource-rich countries than in resource-poor countries.[54]

Saudi Arabia serves as an example of a country that invested heavily in education yet continues to face significant challenges in improving the quality

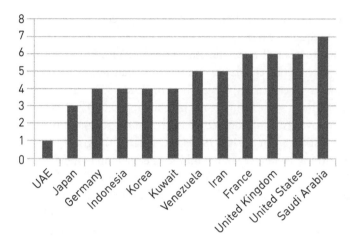

Figure 8.1 Public expenditure on education (% of GDP), 2006. UAE data from 2005 and Saudi Arabia from 2004.

of education and in fostering the economic and business environment that would allow people opportunities to engage in the global labor market. Instead, the government uses energy rents to educate and then employ vast portions of the population in its bureaucracy and government institutions.[55]

The creation of a national education system in Saudi Arabia coincided with the commercialization of the country's oil in the 1950s and 1960s. With illiteracy rates above 95 percent in the 1950s, Kings Saud and Faisal dedicated significant portions of the oil revenues to building a modern education system including ministries, directorates, primary and secondary schools, and universities. In higher education, the government pursued two strategies simultaneously. First, it established multiple universities, enrolling 25,000 students by 1975. Also by that time, more than 5,000 Saudis were studying abroad, largely on government stipends; the students later returned to work in the Faisal and Fahd administrations and gradually displaced traditional bureaucrats and graduates of domestic religious institutions. Many of these higher education graduates also worked in the private sector as well.[56] Between 1970 and 2008, access to primary and secondary institutions increased from 45 percent and 12 percent, respectively, to about 100 percent. Tertiary access increased from 2 percent to 30 percent in this same time period. Spending on education as a percent of GDP totaled 3 percent in 1970 and has since fluctuated between 4 and 9 percent annually, with the most recent data available from 2003 and 2004 at 7 percent.

Although this expansion in access is noteworthy, three factors damp-
ened the impact of education on the country's development trajectory. First,
although educated technocrats and a new middle and upper class had gained
important positions in government and bureaucracy, rising political tensions in other Middle Eastern countries and within Saudi Arabia itself ultimately led to the strengthening of the *ulama* and other religious leaders,
whose power had waned during this period of modernization and education
expansion.[57] These leaders advocated for government support of rural religious institutions as opposed to secular universities and foreign education.
Riots in the late 1970s and petitions to the king in the early 1990s from both
sides of the spectrum—liberal intelligentsia reformers and ulama and religious leaders—signified the intensity of political conflict within the country
regarding the direction of modernization, reform, and Western influence.[58]
In the end, although the country's leadership pushed for modernization
and invested heavily in education, conservative religious and social forces
shaped the content and nature of education within the country.

Second, education quality and relevance for the labor market suffered:
"As demand for trained Saudis in the 1960s and 1970s became almost insa-
tiable, Faisal abandoned any attempt to improve the quality of the education
system and allocated vast funds for its expansion."[59] The expansion of the
educational system largely benefited traditional urban dwellers and newly
urbanized residents and excluded rural populations. Moreover, higher
education focused on the humanities and social sciences, as opposed to
technical and vocational skills. In part this is due to a historic emphasis on
humanities and other such subjects as well as the belief among the population that white-collar jobs are preferable to blue-collar ones.[60] In addition,
these tendencies were reinforced by government emphasis on investing in a
real estate boom rather than manufacturing or agricultural diversification.
Because the domestic population was ill equipped to provide labor for this
boom, foreign laborers skilled in technical, managerial, and vocational areas filled the gaps in the Saudi workforce.[61] The extent of foreign labor in the
private sector is dramatic. In the 1970s, about two million expatriate workers helped to build the modern infrastructure in Saudi Arabia,[62] and as of
1997, only a fraction of the private sector work force comprised Saudi nationals.[63] The growing population of Saudi nationals is untrained for many
professions, and unemployment is a significant concern: "Only 40,000 of
120,000 Saudi nationals who entered the labor market in 1999 were able to
find jobs in the non-oil private sector."[64] As of 2006, unofficial statistics put

the general unemployment rate at 20 percent, and the rate was even higher among the younger population.[65]

Third, and finally, as a result of these political and labor market trends, the government played a significant role in absorbing the educated elite and newly urban population in the country: "Universities were created by the governments to perform a specific job: to prepare citizens for employment in the expanding bureaucracy."[66] The government bureaucracy and more generally, the public sector, employ significant percentages of Saudi nationals.[67] In effect, oil money has allowed the government to employ its own people and provide them with relative wealth, job security, and social status. Consumer spending by the government-paid population further supported the expatriate labor community, which provided the majority of private goods and services. The long-term danger of this arrangement is that given the reliance of the majority of the population on government employment, and more broadly on energy rents, energy shocks or slumps—not to mention a possible transition away from oil and gas and/or rapid population growth—would directly impact the ability of the Saudi economy and its population to adjust. Indeed, during the oil crisis of the 1980s, tens of thousands of university and high school graduates could not find employment in either the coveted public sector or the ailing private sector.[68] Suzanne Maloney sums up these earlier trends in the Gulf states by arguing that despite massive investments, returns were poor: "educational systems produced graduates unprepared for the job market, public sectors were bloated and inefficient, average growth rates were lower than in the pre-OPEC period, non-oil sectors were highly subsidized and unproductive, and the region's share of world trade declined."[69]

During the past decade, Saudi Arabia and other Gulf states and developing countries have led a massive effort to reorient their economies and to partner with leading Western higher education institutions or create top-notch learning centers of their own. The initiative to build high-quality domestic institutions coincides with a broader desire on the part of many well-endowed developing countries to build "World Class Universities (WCU)" that compete with the best universities in the world.[70] Research universities—which combine research and teaching and sit at the intersection of education and scientific development—have received particular attention as "icons of internationally competitive states since the nineteenth century."[71] Harvard University in the United States often tops the list of "best universities in the world," followed by others in the U.S. and UK such as Cambridge, Oxford, MIT, Yale, Stanford, Berkeley, and Princeton, depending on which survey measurement is used.[72] World higher education rankings are followed closely by some developing countries: "Preoccupations about university rankings reflect the general recognition that economic growth and global competitiveness are increasingly driven by knowledge and that universities play a key role in that context."[73]

Energy-rich countries have embarked on grandiose and ambitious plans to build new higher education institutions and form collaborative initiatives with leading Western universities.[74] In the Middle East, one of the largest initiatives is Education City in Qatar, begun in 1998. The Qatar Foundation—a multi-billion-dollar endowment fund—envisioned a world class university comprising campuses of already well-established and renowned western universities. To date, five universities offer degree programs: Virginia Commonwealth University, Weill Cornell Medical College, Texas A&M University, Carnegie Mellon University, and Georgetown School of Foreign Service. The foundation has paid for the construction of new buildings, financed high salaries for Western professors, and provided full scholarships for Qatari students.[75]

Two UAE members—Dubai and Abu Dhabi—have rushed to compete with Qatar's vision. Abu Dhabi's vast wealth has allowed it to build its own University City, with France's Sorbonne campus as the flagship institution. New York University will also have a campus on the new $28 billion Saadiyat Island that is shared with other schools such as the Johns Hopkins University public health program and global business school INSEAD. Dubai is now home to the Dubai School of Government (DSG), a teaching and research institution that aspires to be the leading public policy school and research institution in the Middle East. Established with the help of the Dubai Initiative in 2004, a collaboration between Harvard's Kennedy School of Government and the DSG, the school offers master's-level degrees in public policy as well as executive education certificate programs.[76] Dubai's Academic City and Knowledge Village are "education malls" filled with second-tier academic institutions. Because Dubai does not have the natural resources of Qatar or Abu Dhabi, it makes money by leasing building space to universities and other institutions. Ironically, however, the "education mall" largely caters to the significant number of expats in UAE from India and other parts of Asia who seek educational opportunities.[77] Finally, Saudi Arabia has been planning two new universities,

Al-Faisal University and the King Abdullah University of Science and Technology (KAUST). The king has contributed over $10 billion to KAUST.[78]

These initiatives are in part driven by energy-related construction booms
and the desire to house internationally recognized higher education institutions. Despite modern physical infrastructure, these institutions face common challenges, including attracting and keeping quality faculty, maintaining
high academic standards, and providing jobs for graduates in the private
sector labor market.[79] Moreover, these universities may not be attuned to
the labor market demands of the country and region: in the case of small
countries in the Middle East, needs include technical, infrastructure, and
vocational skills.[80] A 2009 World Bank Report quoted an education specialist in saying: "The paradox of the world-class university . . . is that 'everyone
wants one, no one knows what it is, and no one knows how to get one.'"[81]
Thus, although these countries are investing in human capital, the question
remains as to whether these programs address outmoded education systems
at their core and overcome patronage politics and resistance to economic
diversification.[82]

Summary of Trends and Lessons

The cases of Nigeria and Saudi Arabia confirm that energy-exporting countries have increased access to education for their populations to varying
degrees. Yet both countries confronted the challenge of mitigating the distorting effects of Dutch disease, which often leads to a focus of investment
in education and human capital on the profitable mineral sector. Both
governments confronted political challenges in sustaining long-term investments in quality education: in Nigeria, education spending has been
relatively low on average and has been tied to personal enrichment and patronage politics, and in Saudi Arabia, spending has been higher, though it is
also tied to patronage politics and is "beyond the absorptive capacity of the
economy and beyond [levels] that the government could efficiently and effectively control."[83] For Saudi Arabia and other Gulf states, this has meant
"the efficiency of investment has been steadily declining, reflecting poor
screening of the economic viability of projects."[84] Various indicators suggest
that the type and quality of education has suffered in energy-exporting
countries. These include the relatively small number of people trained in
technical/vocational skills in many energy-exporting countries such as

Nigeria, Kuwait, Qatar, Saudi Arabia, UAE, and Venezuela and the low scores on basic math and science tests.

A key distinction in assessing the impact of education spending is whether an initiative is viewed as a consumption good—an entitlement or a "plum awarded by the government, an enhancement of consumer (and voter) satisfaction"—or an investment good that can improve the lives of individuals, families, and the country as a whole over the long term.[85] Consumption-based education spending can lead to poor-quality schools, inefficient development projects, and little human capital dynamism. Examples of what the World Bank calls an "engineering" approach to education reform, which does not necessarily lead to behavioral changes that improve education quality and capacity of those involved in education (teachers, education authorities, and administrators), include: an overemphasis on testing, curriculum redesign, and physical infrastructure such as buildings.[86] One of the main problems with investments in physical infrastructure such as new schools, universities, and technology is that top government leaders often grant procurement contracts on the basis of patronage, ethnic, or other family loyalties and pay less attention to the "growth-enhancing potential" of the investments.[87]

Due to insufficient opportunities in the labor market for the population, especially the educated segments, governments subsidize employment in public sector bureaucracies and in uncompetitive manufacturing industries.[88] Although average government spending on employee compensation in OECD countries hovers between 10 and 15 percent of total government spending, in some energy-rich countries such as Bahrain, Iran, Kuwait, Malaysia, Qatar, and UAE, the numbers are 30 percent and above.[89] This strategy may work in the short term, but during bust periods or population booms, governments face challenges employing and paying government employees. Employees of bureaucracies come to expect and rely on government employment and have "distorted incentives to work."[90] Moreover, in countries where populations are growing rapidly, such government spending can be unsustainable in the long run.

Education in Post-Soviet Countries: Common Trends

This section investigates to what extent the challenges of education reform and human capital advancement apply to new post-Soviet energy-exporting countries. Azerbaijan and Kazakhstan gained statehood in 1991 upon the collapse of the Soviet Union. Under Tsarist and then Soviet rule in the nineteenth and first part of the twentieth centuries, varied and complex processes, which in some regions of the Caucasus and Central Asia involved the violent eradication of local forms of education and Islamic practices, culminated in the establishment and integration of these republics into the Soviet educational system.[91] The process of creation and the quality of these education systems have been debated, but the vast majority of the Soviet populations in these regions were literate, and many were multilingual by the time of the Soviet Union's collapse.[92] There were, however, important regional differences across Soviet republics not only along education indicators, but also in budgeting and policy choices more broadly.[93] For example, the rate of secondary education enrollment differed across regions by the late 1980s, with Russia and the Baltics having higher rates than the Caucasus and Central Asia. Vocational and other specialized educational opportunities were greater in industrial centers and correspondingly lagged in certain southern regions of the Soviet Union.[94]

Overall, however, the high literacy rates and access to primary and secondary education distinguish post-Soviet countries from other postcolonial Middle Eastern and African countries that became independent earlier in the century. In the latter, independence coincided with low literacy and low educational access rates. Despite these advantages, the post-Soviet countries faced other challenges that resulted from the centralized command economy and the political, social, and economic dislocations of the collapse of the Soviet system.[95]

The new countries in the region faced wrenching budgetary and economic crises to varying degrees in the 1990s, and these were exacerbated by war and political instability in some countries such as Armenia, Azerbaijan, Georgia, and Tajikistan. As a result of these fiscal challenges, many post-Soviet governments struggled to maintain physical infrastructure such as school buildings, fight corruption, keep up enrollment, and combat non-attendance as students fled to the streets to take part in emerging market activities and other new opportunities.

In part to offset state expenditures on higher education, many post-Soviet countries opened their doors to private higher education institutions, though to varying degrees (see Figure 8.2). State schools themselves have increasingly moved toward charging tuition and fees. In some countries, depending on a student's score on the standardized university entrance

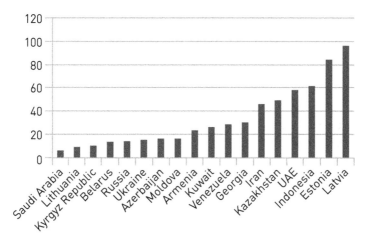

Figure 8.2 Post-Soviet tertiary private enrollment share (%), 2008. Estonia, Armenia, Kazakhstan, Latvia, Lithuania, and Russia data from 2007; Kuwait from 2006; and Indonesia from 2005.

exam, grants and fellowships are available: the higher the score on the exam, the greater the chance the student will receive a government scholarship to study for free. Students who do not score well often must pay to study (which can lead to significant inequalities based on wealth) or go to lower-tier institutions or none at all if they are unable to afford the fees.

The region also faces significant challenges with corruption, cheating, and low-quality teaching in public education institutions.[96] Due to low teacher salaries and the systemic nature of corruption in society, payments are often extracted at various levels. Teachers can receive bribes for giving higher grades. Administrators can receive bribes for passing students and appointing teachers or others and can siphon off state money for personal gain. And national officials can award contracts for textbooks or school construction and repairs to their own businesses or personal interests.[97]

Post-Soviet countries also face challenges in linking the type and quality of education to demands in the labor market; the students who do graduate from domestic education institutions are often unable to find good jobs. In part, this is due to the Soviet educational system's distinct pathologies and inefficiencies that prevented mobility across professions and overemphasized certain priorities while downplaying others.

Finally, as a result of the Soviet education system, research institutions and universities had been divided, and the process of reintegrating them is

still ongoing. In the Soviet system, research institutions were more presti-
gious than universities, which primarily served to teach students. Yet experiences in the U.S. and other OECD countries indicate that important
research takes place at big universities; professors not only teach students
but also involve them in competitively funded research collaborations. The
Soviet Union's particular legacy of separating research from teaching has
also made it difficult to shift to the "emerging global model of the research
university" and to link policy changes in education to a market-oriented
and business-friendly environment.[98] State control of curriculum and administration at universities further hampers attempts to reform the system.

Against this backdrop, foreign and international actors have been reshaping the education systems of these new countries during the past two
decades. These include international organizations such as the United National Education and Science Cooperation Organization (UNESCO)[99] and
OSCE,[100] international financial institutions such as the World Bank,[101] the
Asian Development Bank (ADB),[102] and the European Bank of Reconstruction and Development (EBRD), foreign national governments,[103] and private
foundations such as the Soros Foundation[104] and the Aga Khan Foundation.[105]
Some of these programs offer opportunities within the home countries, and
many also provide funding and administrative support to allow students
and professionals to travel abroad for educational opportunities in donor
countries.

Although the intentions of these various actors in the education sector
often are good, the impact on the countries themselves is not always positive.
According to one view, "independence exchanged one form of politico-
economic dependency (on the Soviet imperial center) for another (international organizations, development bodies, and foreign governments)."[106]
Moreover, the alumni of these programs often network among themselves
upon return, widening the gaps between alumni who have absorbed different
political philosophies in their time abroad as well as between those who do
have foreign education and those who do not. This can not only stymie the
formation of a strong civil society, but also lead to "competing understand-
ings of how national identity should be understood and which development
model their country should end up opting for."[107] In general, analysts have
argued that international institutions and organizations have not been effective in advancing education policy: "While Western governments, multilateral agencies such as the World Bank, and major private foundations have
poured substantial resources into the reform of post-Soviet higher education

since 1991, there was arguably a sense by the end of the decade that much of that technical assistance had been ineffective . . . ."[108]

The remainder of this chapter presents cases of education policy and reform in the post-Soviet region conducted by national governments; this is an especially relevant approach for resource-rich countries (Azerbaijan, Kazakhstan, Russia, and Turkmenistan) that have accumulated significant amounts of capital for development projects and other national priorities. In the sphere of higher education, despite important foreign and privately funded universities in the region, a significant majority of students participate in the state-run education system. The remainder of this chapter shifts the spotlight from the role of international organizations, nongovernmental organizations, and other international actors in the education sphere to the role of national governments in reshaping education policies and opportunities.

Post-Soviet Rentier States in Comparative Perspective

This section compares education indicators in energy-rich post-Soviet countries with other countries in the region and other energy exporters. Of the four energy-rich post-Soviet countries, this chapter focuses on Azerbaijan and Kazakhstan because they are new, accessible, and relatively small countries. Turkmenistan is difficult to research in light of restrictions on scholarly and foreign access, and Russia is a vast country beyond the scope of this chapter.

Primary data were collected in July 2009 and include more than a dozen interviews with academics, analysts, and government officials in each country;[109] government statistics; and reports and analyses from international and nongovernmental organizations. The countries are first compared on spending and enrollment indicators and then on assessment and other qualitative indicators that shed light on education quality and access to the labor market.

The energy-producing post-Soviet countries have one potential advantage in reforming education over other post-Soviet countries in the region: significant revenues available to them since the late 1990s. These are rentier states in the sense that governments rely heavily on energy exports for budget revenues, which have been growing rapidly in the 2000s as a result of increased exports and high energy prices.[110] In Azerbaijan, by 2002, the oil sector provided 89 percent of exports, 30 percent of GDP, 55 percent of government revenues, and only 1.1 percent of employment.[111] In Kazakhstan, by

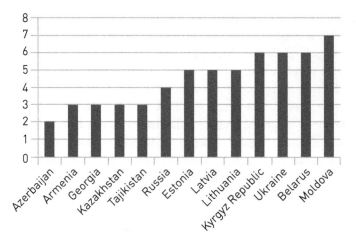

Figure 8.3 Post-Soviet public expenditure on education (% of GDP), 2006.

2002, the oil sector accounted for 56 percent of exports, 18 percent of GDP, 20 percent of government revenues, and less than 2 percent of the work-force.[112] Moreover, signifying the distorting trends of energy exports on other sectors of the economy, both countries have experienced dramatic declines in the value added from the agricultural sector, from 29 percent (Azerbaijan) and 27 percent (Kazakhstan) to 6 percent in both cases.

Three indicators—government expenditures on education, education enrollment ratios, and expenditures on research and development—reveal that post-Soviet energy-exporting countries are on the lower end of the spectrum of post-Soviet countries and in some cases the spectrum of energy exporting countries more broadly. Each is discussed in turn. Regarding to-tal education expenditures, although many post-Soviet countries experi-enced significant declines in the percentage of GDP spent on education in the 1990s, by 2006, the energy-exporting countries were among the bottom half of all post-Soviet countries on this indicator, with Azerbaijan at 2 per-cent, Kazakhstan at 3 percent, and Russia at 4 percent of GDP (see Figure 8.3). As discussed above, OECD countries range in spending from 3 to 6 percent, and energy-exporting countries vary between 1 and 7 percent. The same trend applies to per capita higher education spending: Azerbaijan, Kazakhstan, and Russia are among the lowest in the region, well below spending in OECD countries[113] (see Figure 8.4). Measured by share of gov-ernment expenditure for tertiary education as a percent of total education

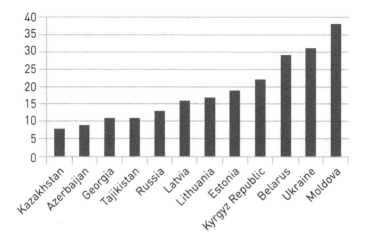

Figure 8.4 Post-Soviet tertiary public education expenditures per student (% of per capita GDP), 2006. Georgia data from 2008 and Estonia from 2005. For comparison, U.S., UK, and French expenditures fall between 25 and 35 percent.

expenditure, Azerbaijan and Tajikistan are the lowest at 7 percent, with Kazakhstan at 16 percent, and Russia above 20 percent. Finally, Azerbaijan and Kazakhstan spend a smaller portion on higher education as percent of GDP (0.2 to 0.3 percent) compared to other middle-income countries such as Russia and China (0.7 to 0.8 percent). OECD and European countries spend between 1 and 2.5 percent of GDP on higher education.[114]

Although enrollment indicators are high at the primary and secondary levels across the region, there is significant variation in higher education. Azerbaijan and Russia are at opposite ends of the spectrum of college-eligible population entering higher education, at 15 percent and 75 percent, respectively, with Kazakhstan in between at 51 percent. In some countries, percentages have increased since the collapse of the Soviet Union (for example Russia and Kazakhstan), and in others percentages have declined (Azerbaijan) (see Figure 8.5). Enrollment in technical or vocational education varies in a similar way among energy-exporting countries in the post-Soviet region (see Figure 8.6).

Finally, spending on research and development among post-Soviet countries varies from 0.1 percent to 1.1 percent of GDP, with Azerbaijan and Kazakhstan among the lowest at 0.2 percent and Russia the highest at 1.1 percent. The OECD average is 2.24 percent, with the U.S. and Korea around 2.6 percent.

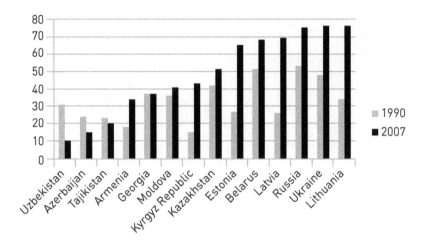

Figure 8.5 Post-Soviet tertiary gross enrollment ratio, 1990 and 2007. Armenia 1990 data are as of 1992.

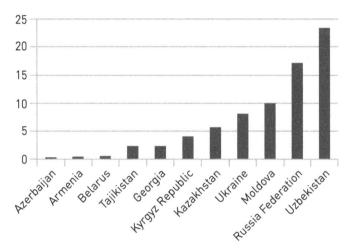

Figure 8.6 Post-Soviet vocational and technical enrollment (% of total secondary enrollment), 2007.

In sum, these indicators suggest that along certain education spending and R&D indicators, Azerbaijan and Kazakhstan rank among the lowest in the post-Soviet region. Along other spending and enrollment indicators, there is greater variation, with Azerbaijan at the lower end of post-Soviet countries, Kazakhstan in the middle, and Russia at the higher end. However, as noted earlier, although these indicators on spending and enrollment give a general sense of budgeting and prioritization of education spending, they do not capture quality of education investments and relevance to the labor market. In other words, they do not tell us if education spending is based on long-term investments in human capital or represents consumption-based expenditures based on other factors such as distributing patronage and short-term decision making. To assess the quality of human capital investments in Azerbaijan and Kazakhstan, the next three sections will focus on recent developments in education assessment and labor market needs, the types of education expenditures, and the role of study abroad programs in the region.

Education Assessment and the Labor Market

International indicators that assess the capabilities and learning achievements of students across countries are available from three main exams and tests.[115] The data for Azerbaijan's first time participation in the PISA test administered in 2006 revealed that although its fifteen-year-old students scored relatively well in math, the country was among the bottom three of the total fifty-seven countries that participated in the test in both science and reading.[116] Kazakhstan participated in the 2007 TIMSS test at the fourth-grade level; the test measures math and science learning outcomes. Kazakhstan's students scored well in math, above other Eastern European countries (Latvia, Hungary, and Russia) and energy-exporting countries (Iran, Kuwait, Norway, and Qatar), and fairly well in science.[117] Although relatively high mathematics scores are encouraging for both countries, analysts are concerned about the literacy and science numbers in Azerbaijan, in part because these numbers reflect a low level of analytical and comprehension skills, those needed for many professions.

Recent statistics from Azerbaijani institutions confirm that the country faces significant challenges in improving the quality of education at all levels. High school students interested in higher education are required to take a university admissions exam administered by the State Students

Admission Commission (SSAC), and recent scores suggest that significant portions of the population are underprepared for higher education. As of 2009, about 108,000 people took this test, and only 33,202 passed the threshold of more than 200 out of 700 total points; in other words, over 60 percent of the applicants who took the test did not score well enough to enter university.[118]

Both countries face the challenge that what students learn is not relevant to the labor market needs in the economy. The OECD sums up contemporary concerns with respect to Kazakhstan: "There seems to be no regular or formal involvement of employers in estimating the numbers of graduates needed in different disciplines; defining the knowledge, skills, and competences required on graduation; or assessing final standards. Nor are there effective links between universities and employers for the purposes of research, fundamental or applied, or commercializing scientific discoveries."[119] As of the mid-2000s, one main problem in Kazakhstan was that people were being educated in law and finance, yet the labor market needed other specialists and technically skilled people.[120] In Azerbaijan, a government official confirmed that the quality of education often does not meet the standards and needs of the labor market.[121]

Education-Related Expenditures

With growing national revenues during the past decade, both Azerbaijan and Kazakhstan have increased education spending. Between 2001 and 2009, Azerbaijan increased state budget spending on education more than fivefold to 8.9 percent of the total state budget in 2009. Spending in Kazakhstan between 2004 and 2008 also grew significantly, increasing threefold to 18.9 percent of the total state budget in 2008.[122] To put these numbers in perspective, OECD countries spend on average 12 percent on education as a percent of government budget, with some Gulf countries considerably higher. Post-Soviet countries vary considerably on this indicator.

In addition to increases in teacher salaries, another important component of spending is building and infrastructure, the physical dimensions of education reform. As discussed in the first section, however, a significant peril for oil countries is that education reform will be driven by a broader construction boom and a concurrent desire to achieve quick results. Azerbaijan has focused investments on physical infrastructure such as schools, computers, and free textbooks at the primary and secondary levels. In particular, the government launched a State School Infrastructure Improvement Program (SSIIP) between 2003 and 2008 that resulted in more than 1,200 new schools, 785 schools undergoing repair, and 71 schools being rehabilitated. In addition, more than 200 schools were built under a program funded by the Heydar Aliyev Foundation. The government has also supported programs in curriculum development, including a program that provides free textbooks for primary students, teacher development and training programs, and increases in teacher wages. Newer programs have included a focus on preschool education development (2007–10) and Information and Communication Technology (ICT) in education program (2008–2010).[123]

Kazakhstan has also embarked upon initiatives to fund school construction and renovation and bring Internet access to all schools. The government is also opening thirty specialized language schools to help the country achieve President Nursultan Nazarbayev's goal of a trilingual society (Kazakh, Russian, and English). Increases in teacher salaries also are expected to continue.[124]

The construction boom at the primary and secondary levels has also reached higher education, where both governments are spending millions of dollars building new higher education institutions from scratch. Kazakhstan has constructed a new public international university in Astana with support from President Nazarbaev. Government members and other advisors traveled to the UK, U.S., Singapore, and Qatar in 2008 to learn about the higher education institutions of these countries and were most impressed by the latter two. The academic focus will be on a handful of high-tech fields, such as biotechnology and nanotechnology, and the university will integrate teaching and research. Each academic program will have an affiliated foreign institution aiding with academic development, and at least half of the faculty will be from abroad. The government contracted with University College London for preparatory courses in English and science, and 500 students began in September 2010. Although the goal is to build the domestic knowledge base in science and engineering, significant questions remained in 2009 regarding what programs will be chosen, how to arrange international contracting arrangements, and how to attract international staff and administrators. Moreover, although $100 million was initially budgeted, international experience suggests that at least $500 million will be needed, if not significantly more.[125]

In Azerbaijan, significant effort is going into the creation of the Azerbaijan Diplomatic Academy (ADA), a new educational institution focused on higher education opportunities for elite students in foreign policy, international relations, and diplomacy. Administrators and leaders of the school visited Georgetown University, Johns Hopkins University, the Tufts University Fletcher School of Law and Diplomacy, Russia's Moscow State Institute of International Relations (MGIMO), and the Diplomatic Academy of Vienna prior to establishing the school and seek to create a leading international institution with U.S.- or Western-trained scholars and administrators. Prior to 2009, the ADA offered professional development courses to diplomats as well as an annual international summer school. Starting in 2009, the ADA admitted its first incoming class of about two-dozen students (40 percent from abroad) for the master's program in international affairs and diplomacy. In the next five years, the school plans to offer a bachelor's degree in addition to a master's in environmental and energy management and an MBA. Funding for the construction of a new "green" campus is coming entirely from the government, and the institution hopes to build an endowment through the ADA Foundation, which has offices in Baku and Washington, D.C., and will soon in Brussels and Seoul. As with Kazakhstan's new university in Astana, this project has the direct backing of the president of the country via the university's rector, former U.S. Azerbaijani Ambassador to the United States and current Deputy Foreign Minister Hafiz Pashayev.[126]

In addition to the ADA, a new tourism institution was recently established to tap into the labor market demands in tourism. The government issued a state program to develop tourism by 2016 and is working toward earning a World Tourism Certificate. The Azerbaijan Tourism Institute is an effort to realize this goal and to link the hotel industry and the education sector. As of 2009, there were about 800 bachelor's students enrolled with about 200–300 entering each year. The school offers an option to get a dual degree from a partner institution, the Austria's IMC University of Applied Sciences at Krems. However, due to the low-level English skills of applicants, there are only about twenty-five students in this program. There are also internship programs to provide practical training abroad. As with other initiatives in the region, the main problems for the Institute include finding qualified teachers (now many are from Turkey) and preparing students in the English language.[127] All of these institutions in both countries have formed partnerships or collaborations with European, Asian, and/or American universities in the hopes of building bridges of human capital and learning.[128]

Despite the efforts of Kazakhstan and Azerbaijan to reform and build new primary, secondary, and higher education institutions, certain patholo-

gies of the existing higher education system remain unaddressed. An analyst of Kazakhstan's reform efforts stated: "the current approach in Astana
of investing limited funds in facilities, while neglecting the people that are
the heart of any university, will simply perpetuate mediocrity."[129] A World
Bank analysis of Azerbaijan's trajectory stated: "If serious education reform
actions are not taken on a large scale and with determination, the investments the government of Azerbaijan is presently making in improving
physical facilities and putting educational technology in the schools will not
improve learning outcomes and the gap between Azerbaijan and comparator countries will widen, leaving its school graduates at a growing disadvantage and the economy ill prepared to compete in a world which relies
increasingly on knowledge and on high-order thinking skills."[130]

Gaps already exist within these countries, and foreigners are filling them
rapidly. Kazakhstan's President Nazarbaev stated that 60,000 foreign specialists came to Kazakhstan in 2007 and that he hopes his new state plan to
improve the status of vocational education and training (2008–12) will help
to reverse this trend.[131] In both countries, this will involve retraining teachers, investing in changing the quality and culture of education, and identifying the fields (whether scientific, technical, agricultural, or service) that
should be emphasized. Both countries are formulating plans to address vocational education and training, but these are still in their infancies.[132] Thus,
the challenges for these two countries involve not only overcoming legacies
of the Soviet system and the crises of the 1990s, but also undertaking a concerted effort to avoid the tendencies that energy-rich countries face; as discussed in the first half of the chapter, rapid spending in the construction
sector (whether on education infrastructure or otherwise) often outpaces
the more challenging, longer-term investments in human capital. Both countries are exhibiting signs that the building and infrastructure sectors have
developed without enough attention to the managers, specialists, and vocational workers who will populate them.[133]

State Study Abroad Programs

Sending students abroad to get high-quality education and training is one
strategy to build human capital when existing domestic institutions are failing or unable to reform fast enough to meet labor market and changing global
demands. Government programs are not the only way to study abroad; other

international fellowships and private money are available to students of the region.[134] However, countries with money from energy exports have the opportunity to build a bureaucratic infrastructure to administer these expensive programs as well as to pay for the tuition, travel, and other expenses associated with each student's educational costs. Kazakhstan implemented an ambitious program to send students abroad in 1993, and Azerbaijan began a similar program in 2007.

In 1993, the Bolashak program was started by the initiative of Kazakhstan President Nazarbayev. Initially, the goal was to send about 250 students abroad to master's-level programs in finance, economics, law, and international relations. About 800 to 1,000 applied annually in the 1990s, and about 60–80 went abroad every year, primarily to France, the UK, Germany, and the U.S. In exchange for government paying for higher education, students agreed (by putting down a house or car as collateral) that they would return and work in the country for five years. In 1997, a scandal revealed that the children of elite members in the government had special priority for these slots—in other words the selection of students for the program was not solely merit based. Leadership and administrative changes in the program resulted.[135] By 2005, almost 800 students had received a Bolashak scholarship, with 600 of them completing their BA and MA degrees and subsequently working in Kazakhstan.[136]

An additional wave of changes occurred against the backdrop of the 2006 presidential elections as the government responded to growing pressure from parents and other citizens to provide more opportunities for the country's students.[137] In response, the Bolashak program expanded to include more than twenty eligible countries and almost 200 schools on the list of approved higher education institutions. The government has also begun to more actively encourage training in engineering, biotechnology, information technology, oil, and public administration—subjects determined by the government to be lacking in the labor market. For example, as of 2009, if a student wanted to study under Bolashak for a BA, the only choices were technical or medical fields; finance and accounting at the bachelor's level were not funded for 2009 as they had been in the past. In another example of how the government prioritizes fields, in 2008 it was deemed that the country needed more specialists in tourism and hotel management in advance of the 2011 Asian Olympic Games to be held in Almaty and Astana. In that year's Bolashak application announcements, the government undertook a major PR campaign to encourage applicants for this sector and got significantly more applicants than it had in the past, even though this had always been an approved field.[138] In this way, the government is trying tailor the Bolashak program to meet the demands of the labor market and education deficiencies of the national system.

A second response by the government has been an increase in the total number of students abroad and the regions of the country they represent. The goal is to have 3,000 abroad in any year, which means that about 500 students are accepted each year out of thousands of applicants. Whereas previous applicants came primarily from major cities in the country, recent initiatives have focused on attracting students from rural regions via a quota system and requiring them to go back to their home regions to work and contribute to the economy and society upon graduation.[139] By 2010, 6,697 students had been granted scholarships. Until 2005, students went primarily to the U.S. and UK and to a lesser extent to France, Germany, Russia, and other European countries. Students were placed in thirty-two countries from 2005–10. In this time period, most studied for either BAs (53 percent) or MAs (41 percent) with enrollment in technical fields (53 percent), humanitarian and social science subjects (42 percent), and medical studies (5 percent).[140]

One challenge for the success of the program in the first decade was that graduates could not find good jobs upon returning home. However, with the 2005 reforms, more emphasis was placed on the program's role in helping returnees find work in any sector, whether private or public. A related challenge is that a fraction of participants ultimately do not return to Kazakhstan or return only to leave again. By 2005, this number had stabilized at 15 to 20 percent of the total.[141] Finally, the biggest systematic weakness in the current applicant pool is often command of the English language. Most students do not have good enough English language skills to directly enroll in foreign universities.[142] The program administrators have now begun to accept students who do not have language proficiency and give them the opportunity to take one semester or a year to build their English skills before embarking on a foreign program.[143]

Azerbaijan has had a history of bilateral education programs with dozens of countries including Turkey and Russia. Thousands of students have been educated in these countries beginning in 1992. More recently in 2007, the government initiated a state study abroad program resembling the Bolashak program that is administered by the Ministry of Education and financed by the State Oil Fund of Azerbaijan (SOFAZ).[144] In the first year, 200 students participated and about sixty graduated with MAs. Despite initial complaints of challenges with funding disbursements and allegations of bribery,[145] as of April 2010, more than 500 students were being educated in economics, medicine, engineering, international relations, and other technical subjects in the UK, Germany, Turkey, France, Russia, South Korea, the Netherlands, the U.S., Canada, and Switzerland. The program aims to send about 5,000 students abroad by 2015.[146]

The ultimate goal of these study abroad programs is that foreign-educated students return home to contribute either to the public or private sector. To the extent that students do not return home or conditions are not created for their productive contribution to society upon return, the programs—while perhaps buying social or political support for the leadership—will not impact reform and development as anticipated. The Umid (meaning "hope") program in Uzbekistan provides a cautionary example. The program began in 1997 and was financed by private companies (Uzbekistan does not have nearly as significant energy reserves as Kazakhstan and Azerbaijan). The program was administered by the state-founded youth organization, Kamolot, and initially encouraged undergraduate students to study abroad. Later, in 2000, the program shifted to focus on graduate studies. By 2002, the program ended after financing ran out and a projected 80 percent of students never returned to Uzbekistan. In its place, the government announced the creation of Westminster International University in Tashkent, accredited by Westminster University in London, in the hopes that it would attract the best students in the country and keep them there.[147]

Not all such programs have foundered, however; there are examples of students and foreign-educated citizens returning and contributing to society and government in East and Southeast Asia. Kazakhstan's Bolashak graduates are working in corporations and in government at the vice ministerial level though some in government have left or been arrested in political reshuffles amidst allegations of financial misdeeds or tax evasion.[148] Although it is too early to measure the success of study abroad programs in Azerbaijan and Kazakhstan, the important point is that people with knowledge have the opportunity to aid growth and development but only if government policies make meaningful opportunities in the bureaucracy and economy available. To date in Azerbaijan, many foreign-educated people—whether educated through the state study abroad program or independent of it—have chosen to work in the private sector in part due to low government wages.[149] Data on wages as a percentage of total government expenditures suggest Azerbaijan and Kazakhstan do not currently spend significant amounts on employee wages in comparison to both

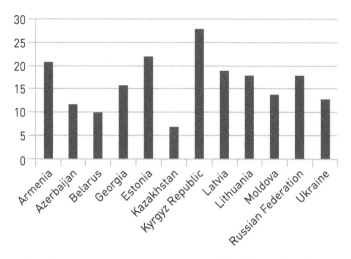

Figure 8.7 Post-Soviet government compensation of employees (% of government expenses), 2008. Estonia data are as of 2007.

other post-Soviet countries and other oil-exporting countries.[150] According to this indicator, these two countries contrast with other Gulf oil-exporting countries that spend significant amounts on government employee wages and are thus far averting this peril. However, some post-Soviet countries— including Azerbaijan, Russia, and to a lesser extent Kazakhstan—do employ high portions of the population in the public sector (through government positions or government-owned companies).[151] See Figure 8.7.

Yet amount spent on wages and percentages of people in government are only part of the story: to the extent that the government work environment stifles "independent and critical thinking"[152] and fails to result in government reforms due to opposing social or political pressures, as the case of Saudi Arabia discussed, the impact of a more-educated population on policy and development goals will be muted. Moreover, corruption in government sectors can be a deterrent for returnees who seek merit-based and performance-based employment standards.[153]

The Politics of Education Reform

Attempts to improve human capital as part of broader development goals are mediated by political constraints and dynamics. As other research on

social welfare in the post-Soviet region has shown, education reform is a
political process that involves multiple stakeholders, often among political
elite and bureaucracies.[154] This final section investigates recent debates in
Azerbaijan pertaining to the higher education sector and highlights how
efforts to improve education quality take place in the context of political
debates among power brokers within the system. Understanding this landscape provides additional insight into the challenges that lie ahead.

Although certain private universities have good reputations for offering
quality education in a noncorrupt environment[155] and certain state institutions such as the Azerbaijan University of Languages have undergone significant reform efforts in the past five years, broader and more comprehensive
reform efforts will include the three main groups and institutions that have
a stake in higher education reform: the Ministry of Education, rectors of universities,[156] and the state admissions committee SSAC. A look at two debates
surrounding the new 2009 education law as it pertains to public universities
and degrees elucidates important dynamics among these institutions and
groups.[157] One controversial debate revolved around the question of who de-
cides which students get admitted to higher education institutions. During
the Soviet period, the Ministry of Education and the rectors had control over
admittance, and this system was riddled with corruption.[158] In 1992, Azerbaijan adopted a centralized and later computerized mechanism for admin-
istering exams for admittance into higher education institutions. This exam,
administered by the SSAC, also established at the same time, was based on a
similar Turkish institution—the Student Selection and Placement Center
(ÖSYM) under the Higher Education Council (YOK).[159] The goal of the
SSAC's establishment was to allow for more equality and less corruption in
the admissions process, and the commission is not under the Ministry of Education but rather under the president. One of the main tensions since this
time has been between this committee and the Ministry of Education, as the
latter has sought to win back control over admissions decisions, though to
no avail as of 2011. Although the centralized exam system established during the past fifteen years has been touted as a success because it has significantly curtailed corruption in the admissions process, others have argued
that it encourages students to learn "for the test" and hire tutors and other
specialists who can help them achieve high scores and that admissions decisions should be in the hands of the rectors.[160]

The second debate involved attempts to improve the quality of higher
education by requiring that students pass a test before graduating from uni-

versity. In the past, the Ministry of Education approved diplomas, and this process gave rise to allegations of corruption in diploma granting. One official at the SSAC pointed out that rectors of universities can admit foreign students—for example from Turkey, Iran, and other developing countries—and grant diplomas in exchange for fees.[161] In order to curtail corruption at this level, the Ministry of Education introduced a centralized graduation exam in 2009, which advocates have argued will help improve standards and quality of education and will prevent students from being able to buy diplomas.

Thus, debate on higher education in Azerbaijan has revolved around who controls entrance and exit to the higher education system, which confirms observations that broader structural reform of higher education will be a political challenge. These examples highlight that the debates do not necessarily revolve around learning outcomes, student achievement or the needs of the Azerbaijani labor market. Consequently, the ability of graduates of the education system in Azerbaijan to find relevant jobs and contribute to the local economy may be suffering.[162]

Conclusions

Commodity-rich countries in the post-Soviet region are different from other energy-exporting developing countries in that they gained independence with literate populations that generally had good access to primary and secondary education. Even so, Azerbaijan and Kazakhstan face common challenges in higher education reform that other post-Soviet countries confront, and they face additional perils as energy-exporting countries.

Increases in energy rents during the past decade are opening doors to financial possibilities in reforming the education systems and reorienting economies. Initial trends indicate that government expenditures have been rapidly increasing in both countries during the past decade though on certain indicators, both countries spend relatively low amounts on education in comparison with other countries. Moreover, to the extent that spending has focused on infrastructure projects such as buildings and technology as parts of the construction boom without adequate attention to linking spending to broader developmental objectives and learning outcomes, these countries face perils similar to those of other energy-rich countries. State-sponsored study abroad programs provide quality education to an increasing number of students in Kazakhstan and Azerbaijan; to the extent that their knowledge is marshaled productively either in government or in the private sector, these programs have the possibility to reshape development and education policy. Yet without considering how education spending ties into the labor market and the needs of local and regional communities, the money may not yield desired outcomes as cases of other energy-exporting countries in the Middle East and Africa highlight.

Future research could elaborate on potentially diverging trajectories of post-Soviet rentier states, including Russia. As of the mid-2000s, higher education and vocational enrollment indicators, as well as education quality assessment indicators, suggest that Kazakhstan may be faring better than Azerbaijan. Concerns about Azerbaijan in particular have focused on the widening gap between the growth of investment in infrastructure and human capital[163] and the decline in Azerbaijan's manufacturing sector: the value added from manufacturing as a percent of GDP declined in Azerbaijan from 24 percent in 1992 to 4 percent in 2008, but in Kazakhstan it increased from 9 percent to 18 percent in the same period. Finally, education and human capital policy in these countries are embedded in broader differences in the countries' institutions, social structures, and the potential amount and timing of energy exports: oil production is expected to plateau in Azerbaijan between 2008 and 2013, and in Kazakhstan between 2016 and 2023. These differences could help to explain diverging education-related expenditures and policies.[164]

Regarding the study of human capital and education reform in energy-rich countries more broadly, assessments of education quality and relevance to the labor market, in addition to education spending levels and enrollment indicators, should continue to be at the forefront of future analyses, because as this chapter has argued, education spending does not necessarily lead to beneficial outcomes for a country's development. An important component of this research could include a deeper understanding through historical and comparative case studies of the conditions under which education spending is managed effectively and results in quality education.[165] This would lead to conclusions about the prospects for policy makers and leaders to overcome institutional, social, and political constraints, thus contributing to ongoing debates about the role of human agency in shaping institutions and development outcomes.[166]

9

Is Norway Really Norway?

Ole Andreas Engen, Oluf Langhelle, and Reidar Bratvold

For many researchers in economics and political science, Norway serves as the archetypal state that has avoided the resource curse. When discussing whether a state's policies will lead it to become a successful or unsuccessful energy exporter, the common refrain is whether it would like to be "Norway or Nigeria." Hence, Norway appears to be a successful example of how it is possible to develop large-scale oil operations in a way that increases the societal wealth and benefits the whole population.

Many contemporary studies of the Norwegian oil industry focus on reasons for the absence of "Dutch disease" and why Norway lacks the structural characteristics of a "petrostate."[1] In general, the explanations have focused on Norway's "political foresight" and its ability to build a sophisticated institutional framework.[2] The country's main political objective has been to further develop the future welfare state through the revenues from the oil business and from the growth of the government pension fund. At the same time, Norway wants to attain the position as a world leader in environmental politics. Due to the tension between climate change targets, biodiversity concerns, and petroleum production, the Norwegian petroleum policy has increasingly been challenged on environmental grounds. A division of interest between the petroleum industrial complex on one hand and environmentalists on the other has emerged to become an important cleavage in the Norwegian political system. Accordingly, while Norway has succeeded in averting many of the typical traits of major oil- and natural gas-exporting states, a number of perils have also afflicted the state. Chiefly, a "petroleum industrial complex" has emerged in Norway that has significant influence on political outcomes in the state. The complex has succeeded in blocking any challenge to the predominance of fossil fuel production and consumption in Norway. Second, this complex has also succeeded in foiling many environmental policies, especially in the sphere of combating climate change.

If Norwegian oil policy appears successful in a historical perspective, it is a result of the fact that it developed within a democratic framework. In the mid-1960s, the Norwegian political system faced powerful multinational companies that were known for taking the law into their own hands wherever they operated. Multinational companies had a free rein wherever corrupted political elites secured control over the channels of wealth. In Norway, strong trade unions, community organizations, a growing environmental movement, and active public opinion contributed to give oil operations a different development trajectory. The democratic forces, however, could hardly have won out if it had not simultaneously been possible to work together with Norwegian companies and utilize Norwegian technological skills to gain the largest possible share of the Norwegian continental shelf. The basic idea of the politics and policies was to ensure that the largest possible proportion of oil revenues remained in Norway. The most important tool for achieving this goal was the establishment of the Norwegian state oil company, Statoil, in 1972.[3]

As the oil and gas fields on the Norwegian continental shelf have matured, Norwegian and foreign petroleum companies increasingly appear to working as a united front. The companies themselves and the suppliers, consultants, stock traders, and public institutions that work hand in hand with the industry have created intricate industrial networks. The privatization of Statoil in 2001, followed by the 2007 merger between Statoil and the second-largest Norwegian oil company, Hydro Oil & Gas, have further strengthened these networks that constitute dominant power constellations in the country.[4] In this chapter, we call these constellations "a petroleum industrial complex."[5] The Norwegian petroleum industry constitutes a power elite that seeks and possesses political influence on a variety of the state's policy decisions, especially those in the environmental sphere. From this perspective, the Norwegian petroleum industry no longer represents an unambiguous force for prosperity and wealth but a possible threat to a more sustainable future.

The remainder of this chapter is structured as follows. The next section provides a brief overview of the development of the petroleum industry in Norway. Then we discuss why Norway has managed to avoid the resource curse and the development trajectories that characterize typical petrostates. The second half of the chapter focuses on Norway's environmental challenges as a petroleum-producing country. Finally, we question whether the powerful oil and gas industry in Norway reduces the country's legitimacy as an environmental leader in a world increasingly concerned about man-made climate change.

The Historical Conditions

In 1962, the medium-sized oil company Phillips Petroleum Ltd. approached the Norwegian government with a request to start exploring for petroleum resources on the Norwegian continental shelf. The Norwegian authorities were taken by surprise. Based on input from the Geological Survey of Norway (NGU),[6] they did not believe in the possibility of finding petroleum. Furthermore, a judicial framework delimiting the Norwegian, British, and Danish borders in the North Sea was nonexistent.

However, the government took action quickly. From 1962 to 1965, a small group of Norwegian civil servants and key executives from oil companies such as Shell, Phillips, and Mobil negotiated and developed an institutional framework that permitted the allocation of licenses and the start of exploratory drilling. At the same time, a negotiation process with Great Britain and Denmark was launched and the dividing lines between the North Sea countries were determined.[7] The Norwegian government enacted tax and concession laws in 1965.

In 1969, Phillips Petroleum declared that it had found a giant oil field on the southern Norwegian shelf. The field was named Ekofisk and turned out to be the largest offshore petroleum field in the world. The Ekofisk discovery led to increased exploration activities and in the early 1970s, the oil company Elf discovered the Frigg field, and Statoil and Mobil discovered and developed the Statfjord field. Investment in Norway's petroleum sector increased exponentially during the 1970s—not only as a result of designing and constructing giant concrete offshore production platforms, but also because of the pipelines that connected the production in the North Sea to European markets. The first oil production began in the mid-1970s and in the first decade of the twenty-first century, Norway is the third-largest oil and gas exporter in the world.

In many respects, Norway was different from other countries that hosted international oil companies in 1960s. Its economy was well organized and heavily reliant on a number of dominant export sectors: wood, pulp, paper, fish, timber, and iron and metal products. Incomes from shipping services and energy-intensive raw materials also played an important role. Politically, Norway had a well-established democratic system based on the country's 1814 constitution. From 1945 to 1965 the social-democratic Labor party was the governing party, and economic policy was characterized by the development of the welfare state. In other words, the oil companies approached a fairly wealthy nation with a strong civil service, a well-educated population, and local industries that could serve the oil companies. Norway was in no respect comparable to the underdeveloped countries that after World War II largely were forced to host an expansive international petroleum industry.

In the first phase of the development of Norway's petroleum industry, international companies established the premises for technology transfer, but public institutions and private actors in Norway negotiated conditions that secured a foundation for "national capacities" in later stages of the industry's development. The first official Norwegian measures for an institutional capacity were composed of concession and taxation laws. The concession laws became the primary way for the state to determine which companies should be granted permission to operate in the Norwegian sector and where their operations were to be concentrated—namely, which blocks were open for tender. These laws were legally binding for all implicated parties and thereby clarified the relationship between the petroleum sector and the Norwegian state. The laws guaranteed companies' rights and simultaneously expressed the sovereignty of the state over the Norwegian area of the continental shelf.[8]

In Norway, these types of "contracts" were not unfamiliar. The main principle was largely similar to the concession system formulated some fifty years previously for the development of hydroelectricity.[9] In the case of both petroleum and hydroelectricity, state policy created incentives for integrating the industry into Norwegian society. The incentives derived partly from the concession system itself, which required foreign companies to employ Norwegian subcontractors. They also derived partly from the authority granted to Norwegian government agencies to distribute rights to the companies and entities they believed would best take Norwegian interests into consideration.[10]

During the first stage of petroleum development, Norwegian industries began to exploit the possibilities created by offshore oil and gas exploration and production. These industries comprised three groups: the engineering industries, shipping, and the only national firm of international scale—Norsk Hydro.

Norway's shipbuilding industry experienced a boom that lasted from the late 1960s into the early 1970s. During this period, the industry's design and construction techniques were transformed to emphasize sectional construction rather than the building of a complete unit from the keel up. In sectional construction, the separate sections are constructed independently and then welded together as a unit. This technique implied greater specialization at each of the yards in design and construction, enabling individual shipbuilders to develop specialized expertise and maintaining the geographically dispersed pattern of the industry. This contributed to the emergence of new groups of shipbuilders that individually executed specialized tasks and together could undertake complex construction operations, such as the building of oil rigs and production platforms.

The second group that became involved with the petroleum industry in the early years of the sector's development was Norwegian ship owners, which consisted of two groups. The first group included those individuals and companies that were already familiar with the workings of the international oil industry. In 1965, 20 percent of the world's tanker tonnage was registered in Norway. Despite the fact that the oil companies themselves transported half of the crude oil from the Near East and North Africa, it was independent shipping companies that transported most of the oil from the Persian Gulf. In other words, Norwegian ship owners were already a part of the international petroleum system and understood the rules of the game. The second group represented Norwegian financial institutions with considerable interests in Norwegian shipyards and the shipbuilding industry, a group that had significant political influence at both the local and national levels.

One of the most international of Norway's companies, Norsk Hydro (or Hydro), played a role in petroleum exploitation in Norway from its inception. Compared to the United Kingdom, Norway lacked strong actors that could play an independent role in the oil system; Hydro was the only Norwegian firm capable of such a role in Norway's embryonic oil industry. Whether the

company actually *had* this ability in the early phase has never been conclu-
sively proved. But there was limited political support for Hydro's playing a
greater role in the oil industry. Instead, the Norwegian government decided
to establish a new, fully integrated state oil company, Statoil—relegating
Norsk Hydro to a secondary role in the early years of the petroleum industry's development. Only in the later phases of the oil industry's development
in Norway did Hydro become an increasingly important participant along-
side Statoil.

To summarize, Norway's petroleum policy has undergone several phases.
In the 1960s, the country's petroleum policy was characterized by establishing institutional arrangements to attract the international oil companies
to the Norwegian shelf. After the early discoveries of petroleum in the 1970s,
the policy became more active and interventionist, symbolized through the
establishment of Statoil and a specialized public administration (to be discussed in the next section). It was officially announced that the public objective was to secure the oil rent for welfare purposes and to build a strong and
independent Norwegian petroleum competence. The petroleum industry in
Norway became a public project organized by politicians in cooperation
with international oil companies. This was indeed "a construction" that
deserves the designation "the petroleum-industrial complex."

The Norwegian Petroleum-Industrial Complex

An independent Norwegian petroleum competence grew in tandem with
high oil prices and positive resource developments on the Norwegian
shelf. In the 1970s, the institutional framework began to take shape with
the establishment of Statoil, the Norwegian Petroleum Directorate (NPD),
and the Ministry of Oil and Energy (MOE). Simultaneously, the state put a
brake on new licenses. This move was directly connected with public officials' wish to have sufficient time to develop Norwegian competence. The
concessions round in the 1980s coincided favorably with a doubling of the
oil price on international markets and gave additional impetus both for
oil companies and public officials to unite on common goals regarding
Norway's competence development and technology choices. Simultaneously,
Condeep—the large integrated concrete-based platform construction—was
manifested on the Norwegian shelf.

Statoil became the main instrument for the development of Norwegian petroleum competence. Politically, the concession system was used diligently to strengthen the company's dominance. Agreements with other companies regarding education, knowledge transfer, and technology were negotiated, and Statoil itself took the role of intermediary in delegating tasks to Norwegian industry. The company utilized traditional industrial networks and functioned as an agent transferring and adapting international petroleum techniques and competences.

This kind of government activity is fully compatible with what Michael Porter calls "infant industry policy."[11] The huge resource potential and outlook for long-term production with significant profits in Norway made the international oil companies more amenable to accepting the government's demands regarding work plans, suppliers, and measures to transfer competence to Norwegian companies and research institutes. Consequently, Norway's petroleum policy induced a gradual integration between international oil companies and Norway's governmental and industrial system. Norwegian competence was in some respects directly shaped by public policy. The development of Norwegian organizations and ambitions for public control were important elements in Norway's petroleum policy, which became a vehicle for both for job creation and regional development. In many respects, this policy succeeded in the sense that the country's regional industrial sectors were closely connected to the oil industry and deindustrialization outside the main industrial centers was thereby avoided. Thus, regional industrial policy and petroleum policy became sides of the same coin. The petroleum-industrial complex represented growth and prosperity for all.[12]

In the 1990s, the Norwegian oil industry experienced economic challenges. Negative price fluctuations appeared to be a permanent phenomenon, and it became clear that new giant discoveries were unlikely. In addition, economic liberalization was further institutionalized through the implementation of the European Economic Co-operation (EØS) agreement, which led to stronger competition for the Norwegian supplier industry. The organizational setting of the North Sea was now ready for changes, and the question was how the relevant actors in the petroleum industry would react. The cost efficiency programs of the 1990s and Statoil's growing interest in establishing a global presence indicated a new era in Norwegian petroleum history. Development of the Norwegian continental shelf was transitioning into a mature phase, and the Norwegian oil business was beginning to integrate gradually into the international network of energy producers. The Norwegian petroleum industry increasingly looked for resources to exploit in other parts of the world and also turned attention to unexploited areas on the Norwegian continental shelf: Lofoten, Vesterålen, and Barents Sea.

The Difference Between Norway and Typical Petrostates

What are the general characteristics of Norway's petroleum policy and what distinguishes these political principles from political principles in other petroleum-producing countries? A key characteristic of a petrostate is the creation of a rent-seeking elite that confiscates large amounts of the oil rent and prevents the capital flow from being reinvested and accumulated in the country's broader economy. Such rent-seeking elites may constitute oligarchies that exclude foresighted economic policy and democratic governance.

Undoubtedly, Norway's petroleum policy has been formed in accordance with the principles of the political system, but because of the importance of the petroleum sector in the Norwegian economy, the petroleum industry also constitutes an elitist power structure. The concept of the "petroleum-industrial complex" shows how networks of financial and political interests create a community between actors from the civil service and the petroleum industry that has the power to influence and sometimes determine political decisions. On one hand, the petroleum-industrial complex has been vital for the development of technical, organizational, and economical projects that are beneficial to the Norwegian economy. On the other hand, it resists and counteracts political movements and policies that challenge the petroleum economy—that is, policies intended to enforce resource management or stronger climate change policies.

The petroleum-industrial complex has strong positive connotations when it is interpreted as an effective network with abilities to organize and plan industrial programs. Scandinavian social scientists have developed a model of how the Nordic countries framed and shaped their economies during the postwar era. This concept (misleading or not) has been denoted as "the Nordic model." It refers to a number of characteristics of politics and society in the Nordic countries but is not a consistent and coherent concept. However, it has been applied to explain the economic and social development of the Scandinavian countries, with an emphasis on some specific national characteristics in explaining economic success.[13]

From a petroleum-industrial point of view, the Nordic model refers to specific ways of organizing production offshore, chief among them the notion that the industry has to accept the same rules of the game as the rest of Norway's industries. This had two fundamental consequences. First, it meant that the average wage level among employees in the petroleum industry to some extent correlated with the average wage level in the rest of the economy. Second, it harmonized the workplace environment. The working conditions offshore were subjected to the same legal framework as the working conditions onshore. The Environmental Act in 1977 gave employees in Norway extended privileges in general and became a powerful instrument for offshore workers in terms of influencing security and safety regulations. A safety deputy, for instance, had the same power as the platform manager to stop the production stream if there was any suspicion of technical or organizational irregularities that could increase the risk of undesirable incidents.

Thus from a more general perspective, the Nordic model refers to a high degree of formalized industrial relations. This implies a centralized organizational structure but at the same time a trinity of cooperation among employers, employees, and the government concerning economic policy, exchange of information, and consultations at different levels of the industry. Such institutional integration also supported a national system organizing the collective negotiations between employers and employees and moreover contributed to the institutionalization of oil companies according to the formal and informal rules of the Norwegian institutional setting. The early decision to divide the power among the MOE, the NPD, and Statoil was essential for the egalitarian and democratic aspects of the companies. In many so-called petrostates, the state oil company (for example, Aramco in Saudi Arabia) grants concessions, approves plans, and collects taxes (while not paying taxes itself), thus completely controlling the petroleum sector.

The Nordic model is further characterized by institutional frameworks organizing and regulating negotiations, wealth distribution, and conflict resolution. Conflicts between parties are solved through extensive laws and systems of agreements. Historically speaking, the Nordic model implied that employers supported unions and their professional activities to a certain degree. Moreover, employers have several times been forced to deemphasize short-term profit goals to advance longer-term managerial objectives. The success of this policy may be explained by the strength of the unions in national and local political processes. From this perspective, we may say that the Nordic model has functioned as a stabilizing factor in Norwegian politics and society. It has formed and shaped the political strategies concerning how to balance a growing resource economy with other economic sectors, how to find balance between the public and private sector, and finally how to consider challenges created by the fact that petroleum is a nonrenewable and exhaustible resource.

With respect to economic policies, Norway has been different from other petrostates in two important ways. First, the prevailing institutional framework in Norway helped to better integrate the international oil industry into the existing industrial structure, created channels for technological transfer and national competence upheaval, and laid the foundation for a Norwegian oil industry that is able to compete in the international arena. Second, the political system has to a certain extent managed to contain itself in order to allocate rents over time and restrict the overspending of a public fortune. The concession policies have, at least to some extent, prevented an excessive petroleum depletion rate, and the main objective of the country's petroleum fund is to prevent politicians from spending too much money for the purpose of being reelected.

Economically speaking, the petroleum industry is the largest single item of the National Account and also an important driver for the industrial structure particularly along Norway's western coast. About 100,000 people are employed in the petroleum industry, and considering that Norway's work force is about 1.5 million people, the significance of the sector is obvious. Other factors are the sunk costs, technological competence, and research activities connected to the oil system. Many of the engineers educated in Norway today have hopes for a future in the oil business. Energy research in Norway is also closely connected to the oil system. About 90 percent of the country's energy-related research focuses on oil and gas. Only a small part of such research money is earmarked for new renewable energy forms.

During the late 1990s, oil and gas companies alone funded 12 percent of Norway's total research and development (R&D) expenditures. The government also supports R&D for the industry through the Norwegian Research Council. Research funded by these organizations has focused almost completely on offshore petroleum production and in recent years has concentrated on improved petroleum recovery, drilling, subsea production, integrated operations, and the like. Although this research has been tremendously successful in the sense that petroleum recovery in Norway is among the best in the world, the competence and facilities necessary for such research (that is, laboratories and test facilities for well drilling) have marginal application in other industries. This form of research unification may thus present an obstacle to directing research toward newer alternative forms of energy.

The economic significance of petroleum production in Norway gives the petroleum-industrial complex considerable force in Norwegian politics. The petroleum industry accounts for about 15 percent of the Norwegian GDP and contributes to regional development, reduced unemployment, and economic and technological growth—factors that are all important considerations for politicians. Yet the dilemma occurs when the continued expansion of petroleum resources is in conflict with other important areas of societal development—most notably, the need to move from fossil fuels to renewable energy to secure an environmentally sustainable trajectory.

Challenging the Petroleum-Industrial Complex: National Fault Lines and Petroleum-Related Environmental Controversies

Although there has been a general agreement among Norwegian political parties on the main developments of the petroleum system, some important political fault lines have emerged and made oil and gas policies one of the most contentious and politically problematic areas in Norwegian politics. In recent years, the most important environmental disputes have revolved around the issue of climate change, the domestic use of natural gas, and the opening of new areas for oil and gas exploitation in the Lofoten areas and in the Barents Sea. At the moment, these issues are part of an ongoing political struggle in Norway that questions both the legitimacy and the future of oil and gas in a world that is increasingly concerned about man-made climate change.

Contrary to many other political issues, the division over energy issues cuts across the traditional left-right axis in Norwegian politics. Traditionally, Norway's parties were positioned as follows on a left-right axis: Socialist Left Party, Labor Party, Liberal Party, Christian People's Party, Centre Party, Conservative Party, and Progress Party. The Centre Party, however, has moved to a position closer to the Socialist Left and Labor parties and is currently in a coalition government with these two parties. However, the energy political cleavage positions the parties as follows: Socialist Left Party,

Liberal Party, Centre Party, Christian People's Party, Labor Party, Conservative Party, and Progress Party.[14]

Crosscutting cleavages on energy and environmental issues are often crucial to building sufficiently broad political coalitions to form a majority government in Norway. In many cases, cleavages on energy even divide political parties internally. The Socialist Left Party and Liberal Party have been the two strongest contenders for filling the space occupied by Green parties in many Western European countries.[15] This political cleavage on energy has played out in all three major environmental disputes regarding oil and gas in Norway.

The Labor Party has played a significant role in building and shaping the Norwegian petroleum industry. The party was the architect behind the establishment of Statoil and also supported policies protecting the domestic petroleum industry during the 1970s and 1980s. It also induced the deregulation of the 1990s and the cost-efficiency programs and internationalization strategies for Norwegian companies. This petroleum policy has largely been accepted by the Conservative Party and the Progress Party. This support from the largest political parties in Norway gives the petroleum-industrial complex additional force. Environmentalists in all political camps have found it difficult to challenge the petroleum economy though many Norwegians see the paradox in expanding petroleum production when there is reasonably broad consensus that at least some global warming is caused by the burning of fossil fuels.

Climate Change

Climate change was placed on Norway's national political agenda in 1987 with the publication of the World Commission on Environment and Development report *Our Common Future*.[16] The commission was lead by Norwegian Prime Minister Gro Harlem Brundtland. In 1989, Norway became the first country in the world to set a stabilization target for carbon dioxide (CO_2) emissions. The goal was to stabilize CO_2 emissions at the 1989 level by 2000.

It soon became apparent, however, that this target not only would be extremely difficult to achieve, but also would be very costly for several reasons. First, Norway's energy structure, with virtually 100 percent of its electricity demand met by hydroelectric power, implied that reduction of greenhouse gas (GHG) emissions would have to be made in other sectors. Second, because of the availability of cheap electricity, Norway had become a major producer of aluminum, steel, methane, cement, and concrete. These industries were also exempted from the carbon tax introduced in 1991 due to concerns over their international competitiveness. Third, emissions from the oil and gas sector were increasing, especially with the increasing production of natural gas and the use of energy to increase petroleum recovery as fields matured. All these developments made it difficult for Norway to meet its stabilization target. The sector where many European nations saw the largest potential for low-cost emissions reduction—power generation—was already emission-free in Norway in 1990.[17]

The Labor government officially abandoned Norway's emissions stabilization target in 1995. The principal justification it offered was that petroleum production was much higher than expected in the late 1980s, making it impossible to reach the stabilization target. Norway's policy dilemma, therefore, was and still is how to combine the roles of being an environmental leader and a fossil fuels exporter. The Kyoto Protocol with its flexible mechanisms—emissions trading (ET), joint implementation (JI), and the clean development mechanism (CDM)—temporarily solved the tension between growing emissions and climate change targets. Through these flexible mechanisms, Norway was able to increase domestic emissions, most notably from the petroleum sector, and still reach the national target of a 1 percent increase in GHG emissions from the 1990 base year. This approach, however, has been far from uncontroversial.

From the early 1990s to the present, Norwegian climate policy debates have been characterized by a confrontation between two conflicting views[18] that reflect the political cleavage on energy described above. The first, promoted by the environmental movement and its political allies, holds that Norway is obliged through international treaties to reduce GHG emissions within the country's borders. The other, promoted by the oil and gas industry among others, emphasizes that mitigation efforts should be introduced through international frameworks such as the Kyoto Protocol in order to be effective as well as cost efficient and that the balance between domestic and international action should primarily be decided by the market. The view emphasizing international implementation has consistently been supported by a political majority composed of the Conservative, Labor, and Progress parties. Still, the minority view emphasizing domestic emissions reductions, usually supported by the smaller Liberal, Christian Democratic, Centre, and

Socialist Left parties and a minority in the Labor Party including its youth branch, has remained influential.[19]

The solution to Norway's policy dilemma—how to combine the roles of being an environmental leader and a major fossil fuels exporter—has been to adapt the country's climate policies to accommodate increased oil and gas production and then justify it by arguing that this strategy makes sense from a global perspective: namely, that Norwegian gas exports make it possible for Europe to switch from coal to natural gas. So, even if Norwegian domestic emissions increase, the global emissions are reduced. This has been the petroleum-industrial complex's principal argument in Norway. Given the fact that all European countries have their own Kyoto targets—independent of Norwegian exports of natural gas—this argument is, however, highly questionable.

In 2007, negotiations in the Norwegian Parliament resulted in a political compromise on emission targets among all parties except the Progress Party. The compromise also called the "Climate Settlement" (Klimaforliket), states that Norway should be "carbon neutral" by 2030, provided that other industrial nations agree to ambitious targets. An interim target for 2020 is to reduce GHG emissions by 30 percent compared with 1990. The compromise suggests that measures within Norway may contribute as much as two-thirds of the difference between the 2020 target and a business-as-usual scenario. It was also decided to overfulfill the Kyoto Protocol emissions reduction commitments for 2008–12 by 10 percentage points (the new target is thus 9 percent under the 1990 level). This will probably be realized by buying permits abroad. There is no comprehensive plan for how Norway will reach its targets, and the affect on the petroleum industry is therefore not yet clear. What is clear is that the petroleum sector will be increasingly challenged by climate change policies.

The Oil Industry as Solver of Environmental Problems—Carbon Capture and Storage

Although climate change represents one of the main challenges for the petroleum sector in Norway, the oil industry—with Statoil as the leading company—has also become part of the solution. Norway is considered to be a pioneer in terms of Carbon Capture and Storage (CCS) policies. CCS involves three basic steps: capturing CO_2 from fossil fuel power plants or large point sources, transporting it to a suitable disposal site, and storing it over the long term. The Norwegian government is currently planning two full-scale CCS projects in Norway: at Kårstø (a gas-fueled power plant) and at Mongstad (Norway's major industrial refinery). The project at Mongstad is considered to be one of the most important instruments in Norway's climate policy. The European CO_2 Technology Centre Mongstad is currently under construction. It will be one of the world's first and largest facilities of its type.

Norway's keen interest in CCS is largely linked to the domestic conflict between climate and energy policy targets described above. In the 1990s, this conflict played out over gas-fueled power plants. In 1994, Statoil, Hydro, and Statkraft entered into an agreement of understanding to build gas-fueled power plants in Norway. The company Naturkraft was established to develop and run two power plants on the western coast of Norway. According to its promoters, gas-fueled power holds the promise of satisfying two key political goals: securing more electric power for households and energy-intensive industries and using more natural gas within Norway's borders as a way to secure industrial expansion.[20]

Initially, it was hoped that gas-fueled power might prove to be a less controversial source of increased electricity-generating capacity. Plans to expand gas-fueled power, however, were opposed by a coalition largely composed of the standard environmentalist coalition in Norwegian politics. The two gas-fueled power plants under consideration would have increased Norway's CO_2 emissions by approximately 6 percent per year, and the environmentalists saw this as unacceptable.

As early as the late 1980s, SINTEF[21] engineer Erik Lindeberg promoted CCS as a potential solution to emissions from offshore activities. CO_2 storage became operational at the Sleipner West field in 1996. At Sleipner, Statoil captures CO_2 from natural gas production in an offshore separation plant and injects it into a water-carrying sandstone formation (that is, an aquifer) nearly a kilometer below the seabed. Both large-scale capture of CO_2 on an offshore installation and CO_2 storage in a saline aquifer were tried for the first time ever in this project. It was also the first commercial-scale CO_2 capture and storage project motivated by reducing emissions (as opposed to projects aimed at producing CO_2 for enhanced oil recovery or other industrial use). The capture and storage process is still in operation and removes about one million metric tons of CO_2 annually.[22]

It was the prospect of onshore, "CO_2-free" power plants fueled with natural gas that eventually propelled CCS technology onto the center stage of

Norwegian politics. CCS technology became part of the formal rules that Naturkraft and other power plant developers had to comply with beginning in June 1997. That's when the Ministry of Oil and Energy made its final decision on Naturkraft's concession to build two power plants after formal complaints from environmental NGOs, most notably the Bellona Foundation, on the earlier decision. In April 1998, one of Naturkraft's owners, Norsk Hydro, surprised everyone by presenting competing plans for a power plant with precombustion CCS.[23] When the Norwegian Pollution Control Authority (SFT) issued Naturkraft an emissions permit in 1999 for the Kårstø plant, it demanded that the company reduce the CO_2 emissions from the project by 90 percent by using the best available technology. Despite warnings that it might cause the Kjell Magne Bondevik government to resign, the majority in the Parliament instructed the government to change the CO_2 emissions guidelines for Naturkraft's power plants. As a direct result of this vote, Bondevik stepped down in March 2000 and was replaced by a short-lived Labor government, which soon gave the necessary permits for CO_2 emissions to the planned gas-fueled power plants.[24]

In the fall of 2006, another gas-fueled power project nearly caused the red-green coalition (consisting of the Labor Party, Socialist Left Party, and the Centre Party) to break up. Statoil's plans for a major upgrade of its refinery at Mongstad in western Norway included a new gas-fueled co-generation facility that would deliver power and heat to the refinery and some additional power to the grid. On one hand, energy integration with the refinery would ensure energy efficiency. On the other hand, the plans for the refinery represented a major new source of CO_2 emissions, and the red-green coalition's platform demanded that new gas-fuelled power should be "based on" CCS.

Simultaneous negotiations among the three governing parties and between Statoil and the government about the timing and stringency of CCS requirements—a process that brought the red-green coalition to the brink of breaking up—concluded with a two-step plan. First, Statoil, the Norwegian government, and an international consortium of energy companies would build a test center for CO_2 capture technologies at Mongstad, operative from 2010 (later postponed to 2011). Second, the government would fund full-scale postcombustion capture of CO_2 from the co-generation plant. Statoil would contribute a sum equal to its alternative emissions costs and assume some risk in case of cost overruns.

To stress the potential importance of improved carbon capture technologies, Norway's Prime Minister Jens Stoltenberg characterized the testing and later full-scale deployment of these technologies at Mongstad as Norway's "moon landing project." This grandiose characterization was used in a newspaper story on October 21, 2006, and again in Stoltenberg's televised New Year's speech on January 1, 2007. Setbacks and news about similar initiatives abroad have led to mocking references to the "belly landing" and "crowded conditions on the moon" from the opposition and various commentators. CCS was supposed to be operative at Mongstad in 2014 but has now been postponed to 2018. The postponing led to increased tensions both within government and between the governing coalition and opposition in Parliament. But the project remains very important for the red-green coalition government headed by Stoltenberg (from the Labor Party).[25] The red-green coalition will govern Norway at least until the election in 2013.

In our view, CCS has a moderating effect on the antagonism against the petroleum-industrial complex in Norway. In fact, CCS has served as political glue among different parties in government and made it possible to transcend the political cleavage over energy and facilitate the formation of government coalitions. The potential of CCS has also made it more politically acceptable to utilize natural gas resources domestically, thus meeting the desires of industry, labor unions, and regional entities without compromising national climate change goals. It has also given the petroleum industry in Norway an important role in GHG mitigation and to some extent increased its legitimacy in relation to climate change. The future development of CCS, including the two CCS projects in Norway, face a host of uncertainties in terms of costs and wide-scale deployment.[26] But most importantly, CCS does not fundamentally challenge the petroleum economy in Norway.

The Creator of Environmental Problems: Opening New Areas for Oil and Gas Exploitation

Although domestic use of natural gas is still controversial in Norway, the issue of whether to open new areas for oil and gas exploration—especially the Lofoten area but also the Barents Sea—is undoubtedly an even more contentious question. It has caused divisions within the current coalition government, consisting of the Labor Party, the Socialist Left Party, and the Centre Party. The Socialist Left Party will probably leave the coalition government if Lofoten and Vesterålen are opened, but the Centre Party's response would be less certain.

The Norwegian Petroleum Directorate has estimated that the Barents Sea and the area outside Lofoten may hold 35 percent of the country's undiscovered oil and gas. This is estimated to be 1,215 million Sm^3 oil equivalents in total, with 485 million Sm^3 as liquid and 730 million Sm^3 as gas. This estimate does not include the area of overlapping claims between Russia and Norway, a disputed area finally resolved on April 24, 2010, after 40 years of negotiations. The maritime delimitation line between Russia and Norway divides the overall disputed area of about 175,000 square kilometers into two parts of approximately equal size. The news of the agreed delimitation in the Barents Sea and the Arctic Ocean was met with enthusiasm by the oil industry as it promised new areas for future exploitation.

Lofoten and Vesterålen are special, however, for several reasons. The oil and gas companies have called these areas the "middle rib steak," and Statoil has argued that there is oil and gas worth NOK 1,500 billion in these areas. Given these circumstances, oil companies have for years tried to get access to and explore these areas, but the political cleavages on this issue have made a final decision impossible. At the same time, oil production in Norway has peaked. The new discoveries are smaller and the reserves replacement rate is declining. On the other hand, natural gas production is expected to increase in the next five years. From representing approximately 30 percent of Norway's petroleum production in 2005, gas production is likely to increase and may eventually represent more than 50 percent of total production by 2014.

Exploration in the Barents Sea has yielded some petroleum discoveries but much fewer than expected. One project is the Snøhvit gas field, northwest of Hammerfest, a city in the county of Finnmark. The project is currently under development and involves subsea-completed wells, a process plant for gas liquefaction (LNG), and a closed system for separating and reinjecting the carbon dioxide into the reservoir. The field started producing in 2007. Another commercial oil field is Goliat, where the production license processing was planned to begin in 2007. The field started up in 2009 and the offshore activities will take place in 2011, 2012, and 2013. Still, it is recognized that most of the resources are on the Russian side of the sea, and the resource potential in the formerly disputed areas of the Barents Sea and the Arctic Ocean is largely unknown.[27]

In 2002, the Norwegian Parliament decided that the government should prepare an Integrated Management Plan (IMP) for the Barents Sea. Parliament approved the Integrated Management of the Marine Environment for the Barents Sea and the Sea Areas off the Lofoten Islands on March 31, 2006. Under the plan, the Lofoten area and the northern Barents Sea remain closed to petroleum activities, and this includes the area around Bear Island, waters farther north, the Tromsø Patch, and the edge of the pack ice. An additional 50 kilometer-wide zone from Troms II and east along the coast of Finnmark would also be protected. The exceptions are where exploration activities have already started and already announced development blocks in the area, which range from 35 to 50 kilometers off the coast.[28] However, the Soria Moria II Declaration, which is the founding document of the present government, states that Lofoten and Vesterålen (Nordland VI, Nordland VII, and Troms II) will not be opened under the current Parliament, implying that it is postponed to after the next elections in 2013. The impact assessment of Lofoten and Vesterålen was further postponed in 2011, but other areas in the Norwegian Sea and Barent Sea were opened up for exploration instead. For the time being it seems that Lofoten and Vesterålen will be protected from exploration, at least a long as the red-green coalition is in government.

The question of opening these areas for oil and gas activities touches upon a number of issues in Norwegian politics: climate change, domestic versus global emission reductions, tensions between the northern and southern parts of the country, tension between oil and gas and fish and fisheries, regional development concerns such as jobs and income, fear of oil spills resulting in loss of biological diversity, indigenous people's rights (the Sami people), the relationship to Russia in the Arctic, perceptions of the future energy mix, and when the transition to non-fossil fuel energy can and should take place.[29] These concerns are what the politicians are currently struggling with, and the petroleum-industrial complex is vigorously fighting to open these areas for exploration.

Given the petroleum-industrial complex's political clout, it is unlikely that the Lofoten area (and the Barents Sea) will remain closed to petroleum exploration. The temporary restrictions on Lofoten in the IMP will be a major source of political controversy in the years to come, and the outcomes of these battles will be settled partially through the elections—which determine the composition of Parliament and possible government coalitions—and partially by the mobilization of interest groups, among them the petroleum-industrial complex. Thus, even people in the Ministry of the Environment do not believe that the management plan would prevent development if a major discovery were made in one of the contested areas. The increasing scarcity of oil and gas resources and the global competition to get hold of them, increasing oil prices, increasing global demand, and a real worry about security of energy supply all pull in the direction of the opening of new areas for development.[30]

Conclusions

The petroleum industry has had—and still has—a significant impact on the Norwegian economy and society. As a result of historical conditions, political abilities, and a capacity to build up independent and competitive technical competencies, Norway avoided the economic traits of a typical petrostate. The success story is confirmed by the fact that the country is among the top economies in all UN and OECD rankings of the world's prosperous economies. The petroleum industry has brought significant wealth into the Norwegian society.

However, the petroleum industry constitutes a substantial power in Norwegian politics, and this has mixed consequences. On one hand, these actors are of crucial importance in developing a petroleum industry that is efficient and vital and has the capacity to develop further in international energy markets. On the other hand, they resist any proposal that fundamentally challenges the petroleum economy and the continued production and consumption of fossil fuels. The conflict between environmentalists and the oil industry in Norway has also been won by the petroleum industry; the petroleum-industrial complex has managed to defeat most opposition, including opposition stemming from political parties in the new red-green coalition. Alternatively, the fact that the political cleavage over energy cuts across the traditional left–right axis in Norwegian politics has given the environmentalists more influence than they would otherwise have.

A sustainable development trajectory and the outcome of Norway's climate change policies will be heavily influenced by the power relations between the petroleum industry and parts of the political system, a network of vested interests that constitutes the petroleum-industrial complex. This complex argues that technology and technological development will make it possible to produce petroleum with minimal environmental costs. The environmentalists argue against petroleum production, but production is only part of the problem. Even more important is the *consumption* of oil and gas, and as long as the petroleum industry gets access to new areas, petroleum will be both produced and consumed.

Although there is reason to believe that technological arguments will overcome environmental opposition to petroleum development and that arguments about regional development will play an important role, climate change represents an important caveat for fossil fuels. The technological and economic gravity and the politically embedded Norwegian petroleum complex give the environmental movement little room to maneuver despite its influence. From a democratic point of view, we may thus say that there are elements that may justify arguments that Norway is developing in the direction of a petrostate—not in the traditional sense but in the sense that its primary interest lies in the continued production and consumption of fossil fuels. Petroleum politics in Norway are part of a democratically based political system. Some actors and interests, however, have more influence and political clout than others, and Norway's oil and gas industry represents one such powerful and vested interest. Petroleum secures revenues for the state and politicians, protects the welfare state, and places Norway in a financial situation quite different from most other European countries.

PART III

Energy Exporters in the International
Political System

10

Energy Exporters and the International Energy Agency

Richard Jones

The International Energy Agency (IEA) was established in 1974.[1] The creation of the IEA followed the 1973–74 oil crisis and was a firm and effective response to this challenge. At its establishment, the IEA encompassed the major oil-importing states and aimed to limit oil exporters' potential economic and political power.

In the years since that crisis, the IEA has protected the interests of energy importers. IEA member states and other oil importers have taken a number of steps that provide them with important counterweights to exporters' ability to disrupt energy markets. One of the most effective measures at the organization's disposal is strategic stocks of oil. These reserves have limited oil importers' potential vulnerability to supply disruptions and thus undermine exporters' potential power.

In contrast to the prevailing perceptions of the 1970s, energy exporters possess limited international economic and political leverage for a number of reasons. First, energy exporters' longer-term interests ultimately depend on the economic prosperity of their customers. This became obvious in the early 1980s when recession in the West hit oil demand and undermined energy prices just as alternative energy sources began to come on stream, further contributing to the reduction of long-term demand for oil. Second, many oil producers recognize they share common interests with oil consumers, such as stable energy markets and investment in new production, and do not want to use their energy wealth to promote political goals and thus endanger cooperation with consumers. Many today have significant economic and financial investments in consuming countries. Third, producers are not a united bloc. Today, more than 60 percent of global oil production comes from states that are not members of OPEC. Even OPEC itself is far from a united entity, as its member states possess very different priorities. Some states, such as Iran and Venezuela, have large populations and a short-term need for higher revenues, yet others take a longer view. Next, most OPEC members recognize that extended high oil prices lead to investments in other forms of energy—coal, gas, nuclear, and renewable energy—that can lead to a permanent reduction in the demand for oil. Thus, extended high oil prices serve as a peril for both exporters and importers of oil. Last, energy exporters worry about "security of demand," especially when faced with concerns about global climate change policies. Many of them realize that they will not obtain continued investment or increased global demand for oil solely by coordinating with other producers. Cooperation between energy exporters and importers can lead to an improved situation for both sides.

The Founding of the IEA

The full-scale energy crisis in autumn 1973 and the perceived threat from OPEC led importing countries to form the International Energy Agency, which undertook the task of ensuring the energy security of oil-importing nations. According to the treaty that led to its founding, the IEA has executive authority to handle major oil supply emergencies. Subsequently, in contrast to the crisis atmosphere of the 1970s, oil exporters have come to understand that the degree to which they can achieve political ends by disrupting oil supply is limited.

OPEC was established in 1960 by five founding members—Iran, Iraq, Kuwait, Saudi Arabia, and Venezuela—to protect energy exporters' interests in what was still a buyers' market. These countries understood they needed to maximize returns on their depleting asset and develop their economies. At the same time, they recognized that they also had an interest in preserving stable energy markets and economic growth among oil-importing countries. Consumers were dependent on their oil, but OPEC members had become equally dependent on the revenue oil exports generated for them. At that time, oil dominated international energy trade, and OPEC countries dominated trade in oil. By the mid-1970s, OPEC had expanded to include Algeria, Ecuador, Gabon, Indonesia, Libya, Nigeria, Qatar, and the United Arab Emirates, and the organization's members exported more than 70 percent of all internationally traded oil.

The selective oil embargo imposed by the Organization of Arab Petroleum Exporting Countries (OAPEC)[2] at the height of the October 1973 Arab-Israeli War presented oil-importing nations with a problem they quickly realized they did not have the institutional structures to handle. So it is not surprising that the IEA was set up as an autonomous body within the framework of the OECD in Paris. Western policy makers normally discussed the industrialized world's energy problems in the OECD Energy Committee. But the OECD lacked adequate powers to handle the crisis that presented itself in 1973, and some countries felt the organization was much too bureaucratic to take on an action-oriented, operational role during a crisis. The energy sector, including major international oil companies, experienced no-holds-barred commercial competition among the industrialized countries. Although commercial competition would always remain part of the picture, a new level of political cooperation was required.

The 1973–74 energy crisis had not come out of the blue but had been building for much of the previous decade. OECD member countries were aware that they had allowed themselves to become highly dependent on imported oil and had not been able to forge a common energy security policy. Second, the oil exporters had—by founding OPEC in 1960—established an organization dedicated to the coordination of oil policy, and industrialized countries were interested in creating a similar institutional capacity to keep this challenge in check.

As former U.S. Secretary of State Dr. Henry Kissinger observed at the time, the energy crisis "is not simply a product of the Arab-Israeli War; it is the inevitable consequence of the explosive growth of worldwide demand outrunning the incentives for supply."[3] Between 1950 and 1973, oil consumption among OECD states had risen fivefold and their oil imports had risen tenfold. OECD import dependency had reached well over 90 percent; even the richly oil-endowed United States of America had begun to import oil by the early 1970s. Oil became a sellers' market, which put pressure on international oil companies to concede price setting to the producer governments and, in some cases, to eventually accept nationalization of their assets. Meanwhile, OECD governments had done little to establish oil-sharing arrangements: there were no serious programs to promote energy efficiency, and there were no plans for diversification away from oil toward coal, natural gas, or nuclear power.

Emergency oil sharing, energy efficiency, and diversification would become three of the IEA's main themes. The agency developed a comprehensive policy to improve global energy security and protect the interests of energy importing states. The IEA's basic aims, still the same today as when the organization was founded, are:

- Maintaining and improving systems for coping with oil supply disruptions;
- Promoting rational energy policies in a global context through cooperative relations with non-member countries, industry, and international organizations;
- Operating a permanent information system on the international oil market;
- Improving the world's energy supply and demand structure by developing alternative energy sources and increasing energy efficiency; and
- Assisting in the integration of environmental and energy policies.

Dealing with Volatile Markets and Price Shocks

The IEA has succeeded in protecting energy-importing countries and thus has limited somewhat exporters' potential power advantage. One of the IEA's most formidable tools is that its member countries are required to hold or control strategic stocks of oil equal to ninety days of the country's net imports from the previous year. In a crisis, these countries must make these stocks available upon a decision of the IEA's Governing Board. These stocks have been formally activated twice in IEA history—in response to the Gulf War in 1991 and Hurricane Katrina in 2005. (Individual IEA Member countries have more often used their own strategic stocks to overcome a domestic supply disruption.) On a number of other occasions, preparations were made to use the collective stocks, but there was not an acute need to actually activate the plans. These emergency arrangements have proven their worth on several important occasions. Sometimes, even the warning that these reserves might be activated had a calming effect on the market or encouraged exporters to increase production.

Since the IEA was founded, its members have also viewed high prices as an energy security concern, because of the economic damage resulting from them. In addition to the obligation to maintain emergency stocks and coordinate their use, the IEA has developed various policies and emergency procedures to deal with different supply disruptions and avert steep oil price increases. Just after the energy-importing states thought they had overcome the challenge of the unprecedented price rises of the early 1970s, oil supply was hit again with a "Second Oil Shock" due to the Iranian Revolution. The collapse of the shah's regime in Iran at the end of 1978 led to a breakdown in Iranian oil production. Prior to this crisis, IEA member countries had agreed that an overall 7 percent oil supply shortfall was the "trigger" for an emergency oil-sharing response. Although the volume of production that was lost in Iran was not enough to trigger the IEA's Emergency Sharing System (ESS), the uncertainty prompted a scramble for oil cargoes, and prices rose very sharply. In response, IEA member countries instituted a period of 5 percent demand restraint, which calmed markets somewhat.

Both energy exporters and the IEA were very conscious that supplies could be disrupted or the market destabilized by chance events, and the IEA maintains a state of readiness to avert these problems. For example, when armed conflict between Iraq and Iran erupted in September 1980, more than four million barrels per day (mbd) of supply were shut out of the market. But with a combination of 5 percent demand restraint in IEA countries and the indication of a willingness to allow member countries' strategic stocks to fall below 90 days, the IEA was able to avoid a panic. In addition, other Gulf states raised their production to compensate for the shortfall in Iraq's production, and Iran was able to sustain a good level of exports from points farther south along the Gulf, out of the range of Iraqi warplanes. As the war dragged on into the mid-1980s, Iraq was able to export oil via new pipelines through Turkey and Saudi Arabia, which allowed Iraqi exports to return to almost prewar levels. When tanker traffic in the Gulf was threatened toward the end of the war, consumer countries and oil-exporting states collaborated to maintain freedom of navigation in a way that seemed unlikely only a decade before.

By the time the next crisis emerged a few years later, just prior to the 1991 Gulf War, the IEA had developed more flexible crisis management systems. After Saddam Hussein's forces occupied Kuwait in August 1990, the United Nations imposed within two days an embargo on all exports of oil from Iraq and Kuwait.[4] This meant that 4.3 mbd of supply were removed from international markets. But other Gulf producers (notably Saudi Arabia) were helpful in quickly announcing production increases that helped fill the gap. The formal IEA ESS was not invoked in this case, but knowledge of its availability helped calm markets.

Oil prices remained relatively high while the crisis unfolded because the risk of a wider war was never far away. But major producers and consumers were working together to resolve the crisis and restore Kuwait's sovereignty. In January 1991, on the eve of the UN deadline for Iraq to withdraw from Kuwait, the IEA had agreed on a contingency plan for drawing on 2.5 mbd of emergency stock if it proved necessary. On January 28, the IEA Governing Board decided that the plan would be implemented flexibly, according to supply and demand developments. Seventeen OECD member countries[5] made oil stocks available according to their national situations. This was transparent to both the energy exporters and the energy markets and had the desired effect of maintaining orderly markets and stable prices. The emergency response policy, developed over a number of years, had proved its value.

The IEA's emergency response policy has shown its value not only during political crises, but also during natural disasters such as Hurricane Katrina and Hurricane Rita. Supply stocks were activated in 2005 to mitigate the impact of those crises. In addition, during the 2008 hurricane season in the Gulf of Mexico, a brief statement from an IEA official on preparedness helped calm jittery markets.

Adapting to Change on Both Sides

Since the 1970s oil crises, a number of developments have emerged that illustrate the perils energy exporters face from the instability of oil exports. First, oil price spikes have led to a long-term decline in the rate of growth in global oil demand. Second, many energy exporters invest a large portion of their revenues in industrialized Western countries. When global recession hits as a result of high oil prices, these oil exporters take a loss on many of their investments. Third, OPEC members have not maintained discipline in their production policies. Fourth, the relative portion of oil in global energy consumption has declined significantly since the 1970s with natural gas use expanding rapidly.

The "Second Oil Shock" of 1979 did serious damage to Western economies but was more perilous for energy exporters in the long run because the ensuing recession led to a reduction in global oil consumption. Global demand slid to 56 mbd, and world trade in oil fell to no more than 24.2 mbd by 1985. In 1986, prices collapsed to less than $10 a barrel.[6]

At the same time that the global recession led to a drop in demand for oil, many of the energy saving measures introduced in the 1970s began to have an effect, leading to further slowing of demand growth. In addition, a number of major nuclear power programs in industrialized countries, which had been under development since the 1960s, began to reach completion. By 1986, nuclear power generation among OECD countries was ten times what it had been in 1971. This would have a permanent effect on global demand for oil. Lastly, the high prices of the 1970s had spurred a good deal of new oil production among IEA member countries themselves—including from completely new oil basins in the North Sea and Alaska. By 1984, total OPEC exports had fallen below 12 mbd from a peak of 27 mbd in 1977. The damage to Western economies affected exporters' economies as well. During the 1970s and 1980s, many OPEC countries made substantial investments in Western financial markets and industries, and these faltered in the global recession.

In the global energy consumption picture, oil's overall importance has declined since the 1970s and will likely continue to do so, giving way to other energy sources, especially natural gas. A number of the world's major producers of coal and natural gas are not OPEC members. The top-three natural gas exporters (Russia, Norway, and Canada) are not OPEC members, and Canada and Norway are IEA members.[7] The world's top coal exporters (Australia, Indonesia,[8] and Russia) are not OPEC members, and Australia is a member of the IEA.

The fall of the Berlin Wall in 1989 and the collapse of the Soviet Union in 1991 also led to significant developments that affected relations between energy exporters and importers. A number of major oil producers that are not members of OPEC—Russia, Azerbaijan, and Kazakhstan—emerged following the Soviet breakup. Russia is the second-largest producer of oil in the world and the largest overall producer of energy. Unlike most of the Middle East oil exporters, post-Soviet producers have welcomed foreign direct investment. In addition, a number of new exporters in the Atlantic basin— particularly Angola and Equatorial Guinea—added to the diversity of oil exporters. Angola is very open to foreign direct investment and cooperation with importers.[9]

The fall in global oil demand in the early 1980s led to a breakdown in the OPEC quota system. As demand for OPEC oil weakened, only Saudi Arabia was sticking to the cartel's price structure, with disastrous results for the country's oil production.

At the same time, the IEA has become stronger over the years with the addition of new members. Since the organization was formed in 1974, a number of other OECD states have joined, including Australia, Greece, New Zealand, and Portugal. Finland and France—which had initially stayed out of the IEA—joined the IEA's emergency planning process for the Kuwait crisis and subsequently entered the organization in 1992. Also, a number of major energy exporters are members of the IEA, including Norway, Canada and Australia (LNG and coal).

The composition of the oil demand side of the world economy, however, is changing. The bulk of rising demand for oil has shifted from IEA members to Asian countries, with China and India taking the lead. The IEA is aware of the significance of this change and has expanded its cooperation with China and India and other nonmember consumers in Asia to continue representing oil-importing countries' interests.

Toward a Real Producer-Consumer Dialogue

In the 1990s, the IEA began to engage intensively in a producer-consumer dialogue on energy trends, recognizing that both sides need security of supply and demand.[10] Seeking ways to ensure adequate investment in the oil sector has been an important strand in IEA thinking since the very beginning. Medium-term investment requirements were on the agenda of the IEA's very first producer-consumer experts meeting in 1992. The aim of the 1994 Energy Charter Treaty, an initiative of the European Union, was promoting and protecting investment. The IEA is a strong supporter, and continues to maintain that free and open energy trade is the best way of allocating resources.

The IEA has been engaged in a number of consumer-producer dialogue meetings to work on issues of mutual interest. In July 1991, the French and Venezuelan governments hosted a "Seminar for Oil Producing and Consuming Countries" in Paris. This was the first ministerial-level conference bringing representatives of producer and consumer states together. Topics for discussion included oil markets, energy policies, industrial cooperation, and the environment. It was agreed in advance that price management and production questions were to be avoided.

The Spanish government, in collaboration with Algeria and Mexico, hosted the third ministerial-level producer-consumer meeting in Cartagena in 1994. More than thirty countries and a number of international organizations attended the meeting, and it represented the first in a series of biennial, ministerial-level meetings that was recognized by the end of the 1990s as the International Energy Forum. The seventh meeting, held in Riyadh in 2000, was the first to be officially called an International Energy Forum (IEF), and saw Crown Prince Abdullah of Saudi Arabia call for the establishment of a permanent International Energy Forum Secretariat based in Riyadh. This proposal was endorsed at the subsequent forum in Osaka (Japan) in 2002 and put in place by the end of 2003. Biennial IEF meetings continue today.

During this period, it had become customary for the IEA and OPEC to host working groups of experts, providing a framework for technical-level exchanges and a way to prepare for IEF ministerial sessions. The 1999 Experts Meeting in Paris focused on the implications of the Kyoto Protocol and on the consequences of the serious oil price declines of 1998. The subsequent meeting in Abu Dhabi in 2002 attracted 130 participants and concentrated on developments in natural gas markets.

IEA Relations with Energy Exporters in the Twenty-First Century

The IEA has widened the spheres of its activity in its mission to promote energy security. A number of risks still exist, but today there is a better appreciation of the extent to which these risks also affect energy exporters.

The IEA remains committed to maintaining the oil emergency response system it has developed over the past thirty-five years. The importance of regular supply and stable prices are recognized on all sides, and the IEA emergency response mechanism is no longer seen as confrontational. Oil will continue to be a vital commodity in international trade. With the balance of proven oil reserves in the Middle East, it is clear that global oil trade remains exposed to a measure of risk. Every day, Gulf countries export 17 million barrels of oil. Moreover, 10 mbd of Gulf oil flows to Asia, nearly half to China and other Southeast Asian destinations such as Thailand and Singapore, which are not IEA member countries. In recent years, advice and training on oil emergency procedures and stockholding systems have become an important element of IEA engagement with non-member countries.

Another new problem that may affect IEA relations with producer countries is the growing importance of natural gas in the global energy supply. When large volumes of gas must be piped through one or more transit countries en route to customers, there is inevitably a risk of supply disruptions. This was highlighted in January 2009 when a financial dispute between Russia and Ukraine shut down gas supplies to many Russian gas customers in central and southeast Europe. This crisis raised a number of issues that are currently under examination in IEA circles.

Recent years have also seen a number of oil-producing countries take a more protectionist attitude toward natural resources. Foreign investment in the energy sector remains politically controversial in OPEC countries such as Kuwait and Iraq, even as their governments seek to attract foreign companies into production. Investment terms in Algeria and Libya have also become more restrictive, though foreign companies have generally done very well in exploration and production in both countries. The civil war in Libya in 2011 and the unrest in the region in this period raise questions about the continued stability and can affect investment in the energy sectors. Russia is also generally considered to have become less welcoming for foreign investors despite the huge resources it has to offer.

Investment is a two-way street, of course. Many producer states have a long record of investment in energy distribution (downstream) in Western markets. Kuwait's Q8 gasoline stations were for many years recognizable in the United Kingdom and continental Europe. Since 1990, Petroleos de Venezuela (PDVSA) has owned 100 percent of Citgo Petroleum Corporation in the United States refining and distribution sector. More recently, a number of producer countries have invested in new joint venture refineries in their more significant markets. For example, Kuwait has invested in a Vietnamese refinery, Saudi Arabia has invested in Chinese refinery capacity, and Algeria has invested in re-gasification facilities in the United States. Many of the new investment funds in the Gulf such as Taqa (the Abu Dhabi National Energy Company) have invested in upstream foreign markets, too. Taqa has now assumed operatorship of the United Kingdom's Brent pipeline system. It is also establishing, in partnership with Gazprom (Russia's largest energy company), the Bergermeer gas storage facility in the Netherlands, one of the largest in Europe. It is important to encourage investment in both directions and avoid raising concerns that security could be used as a justification for protectionism.

Recent discussions between producers and consumers have focused on the possibilities of more collaboration between major international oil companies and producer states' national oil companies (NOCs). There are clearly synergies available: oil majors possess advanced technology perfected in the development of more challenging oil deposits worldwide; the NOCs still have substantial reserves but are beginning to face more challenging geology, too. Recent initiatives by Chevron in the Kuwait/Saudi neutral zone, by ConocoPhillips in Abu Dhabi, and by Occidental and BP in Oman show that such collaboration can be very effective. The IEA has never acted as the champion of Western oil companies, which energetically compete against one another around the world every day. But promoting advanced technology to optimize oil-field recovery rates and minimize environmental damage reflects IEA principles that are in the interest of producers and consumers alike. This is, and will continue to be, an important and fruitful area of the producer-consumer relationship.

Major energy-exporting countries are not shy about articulating their own concerns. The Riyadh Declaration at the third OPEC summit in November 2007 noted that the discussions had centered on three areas: stability of global energy markets, energy for sustainable development, and energy and environment. The first of these areas highlights a problem that will get worse before it gets better. The sophisticated commodity markets that evolved in the 1980s cannot be uninvented and, in many ways, make an important contribution to economic growth and welfare by providing capital to the energy sector and helping energy-intensive industries hedge their risks. Markets are still mainly driven by supply and demand fundamentals, but large capital inflows from speculative funds can accentuate their movements. Whether such flows have been a major cause of recent volatility—and what might be done about it—is still the subject of expert inquiries and political speeches. Suffice it to say that although the understanding of this problem may vary among producers and consumers, all parties have a common interest in maintaining stable international energy markets and are very conscious of the damage large price swings can cause for economies everywhere.

We Are All Consumers Now

One of the factors encouraging this increasing confluence of interests is that today many major energy exporters are also major energy consumers. The 2008 edition of *World Energy Outlook* highlighted the important role the Middle East is now playing in the growth of world demand for energy; it is

surpassed only by China and India. In the states of the Gulf Cooperation
Council, electricity demand is expected to grow by 45,000 megawatts by
2015—equivalent to 45 billion cubic meters per year of gas feedstock. Libya
and Algeria are important gas exporters but are also launching large-scale
electricity and water desalination programs that will consume a large share
of future production. Demand for gas in Iran is rising by 8 to 10 percent per
year. In most energy-exporting countries, domestic fuel prices are heavily
subsidized (see Chapter 4 in this volume). The combination of these subsidies, growing populations, and industrial policies designed to create employment by diversifying economies away from raw materials is a recipe for
alarmingly rapid growth in demand for energy. Regardless of environmental concerns—which are significant—the economic imperative to find ways
of restraining demand and improving energy efficiency is now as strong, or
perhaps even stronger, among the energy exporters than it is in the mature
economies of the OECD.

Producers, of course, have other concerns, too. Although formally accepting the need to curb carbon emissions, they have also warned that when
the world engages in production of expensive alternative energy technologies it reduces the capital available for investment in the huge oil and gas
sectors. In the longer term, both oil and gas exporters share the concern that
pressure to maximize development of low-carbon energy or at least minimize imports of hydrocarbons will eventually leave some exporters saddled
with unused capacity. This is a well-rehearsed concern for producers: that
security of supply for consumers should be matched by security of demand
for exporters. The IEA believes that the best response to this concern is greater
transparency in well-functioning energy markets, which can balance global
energy supply and demand efficiently.

11

Resource Nationalism and Oil Development:
Profit or Peril?

Amy M. Jaffe

The beginning of the twenty-first century was marked by a return to resource nationalism and empowerment of national oil companies that is transforming international relations among major nations and affecting the supply and price of oil. Resource nationalism finds its roots in the ideology that the natural resources of a country belong to the nation and exist as a national patrimony and consequently should be used for the benefit of the nation as a whole and not be exploited for private gain.[1] The reemergence of resource nationalism has large implications for future oil exploration trends and for the role of foreign direct investment in propelling new supplies to market in a timely fashion in the coming decade.

During the next thirty years, $5 trillion in new investments will be needed in the global oil sector to meet rising world demand for oil, according to estimates by the International Energy Agency.[2] The IEA notes in its 2009 World Energy Outlook that as a result of the global financial crisis and related credit crunch, national oil companies (NOCs) have reduced upstream spending by 7 percent in 2009 compared to 2008, and the largest international oil companies (IOCs) have held spending relatively flat.[3] But despite the tremendous capital requirements that will be needed to meet future world oil demand, many governments continue to intervene in national oil sectors in a manner that is slowing or even discouraging needed investment.

Populist trends driven by resource nationalism mean that in many of the most prolific and promising regions for oil resource development, the private sector firms in the best position to amass the capital required to make major risky and long-term investments are being denied access to make them. At the same time, financial and bureaucratic constraints are blocking national governments from making these investments themselves. Some national oil companies such as Mexico's Pemex must turn over such a high proportion of revenue to their federal governments that they cannot undertake sufficient spending in exploration and development. To the extent that national governments force state-owned oil companies to meet socio-economic obligations, such as income redistribution, over-employment, and fuel price subsidization, this means the national oil sectors have fewer incentives and retained revenues for reinvestment in reserve replacement and sustained exploration as well as oil field expansion and development.[4] The role of fuel subsidies has been particularly crippling in oil sectors in countries as diverse as Nigeria, Iran, Indonesia, India, and Venezuela.

The list of NOCs with falling or stagnant oil production in recent years is long. Production has been affected by civil unrest, government interference, corruption, inefficiency, and the large diversion of corporate NOC capital to social welfare. Moreover, violent and nonviolent social movements in major energy-producing nations are raising the costs of investment, disrupting exploration and production, and generally interfering with the flow of primary commodities. This is especially true in Africa where some local communities are resisting oil development on environmental and social justice grounds and where violence by rebel groups has hindered oil development and exports. In Latin America, hypermobilized social movements have also created new political risks, which have in turn had negative consequences for international investment and have also curtailed energy supplies in the region. In the Middle East, resource nationalist sentiment among populations and rulers alike has blocked or slowed investment in a number of countries including Kuwait, Iraq, and Iran.

This chapter will examine the impact of resource nationalism on oil exploration and development trends in key oil producing regions and the consequences for global energy security and future supply. As will be discussed in the chapter, resource nationalism is constraining the timely development of new oil and natural gas resources and therefore could lead to a shortfall of needed future oil supplies for the global economy in the coming decades. Ironically, it will also hurt the prospects for sustained economic development in resource-holding countries and create challenges and perils for future political stability and social justice in those nations.

Economic Rents in Oil and the Roots of Resource Nationalism

For most oil producing countries, the cost of finding, developing, and producing oil is significantly below prevailing market prices. The difference is a windfall gain often referred to as the "economic rent." Throughout the history of the oil industry, the struggle to divide the profits from this economic rent has been fraught with peril.

During the 1940s and 1950s, most of the world's oil was owned and produced by private oil companies that garnered most of the economic rent for themselves. An oligopoly of international oil companies regulated supply and rent sharing in the developing world through a series of geographical market sharing agreements, the most famous of which was the "Red line" agreement. The Red line agreement of 1928 allowed five American firms to join ownership in oil assets in Iraq but included a self-denying clause forcing the companies to act in concert in the Middle East oil development and preventing them from acting unilaterally outside the "red line" limit demarcated on a map of the former Ottoman Empire. Since the majority of oil exporting countries in the Middle East, Asia, and Latin America were not industrialized at that time, they were forced to rely on these large international oil companies to mine and develop their resources. The companies, which included firms such as Standard Oil (now ExxonMobil), Anglo-Persian (now BP), and Royal Dutch Shell, shared economic rents with the host countries through a system of royalties based on a "posted" price for international crude oil that was set by the oligopoly of companies. The hosting oil-producing countries were dependent on the international firms for the production, distribution, and processing of the oil.

As a rising tide of nationalist sentiment and independence movements against European colonialism gained momentum in the post-World War II period, more oil-producing countries began to demand greater control of their national resources and a larger share of oil rents. This clamor for a larger cut of the profits eventually led to the 1960 creation of the oil producer cartel OPEC, whose mission was to garner a larger share of the profits from oil away from the international oil companies. OPEC's original members included Saudi Arabia, Iran, Iraq, Kuwait, and Venezuela. Throughout the 1960s, OPEC focused mainly on serving as an oligopolistic counterweight, providing the bargaining power to help its members wrest higher extraction taxes and a higher "posted" price from the IOCs. But as nationalist political movements took hold across the developing world, many oil-producing nations created national oil companies of their own and began the process of partial, if not outright, nationalization of oil assets in their countries.

In seeking nationalization, the oil-producing countries were influenced by a trend toward command-and-control industrialization policy and import substitution in the developing world. In addition, they also wanted to gain control of their own oil resources from foreign oil companies that were not serving the national interests of the host governments. The idea was that oil resources, controlled and run by the state, could be harnessed to achieve rapid industrialization and infrastructure development. In these cases, such as Iraq, Iran, Algeria, and Libya, NOCs were created to manage state control over the country's partially or fully nationalized oil resources and to gain higher national rents from oil production.

The process of nationalizations was, in many cases, a drawn out one because the new entities lacked funds and technical expertise. Iran's mixed experience with outright nationalization served as a warning for other countries that full nationalization could have negative economic consequences. Prime Minister Mohammed Mossadegh—soon after his election to office on a nationalist platform—moved to implement nationalization in 1951. The move, authorized by a resolution already passed by Parliament, was designed to address failed attempts by Tehran to press the British-controlled Anglo-Iranian Oil Company to increase production and revenue. The move backfired, however, and Iranian oil was subsequently embargoed by the British, leaving the fledgling Iranian government with sinking national revenues and severe economic turmoil. In 1954, Iran was forced to set up a foreign consortium to run the oil industry, and this went on for many years.

The case of Iraq was representative of subsequent efforts at nationalization. Iraq established the Iraqi National Oil Company (INOC) in 1964 as a fully government-run state entity to develop oil concession areas taken over from the international oil majors who constituted the Iraq Petroleum Consortium (IPC). But it was not until the mid-1970s that INOC actually took over any Iraqi oil fields. In the early period of nationalization, INOC was given the exclusive rights to develop Iraq's untapped, undeveloped oil reserves, leaving the international companies to continue to manage the country's existing oil production.

In August 19, 1967, in the aftermath of nationalist sentiment following the Arab-Israeli War, Law 97 was passed to transfer the rights to develop Iraq's huge Rumaila field to INOC. But the progress of INOC in this endeavor did not really take hold until 1968 when the Soviet Union agreed to provide technical assistance worth $140 million for the development of Iraq's national industry. By 1970, INOC began drilling oil at Rumaila in commercial quantities with Soviet financial and technical assistance. By 1975, eleven years after INOC was established, the ruling socialist Baath party of Iraq nationalized all of Iraq's oil industry, turning it over to INOC amid new production from the Iraqi-run Rumaila field. The USSR backed Iraq's nationalization and offered a treaty to protect the Iraqi government from any possible intervention by a foreign power on behalf of the international oil company interests.[5]

Nationalization in Saudi Arabia and the Arabian Peninsula was even more drawn out. For the most part, Saudi Arabia pursued an incremental approach to the nationalization of Aramco, the international consortium that owned the concessions to Saudi oil. The kingdom began by taking a minority stake in Aramco's ownership, which was followed by gradual increases in that stake as well as training and placement of Saudi nationals into key management positions.[6]

As national oil companies increased their hold on domestic oil industries during the 1970s and 1980s, the challenge for governments has been to separate the economic rent accruing from resource ownership from the true economic cost of developing oil resources (including the return on investments by the government) and the opportunity cost of the money that might be spent developing the oil as opposed to other kinds of investments. In addition, oil-producing governments have had to decide how to allocate the accrued economic rent within society, which has fueled tensions (in some countries to the point of violence) among competing stakeholders. Figure 11.1 illustrates the breakdown of classes of costs/revenues for a typical $50 a barrel oil field development. The diagram shows that the cost of capital must be deducted from revenues before calculating the economic rent.

For NOCs in countries with no private oil company participation, the return on investment in the firm by the national oil company is often treated by governments as revenue that can be siphoned off for discretionary use. In countries where direct foreign investment is allowed, investment terms must be negotiated to split the economic rents between the host oil-producing

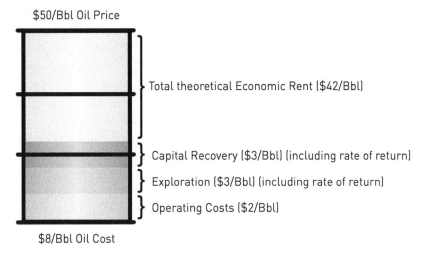

Figure 11.1 Typical breakdown of costs.

government and the international oil company offering investment capital. For developing countries with needs for large amounts of capital, foreign direct investment is one way that the country can increase total investment and hopefully enhance development prospects without sacrificing other government spending requirements. By having foreign companies develop the country's natural resources, the government can spend its revenues on other kinds of investment, including socially oriented investments that would not be likely to be financed by foreign investors. Private investors must be compensated for risk taking so the distribution of revenues will reflect the allocation of risk between private investors and the government. The less risk the direct investor takes in undertaking exploration and development activities, the less the national government will have to share a portion of the economic rent. However, if the investor is absorbing a high level of risk, it will expect a commensurate share of the economic rent. So, for example, in Azerbaijan where investors were facing high geological risk, great distance from markets (Azerbaijan is a landlocked state), and lack of long-established political institutions and governance tradition, higher returns were required to investors than in, say, Abu Dhabi, which has more stable government institutions, existing export infrastructure, and attractive, prolific geology.

Generally speaking, there are three kinds of foreign direct investment contracts: concessions, production sharing agreements, and service contracts. Concession leasing is typically used in industrialized countries where private property rights are firmly established and title to the oil is not subject to arguments that subsoil rights are protected as national patrimony under provisions of a national constitution. Under a concession agreement, the investor receives legal title to the oil and gas, and the state is shielded from all risk, instead collecting fixed royalties and taxes but leaving the investor with the windfall if oil prices rise significantly over the life of the investment. This kind of contract has been widely used in the United States, the United Kingdom, and Australia.

A second kind of contract, production sharing contracts (PSAs), is the most common form of contract where the state and private direct investors share both the economic rents and the investment risk equally. PSAs include terms that allow the host government to take an increased share of the economic rent as oil production rates increase and to get a larger share over time as cumulative targets for revenues and volumes for the projects are reached. Thus, typically under production sharing agreements, the more profitable the venture, the higher the return will eventually be to the host government, but the government also shares in the risks of project costs and long-term oil prices along with the investor. Legal title to the oil and gas remains with the state, and the contractor receives the right to share in ongoing production. Many PSAs have provisions that allow the investor to recover its costs of exploration, development, and operations before the profits from the project are distributed.

Finally, some oil producing countries, especially those with a history of prior nationalization of the industry from the 1950s through the 1970s, have favored offering service contracts where the government retains full ownership of the oil and investors do not share in any economic rent. Rather, investors receive a "fee" for their "services" with payment often linked to the volume of hydrocarbons produced or discovered. These "fee for service" contracts specify a particular type and amount of work to be performed under a field development plan, leaving the government not only with all economic rents, but also with the fullest extent of market and price risk. In the case where there is high cost risk exposure for the development of hydrocarbon resources, a "cost-plus" service contract is sometimes employed where contractors/investors are ensured a fixed profit payment, typically linked to unit production performance.

Within these different contracting structures, the fiscal terms vary from country to country, making some places more attractive to direct foreign investment than others. One of the key variables in the competitiveness of fiscal terms offered to investors is the intensity of resource nationalism present within a country's population and political leadership. In countries where resource patrimony is high, such as Mexico or Bolivia, it can be difficult to fashion any kind of contract open to foreign direct investment. In countries where resource nationalism is localized because indigenous local populations are dissatisfied with their regional share of economic rents, such as Nigeria, internationally competitive fiscal terms might be able to be offered, but local conflict and violence can disrupt ongoing activities of foreign operators. Finally, there have been other cases where resource nationalism was fueled by changing market circumstances as oil-producing countries gained a stronger geopolitical hand in tightening oil markets. In this climate of rising oil prices, some host countries such as Russia and Venezuela sought to wrest back a higher share of the economic rents from existing investors, in certain cases, which led to renationalization of assets back to state control. Oil producers' tendency to harden fiscal and contracts terms or restrict access to foreign direct investment in their resources was clearly demonstrated during the extreme price shock period from 2003 to 2008, and studies show that weaker, less transparent governments are more likely to nationalize resources when prices are high.[7]

As this chapter will discuss, the end result of all three such manifestations of resource nationalism has been a reversal of fortunes, where the country's production profile shifts from a positive growth path to a declining output trend.

Resource Nationalism Defined

Resource nationalism relates to the ideology that the natural resources of a country belong to the nation and exist as a national patrimony and consequently should be used for the benefit of the nation as a whole and not be exploited for private gain. In many countries, a legal basis lays the groundwork for resource nationalism. Through a constitutional provision, subsurface land laws, or a national natural resources or oil law, it is established that natural resources in the ground or under the sea are the property of the nation rather than of the individual who owns the surface land area. For example, in 1938 in Mexico, President Lazaro Cardenas declared that all mineral and oil reserves within Mexico belonged to the government. Mexico's constitution bars foreign participation under Article 27, which reads, "In the case of petroleum, and solid, liquid, or gaseous hydrocarbons no concessions or contracts will be granted nor may those that have been granted continue, and the Nation shall carry the exploitation of these products, in accordance with the provisions indicated in the respective regulatory law."[8] This is in contrast, for example, to the United States where property rights communicate ownership of subsurface resources on private land and where the state or federal government can "lease" its rights to private firms for natural resource development.

During the period between 2003 and 2008 as strong economic growth, especially in the emerging Asian economies, strengthened the position of commodity sellers worldwide, resource nationalism again rose around the world as efforts were taken in many resource-rich nations to use hotly contested bids for sources of oil to garner larger geostrategic or economic gains.

Countries such as Nigeria, Kazakhstan, and Venezuela tightened terms for foreign investors to favor higher shares for the national oil company or higher royalties to be paid to the federal government. In the case of Venezuela, President Hugo Chavez gave notice to foreign oil companies in the spring of 2007 that they had until June 26 to reduce their ownership in Venezuelan Orinoco Belt heavy oil field projects to give the state at least a 60 percent ownership share. As a result, U.S. companies ConocoPhillips and ExxonMobil withdrew from ventures in Venezuela, actions that eventually led to a decline in Venezuelan oil production rates. American company investment was eventually replaced by investment by Chinese and Russian companies who were willing to pay higher rates for entry, driven partly by geopolitical concerns. In a different kind of example that was more geostrategic in nature, in 2006, the Russian government cut off natural gas supplies to the Ukraine, reportedly to increase prices, but the net effect was highly political. The move effectively shifted internal politics and rearranged elective coalitions in Kiev, which led to a turn away from the pro-NATO, anti-Moscow candidate Viktor Yushchenko and toward a governing coalition more to Moscow's liking.

Indeed, the most notable cases of resource nationalism that took place during the upward cycle of the 2000s were those of Venezuela and Russia. As Ian Bremmer and Robert Johnson note in their 2009 *Survival* article:

Both exemplify revolutionary resource nationalism, which is linked to broader political and social upheaval, not merely directed at the natural resource sector. In Russia, this encompasses the broader re-consolidation of state power under the Putin Presidency beginning in 2000 and the larger rollback of privatization in strategic sectors. In Venezuela, oil resource nationalism was an important feature of the "Bolivarian Revolution" in which political and economic power was transferred under the Chavez presidency from the technocratic business class to the poorer segment of the population.[9]

During the second term of his presidency, Vladimir Putin implemented a wave of consolidations in Russia's oil industry that was designed to reassert state control over the Russian oil sector in effect to both reallocate resource rents back to the Kremlin and reduce the political power of privately owned oil firms in Russia. With resource nationalism as a popular backdrop, the Kremlin tapped prosecutions of tax "problems" or "environmental investigations" of privately held firms, including foreign firms, to force renegotiation of fiscal regimes or even to force strategic mergers that shifted control of assets to Russia's two state-controlled energy giants, Rosneft and Gazprom. The cozy relationship between the Kremlin and its state-owned firms such as Gazprom meant that the state could pursue prosecutions of foreign investors as a means to force foreign firms to cut in Russian NOCs as a hedge against losing the entire investment. As a result, many foreign oil companies have either withdrawn from Russia or greatly reduced their exploration and development spending there. Like in Venezuela, this nationalist policy has led to a drop in investment in Russian oil and natural gas exploration, thwarting rises in hydrocarbon output.

The consolidation frenzy of the Kremlin directly and dramatically impacted foreign direct investors. TNK-BP, which owned the license to develop the East Siberian Kovykta natural gas field through its acquisition of RUSIA Petroleum,[10] was forced to sign over its rights to Gazprom in 2007 after Rosprirodnadzor, Russia's state-owned environmental protection agency, launched an investigation against it. The agency maintained that since the company extracted 33 million cubic meters—instead of 9 Bcm, or 272 times less than originally planned—its license should be forfeited. From its perspective, TNK-BP's delay in extraction rates was related to its inability to finalize an export route for the natural gas, which in turn related back to

Russian foreign policy. But in the end, TNK-BP realized its only option was to sell its stake to Gazprom because practically speaking, it would never be able to develop or monetize the field in any other manner.

For the Sakhalin Island investors, Royal Dutch Shell wound up halving its 55 percent stake in Sakhalin-2 to 27.5 percent, with Gazprom buying in to take a controlling government majority share, again in the aftermath of a battle with Rosprirodnadzor, which was seeking $30 billion in fines or threatening to take away the foreign consortium's development license.[11] The revision of financial arrangements for Sakhalin-2 was a clear example of Russia revising the terms of a PSA that had previously favored foreign investors in light of changing leverage in a higher oil price environment.[12] The move reflected the state's insistence on controlling strategic export projects, and Gazprom asserted itself into Sakhalin-1 as well by effectively preventing investor ExxonMobil from marketing the output from Sakhalin-1 to China and announcing that all the natural gas from the project needed to be sold directly to Gazprom.[13]

The end result of the Putin reign has been that many of the privatizations of the 1990s have been undone. Whereas before Putin came to office, a vast majority of Russia's reserves were privately held, now nearly half are again under state control.[14] By the same token, state intervention did not bode well for production trends. As the industry was privatizing, production recovered from a low of 6 million in the mid-1990s to a high of 9.9 million b/d in October 2007. Russian production had slipped to an average of 9.6 million b/d by the autumn of 2009.

The case of Hugo Chavez in Venezuela's climb to power has similar circumstances. In the 1990s, prior to Chavez's rise to power, Venezuela opened its doors to foreign direct investment with a target to increase output from 2.5 million barrels in a day in 1990 to close to 7 million b/d by 2010. To achieve this goal, the Venezuelan government reopened the country's nationalized and monopolized petroleum sector to international investment via association agreements to rehabilitate old fields as well as some projects involving untapped fields not previously in production. Venezuela utilized an "operating service contract," which granted operating rights to foreign companies for marginal fields and gave the foreign contractor a cash fee per barrel of oil produced.[15] With the combination of higher capital expenditures by state company PDVSA and the foreign contracts, Venezuela progressively upped its production so that by mid-1997, the country's production capacity had increased to 3.7 million b/d against its OPEC quota of 2.3 million b/d.

After the election of Hugo Chavez in 1998, the Venezuelan populist leader began to implement policies that would transfer more of the economic rent to the Venezuelan state, and this was accompanied by resource nationalism public rhetoric. First, under Chavez, Venezuela raised taxes and royalties. Then Venezuela announced that all private sector companies had to convert their operating contracts into joint venture agreements that made PDVSA the majority shareholder. A new hydrocarbons law was passed that gave the government financial and operative control (that is, more than 50 percent) of all operational and strategic association agreements. The new framework granted the government "no less than 83 percent of the value created by upstream projects."[16] As discussed above, during this renegotiation process several international firms, including ExxonMobil, Total, and ConocoPhillips, chose to liquidate their stakes rather than accept the less attractive terms imposed by Venezuela.

The exit of these foreign firms, combined with the reduction in incentives for remaining foreign investors to increase the level of their investment in Venezuelan fields, has hurt Venezuelan production trends. Third-party production, after peaking in April 2005 at 1.25 million b/d, has been declining and averaged only 875,000 b/d in 2006. Combined with a sharp decline rate in fields operated by PDVSA, Venezuelan production overall has dipped to close to 2 million b/d, down well over 1.5 million b/d since Chavez took office.

Some cases are less extreme than those of Russia and Venezuela, where control and ownership structures were revised. Instead, renegotiations involve less ambitious restructurings of rents through a larger stake or greater fiscal take for the host government, but they fall short of regaining control of the venture. Such was the case with Kazakhstan, which sought more returns for its state firm Kazmunaigaz.[17] In Algeria, a stiffening of contract terms included a new windfall profits tax on upstream operations by foreign operators. These kinds of changes have smaller long-term impacts on the production profile of the oil producing country; they bring a delay to investment instead of more debilitating cancellations of upstream plans.

One of the major emerging challenges of resource nationalism is coming from a new more localized source of discontent. In Africa and Latin America, there have been an increasing number of claims by indigenous tribes that subsoil rights belong to them, not to the nation. Indigenous movements in Latin America are advocating for redress of 500 years of exploitation by colonial and national governments with the assistance of nongovernmental organizations (NGOs) from the U.S. and Europe. In countries such as Bolivia and to a lesser extent Ecuador, the lingering tensions between indigenous and national rights have negatively impacted exploration and production activity.[18]

In the Niger Delta of Nigeria, violent conflicts have developed in recent years resulting from "the exclusion of the local communities from participating in the exploitation and benefits of the resources."[19] The violence in the region has at various times in recent years shut down exports from the region and is certainly restraining future investment rates by foreign companies. In 2002, Nigeria set its sights on increasing oil production to 4 million b/d with the help of increases in foreign direct investment. But violence in the Niger Delta has curbed the country's production rates, with monthly output in 2009 ranging from a low of 1.51 million b/d in August to a recovery to 1.7 million b/d by October. About two-thirds of Royal Dutch Shell's production fields in Nigeria or about 800,000 b/d were closed in November 2009.[20] Infrastructure in the region has been heavily damaged by the fighting.

There is growing evidence that intrastate competition among subnational groups/militias inside oil-producing countries has led to violence and civil war, with internal attacks motivated by parties wishing to get control of resource rents. The examples of such conflict involve many oil states such as Colombia, Nigeria, Indonesia, Iraq, and Angola. But these conflicts also have other underlying causes related to ethnic unrest, religious divisions, failed institutions of government, social inequality, and criminality and lawlessness. Again, rising oil prices may have contributed to the trend by giving a greater incentive to subnational groups to gain international attention by attacking energy facilities, not only to gain control of oil, but also to further wider political aims.

Internal civil war or conflict over resource rents will undoubtedly be an emerging challenge to global oil supply, as has already been seen with temporary supply cutoffs from Indonesia and Nigeria. As author Michael Ross notes, although the world has become more peaceful now than it was fifteen years ago, with the number of major civil wars dropping dramatically, there has been no similar drop in the number of conflicts in countries that produce oil. Oil-producing states now contain over a third of the world's internal conflicts, up from only one-fifth in 1992. As new countries such as Congo, Chad, Mauritania, Namibia, Cambodia, East Timor, and Vietnam become oil producers in the coming years, the prospects to manage a sudden influx of oil wealth look dim given the weak governance structures in many of these nations. Oil wealth often helps support insurgencies by giving rebels the opportunity to steal and smuggle oil or to extort money from foreign oil companies operating in regions distant from the central government. It can also invite separatism from localized groups who feel secession would leave them in control of the oil (and the related economic rents) under the ground where they live. Such conflict can be seen in Bolivia, Indonesia (such as in Aceh), Iraq (in Kurdish regions), Nigeria, and Sudan.

Some analysts, such as Bremmer, argue that resource nationalism will subside in the event of a moderate oil price correction, such as seen in the second half of 2008. Faced with lower oil revenues and rising social pressures, Venezuela's Chavez, for example, launched a new bidding round for foreign direct investment in the oil-rich Orinoco Belt in late 2008 in a sign that he was being forced to be more practical than ideological to stay in power.[21] Iraq is also increasing the number of new oil-for-fee service agreements with international companies and has declared a desire to increase production to over 10 million b/d during the next six years with foreign assistance. The Iraqi oil ministry has awarded twelve technical service contracts to IOCs since re-opening its upstream doors to foreign firms. Eleven contract awards resulted from the two 2009 crude licensing rounds,[22] while Baghdad had already awarded a $3 billion contract to Chinese state firm China National Petroleum Corp. (CNPC) in November 2008 to develop the al-Ahdab field, the first major oil contract Iraq had inked with an IOC since the 2003 U.S. invasion.[23] Although Iraq conducted its first two licensing rounds—in June and December 2009—and forecast that its technical service contracts with the IOCs would increase Iraq's oil production capacity by nearly 10 million b/d by 2017 from its 2009 capacity of 2.4 million b/d, questions remain about whether all of the contract holders can actually hit plateau production goals set forth in the contracts.

Even Mexico is attempting to reform its oil industry to allow foreign participation under service contracts. But Mexico is stymied by a resource nationalist past and its underlying tenet that the commodity itself has an intrinsic value, not one determined by the market, and this value ("rents") belongs to the nation.[24] Thus, any movement toward a service contract for existing fields such as Chitequipec or for deep water exploration would have to exclude foreign oil companies from participating in any way in the upside share of the rising value of oil market prices. This might make it difficult for Mexico to develop commercial fiscal terms that are competitive internationally. Without reform to its oil sector, the outlook for Mexico's oil production is particularly dim. The country has seen its output fall from 3.2 million b/d in 2002 to about 2.6 million b/d in late 2009, as a lack of investment, mismanagement, and maturing of its oil fields have taken their toll.

Policy Frameworks to Deal with Resource Nationalism

Studies show that government-owned oil companies perform better when they have a more independent oversight structure closer to the governance of private sector firms that must respond to commercial competition and private shareholders.

One key finding of the Baker Institute study on NOCs is that the structure of governance for an NOC can have significant impact on its abilities to "focus efficiently on its core businesses" and "greatly reduce the prevalence of corruption and wasteful spending." The Baker Institute study concludes that the members of an independent corporate board of directors "play a positive role in bringing transparency and performance measures into the oversight structure of NOCs such as Statoil, Saudi Aramco, and CNOOC [Chinese National Offshore Oil Corporation]."[25] The study also finds that competition also plays a strong role in promoting best practices and that privatization or public offerings of shares can increase the efficiency of the firms. This finding is supported by research conducted by the University of Texas's Center for Energy Economics, which concludes that for commercialization goals, "upstream competition matters." The center's researchers found that "the coordination and competition among commercial players often yields the best results in activities that include many complicated decisions of a commercial and technical nature." The study also concludes that in places where NOCs compete or cooperate directly with foreign direct investors, "there was an initial strong element of knowledge transfer from foreign oil companies and supply/service companies."[26]

Christian Wolf and Michael G. Pollitt have applied a similar framework to oil companies using a much more detailed database that allows them to use some twenty-two measures of firm performance.[27] Their work also supports the idea that partial or full privatization enhances the operation of a state-owned firm: "Over a seven-year period around the initial privatization offering, return on sales increases by 3.6 percentage points, total output by 40 percent, capital expenditure by 47 percent, and employment intensity drops by 35 percent." The study demonstrates that most of the improvements in profitability and employment intensity begin to occur several years before the sale of shares but taper off afterwards. These gains occur despite the fact that the government may still hold the majority of shares and hence operating control. Significantly, Wolf and Pollitt do not find comparable efficiency gains with subsequent share sales as governments reduce their stakes in the firms. These studies have implications for policies that could increase transparency and governance and thereby the stability of investments and access to foreign direct investment in resource-rich countries.

There is no doubt that at least some of the rapid increase in world oil prices in 2007–2008 and again in 2010–2011 was the result of insufficient investment in oil-producing capacity in regions such as Latin America, the Middle East, and Africa, hindered in part by resource nationalism. In most cases, the countries in question had oil industries dominated by a national oil company.

The global community has a shared interest in seeing the promotion of good governance, social justice, and the efficient operation of oil-producing governments and their national oil companies. Data suggest that a higher level of government ownership reduces the ability of a firm to produce revenues for a given quantity of inputs.[28] For those national oil companies that access international capital markets, there are pressures to engage in more transparent accounting and financial record keeping. Offerings of IPO shares, partial privatizations, and even commercial bonds can bring NOCs into the monitoring systems of international financial markets, improving transparency, accounting and public reporting systems, and corporate governance. Once shares are publicly traded, government interference in NOC activities will damage the value of the firm's shares and thereby invite public criticism and exposure. Increased transparency is a constructive means to reduce the opportunities for corruption and other problems that can fuel conflict over rents inside an oil-producing country. Better governance can discourage a diversion of rents to a favored political group, thereby reducing the possibility of internal national conflicts that might be generated by an unfair distribution of oil rents within society. As Ross notes,[29] "A second way to limit the effects of the oil curse would be to encourage the governments of resource-rich states to be more transparent. Their national budgets are unusually opaque; this facilitates corruption and reduces public confidence in the state, two conditions that tend to breed conflict."

It seems likely that during periods when oil prices are moderating, more resource-holding governments will want to tap IPOs as a means of raising capital for investment or to retire debt. If oil prices remain relatively low for a period of time, many oil-producing countries will be under greater pressure to generate revenues to maintain social investments and services to rapidly growing populations. Borrowing money will be costly given the quantities involved and the perceived risk of government debt. Selling off part of the NOC will be seen as a politically palatable way of raising cash without sacrificing "control" over the country's patrimony.

Oil-consuming countries can also promote best practices for NOCs through existing and emerging bilateral and multilateral trade mechanisms such as the World Trade Organization, the Energy Charter, NAFTA, and other new international architectures. These would be important elements in ensuring that there is sufficient investment to meet global demand in the years and decades ahead. Michael Collier suggests in his book *The Bottom Billion* that the international community should set up a global "natural resources charter" that would set standards for the governance of resource revenues.

Multilateral discussions of trade in energy goods, though technically covered by WTO rules, could be strengthened to allow for improved global rule making on international trade and investment in oil and natural gas.[30] An opportunity to put energy more front and center to international trade talks is better today than at any time in recent years because the negative impact of extreme oil and gas price volatility in 2008 has harmed the economies of both consumer and producer nations equally, highlighting the benefits to both sides of a more stable future for global oil markets. Although oil producers may have enjoyed rising state revenues from 2004–7, the sudden collapse in oil prices in 2008–9 left state budgets and national economies in many oil-producing countries in crisis. So although producing countries might appear to have a short-term interest in unilateral pricing and investment policies, it is clear that securing more stable, long-term revenues would be preferable to the peaks and valleys seen in the last two decades. Russia's default on its sovereign debt during the oil price plunge in 1998 is but one example. The current financial problems of Venezuela and Iran are others.

International architecture that would promote adequate, steady investment in oil and natural gas resources is sorely lacking in the existing financial and global economic system. More consideration should be given as to how to remedy this deficit. Trade agreements need to seek to not only regulate fair competition within energy sectors, but also promote the conditions that will be conducive to adequate investment in upstream sectors. The

G-20's 2009 announcement of member countries' intentions to work to phase out fuel subsidies is a good example.[31] Such subsidies have had a debilitating effect on the ability of national oil companies to reinvest in new productive capabilities. The G-20 should also discuss the means for a multilateral agreement on cross investment that would guarantee removal (or even easing) of investment restrictions inside many major oil-producing countries in exchange for favorable trade terms between the industrialized countries and those oil-producing countries. Such agreements could take the form of new energy charters or treaties or adjustments to existing trade agreements and rules. Initiatives such as the United Nations Global Compact and the Extractive Industries Transparency Initiative (EITI) provide excellent examples of starting points to create new rules of international engagement for hydrocarbons investment worldwide. New international law needs to be created to guide and regulate both transnational corporate practices globally and the practices of host countries with regard to international contracts for resource investment. The United States and other major consuming countries should take a lead role in pressing debate on these important issues. All countries need to recognize that, given the bureaucratic inefficiencies and domestic political interference in oil sectors around the world, future oil resources simply might not materialize in the volumes they expect and need. The outcome will be negative for both the economies of oil-producing and oil-consuming states, and therefore the problem needs to be tackled to prevent the kind of economic dislocation seen both in 1998 in the developing world and in 2007–8 globally.

12

Natural Resources, Domestic Instability, and International Conflicts

Elnur Soltanov

The resource curse literature, which the present volume builds upon and contributes to, highlights the counterintuitively negative consequences of resource richness. This debate over the "curse of the plenty" has tied the presence of abundant resources to a myriad of undesirable consequences from weak state-society linkages[1] to authoritarian regimes,[2] to slow economic growth,[3] and the like. This chapter tries to shed light on the effects of natural resource abundance on militarized conflicts.

There have been numerous works studying the association between natural resources and domestic conflicts.[4] Several scholars also looked into the association between resources and international conflicts, though not as systematically.[5] In the current chapter I build an association between resources, domestic conflicts, and international conflicts simultaneously, tracing the path from resources to civil and then international conflicts. More concretely, I am looking at whether and how the interaction between resources and domestic disturbances brings about international conflicts. There are two broad hypotheses I propose. Either resources cause domestic conflicts that in turn bring about international ones, or, alternatively, resource-rich nations experiencing civil wars (whether because of resources or not) become involved in international military conflicts because of resources.

I do not find a statistically significant association between resources and civil wars. This naturally means the lack of empirical support for the first hypothesis. Because natural resources are not associated with domestic conflicts, they could not lead to international conflicts *through* domestic strife. But I do find empirical support for the second hypothesis. Nations that are experiencing domestic instabilities and also happen to be resource rich are more prone to international conflicts than resource-poor nations with the same domestic instabilities. To put it differently, the richer a country is in terms of hydrocarbons, the more likely it is to get involved in international disputes when experiencing domestic disturbances.

There is no shortage of anecdotal evidence that shows a resource-rich state finding itself simultaneously under the double threat of domestic and international conflicts. The military struggle for power in the Republic of Congo in 1997, for instance, which revolved around the offshore oil sector that represented 85 percent of the export revenues of the country, could be a case in point. As Philippe Le Billon observes, the conflict eventually resulted in the military intervention of the Angolan government, "eager to protect its claims over the oil-rich enclave of Cabinda and prevent the use of Congo as a platform for UNITA diamonds-for-arms deals."[6] Saddam Hussein's intervention in oil-rich Iran in 1980 while the shockwaves of the Islamic Revolution were still reverberating would easily fit into the same category. Similar examples abound.[7]

The question is how exactly do natural resources and civil wars interact in bringing about international conflicts, if at all? Is it because resources result in internal instabilities that eventually spill over their initial boundaries and become internationalized? What if resources generate an additional push for countries undergoing civil wars? That is, whether a country experiencing domestic strife (whether the natural resource variable is or is not the cause) could become more susceptible to international conflicts due to natural resources. For instance, such resources could generate an extra incentive for outsiders to intervene or make domestic governments more willing to divert their societies' attention from internal problems; in both cases the presence of valuable natural resources will increase the stakes.

I want to give a few words on what this chapter does not do. There are other theoretically plausible associations in the triangle between civil wars, natural resources, and international conflicts that are beyond the scope of the current study. For instance, it is possible that it is the interaction between resources and international wars that result in civil wars. On the other hand, though nonintuitive at first glance, civil and international wars could shrink the industrial sectors of an economy such that it could become more and more resource dependent; in other words, the causal arrow could run from wars to resource dependence. This chapter is not sorting out and testing all potential causal linkages among these three variables. The specific question is: how do natural resources and civil wars interact to bring about international conflicts, if at all? To put it in Waltzian terms with little modification, are natural resources a *permissive* (indirect) and/or an *immediate* (direct) cause of international wars?[8]

If resources result in domestic conflicts, which in turn facilitate involvement in international conflicts, resources become a permissive cause. If resources increase the likelihood of international conflicts in societies undergoing domestic conflicts by increasing the stakes for the insiders and/or the outsiders (through diversion, protection, and opportunism), then it becomes an immediate cause. It should be noted that these two causal mechanisms are not mutually exclusive. Resources could get linked to international conflicts both ways.

As referenced above, since the seminal work by Paul Collier and Anke Hoeffler,[9] numerous studies have made important contributions to our knowledge on how natural resources affect civil war.[10] Yet the relationship between natural resources and international wars has not been researched as thoroughly.[11] Studies of more complex associations between resources and international conflicts (involving civil wars, for instance) are virtually absent. The current chapter aims to fill this gap in the literature.

Literature, Theory, and Hypotheses

The first hypothesis of this chapter is built around the expectation that resource-rich states are more prone to international conflicts simply because they are more prone to domestic conflicts in the first place. The theoretical basis for this hypothesis gets its inspiration from the tax linkage phenomenon of the rentier state literature—the observation that rents that accrue from resource extraction free the state from taxing the society. This translates into the absence of a competent bureaucratic apparatus that has historically sustained the tax link between state and society. A related issue that hinders the build up of an efficient bureaucratic entity is the fact that only a small portion of the society is employed (and thus could be effectively taxed) due to the capital-intensive nature of nonrenewable resource sectors. Taxing such a small number of people does not require a powerful bureaucracy and does not justify the considerable cost of its establishment. All in all, the weak state institution eventually becomes unable to tackle society's problems and concomitant internal instabilities that ensue. In the second stage of this mechanism, states mired with domestic instabilities become predisposed to international conflicts.

The principal source of the problem is resource revenues flowing in from abroad, which, in Jacques Delacroix's words, brings about the emergence of a "distributive state," a deviation from the historical "extractive" West European state.[12] The idea is that the extractive potential of the traditional state relied on an invasive tax bureaucracy, which generated not only revenues but also crucial information about society and thus the capacity to govern the society. The lack of the incentive to collect taxes comes with the lack of the competent bureaucratic apparatus and the consequent weakness of the state institution.[13]

As Dirk Vanderwalle argues, in this situation the state becomes capable of governing simply by virtue of the rents it receives. What it needs are a few professionals who can negotiate the size of the rents with the producers. There is hardly a place for "an elaborate bureaucracy," because the multinational companies providing the rents also act as tax-collecting arms of the host governments. The same pattern applies when resource sectors are controlled by national governments. That is, when the state is the direct recipient of resource revenues it just has to control that same sector, without having to build institutions for tax collection purposes. In Vanderwalle's words, the "rentier nature of state revenue thus militates against the creation of a strong state."[14]

The second main reason that stands behind the "no significant taxation of society" argument is that natural resource industries are capital extensive, employing only a small portion of the society. Oil and coal, for example, top the list of economic sectors in terms of capital intensity.[15] Oil especially has been given a prominent position among other minerals. In Giacomo Luciani's words, "oil production is a highly automated business, in which few are employed, and a relatively high percentage of those few are specialized full-time labor. The vast majority of the population is not involved at all in oil operations."[16] With few exceptions (for example, secondary diamonds found in alluvial plains), the great majority of nonrenewable natural resources can be assessed similarly. Assuming that such sectors make up the bulk of the national income, the only taxable portion of the society would be those employed therein. Yet because there are relatively few employees clustered around few resource sites, they can hardly justify the considerable investment in a tax collecting bureaucracy.

Another point of essence in this context could be the concurrence of state formation with the emergence of nonrenewable resource sectors. As Terry Karl aptly puts it regarding "capital-deficient oil exporters," when natural resource exploitation coincides with the beginnings of modern state formation, the dynamics of production for export shape states in "fundamental ways" and give rise to "specific structures of choice, uneven capacities, and birth defects that endure long past the moment of their creation."[17] To be sure, state formation in modern history cannot be detached from the history of colonization. In fact, the first indications of weak state capacity associated with the absence of tax institutions can be traced back to the colonial period.

According to Terry Karl, due to the localized nature of revenue sources, colonies with minerals tended to have localized foreign control. This meant the absence of pre-state bureaucracies permeating the land, and this was consequently perpetuated in the postcolonial period by native rulers.[18] Daron Acemoglu and his colleagues explain the emergence of "extractive institutions" in some colonies as the alternative option to direct European settlements, that is, when colonizing communities failed to survive due to diseases.[19] All the same, they are in line with Karl in pointing to the weaknesses of these extractive institutions (once they had been established somehow) and attributing to them poor economic performance in the post-colonial period.

Only a handful of about two hundred nation-states today have not been subject to colonization. For the majority of states, colonization, state formation, and industrial-level exploitation of resource sectors have occurred simultaneously. Therefore, in most cases where the amount of resources could be considered abundant, the chances are high that the owner state experienced colonization and its resource sectors' emergence coincided with its state-building process. All in all, I argue that the nature of the resource sector combined with the legacy of colonization and state building leads to the emergence of a weak state institution.

But the weak state institution is not the outcome I am concerned with. It is significant as a determining factor of another phenomenon. One of the reasons the rentier state approach emphasizes this point is that weak governments become vulnerable and unable to effectively handle domestic, economic, and social problems.[20] James Fearon argues that states with a lot of oil revenues do not have the motivation to build "administrative competence and control throughout their territory," despite having more financing available to them.[21] Accordingly, he claims that "an empirically more plausible and internally consistent explanation" is that oil-exporting nations are more prone to civil wars because of "weaker state institutions than other countries with the same per capita income."[22]

Even if economic and social problems occurred randomly, such weak distributive states would be less capable of resolving them compared to their more powerful counterparts. But the overreliance on natural resource rents may make the former face more problems on average, overburdening their already limited capacity. For instance, the volatility of natural resource prices in the international market is known to make resource exporters vulnerable to trade shocks.[23] In addition, boom periods could destabilize the economy due to such factors as inflation, and bust periods may generate political tension by putting an end to patronage networks.[24] Combined with other effects of natural-resource dependence such as inequality, forced migration,[25] and slow economic development,[26] these factors may increase internal societal grievance and domestic instability in resource-reliant countries.

In her study of petrostates, Karl draws attention to the political turmoil that followed the oil windfall of the 1970s:

> In the earliest and most dramatic case, the Shah of Iran was overthrown in 1979 in an Islamic revolution that bitterly criticized the rapid industrialization and Westernization characteristic of his "Great Civilization." Nigeria oscillated between military and civilian rule without being able to consolidate either. One-party domination was shaken in Mexico. By the 1990s, once stable Algeria teetered on the brink of civil war, while Venezuela, Latin America's second oldest democracy, struggled desperately to preserve its competitive party system. Indeed, less than two decades after the oil price increase, all major oil-producing developing countries except Indonesia and the scarcely populated Arab nations experienced serious disorganization in their state bureaucracies and severe disruption in their political regimes.[27]

This brings us to the last leg of the argument for this section. I hypothesize that such weak states mired with instability could become susceptible to international conflict involvement. This could be driven by the domestic

Figure 12.1 Model of linkages formulated in the first hypothesis.

elite's strategy to distract domestic discontent, as elaborated in the diversionary conflict literature.[28] Alternatively, surrounding countries of these unstable nations may feel the need to protect themselves or may simply be motivated by opportunism.[29] Perhaps both of these factors were at work in the tension between Iran and Iraq following the Iranian Islamic Revolution, which eventually resulted in the war between these nations. The second point is relatively less emphasized in the literature, but there is no shortage of examples for it.

An example mentioned above regarding the intervention of the Angolan government in the internal oil-related dispute in the Republic of Congo in 1997 is relevant at this point. The Angolan government is believed to have been motivated to protect its oil-rich Cabinda enclave and prevent the instability in Congo from spilling over into its lands.[30] According to Arthur Westing, the war of unsuccessful secession by Katanga from the Democratic Republic of Congo that lasted from 1960 to 1964 was "in large part fomented by Belgian and other foreign interests so as to protect their investments in copper and other minerals."[31] The purpose of the foreign intervention does not have to be about the resources per se. It could stem from the urge to contain or end a potentially dangerous neighboring conflict. Algeria, due to the insecurities concerning its own population and its failure to economically gain from the internal conflict in Mali, placed pressure on the rebels, which, in Macartan Humphreys's words, was probably "the greatest international influence on the duration of the Mali conflict."[32] All in all, an internal dispute associated with a resource windfall may spill over a country's borders and result in increased likelihood of international involvement (see Figure 12.1). This discussion brings us to the first hypothesis:

H1: States richer in terms of natural resource endowments are more likely to be involved in international conflicts through increased domestic instabilities.

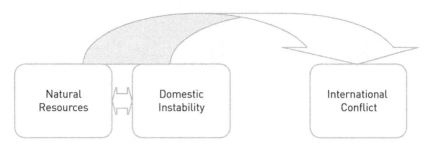

Figure 12.2 Model of linkages formulated in the second hypothesis.

Whatever the determinants of domestic instabilities are, that is, even though they are not caused by energy rents, could they still have a different effect on interstate conflicts at higher levels of energy revenues than at lower levels of energy revenues? I still expect that civil wars, without involving natural resources, are likely to expand beyond national borders and get international-ized due to diversion, protection, and opportunism (this association is going to be tested). The point is, civil wars accompanied by natural resources will increase the incentives for domestic and international actors to internation-alize domestic wars. In other words, higher energy income is expected to amplify the effect of domestic instabilities on interstate conflicts. In this situation the point is still some kind of interaction between two indepen-dent variables that makes a difference in terms of their effect on the depen-dent variable (see Figure 12.2).[33]

H2: States richer in terms of natural resource endowments are more likely to be involved in international conflicts while experiencing domestic insta-bilities than similarly unstable countries that are poorer in terms of natural resources.

Variables

The dependent variable, Force Use Onset, is taken from the Militarized In-terstate Disputes Dataset.[34] Force Use Onset includes only militarized inter-state disputes that involve the use of force. All incidents within the use of force category share the "commonality of active military operation." There is a tangible impact on a target whenever force is used; "blockades, clashes, occupation of territory, all, by the nature of the action, have a direct effect on the receiving state."[35]

Kirk Hamilton and Michael Clemens created the primary energy data used in this study, which is annually updated by the World Bank.[36] Ross refers to it as one of the best measures available.[37] The main independent variable, Energy Rent, "covers crude oil, natural gas, and coal" and is measured as the percentage of GNI. Unit resource rents are calculated by subtracting the extraction cost of each commodity for each producing country from its global prices.

There are several additional factors that are theoretically relevant as controls. This study's models include five that tend to be in common use in the related literature: Democracy, Trade, Level of Income, Economic Growth, and Domestic Instability. Democracy is Polity2 from the Polity IV project.[38] All three economic variables, Trade (percentage of GDP), Level of Income (GDP per capita in constant 2000 $US),[39] and Economic Growth (annual percentage), are taken from the World Development Indicators dataset of the World Bank (2006). Domestic Instability is Arthur Banks's Conflict Index, generated from a combination of assassinations, general strikes, guerrilla warfare, government crises, purges, riots, revolutions, and antigovernment demonstrations.[40]

Empirical Tests

The first hypothesis of this chapter, to repeat, is that natural resources are correlated with international conflicts not only because they may exert a direct effect upon them, but also because they cause changes in the intervening factor, which is domestic instability in this case, and the intervening factor in turn affects the likelihood of military disputes. Theoretically, the correlations between all factors must be positive. That is, more resource revenues are supposed to give rise to more intense domestic instabilities, and more of the latter are expected to increase the odds of interstate conflict involvement.

Although political science literature has been relatively indifferent to the mechanisms inherent to the intervening effect, other disciplines have shown considerable interest and made useful improvements.[41] I use one of the most relevant and widely used approaches to test for the presence of this effect—the Causal Steps approach. It specifies a series of tests of linkages in a causal network.[42] In this approach there are three basic chains and four requirements for finding support for the presence of an intervening variable: the main independent variable must be correlated with the dependent variable; the same main independent variable must be correlated with the intervening variable; controlling for the main independent variable, the intervening variable must still be correlated with the dependent variable; and lastly, in the case of complete intervention/mediation, the association between the independent and dependent variables is expected to disappear, and if there is only a partial mediation, the correlation is expected to diminish. There are a number of works that utilize the Causal Steps approach to an extent.[43] I will try to apply all the criteria of the approach (four) before drawing conclusions.[44]

Regression analysis indicates that states with an abundance of fuels are more likely to get involved in interstate conflicts compared to their poorer counterparts (see Table 12.1, column 1). This finding is in line with the general intuition and expectations in the related literature.[45]

Table 12.2, column 1 replicates Table 12.1 with a restricted number of cases; Energy Rent is still positively and significantly associated with Force Use Onset. The first requirement of the Causal Steps is fulfilled. Then I add the theorized intervening variable, Domestic Instability (see column 2 in Table 12.2). In the Causal Steps approach the added intervening variable itself is supposed to be significant vis-à-vis the dependent variable. This second condition, too, is satisfied. The third requirement is either a complete disappearance of or a reduction in the value and significance of the Energy Rent coefficient after the addition of the intervening variable. This requirement is not fulfilled. The fourth requirement is whether the main independent variable is a significant determinant of the hypothesized intervening variable. In Table 12.3, the energy variable fails to be a positive determinant of domestic conflicts. Thus, two of criteria of the Causal Steps approach are not fulfilled, which means that there is no indirect effect between energy resources and international conflicts through the domestic conflict link. The first hypothesis is rejected.

At this point Luciani's observation about two decades ago deserves attention. According to him the lack of association between resources and domestic instability could be related to the "state's ability to buy legitimacy through allocation" with even limited revenue from abroad, which would

Table 12.1 Energy Rent and Force Use Onset:
Interactive Test 1

DV: Force Use Onset	
Energy Rent$_{(t-1)}$	0.014***
	(0.005)
Trade$_{(t-1)}$	−0.006**
	(0.003)
Level of Income$_{(t-1)}$	−0.019
	(0.136)
Economic Growth$_{(t-1)}$	−0.002
	(0.008)
Democracy$_{(t-1)}$	−0.007
	(0.010)
Peace years	−0.331***
	(0.116)
Constant	−0.629***
	(0.191)
Observations	3,511
Countries	144
Model Chi^2	89.68
ROC area	0.7470

Standard errors in parentheses.
* significant at 10%; ** significant at 5%;
*** significant at 1%.

Table 12.2 Energy Rent and Force Use Onset: Interactive Test 2

DV: Force Use Onset	(1)	(2)
Energy Rent$_{(t-1)}$	0.011**	0.012***
	(0.004)	(0.004)
Domestic Instability$_{(t-1)}$		0.040***
		(0.014)
Peace years	−0.291**	−0.295**
	(0.120)	(0.119)
Constant	−1.139***	−1.195***
	(0.147)	(0.147)
Observations	3,456	3,456
Countries	144	144
Model Chi^2	54.79	74.06
ROC area	0.7393	0.7464

Standard errors in parentheses.
* significant at 10%; ** significant at 5%; *** significant at 1%.

Table 12.3 Energy Rent and Force Use Onset:
Interactive Test 3

DV: Domestic Instability	(1)
Energy Rent$_{(t-1)}$	−0.0001
	(0.009)
Constant	1.344***
	(0.144)
Observations	3,476
Countries	144
Model Chi^2	0.001

Standard errors in parentheses.
* significant at 10%; ** significant at 5%;
***significant at 1%.

dramatically increase regime stability. It is no surprise, argues Luciani, that "Iraq since the early seventies and Algeria almost since independence have had remarkably stable power structures." The major exception is Iran of 1979. But in the case of Iran "the Shah was more preoccupied with promoting aggressive industrialization, even at the cost of exacerbating class conflict, than with buying political support." His religious successors have not done much regarding democratization, "but their concoction of populism, Islamic revival, and appropriate use of oil money to buy consensus at the retail level seems to be working quite a bit better than most observers expected."[46]

Benjamin Smith, too, does not find an empirical association between oil and domestic instabilities. His point is vindicated here.[47] Moreover, this finding is in concordance with the increasing number of challenges qualifying the explanatory potential of natural resources in the civil war literature.[48] When I use alternative methods, namely the Product of Coefficients approach and the path analysis, the non-finding is repeated regarding the intervening effect of domestic conflicts (not reported).

As Table 12.1 shows, higher levels of domestic instability do increase the likelihood of international conflicts. Yet it became clear that such instabilities are caused by factors other than energy revenues. Hence a conclusion was made that Domestic Instability does not qualify as an intervening variable between Energy Rent and Force Use Onset. But this does not rule out that this variable's effect on interstate conflicts is still conditional on increased levels

Table 12.4 Energy Rent and Force Use Onset: Multiplicative Regressions

DV: Force Use Onset	(1)	(2)
Energy Rent$_{(t-1)}$	0.014***	0.010**
	(0.005)	(0.005)
Domestic Instability$_{(t-1)}$	0.040***	0.022
	(0.014)	(0.016)
Energy Rent x Domestic Instability$_{(t-1)}$		0.004**
		(0.002)
Trade$_{(t-1)}$	−0.006**	−0.007***
	(0.003)	(0.003)
Level of Income$_{(t-1)}$	0.002	0.027
	(0.135)	(0.132)
Economic Growth$_{(t-1)}$	0.005	0.006
	(0.008)	(0.008)
Democracy$_{(t-1)}$	−0.008	−0.009
	(0.010)	(0.010)
Peace years	−0.298**	−0.286**
	(0.116)	(0.115)
Constant	−0.771***	−0.754***
	(0.187)	(0.188)
Observations	3,456	3,456
Countries	144	144
Model Chi^2	98.63	117.96
ROC area	0.7531	0.7536

Standard errors in parentheses.
* significant at 10%; ** significant at 5%; *** significant at 1%.

of Energy Rent. Table 12.4 displays models that test for the multiplicative effect, or the second hypothesis.

Column 1 of Table 12.4 includes both energy and instability variables, and column 2 adds their product term to the previous model. Both Energy Rent and Domestic Instability are (as expected) positively and significantly associated with Force Use Onset in the first model, as has been shown in the previous models. When included together with their product term in column 2, separate energy and instability require entirely different interpretations. In this case, neither Energy Rent nor Domestic Instability is significant, meaning that Energy Rent's effect on Force Use Onset is insignificant if there is no domestic conflict (when Domestic Instability is zero). When there is no energy rent available to a country, the effect of domestic instability on

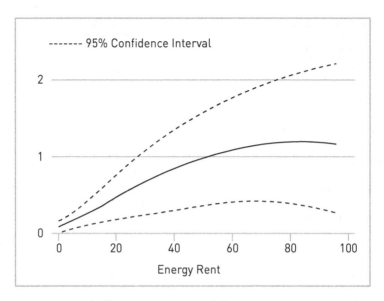

Figure 12.3 Marginal effect of Domestic Instability on Force Use Onset at different levels of Energy Rent.

international conflict is not distinguishable from zero either. These are interesting results in their own right because both energy and instability variables can theoretically and empirically be zero.

When the multiplicative term is added in column 2, it becomes positive and statistically significant at a 5-percent level. This suggests that the effect of domestic instabilities on international conflict onsets is not uniform across all levels of energy revenues accruing to a country-year. In other words, instabilities spill over the borders of a certain country at a higher rate if it is richer in terms of energy resources.

Note that in Figure 12.3, which is consistent with column 2 of Table 12.4, when energy revenues are zero, the effect of domestic tensions on international conflict is not statistically different from zero, indicated by the lower boundary of the confidence interval line falling below the X-axis at that point. When Energy Rent is around 30 percent, a one unit increase in Domestic Instability changes the likelihood of international conflict involvement by about 5.1 percent; whereas, when Energy Rent takes a value of about 50 percent, a one-unit change in Domestic Instability changes the odds of fighting by 10.5 percent. The marginal effect is always positive, and the confidence interval lines around the marginal effect graph suggest that it is always statistically significant except when Energy Rent equals zero. In the graph of interactive effects I keep all of the control variables at their mean values as suggested by the literature.[49]

The finding makes intuitive sense. There are reasons why domestic instabilities could be more likely to end up as interstate conflicts as rents obtained from energy endowments increase. One of them could be that because energy resources would increase stakes in countries that are relatively rich in those terms, foreign nations would have more tangible grounds to act when internal problems destabilize these countries (compared to resource-poor countries). Civil strife ripping the resource-rich Democratic Republic of Congo apart in the late 1990s and early 2000s could be a good example, indicating opportunistic behavior by neighbors.[50] Throughout their course, the violent domestic instabilities have been accompanied by interventions from Rwanda, Uganda, Zimbabwe, and other countries in proximity. According to a UN Security Council report, these interventions were intimately related to the plunder of the natural resources of the country by the high-ranking officers of the invading armies.[51] But the current chapter does not test for the specific mechanisms regarding *how* exactly the civil conflicts become internationalized. Other possibilities are equally likely. For instance, the initiator of the international conflict could very well be the country undergoing the civil war because of the diversionary pressures.

The control variables behave consistently. Only trade and years spent in peace are statistically significant and appear to decrease substantially the chances of international conflict involvement. A 1 percent increase in the trade level of a country diminishes its likelihood of conflict involvement by 10.5 percent, and one year spent in peace diminishes it by 35 percent. The remaining three variables, however, change signs and are never statistically significant at accepted levels.

To summarize, Energy Rent is not a significant determinant of Domestic Instability. Therefore, the latter's effect on international conflict cannot be ascribed to energy revenues. However, at higher levels of Energy Rent, the effect of Domestic Instability on Force Use Onset increases. These findings are not contradictory. The fact that energy revenues do not systematically affect the domestic strife level does not mean that at different levels of energy earnings a unit change in Domestic Instability will not have a different effect on interstate conflicts. Both statistically and substantively, energy-rich nations going through domestic instabilities tend to have a greater likelihood of international conflict involvement.

Conclusions

The linkage between conflicts and natural resources has been long suspected, and recently there have been important studies analyzing the association professionally. Especially widespread are works that look at the relationship between resources and domestic conflicts. The study of international conflicts from the same prism has been limited, yet it is difficult to miss the fact that there are a number of cases where resource abundance coincides with both domestic and international conflicts. The question that I tried to answer in this chapter was related to this triangle of associations. More concretely, I attempted to see how exactly international conflicts are tied to domestic conflicts in resource-rich nations. The main two directions that I focused on were that this must either stem from the fact that resources cause domestic conflicts, which in turn bring about international ones, or, alternatively, that resource-rich nations experiencing civil wars become vulnerable to international military conflicts *due to* the increasing stakes generated by natural resource abundance.

The results were surprising in the sense that I did not find a statistically significant association between resources and domestic conflict, despite a number of scholarly works that did find such a linkage. The outcome is not that surprising given the recently increasing number of non-findings, which has started to challenge the previous positive findings since Collier and Hoeffler's seminal work.[52] Yet there was empirical support for the second hypothesis. Resource-rich nations going through domestic instabilities are more likely to get involved in interstate disputes than resource-poor nations with the same domestic problems. The substantive effect is noteworthy. When Energy Rent is around 30 percent, a one-unit increase in Domestic Instability changes the likelihood of international conflict involvement by about 5.1 percent. Whereas, when Energy Rent takes a value of about 50 percent, a one unit change in Domestic Instability changes the odds of fighting in a military conflict by 10.5 percent.

Why are domestic instabilities more likely to end up as interstate conflicts when rents obtained from energy endowments increase? One of the reasons could be that as energy earnings increase, foreign nations will have more tangible grounds to act opportunistically when internal problems destabilize resource-rich countries. In other words, they have more to gain given the resource riches of the target country. The intervention by Angola in the Republic of Congo in 1997 and interventions by Rwanda, Uganda, and Zimbabwe in the Democratic Republic of Congo in the late 1990s and early 2000s are examples to the point. In both cases the invaded country had two overlapping characteristics: they were both were resource rich and going through civil strife. Alternatively, resource-rich nations, in light of their legitimacy problems, among other things, could be more willing to externalize their domestic problems compared to resource-poor countries. This line of reasoning would fall within the realm of the diversionary conflict literature. But a more refined dataset and models are required to determine such details. What the tests of this chapter reveal is that, the richer a country is in terms of hydrocarbons, the more likely it is to get *involved* in international disputes when experiencing domestic disturbances.

This finding shows that the international community must be especially concerned about and try to forestall domestic instabilities in resource-rich nations. True, a civil war or lesser forms of domestic conflicts are issues in their own right and need to get the attention of the world in any case. But if such domestic problems are plaguing oil-rich nations, then the likelihood for them to spill over into the international arena and draw more nations into the orbit of the conflict will increase. Therefore, preventing domestic strife in a hydrocarbon-rich country not only will bring stability to that particular nation, but also will prevent it from falling prey to opportunistic foreign nations or making other nations pay for its problems.

13

Petroleum, Governance, and Fragility:
The Micro-Politics of Petroleum
in Postconflict States

Naazneen H. Barma

Contemporary political economy research suggests that whether a country falls prey to the resource curse depends on a number of structural and economic factors. The cumulative body of large-N analyses of resource-rich developing countries indicates that the quality of existing institutions is perhaps the key factor that mediates a resource-rich country's economic outcomes.[1] Yet there is a gap in the political economy literature in terms of the subsequent causal reasoning about *why* institutions play this crucial intervening role in the resource curse. In this chapter, I examine the micro-politics of petroleum in Cambodia and East Timor through a framework rooted in the natural resource value chain to develop a sense of the mechanisms underpinning the resource curse in fragile nations.[2] Postconflict states offer fertile ground for generating hypotheses about the causal interplay between fragile political institutions, limited state capacity, and resource riches as they impact economic outcomes.

Political Economy and the Resource Curse

A wide and growing body of scholarship has emerged in the economics and political science disciplines that attempts to understand the mechanisms underlying the resource curse and illuminate policy fixes to help poor countries avoid it. Broad agreement exists on the appropriate macroeconomic, technical, and institutional mechanisms to put in place to manage the resource curse successfully. Even when the menu of policy options varies, the institutional prescriptions to ensure good governance of the national resource sector all emphasize clear organizational mandates, transparency of processes, and strong built-in accountability measures.

The true puzzle is *why* governments are unable to implement such corrective policy measures to mitigate many of the patterns that cumulate into the resource curse. This, then, is where politics enters the picture, and a complementary political science literature emphasizes how different political economic systems deal with resource rents, focusing on the nature and role of state institutions and how dynamics such as state capture and patronage networks influence the management of natural resource rents.[3] When a state has resources such as petroleum, the main political and economic impacts come via the effect that resource rents have on the state's patterns of revenue collection and expenditure.[4] Natural resource booms turn countries into "rentier states," which live off unearned income; the state is resourced through rents rather than taxes and requires correspondingly little organizational effort from the state apparatus.

Politically, natural resources generate significant windfall resources for the state and therefore a valuable prize for those who control political power.[5] By limiting a government's need for other forms of revenue generation, such as tax collection, natural resources can lead to the attenuation of state-administrative and institutional capacity building. A core logic of the political effects of the resource curse hence derives from what Mick Moore has dubbed the "fiscal sociology" paradigm.[6] This has been crystallized recently by Robert Bates in his examination of state failure in Africa: if political elites calculate that their own best interests are served by collecting tax revenues and protecting producers with the rule of law to maximize the tax base, they will establish bureaucratic infrastructure to enable them to do so; if not, they will be prone to turning the state apparatus into a predatory instrument that extracts rent from society and dispenses that rent through patronage networks.[7] Terry Karl articulates how this dynamic unfolds in her seminal book *The Paradox of Plenty*:

> Dependence on petroleum produces a distinctive type of setting, the petro-state, which encourages the political distribution of rents. Such

a state is characterized by fiscal reliance on petrodollars, which expands state jurisdiction and weakens authority as other extractive
capabilities wither. As a result, when faced with competing pressures, state officials become habituated to relying on the progressive
substitution of public spending for statecraft, thereby further weakening state capacity.[8]

Supporting hypotheses advanced in the contemporary political economy
literature suggest that a resource curse is made more likely when: (1) natural
resources constitute the "only game in town"; (2) the distribution of resource rents aligns with existing political-economic cleavages; (3) political
power is concentrated in the executive; and (4) policy commitment is made
more difficult by price volatility or political instability.[9]

The resource curse is particularly acute in the case of petroleum (compared to other natural resources such as hard-rock minerals) because of petroleum's "point source" nature with highly concentrated ownership.[10] Such
point source resources foster a higher concentration of power and, consequently, weaker accountability of political elites and potentially poorer policy decisions.[11] Point source resource extraction is easier for governments to
regulate and tax; in practice, this means that the rents are high and pass
through the hands of a relative few. More highly concentrated resource
ownership facilitates the collective action of resource developers—meaning
they are more likely to have disproportionate access to government agencies
and be able to defend their vested interests. Petroleum tends, moreover, to
be highly lucrative in relation to production costs so that the magnitude of
the rent streams is high and the consequent resource curse is often greater.

The bulk of the political economy literature thus identifies institutions as
key intervening variables affecting a country's susceptibility to the resource
curse and, most importantly for the purposes of this chapter, attributes a bi-
directional causality to them. Resource dependence actually shapes state institutions and decision-making frameworks in predictable patterns; in turn,
those political and institutional constellations have predictable effects on
economic outcomes. Karl again offers a concise summary of the logic:

Petro-states suffer from a double perverse effect: their states, so often
formed during the period of oil extraction, are skewed by the impera-
tives of resource extraction, but the intensification of the resource

dependence that accompanies state-building subsequently produces even further decay in critical areas such as non-mineral-based revenue raising, expenditure patterns, fiscal accountability, and citizen participation. A vicious cycle between mineral extraction and state making is set in motion.[12]

At the core of this chapter's argument is the explicit recognition that natural resources interact with governance and state institutions in two interrelated ways. First, extraction of natural resources might erode the quality of governance. One line of logic is that dependence on natural resource wealth limits other forms of government revenue generation, such as tax collection. This, in turn, can lead to a decline in administrative and institutional capacity building, particularly as the core tax-accountability linkage between state and society is weakened.[13] Additionally, resource wealth might adversely impact the quality of governance by intensifying battles between political and economic elites for control over natural resource rents and the state institutions responsible for collecting and distributing them.[14]

Second, even if resource abundance does not cause deterioration in governance, the quality of institutions and governance will most likely condition the quality of the economic and natural resource management policies adopted as well as their implementation across the value chain.[15] From this viewpoint, institutional quality and the government's ability to make policy effectively, minimizing discretion and rent seeking, affects outcomes in the natural resource sector much as they do other development outcomes. In addition, because natural resources generate revenue windfalls, governments can be tempted to make policy and public spending decisions with adverse long-term consequences.

Both these interactions are of interest to the study, and I attempt to treat them as distinct through a twofold analytical approach. I use the micropolitical lens of the natural resource value chain to focus on the detailed institutional and governance arrangements that frame the process of rent extraction and distribution. At the same time, I build causal narratives rooted in the contemporary political context in an attempt to unravel the endogeneity inherent in the institutional quality puzzle. In order to develop the argument, I examine two oil-rich postconflict countries, Cambodia and East Timor, as their nascent and fragile institutional architecture throws the issues into sharp relief.

A Micro-Political Economy Framework: Value Chain Analysis

The political economy literature recognizes, as discussed briefly above, that the main factors determining the success of oil-rich countries are inherently related to a country's overall governance framework and political economy of rent extraction and distribution. In other words, managing the resource curse is a governance challenge—the quality, transparency, and accountability of policy-making processes, the legal and regulatory climate, and general public as well as natural resource sector institutions are major determinants of how successfully countries can turn the resource curse into a blessing.[16] Yet the macro viewpoints outlined above fall short of translating broad agreement on the "right" policies into concrete steps to navigate the institutional and political obstacles that are associated with governing the resource curse. In other words, what state-of-the-art scholarship on the resource curse lacks, and what this chapter seeks to elaborate, is a fine-grained micro-political framework that demonstrates how and where rent generation and extraction actually occur in practice.

The World Bank and its development partners have recently elaborated a "value chain" approach to systematically diagnosing the institutional and governance challenges in the natural resource sector.[17] The approach pivots on the Extractive Industries Transparency Initiative (EITI), which seeks to encourage governments to publish their natural resource revenues and resource developers to publish their payments to governments so that the figures can be independently reconciled. EITI has made great steps in improving transparency in natural resource management, yet it does not cover the full value chain spanning from how resources are developed to how the revenue generated is ultimately spent. In the language of political science, EITI alone does not cover the full range of rent generation and distribution in the natural resource sector.

The natural resource management value chain approach is an attempt to develop a comprehensive analytical framework for better understanding the governance of the natural resource sector, which I will now refer to as "sector governance." It encompasses and integrates (as depicted in Figure 13.1) the institutional arrangements across four key steps spanning the full range of an extractive industry's value chain: (1) award of contracts/licenses and organization of the sector; (2) regulation and monitoring of operations; (3) collection of taxes and royalties; and (4) revenue distribution and economic management.[18]

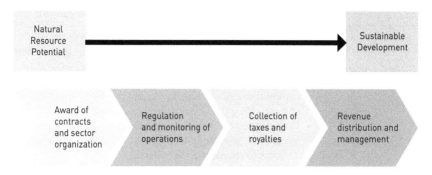

Figure 13.1 Natural resource management value chain.

The World Bank has adopted this approach with the primary objective of prescribing an integrated sequence of feasible policy remedies and reforms to help countries address the resource curse. In this chapter, I propose that this framework, when grounded contextually, offers the potential for a comprehensive micro assessment of the domestic politics of petroleum exporters. It identifies a series of institutional and governance good practices for each pillar of the value chain (see Table 13.1).

This set of criteria forms the backbone for a structured characterization of the micro-politics of how petroleum rents are generated and distributed in a country. A deeper look at the underlying political and institutional context can then be used to generate a causal picture of the fate a petroleum-rich country faces vis-à-vis the potential resource curse. The following empirical sections of this chapter discuss the cases of Cambodia and East Timor, two hydrocarbon-rich states in East Asia and the Pacific, using the organizational logic of the natural resource value chain. In each case, I move from upstream to downstream issues, focusing on key institutional and governance dimensions of the four consolidated pillars of the value chain: (1) the legal, regulatory, and institutional framework surrounding the granting of petroleum concessions and sector organization; (2) oversight and monitoring of resource exploitation; (3) the collection and management of revenues from the petroleum sector; and (4) some aspects of expenditure management.

Cambodia and East Timor have both recently discovered large petroleum reserves and both also have recent postconflict state-building experiences that attempted to strengthen state institutional capacity. They thus provide fertile empirical ground for testing Karl's observation of the vicious

Table 13.1 Natural Resource Management Value Chain Framework

Value chain stage	Good practice institutional and governance arrangements
Award of contracts and sector organization	• Clear legal and regulatory framework that gives private developers consistent expectations and enables government departments to know whether the law is being enforced • Transparent and nondiscretionary framework for awarding exploration and production rights (contracts/licenses), encompassing the national petroleum authority (if it exists) • Well-defined institutional responsibilities so government agencies at central and local levels are aware of their mandates and able to coordinate with each other
Regulation and monitoring of operations	• Clearly defined monitoring and inspection responsibilities in appropriate government agencies • Commensurate institutional capacity and resourcing • Monitoring of community development and environmental impact, with remediation programs in affected communities
Collection of taxes and royalties	• Transparent and nondiscretionary fiscal regime for concessions, preventing revenue leakage and empowering government vis-à-vis private sector by encouraging competition on the terms of the deal • Adequate administrative and audit capacity for revenue collection agencies • Adherence to internationally accepted accounting and reporting standards • Channeling of resource revenues into formal budget process such that they are subject to normal scrutiny and accountability mechanisms
Revenue management and distribution	• Appropriate macroeconomic policy responses to mitigate negative consequences from exchange rate appreciation • Transparent savings decisions to smooth public expenditure in the face of commodity price volatility and to accumulate assets as finite resources are extracted • Strong public financial management and procurement systems • Judicious allocation of public expenditures—e.g., within a medium-term expenditure framework and aligned within a national development strategy • Adequate scrutiny, appraisal, and audit of public investment decisions

Adapted from Eleodoro Mayorga Alba, "Extractive Industries Value Chain: A Comprehensive Integrated Approach to Developing Extractive Industries," Oil, Gas, and Mining Policy Division Working Paper 3 and Africa Poverty Reduction and Economic Management Department Working Paper 125, World Bank (2009).

cycle between mineral extraction and state making. A brief discussion of the two countries' recent political histories provides the context within which to consider governance and institutional strengths and vulnerabilities in the petroleum sector. Through an application of the value chain framework, then, I attempt to unravel the micro-political economy underlying the bi-directional interaction of institutions with resource wealth. On one hand, the two cases show how preexisting institutional quality affects policy making and governance outcomes in the petroleum sector. On the other hand, I trace the impacts of petroleum and its rents back on the broader institutional context.

Cambodia: The "Shadow State" and Rent-Seeking Networks

From 1970 onward, Cambodia underwent two decades of political instability, auto genocide, and civil war. Beginning with the Khmer Rouge's brutal regime from 1975 to 1979, which strategically dismantled and destroyed the political and social fabric of the country, and continuing into the Vietnamese-backed regime that took power in 1979, the conflict for political control over the country developed out of the Cambodian state's collapse of legitimacy. The Cambodian peace accords of October 1991 provided a roadmap for building state capacity and a transition to an elected government. Elections were held successfully, but the political and administrative landscape has since been increasingly dominated by the powerful Cambodian People's Party (CPP) led by Hun Sen. The CPP's main source of leverage in achieving this result was its grip on the institutions and human resources of the state apparatus.[19]

The power-sharing coalition that emerged from Cambodia's first post-conflict elections in 1993 created persistent legislative and executive gridlock. Despite having won the elections, the royalist party Funcinpec's governing power was restricted to the cabinet level; administrative power further down the state hierarchy remained in CPP hands. Continuing bureaucratic factionalism has prevented Cambodia's development of national institutional capacity to this day. The power-sharing system failed to foster reconciliation among the factions and build a new political system and effective state apparatus based on compromise and inclusion; worse still, it created dual governments, as Funcinpec brought its supporters into the already bloated state structure. This arrangement deadlocked decision making and governance and perpetuated parallel crony-based political networks that operate both within and outside the state, such that "Hierarchical patron-client networks . . . have expanded and subsumed the formal state structure."[20] In the absence of an institutional power base or the ability to seek legitimacy through the public sector, Funcinpec leaders chose to mimic and partner with the CPP in rent extraction and distribution networks. In turn, these networks continued to undermine state capacity, perpetuating a self-reinforcing vicious cycle of institutional decay.[21]

The consensus principle of Cambodia's coalition government endowed the CPP, with its control of the state, with de facto veto power over any reforms that threatened its political, financial, or institutional interests. State capacity was weak under the CPP's grip, and no structural reform of the state was possible. Both parties were anxious to ensure that their own supporters were not removed as part of a bureaucratic retrenchment process, and attempts to increase state revenues threatened the ability of the two patronage networks to extract rents. The state had no nonpartisan, technocratic constituency to defend itself against the sociopolitical elite and to support institutional reform and the building of state capacity. This lack of a reform coalition has continued to hamper the international community's efforts to build state capacity and improve Cambodian governance to the present day.[22] Time-series data of government effectiveness in Cambodia demonstrate that although state capacity may have improved slightly in the late 1990s, it has since remained consistently quite low (see Figure 13.2).

The consolidation of two parallel state structures in Cambodia also affected internal party dynamics, concentrating power in the hands of leaders. The two sets of elites managed to work together for the first three years of their coalition government, avoiding contentious issues and pursuing enough economic liberalization to blind foreign observers to the political decay taking place. But this greater openness came at the price of dual party-based rent extraction networks—with both networks carrying out land grabs, deforestation, corruption, and violent crime in an environment of weak legal institutions.[23] As we shall see, this mode of affairs has also permeated Cambodia's petroleum sector. Yet the CPP and Funcinpec's mutually beneficial arrangement of dual rent-seeking was not enough to prevent deterioration in the relationship, as Funcinpec began to voice its frustration over the CPP's increasing stranglehold on power. In response, Prime Minister Hun Sen and the CPP staged a coup d'état in 1997, which marked the breakdown of a system of power sharing between distinct elite groups. In subsequent coalitions,

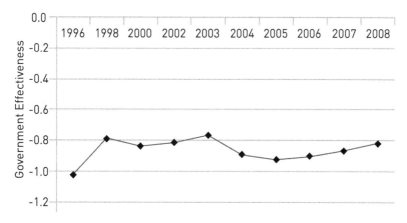

Figure 13.2 Government effectiveness in Cambodia, 1996–2008. Daniel Kaufmann, Aart Kraay, and Massimo Mastruzzi, "Governance Matters VIII: Aggregate and Individual Governance Indicators for 1996–2008," World Bank Policy Research Working Paper 4280 (Washington, D.C.: World Bank, 2009), http://info.worldbank.org/governance/wgi/index.asp. The *government effectiveness score* in the World Governance Indicators dataset measures "the quality of public services, the quality of the civil service and the degree of its independence from political pressures, the quality of policy formulation and implementation, and the credibility of the government's commitment to such policies." The indicator is aggregated from a series of underlying indices and scored from –2.5 for least effective to 2.5 for most effective states. This indicator should be treated with caution, as its composition varies from one year to the next, but it provides a reasonable sense of evolution in a country's government effectiveness over time.

Funcinpec's ostensible role in power sharing has been little more than window dressing for the emergence of a de facto one-party system led by the hegemonic CPP.

The CPP's grip on Cambodia's political system has subsequently thwarted any meaningful progress in the state's (human or institutional) capacity building or democratic consolidation. What manifests as state hollowness or failure can thus actually be viewed as the result of a deliberate elite strategy to assert its control over key sources of resource wealth (forestry) and other rents, thereby assuring its hold on power. This "shadow state"[24]—a system where ruling elites draw power from their ability to control high-rent economic activity—had firmly established itself in Cambodia by the time oil was discovered there.

Since 2004, when Chevron struck oil 200 kilometers offshore in Cambodia's Khmer Basin in the Gulf of Thailand, the country has been awaiting the promise of billions of dollars of oil wealth. There are six potential offshore fields in Cambodia's territorial waters in the gulf plus a number of potential exploration areas in regions disputed with Thailand. Chevron confirmed its find in one of these fields, Block A, in late 2004, and the World Bank provisionally estimated that the explored portion contains 400–500 million barrels of oil and 2–3 trillion cubic feet of gas.[25] Although the volume in question is low in comparison to other oil-producing developing countries, these anticipated petroleum reserves are substantial given Cambodia's size. The projected revenue flow could easily place Cambodia squarely within the ranks of resource dependence.[26] In 2007, the IMF estimated that Cambodia's government oil revenues could begin flowing in 2011 and reach up to $1.7 billion annually ten years after production commences, almost matching the Cambodian government's 2009 overall budget of $1.9 billion.[27] This revenue would be particularly significant in the current aid context, in which donors provide about half of Cambodia's annual budget.

Yet the initial decisions that Cambodian officials have made regarding the management of their nascent petroleum sector across the value chain do not bode well for a channeling of projected wealth into sustainable development outcomes for the country. A snapshot of key institutional and governance arrangements in the sector is provided in Table 13.2. Upstream in the value chain, the legal and regulatory framework for the oil and gas sector, with no comprehensive petroleum law, is incomplete, and the government lacks a comprehensive sector strategy. Moreover, the management structure of the sector is formally fragmented—with opaque institutional mandates for formulating policy, awarding contracts, and interacting with the private sector. Ambiguities also exist in terms of regulation, fiscal and taxation matters, and the handling of petroleum sector externalities.[28]

In practice, the dominant agency in petroleum sector management is the Cambodian National Petroleum Authority (CNPA), which is directly under the control of Prime Minister Hun Sen and Deputy Prime Minister Sok An, the two leaders at the helm of the most powerful faction within the CPP. In 1998, the CNPA was created by royal decree (instead of an act of parliament) as an independent body and took over petroleum sector governance from the Ministry of Industry, Mines, and Energy. Its operations are not subject to scrutiny from the National Assembly, Senate, or any other government body. The CNPA acts as policy advisor to the government on oil and gas sector development, functions as the regulatory body for the sector, and plays a commercial role as the agency that negotiates exploration and production

Table 13.2 Key Governance Outcomes in Cambodian Petroleum Sector

Value chain stage	Institutional and governance arrangements
Award of contracts and sector organization	• Underdeveloped legal and regulatory framework; lack of clarity about institutional mandates • Cambodian National Petroleum Authority (CNPA) dominant; governed directly by prime minister and deputy prime minister • Multiple roles of CNPA—policymaking, regulatory, commercial—with no firewalls between roles • Nontransparent, discretionary award of contracts; companies report having to pay large bribes for licenses that fail to materialize
Regulation and monitoring of operations	• CNPA shares little to no information necessary for effective inspection and monitoring, within agency or with other government bodies • Weak administrative capacity across government • CNPA bypasses accountability controls; not subject to parliamentary or other scrutiny
Collection of taxes and royalties	• Opaque financial flows—fiscal regimes and fees vary considerably in practice; no mechanisms for verifying receipt of revenues • Millions of dollars companies have reported paying to government for oil concessions are missing from official revenue reports
Revenue management and distribution	• Ministry of Economy and Finance out of loop on revenue management • Procurement problems in public investment program • A significant proportion of revenues retained in CNPA and used for rent distribution networks, rather than channeled into formal budget process

contracts, including joint-venture agreements, on behalf of the government. Although this multiple and often conflicting functionality is not uncommon practice for petroleum authorities in the developing world, the lack of firewalls between the CNPA's different roles is extremely problematic in terms of transparency and accountability.

The deputy prime minister, as chair of the CNPA, has almost complete control over its operations, and the organization is run with a premium on secrecy rather than transparency. The agency's capacity is weak, as is the case with the bulk of Cambodia's bureaucracy, and decision making is confined to a handful of people. Although offshore oil development concessions are formally awarded through a competitive bidding process, all exploration contracts to date have been allocated at the discretion of the powerful players at the helm of the CNPA. Some companies have reported paying large bribes for permits that failed to materialize.[29] CNPA claims to use a model production-sharing contract, but the final terms of exploration agreements and other documents are not shared within the agency, let alone shared with other government bodies or the public. This means that any genuine form of impartial monitoring and inspection of petroleum contracts is almost impossible to implement.

Governance and institutional outcomes are no better further downstream in the Cambodian petroleum sector's value chain. The fiscal regimes and fees associated with exploration contracts are reported to vary considerably; furthermore, because contractual terms are not made public, it is extremely difficult to verify fiscal receipts from the petroleum sector.[30] Companies report that millions of dollars they have paid to the government for oil concessions are missing from official revenue figures.[31] Because petroleum revenues have yet to come onstream, a sector-specific assessment of the public financial management system would be premature. In general, the public financial management system has long been an area of major donor attention in Cambodia, but serious problems persist with the procurement system, which is a common mechanism for rent distribution to patronage networks. Moreover, there is no way of estimating what volume of rents is being distributed outside the formal budget process, or "off budget," through the CNPA itself or is being siphoned off into the hands of individuals.

Even in the early stages of its petroleum development, Cambodia's management of the natural resource sector demonstrates how broader institutional quality conditions governance outcomes in the sector. In a similar manner to the use of forestry rents in the contemporary political context, it appears that a significant portion of oil revenues are being captured by political elites, with some portion being used to cement loyalties and pay off the opposition.[32] Mirroring the governance dynamics associated with the forestry sector, the petroleum sector has become co-opted in the patronage extraction and distribution that is the hallmark and basis of the CPP's grip on power. Because Cambodia's oil potential was only discovered a few years ago, however, the feedback effects of the petroleum sector on the broader institutional landscape are not yet obvious. Both interactions are evident in East Timor, to which I now turn.

East Timor: From Best Practice to "Buying the Peace"

Following an almost twenty-five-year guerrilla resistance movement against Indonesian occupation, the East Timorese people voted for their independence in 1999. In the wake of the scorched earth violence that followed that vote in the tiny nation, the United Nations mounted its most ambitious peace-building exercise. East Timor was in numerous ways the poster child for the international community's state-building efforts, and many observers found cause for cheer when the country passed the five-year mark without renewed violence.[33] At that point, it appeared that the Revolutionary Front for an Independent East Timor (Fretilin, by its Portuguese acronym) had successfully seized the mantle of the national resistance front and channeled its organizational strength into a popularly elected administration. Yet during the transitional phase, state capacity building was underemphasized and remained severely attenuated, with elite attention focused on the political rather than the administrative arena.[34]

Even though the United Nations Transitional Authority for East Timor (UNTAET) had established the East Timor Public Administration by 2001 as part of an all-Timorese transitional government, the capacity of this embryonic civil service was woefully weak and failed to incorporate East Timorese participation in planning and administration. The civil administration was highly dependent on international assistance to make up for low professional skills, particularly in the central government functions of public finance and human resource management.[35] This has meant that some core government functions in East Timor are carried out surprisingly well relative to everything else; as we shall see, this seems to be the case in the petroleum sector. Yet overall, Timorese political leaders' emphasis on political incorporation has meant that not enough attention was paid to the state-strengthening dimension of the peace-building program. Time-series data of government effectiveness in East Timor demonstrate that although state capacity spiked in the immediate period after the transition to independence, it has since declined and remains quite low (see Figure 13.3).

Fretilin, the political party led by the returned Timorese diaspora elite, dominated the political process after the transitional period, which proved

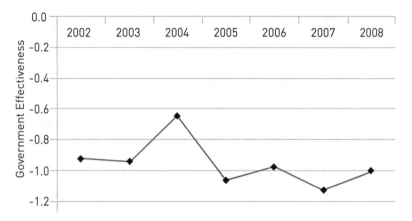

Figure 13.3 Government effectiveness in East Timor, 2002–2008. Kaufmann, Kraay, and Mastruzzi, "Governance Matters VIII." See caption to Figure 13.2 for a description of the indicator.

problematic for state strengthening and the longer-term consolidation of democracy in East Timor. Fretilin, in essence, "placed the new National Parliament in clear subordination to a government intent on using its majority to push through its ambitious legislative program."[36] It also quickly began to consolidate its patronage networks throughout the country by politicizing civil service hiring in district administration throughout the country, which ensured that positions were filled by Fretilin cadres.[37] Although the Fretilin party retained its dominant presence throughout the country, it soon became apparent that the population at large did not necessarily share all of its goals. Timorese civil society representatives have criticized the hierarchical and closed-command culture in Timorese political life, recognizing that it led to the success of a national resistance movement but arguing that it is detrimental to democracy.[38] Moreover, Fretilin's own institutional legacies increasingly compromised its political legitimacy. Politically motivated violence erupted in April 2006; after several months of severe political instability, the Fretilin leadership was forced out of office at the behest of revolutionary leaders. New presidential and parliamentary elections, respectively, were held in May and June 2007, with former President Xanana Gusmão taking the prime minister's seat at the head of a volatile new coalition government.

Decisions around the institutional arrangements in East Timor's petroleum sector have interacted with this fast-evolving political context. East Timor is one of the most petroleum revenue-dependent countries in the world, with oil and natural gas revenues providing more than 98 percent of government revenues and constituting around 480 percent of non-oil GDP (about 80 percent of GDP).[39] Petroleum production began in 2004 at the Bayu-Undan gas field located in the offshore Joint Petroleum Development Area (JPDA) shared with Australia. East Timor's portion of the future revenue stream from Bayu-Undan is estimated at $15.2 billion in present value terms, in comparison with the government's overall budget of about $680 million in 2009.[40] East Timor's sources of petroleum revenue are expected to proliferate in the future—beginning with the Greater Sunrise field, estimated to hold reservoirs as large as Bayu-Undan, and the smaller Kitan field, due to commence production in 2011. Additional exploration in both the JPDA and East Timor's exclusive zone is also expected to result in further commercially viable petroleum discoveries.

Given its extreme petroleum dependence and postconflict institutional fragility, East Timor is very vulnerable to the resource curse. Yet the institutional and governance arrangements the East Timorese government made for the management of the petroleum sector during the country's early stages of independence appear to bode quite well for the country's ability to channel oil and gas revenues into sustainable development (see Table 13.3).[41] More recently, however, some of the institutional safeguards and quality initially designed into the petroleum sector architecture are on the verge of unraveling somewhat, which demonstrates the intense political pressures on the system as well as the impact of the shift in power from the first Fretilin government to the current coalition government. The petroleum sector's evolving institutional architecture has, in turn, begun to have a series of noticeable effects on the macro political and governance landscape as well.

Upstream in the value chain, East Timor has thus far opted for maximum transparency in the petroleum development process—handling all exploration contract bidding rounds with model contracts, publicly advertised terms, and competition based on only one bid variable (reducing the opportunity for discretion in the decision).[42] In addition, the final contracts are public documents. Currently, however, the government is reported to be engaging with regional oil companies and consortia in several strategic investment partnerships—such as the construction of a liquefied natural gas plant and establishment of a supply base as well as storage and port facilities on the south coast of the country.[43] The government has not disclosed what it would offer in return for these proposed investment partnerships, but observers agree that a number of secret memoranda of understanding for exploration

Table 13.3 Key Governance Outcomes in East Timorese Petroleum Sector

Value chain stage	Institutional and governance arrangements
Award of contracts and sector organization	• Best international practice Petroleum Fund Law (2005), widely heralded as robust and transparent • Acreage releases to date with publicly advertised, transparent, open bidding procedures; contracts made public • New, nontransparent deals potentially being negotiated with regional companies • Intention to create National Oil Company (NOC); would change sector organization considerably
Regulation and monitoring of operations	• To date, strong, using Joint Petroleum Development Area (JPDA) mechanisms; but not set up for future contracts • Weak overall administrative capacity and dominance of particular oligarchic interests constrain regulatory capacity • National Petroleum Authority has best administrative capacity in-country, but still weak; brought closer to government, which seems to be affecting neutrality of regulatory decisions
Collection of taxes and royalties	• Revenue collection capacity weak; to date heavily reliant on international technical assistance • To date, transparent, through JPDA mechanisms; potential for revenue leakage with other contracts • Petroleum Fund revenue management is state of the art, with robust independent audits; but there is some pressure for potential reforms • NOC creation could potentially take significant revenues out of the formal budget process, diluting transparency and accountability controls
Revenue management and distribution	• All government expenditure of resource wealth is channeled into the formal budget process, providing full fiscal accountability through budget scrutiny by Parliament • Estimated Sustainable Income can only be exceeded via justification to Parliament • Dysfunctional, centralized public financial management system and constrained budget execution; pressure to spend has opened up possibility of more rent distribution • "Buying the peace" push in 2007 and 2008, using cash transfers, subsidies, and, increasingly, public investment budget • NOC could potentially become an alternate, off-budget source of public investment and rent distribution

contracts may have already been signed in advance of the next scheduled acreage release. Such exclusive terms on high-value sites would represent an unraveling of the hitherto exemplary bidding process and a cause for concern in terms of transparency and accountability.

In terms of petroleum sector organization, the Secretariat of State for Natural Resources handles policy. The National Petroleum Authority (NPA), created in 2008, is responsible for regulating and monitoring activities in both the JPDA and East Timor's exclusive zone.[44] It is widely agreed that the NPA is currently one of the most highly capacitated Timorese state agencies, which is a sign of the government's recognition of the strategic importance of the petroleum sector as well as the premium placed on the regulatory function. The NPA reports to a board of directors, which is in turn supervised by the Secretariat of State for Natural Resources. There is thus concern that the NPA's independence is somewhat compromised due to its proximity to the executive; observers worry, for example, that the forthcoming decision on the development plan for the Sunrise field will be made through a political lens.[45]

Moving across the value chain to revenue-management arrangements, the Fretilin government in 2005 established a state Petroleum Fund for fiscal receipts from the sector along with a complementary legislative framework that are widely heralded as examples of best international practice and even, to some, the finest legacy of the first East Timorese government. With heavy advisory involvement from the Norwegian government, Fretilin Prime Minister Mari Alkatiri articulated a Petroleum Fund based on the Norwegian model. Norway's State Petroleum Fund was established with the aim of ensuring that some proportion of the finite stream of revenues accruing to the country from its North Sea oil deposits would be saved for future generations. East Timor's Petroleum Fund is similarly an exemplary architecture for intergenerational savings, and its receipts can also be used, if necessary, for expenditure smoothing in the face of petroleum price volatility. According to the Petroleum Fund Law, all petroleum revenues—fees, royalties, and taxes—are directed to the Petroleum Fund without exception.[46] There are none of the off-budget petroleum accounts or special purpose funds that are common in many hydrocarbon-rich developing countries. Parliament unanimously passed the Petroleum Fund Law in 2005, and it is the only legislation ever to have received no opposition in East Timor. In this respect, Alkatiri used his technocratic orientation, the considerable postindependence legitimacy afforded to his government, and advice from the international community to establish best practice institutional arrangements for upstream sector governance. The forward-looking logic of the Petroleum Fund was also likely enabled, in part, by the fact that immediate revenues were relatively low: Bayu-Undan had just started producing, and oil prices had not yet spiked.

Enshrined in the Petroleum Fund Law is the concept of Estimated Sustainable Income (ESI)—defined as the maximum amount that can be appropriated from the fund in any given fiscal year, leaving enough revenue in the fund such that the same value can be appropriated in all subsequent years. In short, this principle ensures intergenerational saving. The law sets ESI at 3 percent on the assumption that the fund will generate an annualized 3 percent return on investment, and each year Petroleum Fund advisors at the Ministry of Finance calculate the dollar amount on the basis of fairly conservative revenue projections based on proven reserves. In 2009, East Timor's ESI was just over $400 million (in comparison to the country's total budget that year of $680 million). All revenue coming out of the fund is appropriated through and integrated fiscally with the formal budget process, which means that the use of all resource revenues is subject to parliamentary scrutiny and regular budget accountability measures.

The Petroleum Fund Law enables the government to request an appropriation to the budget exceeding ESI, as long as it provides justification to Parliament; this has now happened twice, in 2008 and 2009. Yet this flexibility may not make the Petroleum Fund resilient enough. A recent development of concern is that the government is considering tabling amendments to the Petroleum Fund Law that would increase ESI over 3 percent, which (particularly in the current low-return global financial context) would almost certainly deplete the fund over time. The initial design was likely enabled by relatively low petroleum revenues; by contrast, the current government appears to be under pressure to demonstrate to a restless public the dividends from both newly reestablished peace and increasing petroleum wealth. The coalition government is unlikely to be a lasting one, moreover, and there are increasing signs that uncertainty about the next set of electoral results has shortened the time horizon of some in government and put in place a short-term personal enrichment calculus. In this respect, reports of corruption are increasing—particularly through the public procurement process, because lack of recourse to off-budget sources of rent puts enormous pressure on the formal public expenditure system.

The formal public financial management system in East Timor complicates petroleum-sector governance because it has been relatively dysfunctional. A complex, centralized design with ex ante spending controls contributed to extremely poor budget execution during the past several years. In turn, increasingly frustrated by the inability of the public financial management system to demonstrate results and to service important constituencies (especially veterans), the government opened a multitude of other spending channels—including subsidies, cash transfers, pensions, and decentralized and shortcut procurement procedures—so that by mid-2008 it was spending seven to eight times more each month than the year before.[47] More recently, in October 2009, $70 million of an unutilized budget allocation for construction of a heavy oil power plant was channeled by executive decree into what was known as the "Package Referendum." These funds were intended to be used for targeted, small- to medium-size public investment programs, such as irrigation and roads. The allocation of the resources was entirely off budget in the hands of a recently formed business association not subject to any form of transparency or accountability controls—heightening the risks of rent seeking and rent distribution.

A preliminary analysis of the geographic allocation of public spending in East Timor could not falsify the hypothesis that the government was spending more—in terms of both cash transfers and public investment allocation—in the districts most strongly supportive of the coalition partners in the 2007 election. Viewing these various public spending measures in the best possible light, the government is acting to "buy the peace" with the country's best interests in mind; in this telling, distributing rents in the form of public expenditures to key constituencies can pacify dissent, control elite conflict, and maintain stability. Nevertheless, elite capture of major rent streams, along with constituency-targeted public spending patterns, are troubling signs that the petroleum sector is indeed having an impact on the macro political and institutional landscape of East Timor through the simple fact that these rent streams make up such a large proportion of the government's revenues and make the spending increases possible.

A final development in East Timor's petroleum sector governance is the government's plan to establish a National Oil Company (NOC) that could take equity shares in any new petroleum development activities. This impetus is driven in part by frustration with the formal public financial management system and its constraints and possibly also by a desire to increase the country's take from the petroleum sector to continue to service emerging expenditure pressures. NOCs are certainly common in hydrocarbon-rich developing countries; unfortunately, they are also notorious sources of inefficiency and corruption.[48] The Timorese government has yet to decide how it would structure its NOC and has accepted Norwegian assistance in studying various potential models.

The double-edged danger, from a governance point of view, is that the creation of a NOC would enable political elites to: (1) divert potentially major streams of petroleum revenue away from the Petroleum Fund;[49] and (2) bypass the fiscal accountability measures embedded in budget appropriations from the fund by creating multiple other channels of public investment and expenditure through NOC subsidiary operations. In short, the NOC could be set up to receive a significant share of petroleum revenues and spend those funds in whatever manner its management and board were to choose, with no other executive or legislative oversight. In the worst-case scenario, this could—as is the case in other oil-rich developing countries such as Angola—make the NOC a mini-state within the state that operates on its own terms and plays an outsized political role because of the sheer volume of petroleum revenues it controls and its potential to distribute rents to patronage networks. The petroleum sector could thus, in very tangible ways, reshape the political and institutional landscape of East Timor.

Conclusions

In this chapter, I have introduced the natural resource value chain concept as a micro-political lens through which to unravel the bi-directional causality attributed to institutions in the resource curse. I have examined petroleum governance arrangements in Cambodia and East Timor in light of the fragile postconflict institutional context in both countries. For both, I have attempted to illustrate how the impact of the macro political environment and overall institutional quality can be seen in the choices made for petroleum-sector governance. Moreover, in East Timor, where petroleum production has begun and revenues have already altered the public expenditure equation, the impacts of petroleum feeding back into the broader political and institutional landscape are already becoming evident.

Developing countries are particularly vulnerable to the resource curse because of their low institutional quality at the outset of petroleum production. These concerns apply even more to fragile postconflict states. The experience of poor countries rich in hydrocarbons has shown that adverse political incentives are exacerbated when oil is the "only game in town," and a lack of access to other revenues constrains the accountability of the state to society and concentrates rent seeking and rent distribution in the natural resource sector. The Cambodia and East Timor cases demonstrate that the logic of zero-sum politics and short-time horizons facing political elites are extremely acute in fragile institutional contexts.

In support of the rich theoretical scholarship that articulates the interaction between natural resources and institutions, these two cases and the value chain concept also demonstrate the potential for containing the resource curse through intelligent and resilient institutional design. Resource curse dynamics can be mitigated through, for example, an institutional setup that guards against the concentration of power; a transparent legal and regulatory framework for the petroleum sector that, in particular, sets out clear institutional mandates and lines of accountability; a forward-looking revenue management architecture that saves some portion of resource wealth for future generations and safeguards it, as much as possible, from being distributed as rent; and an attention to administrative capacity building across the natural resource value chain that cumulates to enhanced institutional quality. Once an adverse resource curse pattern has been set in place, however, it can be extremely difficult to break the vicious cycle of its micro-political dynamics, as can be seen in Cambodia. On the other hand, East Timor is poised to demonstrate whether it might be possible to avoid the worst forms of the resource curse through conscious institutional design. Both countries evidence what Karl articulated as one of the hallmarks of the petrostate: the progressive substitution of public spending and rent distribution for statecraft and the consequent weakening of state capacity. For petroleum-rich poor countries, this is a very real sociopolitical peril that can be extremely hard to escape.

Conclusion: Constant Perils, Policy Responses, and Lessons to Be Learned

Taleh Ziyadov

This volume is an attempt to draw closer attention to the particular and consistent challenges facing resource-exporting states and to contribute to a better understanding of these perils through a number of recent case studies. It aims to add to a growing number of new studies that shed light on specific developmental problems of resource-rich states around the globe. As was highlighted in the introduction, the perils faced by energy producers are in many ways distinct and deserve closer examination.

The constant perils of resource abundance have often been linked to economic, political, and social aspects of development in resource-rich countries. In the resource curse literature, these perils have been analyzed under three subcategories that: (1) look at the relationship between natural resource wealth and economic growth; (2) consider linkages between natural resources and wars; and (3) focus on the relationship between natural resources and various political regimes.[1] The chapters in this volume focus on issues and cases that run across all three subcategories and in some cases go beyond. Yet the major interest of *Beyond the Resource Curse* is in the problems of energy exporters and in persistent and interrelated perils that have emerged in almost all resource-exporting countries.

The chapters have tried to highlight a number of constant pitfalls and challenges facing resource-exporting states and the ways to overcome them.

Among other things, the perils have been associated with the changes in the terms of trade, price volatility, uncertainty in hydrocarbon markets and price, Dutch disease, development of the tradable non-oil sector, monetary and subsidy policies of resource-rich governments, windfall misallocation and structural adjustments, lack of institutional capacity, rent-seeking activities, and human capital development and societal issues. After giving brief background information about the perils of energy exports, this chapter will go over each constant peril and then discuss policy responses and lessons to be learned.

It would be fair to say that those resource-rich states that are eager to learn from the mistakes of others and recognize the constant perils of resource dependence are more likely to succeed and prosper than those countries that fail to do so. Moreover, the extent to which a resource-rich state succeeds or fails is not due to the mere existence of abundant resources; it is dependent, among other things, on how the government goes about managing these resources and the revenues from their sale.

Background

Export-led growth was a particularly popular economic strategy prior to the 1970s, at the time when most developing countries thought that their comparative advantage lay in exporting the raw materials with which they were endowed. The historical engine-of-growth theory by Ragnar Nurkse claimed that exports of natural resources played a positive role in the economic development of nineteenth-century developing states such as the United States, Canada, Argentina, and Australia. Nurkse argued that these countries grew thanks to the dramatic increase in the demand of Western Europe, particularly of Great Britain, for the "foodstuff and raw materials" that those countries "were well suited to produce."[2]

Nurkse, however, was less optimistic about mid-twentieth-century export-reliant developing countries, as global demand for their primary products had diminished.[3] Only oil-rich countries were an exception, because the demand for oil in the world was still high and these countries were able to attract foreign investment. In his discussion of trade trends and international investment, Nurkse drew a parallel between the nineteenth-century developing countries ("new countries") and the oil-rich states of the twentieth century:

Both show a rising share in world trade. Both exert a strong attraction for private foreign capital. Both happen to be, on the whole, sparsely populated. The new countries banished the world food crisis that worried [Thomas] Malthus. The oil countries banished the fuel crisis due to the exhaustion of coal supplies which in England worried [John Stuart] Mill and [William Stanley] Jevons.[4]

In short, twentieth-century resource-rich developing states had better chances to grow and develop than resource-poor developing countries. Yet, this was not the case.

After the surge in oil prices of the 1970s, many scholars started to observe a number of negative developments in resource-rich countries. The literature on Dutch disease and the resource curse grew rapidly, especially after the 1980s, as more data on the economic performance of resource-rich states became available. The negative developments led many economists and political scientists to question the role of resource exports in the economic growth of resource-abundant countries, and they produced a series of papers investigating problems associated with resource dependence.[5]

The consistent presence of Dutch disease symptoms in most resource-abundant states demanded investigation of the phenomenon over time using statistical tools. The earlier works investigating economic development in resource-rich countries have been static cross-country comparisons. Later studies have employed large-N quantitative analysis using data on trade and economic indicators provided by the World Bank and other international organizations. Throughout the 1980s and 1990s, a series of studies pointed to a negative correlation between resource abundance (especially mineral abundance) and economic performance.[6] But it was the comprehensive work of Jeffrey Sachs and Andrew Warner analyzing a larger sample of countries that showed that resource-rich countries tend to grow slower than resource-poor states over time, thus confirming the existence of the resource curse.[7] Other quantitative studies followed—some confirming the phenomenon and some disputing it.[8]

These statistical studies have provided a number of essential insights into the developmental challenges resource-rich states face. Yet these studies also had some limitations. The resource-abundant countries selected for large-N studies have varied from each other significantly, and specifics of individual cases were mostly neglected. As Thorvaldur Gylfason wrote in reference to his eighty-five-country-sample study, "The resource-rich countries . . . [in the sample] vary so greatly from one another . . . with regard to their stage of development and type of government, that it could be regarded as highly questionable whether all of them—from Nigeria to Norway! —should be grouped together for drawing general conclusions."[9]

Sachs and Warner's findings, though important, did not tell us much about the hidden intervening factors that often determine poor or successful economic performance of individual resource-rich countries. More recently, their results have been challenged,[10] and the findings of other predominantly quantitative studies on the resource curse have been labeled as "inconclusive."[11] Likewise, although the qualitative studies have provided a more in-depth understanding of the political and social aspects of the resource curse through cognitive, societal, and statistical theories, they, too, have suffered from a lack of adequate tests.[12] Hence, as Ragnar Torvik contends, "The theoretical modeling of the political economy of the resource curse" is "still in its infancy," and more research needs to be done to better explain divergence in resource-rich states' economic and political development.[13]

Nonetheless, Sachs and Warner's key finding that the resource-rich states tend to grow more slowly has heralded a new era in the research on resource-rich states. The evidence of the resource curse has raised many important questions: What were the factors behind the poor economic performance of resource-rich states? Why have some resource-rich states managed to grow, yet others have failed to do so? What were the determinants of successful economic development for these states? Is resource abundance per se an obstacle to successful development, or are there other intervening factors that come into play in determining the outcome? And more importantly, what are the persistent pitfalls and perils facing resource-rich states and how can these challenges be overcome?

Constant Perils

External Shocks and Price Volatility

During the past sixty years, the world economy has witnessed a number of cyclical upturns and downturns in the demand for and prices of natural resource commodities, including hydrocarbons and minerals. The price jumps and collapses in the 1970s, 1980s, 1990s, and most recently in the 2000s have made a number of countries rich, then poor, and then rich again. Some resource-abundant countries have succeeded in utilizing temporary windfalls from rising oil prices and continued to prosper, but others have failed to do so.

The unfavorable terms of trade and the volatility of the world market prices for natural resources are often cited among the economic explanations for the resource curse.[14] Most resource-rich states are export-reliant developing countries, and they depend on the sale of one or two primary commodities such as oil and natural gas. These depletable hydrocarbons usually constitute the bulk of these countries' exports and generate the lion's share of their GDPs. The economies of these countries become oversensitive to external fluctuations and trends in world demand and hydrocarbon prices. Most importantly, there is not much these countries can do to influence these global changes. As Jeffrey Frankel (Chapter 1) notes, the majority of resource-rich states end up being "price takers" in the exports of their commodities.

The early warning that the demand for developing countries' primary products would diminish came from mid-twentieth-century economists.[15] This argument was reinforced by the important works of Raul Prebisch and Hans Singer[16] on Latin American economies. Their studies were an attempt to address deteriorating terms of trade by proposing an "inward-looking" development model, which led many developing countries to question the export-led hypothesis and turn to import substitution, adopting protectionist policies in the process. Prebisch and Singer were among the first to point to changing terms of trade that had worked to the "secular disadvantage" of developing countries heavily reliant on primary commodity exports and to the advantage of developed nations that specialized in manufacturing.[17] They argued that these unfavorable terms of trade were, and would remain, "the cause of [an] ever-widening gap in [developing and developed countries'] per capita incomes."[18] Studies have shown evidence in support of this hypothesis but admit that the condition does not apply to oil and minerals.[19] Moreover, despite many developing countries' advances in production and export of manufacturing products in the last fifty years, the proponents of the Prebisch-Singer thesis have continued to claim that "unequal exchange with the developed countries" persists to this day,[20] albeit for technological and other reasons rather than the secular disadvantage of trade terms.

Although some previous studies have pointed to a link between the terms of trade and economic growth,[21] more recent studies have shed doubt on the relationship between export instability and the resource curse.[22] Yet oil market disruptions in particular have been thought to exert influence on macroeconomic activity, not only by raising oil prices, but also by increasing oil price volatility.[23] In addition, extended high oil prices can potentially be perilous for both energy exporters and energy consumers and have a long-term effect on energy demand (see Jones, Chapter 10). Therefore, external shocks and price volatility remain the two important perils facing resource-rich states, especially those that fail to diversify and generate positive externalities for the tradable sectors of their non-oil economies. So long as a country depends on the sale of one or two natural resources such as oil and natural gas, which do not require much of "learning by doing" skills,[24] its macroeconomic vulnerability will persist. This will be not so much because of unfavorable terms of trade but due to the country's overdependence on a single product—a product that's external demand and price tag are not decided by the resource-rich state.

Unpredictability

The so-called boom and bust cycles in the demand and price of hydrocarbons are often accompanied by another peril: unpredictability. Many resource-rich states would prefer to have more predictable terms of trade and long-term agreements whereby they can set the prices for their oil and gas. These governments would make concessions when the prices of oil or natural gas were low, but they could also develop a growing appetite for mounting revenues when the prices go up. This could lead to bullying foreign companies (as happened in Russia with the TNK-BP joint venture project when BP had to sell its major stakes to Russia's gas giant Gazprom), renegotiating the terms of previously signed energy contracts (that is, introduction of new windfall profits taxes [Algeria] or amendments to national law allowing change to the terms of production sharing agreements [Kazakhstan], annulling medium-term supply contracts, gradually (re)nationalizing the entire energy industry [Venezuela; see Jaffe, Chapter 11], or increasing chances for entrenched rent-seeking activity [see Auty, Chapter 3]).

The uncertainty in oil and gas prices, in particular, could also affect resource-consuming developed countries, which usually rely on consumption of hydrocarbons and minerals from abroad (see Jones, Chapter 10). The slowdown in economic growth has been registered in the developed states in the aftermath of every oil price shock since the 1970s.[25] For example, James Hamilton notes that since World War II, nine out of the ten recessions in the United States were preceded by a jump in oil prices.[26] Moreover, the changing nature of oil price volatility from demand-driven shocks to expectations-driven future shocks makes energy markets even more unpredictable.[27] As Lutz Killian asserts:

> while no two oil price shocks are alike, most oil price shocks since the 1970s have been driven by a combination of strong global demand for industrial commodities (including crude oil) and expectations shifts that increase precautionary demand for crude oil specifically. These expectations shifts reflect the market's uncertainty about future oil supply shortfalls, which in turn reflects expectations about both future demand for crude oil as well as future supplies of crude oil.[28]

These and other perils call out for more predictable and sustainable arrangements or a "Producer-Consumer Dialogue" (see Jones, Chapter 10) that could benefit all interested parties, including resource suppliers, multinational energy-producing companies, and resource-consuming states. An indexation method proposed by Frankel (Chapter 1) to avoid a threat of nationalization and contract annulations by resource-rich governments could also be extended to address the issue of uncertainty in price and supply of hydrocarbons. Sharing the profit and loss between resource exporters and resource consumers could result in a more predictable arrangement whereby resource-exporting countries would not need to worry about the changing terms of trade and "unfair" pricing, and resource-consuming states would be guaranteed a continuous flow of the most wanted commodity in the world.

Dutch Disease and the Non-Oil Sector

Dutch disease is probably the most recurring economic "sickness" threatening almost every resource-rich country. As more and more countries became infected by this "disease," a number of antidotes have been developed. Yet the disease has developed a high level of endurance over the past four decades and requires more carefully crafted policy responses to neutralize it. What starts essentially as a foreign exchange problem with the appreciation of the local currency (as a result of a massive influx of revenues from the sale of hydrocarbons) soon turns into an unruly fiscal and monetary challenge that puts pressure on the non-oil sector of the economy, diminishing its international competitiveness and its previous employment levels.[29] Joseph Stiglitz sums up the occurrence:

> The problem, known as the Dutch disease in honor of the country where it was first analyzed, had plagued resource-rich countries around the world as they sell their resources and convert the dollars they earn into local currency. As their currency appreciates, they find it difficult to export other products. Growth in the nonresource sector slows. Unemployment increases, since the resource sector typically employs relatively few people.[30]

In addition to causing the appreciation of the real exchange rate of the local currency, Dutch disease also leads to factor misallocation in the economy. This problem was first observed in export-dependent states of the mid-twentieth century when their export sectors witnessed a rapid boom but often to the detriment of other sectors in the economy. Exports of primary products were seen as a comparative advantage for resource-abundant developing countries in the twentieth century, and these states were encouraged to continue their specialization in the production and export of their primary products. Nonetheless, the stimulus from exports was limited to one sector—the booming export-based sector—and did not spread across the whole economy.[31] The scholars studying oil-rich states have also reached a similar conclusion.[32] Sachs and Warner note that "except for the direct contribution of the natural resource sector itself . . . natural resource abundant countries systematically failed to achieve strong export-led growth or other kinds of growth."[33]

Resource-poor countries are less threatened when existing resources from less efficient, non-export sectors are moved to more productive export sectors of the economy. In fact, this reallocation of resources from one sector to another may lead to increases in export output and economic growth.[34] In a resource-rich state, however, this shift usually occurs by default when swelling revenue from natural resource sales "shifts factors of production away from sectors generating learning by doing,"[35] thus exacerbating Dutch disease, sometimes with long-term consequences.[36]

Resource-rich states that fall prey to this trap often do so due to their governments' erroneous policies. These governments are interested in developing the resource-driven—or most rent-generating—sector of the economy because it is their "cash cow." However, they sometimes disregard the development of other sectors of the economy that are not as attractive for rent-seeking activity. A number of studies have pointed out that countries that diversify their economies away from the primary export commodity are more likely to succeed in the long run.[37] The successful resource-rich countries are those that "diversify their exports, improve public finance management, and build on the accumulation of knowledge and infrastructure."[38] Thus, the significance of diversification and the strengthening of the non-oil sector in resource-rich states cannot be overstated. It is vital to continue further research in trying to better understand the determinants of non-oil GDP growth in resource-dependent countries.

Windfall Misallocation and Structural Adjustments

If they make good policy choices, oil-exporting countries may benefit from temporary price hikes and run surpluses during boom periods. But once a boom cycle ends, resource-rich countries start to experience serious fiscal and monetary problems and run the risk of becoming overindebted due to overexpansion in the public sector, overspending, and erroneous investment projects.[39] In addition, resource dependence has a long-term structural impact on the economy of resource-rich states. It slows down economic growth and competitive industrialization, delays critical economic and political reforms, and retards the development of the non-oil sector and human capital generation.[40]

The influx of revenues creates a temporary surplus that many resource-rich governments often misuse or misallocate by building investment projects that have a negative social surplus (that is, white elephants).[41] They expand the inefficient public employment sector in an attempt to deal with unemployment and popular dissatisfaction; invest in financially dubious, unsustainable, and costly infrastructure projects; and sometimes opt for import substitution in sectors that fail to compete internationally even after a protracted period of government protection.[42] This leads to the introduction of "new politics of rising expectations, social welfare largesse, and greater state paternalism."[43]

Once the booms turn into busts, the governments of resource-rich states can no longer maintain high public expenditures and struggle to adopt "correct" structural adjustment policies to reclaim the pre-bust economic growth rate. Even if these governments realize that they need to introduce severe cuts and downsize the inefficient public sector, they are unable to make these politically sensitive changes. Instead, the governments of resource-rich states often choose to maintain the status quo and borrow externally from the IMF and the World Bank in the hope that a "bailout" will be a temporary measure and that the debt will be quickly repaid once oil prices go up again.[44] The time gap between the booms, however, is usually long enough to erode the essential economic base of any unprepared resource-rich state, which could end up being heavily indebted and losing its comparative advantage in world markets. This, in turn, could result in "a permanent loss of competitiveness"[45] whereby any resource-dependent country's ability to strengthen its non-oil economy and diversify its production base away from hydrocarbons is halted. Jahangir Amuzegar sums up the dangers in the example of OPEC member states:

> A combination of "wrong" policies at the state level often ended up in unrealized targets, a multitude of white-elephant projects and widespread inefficiency. The absence of foresight and prudence in the selection of policy alternatives during oil booms made it doubly difficult to shift gear, correct mistaken policies, or adopt counteracting adjustment measures once booms turned inevitably into busts. The reversal of fortune during periods of depressed oil prices frequently resulted in painful economic deterioration, bankruptcies, and debt moratoria.[46]

Subsidies

Another common peril worth mentioning separately is the mismanagement of state subsidies in resource-rich countries. State subsidies are one of the common incentives used by both resource-rich and resource-poor countries across the globe. They usually aim to: (1) provide socioeconomic benefits to the poor; (2) develop rural areas through delivering access to better quality energy and other infrastructure services; (3) protect local businesses and firms from external competition (that is, import substitution); and/or (4) support domestic firms in global competition (that is, export promotion). These explicit and implicit subsidies come as the subsidized cost of food, housing, and energy (in other words gasoline, electricity, natural gas, etc.), tax credits, and direct or indirect financial assistance to private firms[47] (see Mojtahed, Chapter 4 and Sabonis-Helf, Chapter 6).

In most resource-abundant countries, the state is the primary benefactor of revenues generated through the sale of hydrocarbons. The decision on how, when, and where to invest is usually centralized in the hands of an elite. The windfalls are channeled to "priority regions, sectors, and projects in a centralized, force-led and often ad hoc manner,"[48] which more often than not turns state subsidy policy into a bureaucratic swamp and an ineffective and wasteful enterprise. Moreover, sometimes providing costly subsidies is not a choice but an obligation a government feels compelled to fulfill due to socioeconomic factors (refugees, pensioners, etc.).

Although the main purpose of subsidies is to assist the poor, subsidies can easily become untargeted and indiscriminate and create a number of challenges.[49] They could give birth to strong interest groups that depend on subsidies and lobby for their continuation, even when these subsidies are no longer effective (see Auty, Chapter 3 and Barma, Chapter 13).[50] Moreover, due to a common view among the citizens of resource-rich countries that the state should provide and pay for the socioeconomic needs of the population, discontinuing subsidies becomes a politically sensitive issue, which makes it almost impossible to change previously adopted policies for fear of sparking political discontent (see Mojtahed, Chapter 4).

In general, a government's decisions on public investment and the implementation mechanism and efficacy of a subsidy are important determinants of a successful subsidy strategy. Public investments in resource-rich states are sometimes directed to areas that are not an immediate priority. Yet large investment projects are approved, and huge sums of funds are spent on these projects during and after boom periods. Hence, the level of development in oil-rich countries becomes a critical factor in assessing whether a particular project or investment is sustainable and needs a subsidy. Prioritizing public investment and state subsidies according to resource-rich countries' needs could help these countries better manage their budgets and adopt appropriate policies during the boom and bust cycles.[51]

Rent Seeking

Most scholars agree that resource abundance is correlated with the emergence of a particular type of petrostate that is often known for rent-seeking behavior. Although rent-seeking activity is not limited to resource-rich states,[52] the very nature of hydrocarbons such as oil and natural gas makes rent seeking particularly perilous for resource-rich states. Although "low rent motivates governments to provide public goods and efficiency incentives that align the economy with its comparative advantage" (see Auty, Chapter 3), dependence on rents from hydrocarbons "produces a distinctive type of institutional setting...which encourages the political distribution of rents."[53] It allows resource-rich governments to delay essential economic and political reforms needed for sustainable development. Rent seeking may become self-sustaining activity,[54] and this, as Richard Auty stresses, could "risk feeding rent-seeking activity at the expense of sustained economic growth."

Unlike other goods and commodities, hydrocarbons such as oil and natural gas are nonrenewable and do not require much effort for production, as they are extracted from the ground in isolation from other sectors of the economy and sold without going through a production process. This feature makes them "less like a source of income and more like an asset" and increases the risk of rent-seeking activity in resource-rich countries.[55] The depletable, low-cost, but highly profitable nature of petroleum affects oil-rich states' economic and political behavior. This behavior generates particular types of social classes, interest groups, and business circles that reinforce a self-serving "pertolization" strategy and depend on the state for oil rents.[56] Moreover, in time some petrostate governments isolate themselves from the rest of the public by creating their own support base and become "rentier states" that continue to "live largely off unearned income."[57]

The abundance of valuable hydrocarbons also increases the chance of "rent capture" activity by both domestic and external actors. As Terry Karl notes, "The exceptional value of their leading commodity [means] *unusually high level of external intervention* in shaping their affairs and capturing their resources by dominant states and foreign private interests" (emphasis in original).[58] In addition, weak and unstable resource-rich states appear more likely to get involved in international conflicts than states with stable governments (see Soltanov, Chapter 12).

The peril of rent seeking has been observed, in one form or another, in almost all resource-rich states regardless of regime type. Whether through a dominant petroleum industry in Norway, political factions and interest groups in Trinidad and Tobago, rent-extraction patronage networks in Cambodia and East Timor, or oil monarchies and autocratic ruling elites in the Middle East, Central Asia, and Latin America, these politically and economically diverse resource-rich countries have all experienced rent-seeking activity. Yet the extent to which the rent-seeking activity hinders economic growth and leads to a resource curse often depends on the country's level of development and the quality of its institutions and governance.[59]

Lack of Institutional Quality and Poor Governance

The ability to effectively manage perils facing resource-rich states, including rent seeking, often depends on institutions and effective governance.[60] Some scholars have claimed that resource abundance is associated with a deteriorating quality of governance[61] and that there is a strong causality between better governance and higher per capita incomes, with the former having a positive causal effect over the latter.[62] More recent studies, however, found contrary results showing that "greater abundance leads to better institutions and more rapid growth."[63] Others have stated that regardless of the level of natural abundance, it is the quality of institutions, economic management, and the management of the resources that are essential for a country's economic growth.[64] And resource-rich states that have "institutions that promote accountability and state competence . . . tend to benefit from resource booms since these institutions ameliorate the perverse political incentives that such booms create."[65]

Resource-rich states experience consistent problems in attempting to create the quality of institutions needed for sustainable economic development. Most of these problems stem from the inherent structural challenges in a resource-rich economy. Due to a heavy dependence on export of hydrocarbons, the oil sector of the economy is always dominant. This dominance usually hurts the non-oil sectors of the economy, but it could also have a long-term institutional impact.[66] Some resource-rich governments focus on developing the resource-driven—or the most rent-generating—sector of their economies because it is their "cash cow," and the non-oil sector of these economies—not so attractive for rent-seeking activity—remains "less efficient" and neglected.[67] In time, "state officials become habituated to relying on the progressive substitution of public spending for statecraft, thereby further weakening state capacity."[68] In other words, the prolonged dominance of the "oil" sector, which is usually under state control, weakens the overall quality of institutions in the long run. This is particularly problematic for resource-rich countries that began their development with no proper institutional heritage or previous experience of a market economy (that is, postcolonial resource-rich countries in the second half of the twentieth century and newly independent post-Soviet transition economies). Moreover, the governments of resource-poor countries are more likely to support open trade regimes, align their interests with those of the majority of population, and redistribute revenues and assets more efficiently than the governments of resource-rich states.[69]

The more recent explanation for the resource curse related to a country's quality of institutions and governance is the structure of ownership within the hydrocarbon industry. The question of who owns the rights to natural resources and resource production industries is a significant one, as it "has implications for rent appropriation, exploration, and production decisions, and even for the exposure to market price fluctuations."[70] Some studies have shown that state ownership of resources affects the quality of institutions negatively (see Frankel, Chapter 1). But these studies, including the most recent one on oil-rich transition economies,[71] have been inconclusive. What most of them point out, however, is the importance of the quality of institutions, which often determines whether a particular type of ownership structure is bound to succeed or fail. As Amy Jaffe points out in Chapter 11, "government-owned oil companies perform better when they have a more independent oversight structure closer to the governance of private sector firms that must respond to commercial competition and private shareholders."[72] Hence, strengthening state institutions and implementing good governance policies could help resource-rich states avoid negative consequences of resource dependence.

Human Capital and Societal Issues

"It takes good educational institutions . . . to build the human capital stock that is essential for economic progress," notes Gylfason.[73] Accumulation of human capital through education and training is one of the essential ingredients of successful development of resource-rich states. It is also one of the most difficult ones. The perilous nature of human capital is hidden not in its abundance but in its shortage. Because the oil sector is limited in scope and only requires a particular type of human capital, developing "learning by doing"

skills in resource-rich states becomes a challenge. Unlike high-tech producing states that generate greater economic growth through "technological
spillovers," producers of low-tech commodities such as oil and natural gas
are in a disadvantageous position vis-à-vis the countries that concentrate on
manufacturing and exporting high-tech products.[74]

In Chapter 8, Regine Spector asserts, "A better-educated and well-
trained population can increase productivity as well as innovate and/or
adopt new technologies that—if accompanied by favorable macroeconomic
conditions and opportunities to engage in relevant work—will allow the
country to gain a competitive edge in the global economy." In the example
of the resource-rich Persian Gulf countries, Patrick Clawson (Chapter 2) illustrates how resource abundance, if developed properly, can have a positive
impact on human capital development. But most resource-rich governments tend to view their natural resources as "their most important asset"
and in time they start to "inadvertently—and perhaps even deliberately!—
neglect the development of their human resources, by devoting inadequate
attention and expenditure to education."[75]

Even when resource-rich states understand the importance of human
capital, achieving a successful level or quality of education is not always an
easy task. Spector highlights the challenges governments face when trying
to increase the human capital and quality of education in resource-rich developing countries such as Azerbaijan and Kazakhstan. Her findings reveal
that recognizing the importance of human capital accumulation and investing in the educational sector, though important, do not necessarily produce
"better education-related spending" or translate into better quality education
in resource-rich states.

Finally, regarding why some resource-rich states convert their "black
gold" into "human gold" yet others do not, one answer is hidden at the societal
level. As mentioned earlier, resource-rich states tend to produce particular
types of elites and institutions. The mechanism through which these formal
and social institutions are formed in resource-rich countries deserves closer
investigation and more in-depth research. Sometimes the initial conditions,
past experiences, and a number of domestic and external factors affect the
way a resource-rich society as a whole develops. In Chapter 7, Murad Ismayilov
attempts to explain how resource-rich Azerbaijan and research-poor Georgia
have used pipeline politics in post-Soviet Central Eurasia differently in their
struggles for recognition and how having or lacking a natural resource affected

the collective identity formation and orientation of these countries. Such studies draw attention to the significant perils resource abundance can present for a society, perils that go beyond just a few ruling elites.

Policy Responses

Many scholars have offered a number of economic and political antidotes for avoiding the resource curse and Dutch disease. These remedies could be classified under four categories: (1) direct distribution of revenues to all citizens; (2) sound macroeconomic and monetary policies, including setting up intergenerational wealth funds; (3) good governance policies; and (4) economic diversification and the strengthening of the tradable non-oil sector.[76]

Direct Distribution of Revenues

Xavier Sala-i-Martin and Arvind Subramanian, who examined the case of Nigeria, have suggested distributing oil revenues directly to all citizens of the country. The authors claim that their proposal "could fundamentally improve the quality of public institutions and, as a result, transform the economic landscape in Nigeria for decades to come."[77] They are also convinced that this strategy is "superior to the status quo." Similarly, Jesper Jensen and David Tarr advocate the distribution of rents directly to firms and the poor in Iran, arguing that "the poor will be better off and the rich worse off under [their proposed] distribution mechanism."[78] Moreover, pointing to an "an urgent need for political and economic reform in Iraq," Thomas Palley has supported direct distribution of oil revenues to Iraq's citizens, claiming that this would transform the country and "empower citizens to take charge of the process of economic growth and . . . give [them] an incentive to engage in democratic politics."[79]

Although these propositions may sound appealing in theory, they do not address the chronic problems of underdeveloped resource-rich states. Nor do they tackle any of the fundamental issues that would supposedly transform and sustain the economies of resource-rich states. Sachs, for instance, points to a "poverty trap" that exists in many resource-rich developing countries and cannot be broken by distributing oil earnings directly to the public.[80]

The experience of Papua New Guinea, which distributes mineral rents to its population through its parliamentarians,[81] has shown that "an estimated 85 percent in revenue went into immediate consumption rather than skill acquisition or produced capital."[82] Moreover, because most of the distributed revenues are spent immediately without considering future generations, the practice also runs against the sustainability principle, which is essential for continuous growth and the generation of positive genuine savings.[83] In short, there is almost no evidence (that is, Alaska is not an appropriate or sufficient example) to suggest that direct distribution of proceeds from oil to the general public leads to sustainable and long-term economic growth. A partial direct distribution of windfalls could be considered only if a resource-rich country achieves a level of per capita income and development of an advanced country such as Norway and only if the government can assure a fair and efficient delivery, which is rarely the case.[84]

Monetary Policy and Oil Funds

Instead, sound macroeconomic and monetary policies by governments in resource-rich states can create positive and sometimes long-term effects (see Clawson, Chapter 2 and Nurmammadov, Chapter 5). To avoid Dutch disease, some resource-abundant states (for example, Saudi Arabia, Kuwait, Brunei, and other Persian Gulf states) have kept the bulk of their streaming revenues in offshore financial reserves and spent on foreign asset acquisition and purchase of capital-intensive imports.[85] Another solution has been the practice of establishing intergenerational (oil) funds or sovereign wealth funds that isolate surplus oil money from the rest of the economy and prevent the potential shocks of large currency inflows into domestic markets. This measure helps to spread the wealth across time for future generations, stabilize expenditures during the boom period, and avoid borrowing during unforeseen crisis. These policies help resource-rich states "insulate the domestic economy from the volatility of commodity revenues and generate budget stability."[86] Azerbaijan and East Timor established their state oil funds prior to the major influx of oil and gas revenues, which helped them better manage the revenues and stabilize their economies (see Nurmammadov, Chapter 5 and Barma, Chapter 13).

Good Governance Policies

The active involvement of the public in oil management and the issues of transparency and accountability in resource-rich states have become relevant, particularly in recent years. As a result of an active push from a number of international NGOs and foreign governments, the World Bank and the International Monetary Fund have started to urge the governments of resource-rich states to adopt more open policies in disclosing windfall rents and expenditures. They have also encouraged multinational energy companies to publish their transactions with resource-rich states.[87] This led to introductions of various initiatives such as the EITI that sets a global standard for transparent and accountable management of resource revenues in oil, gas, and mining countries (see Barma, Chapter 13). Backed by a coalition of governments, companies, and civil society groups, the EITI aims to improve good governance in resource-rich states "through the verification and full publication of company payments and government revenues from oil, gas, and mining."[88] Currently, thirty-five resource-rich countries follow the EITI initiative and try to meet its standards for transparency and accountability.

Diversification and Tradable Non-Oil Economy

Finally, the most important challenge for resource-rich states—and the most commonly proposed remedy to avoid Dutch disease and the resource curse—has been economic diversification and strengthening of the non-oil economy. A number of studies have pointed out that countries that diversify their economies away from their primary export commodity are more likely to succeed in the long run.[89] A recent World Bank report cites successful experiences of several previously export-dependent states that managed to diversify their economies and grow at the same time. In 1980, oil and natural gas constituted 32 percent of Malaysia's total exports. This figure was only 13 percent in 2006, but the country's GDP per capita reached $12,536, an increase of more than 150 percent between 1980 and 2006. The report notes that in early oil booms, the governments of resource-rich states should "take concentrated action to reverse the unfavorable trends in non-oil private investment, non-oil exports, and non-oil FDI [foreign direct investment]."[90] It is therefore vital to better understand the determinants of non-oil GDP growth, particularly the non-oil tradable sector.

Lessons to Be Learned

When explaining the reasons behind resource-abundant states' failures, the proponents of the resource curse thesis often argue that resource-rich states are different in many ways from resource-poor countries and that these differences, explicitly or implicitly, affect the way the politics and economies of these states evolve. As has been presented throughout this volume, energy-exporting states do indeed face a number of constant and particular perils that are specifically linked to the abundance of resources they are endowed with. Yet the critical elements that determine whether a resource-rich state becomes a "Norway or a Nigeria" are undoubtedly hidden in intervening factors, which are often missed in large-N quantitative studies.

There is an "emerging consensus" among political scientists that a number of "political and social variables mediate the relationship between natural resource wealth and development outcomes."[91] Dutch disease is "not automatic,"[92] and the idea of oil being a "curse" could be "only partly true" and could be avoided by promoting a correct and "long-run growth-focused investment strategy."[93] As some chapters in this volume reveal, the experience of resource-rich latecomers differs from that of their predecessors, which experienced the evils of resource dependence but left meaningful lessons from which their successors could learn. The relatively new resource-rich countries such as Azerbaijan and East Timor—which worked closely with international organizations to mitigate the potential economic risks of a large influx of oil revenues by establishing oil funds and adhering to monetary discipline—seem to have shown a healthier economic performance in the early stages of rent generation. So did the majority of resource-rich countries in the Persian Gulf.

Yet many political and socioeconomic considerations that misled earlier resource-rich countries and brought about their downfall also seem to confront the latecomers. Inefficient public spending and subsidies, investment in wasteful projects, increased rent-seeking activities and corruption, neglect for human capital accumulation, and reluctance to introduce tough precautionary measures for the sake of short-term political dividends are still important challenges that resource-rich states need to tackle.

NOTES

Introduction

1. Jan Dehn, "The Effects on Growth of Commodity Price Uncertainty and Shocks," World Bank Policy Research Working Paper 2455 (2001).

2. This is based on the definition of energy security presented in Brenda Shaffer, *Energy Politics* (Philadelphia: University of Pennsylvania Press, 2009), 93. In *Energy Politics*, the third component was referred to as *environmental friendliness*. The revised term *environmental sustainability* more accurately describes this factor.

3. *Emirates Business 24/7*, December 7, 2009.

4. BBC news, January 4, 2010, http://news.bbc.co.uk/2/hi/science/nature/8440181.stm, accessed July 1, 2010.

5. Benjamin Smith, "Oil Wealth and Regime Survival in the Developing World, 1960–1999," *American Journal of Political Science* 48:2 (April 2004): 232–46.

6. The 1973–74 boycott was called by the Organization of Arab Petroleum Exporting Countries (OAPEC), the Arab group of states within OPEC.

7. GECF was founded in Tehran in 2001. In its official documents it declares, "The Gas Exporting Countries Forum (GECF) is a gathering of the world's leading gas producers aimed at representing and promoting their mutual interests. The GECF was set up with the objective to increase the level of coordination and strengthen the collaboration between member countries." Member states are Algeria, Bolivia, Brunei, Egypt, Equatorial Guinea, Iran, Libya, Nigeria, Qatar, Russia, Trinidad and Tobago, and Venezuela. Kazakhstan, Netherlands, and Norway are observers.

8. Iran is a net importer of natural gas. It exports modest quantities of natural gas to Turkey and Armenia but imports larger quantities from Turkmenistan and Azerbaijan.

Chapter 1

The author would like to thank the Azerbaijan Diplomatic Academy in Baku and the Weatherhead Center for International Affairs at Harvard University for support and Rabah Arezki, Sebastian Bustos, Oyebola Olabisi, Lant Pritchett, and Jesse Schreger for comments.

1. See Richard Auty, *Sustaining Development in Mineral Economies: The Resource Curse Thesis* (New York: Oxford University Press, 1993) and Richard Auty, *Resource Abundance and Economic Development* (New York: Oxford University Press, 2001).

2. See Paul Stevens, "Resource Impact: Curse or Blessing? A Literature Survey," *Journal of Energy Literature* 9:1 (June 2003): 1–42 and Frederick van der Ploeg, "Natural Resources: Curse or Blessing?" *Journal of Economic Literature* 49:2 (June 2011): 366–420. The surveys by Stevens and van der Ploeg are written for energy specialists and economic theorists, respectively. The present survey casts a wider net, is intended for a more general audience, and offers policy prescriptions.

3. See Raymond Mikesell, "Explaining the Resource Curse, with Special Reference to Mineral-Exporting Countries," *Resources Policy* 23:4 (December 1997): 191–99; Stevens, "Resource Impact: Curse or Blessing?"; Daniel Lederman and William Maloney, "In Search of the Missing Resource Curse," *Economia* 9:1 (Fall 2008); Gavin Wright and Jesse Czelusta, "Mineral Resources and Economic Development," Conference on Sector Reform in Latin America, Stanford Center for International Development, November 13–15, 2003; Gavin Wright and Jesse Czelusta, "The Myth of the Resource Curse," *Challenge* 47 (March–April 2004); Gavin Wright and Jesse Czelusta, "Resource-Based Growth Past and Present," in Daniel Lederman and William F. Maloney, eds., *Neither Curse Nor Destiny: Natural Resources and Development* (Stanford, Calif.: Stanford University Press and World Bank, 2006); Pauline Jones Luong and Erika Weinthal, *Oil Is Not a Curse: Ownership Structure and Institutions in Soviet Successor States* (Cambridge: Cambridge University Press, 2010); and van der Ploeg, "Natural Resources: Curse or Blessing?"

4. If OPEC functioned effectively as a true cartel, then it would possess even more monopoly power in the aggregate. We assume here, however, that OPEC does not currently exercise much monopoly power beyond that of Saudi Arabia, because so many nonmembers now produce oil and because even OPEC members usually do not feel constrained to stay within assigned quotas.

5. See Raul Prebisch, *The Economic Development of Latin America and Its Principal Problems* (New York: UN Department of Economic Affairs, 1950) and Hans W. Singer, "U.S. Foreign Investment in Underdeveloped Areas: The Distribution of Gains Between Investing and Borrowing Countries," *American Economic Review, Papers and Proceedings* 40 (May 1950): 473–85.

6. Insecure ownership rights are seen to inhibit investment in natural resources in Henning Bohn and Robert Deacon, "Ownership Risk, Investment, and the Use of Natural Resources," *American Economic Review* 90 (June 2000): 526–49.

7. See Harold Hotelling, "The Economics of Exhaustible Resources," *Journal of Political Economy* 39:2 (April 1931): 137–75.

8. The same arbitrage condition that implies a positive long-run price trend also can explain a major source of shorter-run price swings. The real price of oil should be unusually high during periods when real interest rates are low (e.g., due to easy mon-

etary policy), in order that a poor expected future return to leaving the oil in the ground offsets the low interest rate. By contrast, when real interest rates are high (e.g., due to tight monetary policy), current oil prices should lie below their long-run equilibrium, because an expected future rate of price increase is needed in order to offset the high interest rate. Very low U.S. real interest rates boosted commodity prices toward the end of the 1970s, especially in dollar terms, and high U.S. real interest rates drove prices down in the 1980s, again especially in dollar terms. In the years 2003–11, low interest rates may again have been a source of high commodity prices. See Jeffrey Frankel, "Expectations and Commodity Price Dynamics: The Overshooting Model," *American Journal of Agricultural Economics* 68:2 (May 1986): 344–48; Frankel, "The Effect of Monetary Policy on Real Commodity Prices," in John Campbell, ed., *Asset Prices and Monetary Policy* (Chicago: University of Chicago Press, 2008); Frankel, "An Explanation for Soaring Commodity Prices," *Vox* (March 2008); Frankel and Gikas Hardouvelis, "Commodity Prices, Money Surprises, and Fed Credibility," *Journal of Money, Credit, and Banking* 17:4 (November 1985), Part I: 427–38; Frankel and Andrew Rose, "Determination of Agricultural and Mineral Commodity Prices," in Christopher Kent and Renee Fry, eds., *Inflation in an Era of Relative Price Shocks* (Sydney: Reserve Bank of Australia, 2009); Robert Barsky and Lawrence Summers, "Gibson's Paradox and the Gold Standard," *Journal of Political Economy* 96:3 (June 1988): 528–50; and Ricardo Caballero, Emmanuel Farhi, and Pierre-Olivier Gourinchas, "Financial Crash, Commodity Prices, and Global Imbalances," *Brookings Papers on Economic Activity* 2 (2008): 1–55.

Some authors believe that many of the big oil price "shocks" have in reality been endogenous with respect to monetary policy. See Robert Barsky and Lutz Killian, 2002, "Do We Really Know that Oil Caused the Great Stagflation?" A Monetary Alternative," *NBER Macroeconomics Annual 2001*, vol. 16 (MIT Press: Cambridge): 137–83; and Lutz Killian, "Not All Price Shocks Are Alike: Disentangling Demand and Supply Shocks in the Crude Oil Market," *American Economic Review* 99:3 (June 2009): 1053–69. Some, of course, believe that destabilizing speculators are to blame for price swings.

9. See Thomas Malthus, *An Essay on the Principle of Population* (London: J. Johnson, 1798).

10. Even though Malthusianism predicts rising prices for commodities and structuralism predicts falling prices, both Malthus and Prebisch supported protection against imports. The resolution of the paradox is that Malthus had in mind England, where grain would be the import, while Prebisch had in mind Argentina, where grain would be the export and manufactures the import.

11. See Jeffrey Krautkraemer, "Nonrenewable Resource Scarcity," *Journal of Economic Literature* 36 (December 1998): 2065–2107; Wright and Czelusta, "Mineral Resources and Economic Development"; Wright and Czelusta, "The Myth of the Resource Curse"; and Wright and Czelusta, "Resource-Based Growth Past and Present."

12. See, for instance, Kenneth Deffeyes, *Beyond Oil: The View from Hubbert's Peak* (New York: Hill and Wang, 2005).

13. Although prices do not always move together for oil, other minerals, and agricultural products, there is a surprisingly high correlation. See Robert Pindyck and Julio Rotemberg, "The Excess Co-Movement of Commodity Prices," *Economic Journal* 100:403 (December 1990): 1173–89.

14. See John Cuddington, "Long-Run Trends in 26 Primary Commodity Prices," *Journal of Development Economics* 39:2 (October 1992): 207–27; Cuddington, Rodney Ludema, and Shamila Jayasuriya, "Prebisch-Singer Redux," in Daniel Lederman and William F. Maloney, eds., *Natural Resources: Neither Curse Nor Destiny* (Stanford, Calif.: Stanford University Press and World Bank, 2007), 103–40; Cuddington and C. M. Urzua, "Trends and Cycles in the Net Barter Terms of Trade: A New Approach," *Economic Journal* 99 (June 1989): 426–42; Enzo Grilli and Maw Cheng Yang, "Primary Commodity Prices, Manufactured Goods Prices, and the Terms of Trade of Developing Countries: What the Long Run Shows," *World Bank Economic Review* 2:1 (1988): 1–47; Pindyck, "The Long-Run Evolution of Energy Prices," *Energy Journal* 20:2 (1999); Yael Hadass and Jeffrey Williamson, "Terms of Trade Shocks and Economic Performance, 1870–1940: Prebisch and Singer Revisited," *Economic Development and Cultural Change* 51:3 (April 2003): 629–56; Carmen Reinhart and Peter Wickham, "Commodity Prices: Cyclical Weakness or Secular Decline?" IMF Staff Paper 41 (June 1994); Neil Kellard and Mark Wohar, "On the Prevalence of Trends in Primary Commodity Prices," *Journal of Development Economics* 79:1 (February 2006): 146–67; Joseph Balagtas and Matthew Holt, "The Commodity Terms of Trade, Unit Roots and Nonlinear Alternatives: A Smooth Transition Approach," *American Journal of Agricultural Economics* 91:1 (February 2009): 87–105; and David Harvey, Neil Kellard, Jakob Madsen, and Mark Wohar, "The Prebisch-Singer Hypothesis: Four Centuries of Evidence," *Review of Economics and Statistics* 92:2 (May 2010): 367–77.

15. Three "super cycles" in metals prices over the 150 years from 1850–2000, followed by the beginnings of a fourth, are discerned by John Cuddington and Daniel Jerrett, "Super Cycles in Real Metals Prices?" *IMF Staff Papers*, 55 (December 2008): 541–65.

16. The same phenomenon is evident in real exchange rates, stock prices, and housing prices.

17. See Christopher Blattman, Jason Hwang, and Jeffrey Williamson, "Winners and Losers in the Commodity Lottery: The Impact of Terms of Trade Growth and Volatility in the Periphery 1870–1939," *Journal of Development Economics* 82:1 (January 2007): 156–79; Ricardo Hausmann and Roberto Rigobon, "An Alternative Interpretation of the 'Resource Curse': Theory and Policy Implications," in Jeffrey Davis, ed., *Fiscal Policy Formulation and Implementation in Oil-Producing Countries* (Washington, D.C.: IMF, 2003), 12–44; and Steven Poelhekke and Frederick van der Ploeg, "Volatility, Financial Development, and the Natural Resource Curse," Center for Economic Policy Research DP6513 (October 2007).

18. See Jeffrey Sachs and Andrew Warner, "Natural Resource Abundance and Economic Growth," in Gerald M. Meier and James E. Rauch, eds., *Leading Issues in Economic Development* (New York: Oxford University Press, 1995) and Sachs and Warner, "The Curse of Natural Resources," *European Economic Review* 45:4–6 (May 2001): 827–38.

19. See Mary Kaldor, Terry Karl, and Yahia Said, *Oil Wars* (New York: Pluto Press, 2007); Michael Ross, "Does Oil Hinder Democracy?" *World Politics* 53:3 (April 2001): 325–61; Xavier Sala-i-Martin and Arvind Subramanian, "Addressing the Natural Resource Curse: An Illustration from Nigeria," IMF Working Paper WP/03/139 (2003); and Benjamin Smith, "Oil Wealth and Regime Survival in the Developing World, 1960–1999," *American Journal of Political Science* 48:2 (April 2004): 232–46.

20. See Erling Røed Larsen, "Escaping the Resource Curse and the Dutch Disease? When and Why Norway Caught up with and Forged ahead of Its Neighbors," Statistics Norway, Research Department, Discussion Paper 377 (May 2004). Norway is literally ranked No. 1 of 182 countries in the UN Human Development Index (HDI). Kuwait, Qatar, and the United Arab Emirates are also in the top fifth on the list. In terms of real income, Norway is ranked No. 5, just behind Qatar and the United Arab Emirates. For comparison, the United States is No. 9 in real income and 13 on the HDI.

21. Among those noting Botswana's conspicuous escape from the resource curse that has afflicted some of its neighbors are: Pierre Englebert, *State Legitimacy and Development in Africa* (Boulder, Colo.: Lynne Rienner, 2000); Maria Sarraf and Moortaza Jiwanji, "Beating the Resource Curse: The Case of Botswana," Environmental Economics Series Paper 83 (October 2001); Daron Acemoglu, Simon Johnson, and James Robinson, "Colonial Origins of Comparative Development: An Empirical Investigation," *American Economic Review* 91:5 (December 2001): 1369–1401; and Atsushi Iimi, "Did Botswana Escape from the Resource Curse?" IMF Working Paper 06/138 (June 2006).

22. Most African countries grew more strongly in 2000–2010 than previously, in part due to rising mineral prices. See Laura Beny and Lisa Cook, "Metals or Management? Explaining Africa's Recent Economic Growth Performance," *American Economic Review* 99:2 (May 2009): 268–74. But countries such as the Congo and Chad remain in the bottom 5 percent of countries in the UN Human Development Index. Oil-rich Nigeria ranks 142nd of 169 (2010 figures). See UN Development Programme, *Human Development Report* (New York: Palgrave Macmillan, 2010).

23. See Jacques Delacroix, "The Export of Raw Materials and Economic Growth: A Cross-National Study," *American Sociological Review* 42:5 (October 1977): 795–808; Graham Davis, "Learning to Love the Dutch Disease: Evidence from the Mineral Economies," *World Development* 23:10 (October 1995): 1765–79; and Michael Herb, "No Representation without Taxation? Rents, Development, and Democracy," *Comparative Politics* 37:3 (April 2005): 297–317.

24. See Michael Alexeev and Robert Conrad, "The Elusive Curse of Oil," *Review of Economics and Statistics* 91:3 (August 2009): 586–98.

25. See Francisco Rodriguez and Jeffrey Sachs, "Why Do Resource-Abundant Economies Grow More Slowly?" *Journal of Economic Growth* 4:3 (September 1999): 277–303 and Alexeev and Conrad, "The Elusive Curse of Oil."

26. See Wright and Czelusta, "Mineral Resources and Economic Development"; Wright and Czelusta, "The Myth of the Resource Curse"; and Wright and Czelusta, "Resource-Based Growth Past and Present." Even recorded reserves, the most common measure of endowments, are somewhat endogenous as well because they reflect discoveries, which in turn respond to both world prices and the productivity of the exploration industry, global and local.

27. See Paul David and Gavin Wright, "Increasing Returns and the Genesis of American Resource Abundance," *Industrial and Corporate Change* 6:2 (March 1997): 203–45.

28. See Wright and Czelust, "Mineral Resources and Economic Development."

29. See Ricardo Hausmann, "Venezuela's Growth Implosion: A Neo-classical Story?" in Dani Rodrik, ed., *In Search of Prosperity: Analytic Narratives on Economic Growth* (Princeton, N.J.: Princeton University Press, 2003), 246.

30. See Kiminori Matsuyama, "Agricultural Productivity, Comparative Advantage, and Economic Growth," *Journal of Economic Theory* 58 (December 1992): 317–34.

31. Ricardo Hausmann, Bailey Klinger, and Jose Lopez-Calix, "Export Diversification in Algeria," World Bank, MNSED (April 2009) advise Algeria to diversify its exports beyond oil, not only in anticipation of the exhaustion of oil reserves, but also because identifying the right directions to move within the "product space" will enhance long-term growth.

32. See Ragnar Torvik, "Learning by Doing and the Dutch Disease," *European Economic Review* 45:2 (February 2001): 285–306; and Efil Matsen and Torvik, "Optimal Dutch Disease," *Journal of Development Economics* 78, no.2 (2005).

33. See Wright and Czelusta, "Mineral Resources and Economic Development."

34. See Ricardo Hausmann, Bailey Klinger, and Robert Lawrence, "Examining Beneficiation," Center for International Development at Harvard University Working Paper 162 (May 2008). The authors warn of the pitfalls of assuming that South Africa, for example, can move from diamond mining to diamond cutting. They are not opposed to industrial policy but rather believe that linkages are more likely where factor intensities and technological requirements are similar across sectors, rather than to upstream or downstream industries.

35. See Robert Barro, "Economic Growth in a Cross Section of Countries," *Quarterly Journal of Economics* 106 (May (1991): 407–44 and Douglass North, "Economic Performance Through Time," *American Economic Review* 84:3 (June 1994): 359–68.

36. See Daniel Kaufmann, Aart Kraay, and Pablo Zoido-Lobaton, "Governance Matters II—Updated Indicators for 2000/01," World Bank Research Department Working Paper 2772 (2002).

37. See Acemoglu, Johnson, and Robinson, "Colonial Origins of Comparative Development."

38. See Daron Acemoglu, Simon Johnson, James Robinson, and Yunyong Thaicharoen, "Institutional Causes, Macroeconomic Symptoms: Volatility, Crises, and Growth," Journal of Monetary Economics 50:1 (January 2003): 49–123.

39. See Acemoglu, Johnson, Robinson, and Thaicharoen, "Institutional Causes, Macroeconomic Symptoms" and Acemoglu, Johnson, and Robinson, "Colonial Origins of Comparative Development."

40. Edward Glaeser and his coauthors argue against the settler variable. See Edward Glaeser, Rafael La Porta, Florencio Lopez-de-Silanes, and Andrei Shleifer, "Do Institutions Cause Growth?" *Journal of Economic Growth* 9:3 (September 2004): 271–303. Robert Hall and Chad Jones consider latitude and speaking English or other Western European languages as proxies for European institutions. They do not distinguish an independent effect of tropical conditions. See Robert Hall and Chad Jones, "Why Do Some Countries Produce So Much More Output per Worker Than Others?" *Quarterly Journal of Economics* 114:1 (February 1999): 83–116.

41. See Daron Acemoglu, Simon Johnson, and James Robinson, "Reversal of Fortune: Geography and Institutions in the Making of the Modern World Income Distribution," *Quarterly Journal of Economics* 117:4 (November 2002): 1231–94. William Easterly and Ross Levine group openness together with other policies. See William Easterly and Ross Levine, "Tropics, Germs, and Endowments," NBER Working Paper 9106 (2002); Carnegie-Rochester Conference Series on Public Policy; and Hall and Jones, "Output per Worker."

42. See Roland Hodler, "The Curse of Natural Resources in Fractionalized Countries," *European Economic Review* 50:6 (August 2006): 1367–86 and Francesco Caselli, "Power Struggles and the Natural Resource Curse," LSE Research, London School of Economics (2006).

43. See Carlos Leite and Jens Weidmann, "Does Mother Nature Corrupt?" IMF Working Paper 99/85 (July 1999).

44. See Elissaios Papyrakis and Rever Gerlach, "The Resource Curse and Transmission Channels," *Journal of Comparative Economics*, 32, no.1 (March 200): 161–193.

45. See Thorvaldur Gylfason and Gylfi Zoega, "Inequality and Economic Growth: Do Natural Resources Matter?" CESifo Working Paper 712 (April 2002) and Gobind T. Nankani, *Development Problems of Mineral Exporting Countries* (Washington, D.C.: World Bank, 1979).

46. Thorvaldur Gylfason finds a negative effect on growth via education, and Gylfason and Gylfi Zoega find it via crowding out investment. See Gylfason, "Natural Resources, Education, and Economic Development," *European Economic Review* 45:4–6 (May 2001): 847–59; and Gylfason and Zoega, "Natural Resources and Economic Growth: The Role of Investment," *World Economy* 29:8 (August 2006): 1091–1115. Gylfason also finds a resource curse at work in Eastern Europe and Central Asia through

rent-seeking and policy failures. See Gylfason, "Resources, Agriculture, and Economic Growth in Economies in Transition," *Kyklos* 53:4 (2000): 545–79.

47. See Macartan Humphreys, Jeffrey Sachs, and Joseph Stiglitz, *Escaping the Resource Curse* (New York: Columbia University Press, 2007), 2.

48. See Richard Auty, *Resource-Based Industrialization: Sowing the Oil in Eight Developing Countries* (Oxford: Clarendon Press, 1990); Auty, *Sustaining Development in Mineral Economies: The Resource Curse Thesis* (New York: Oxford University Press, 1993); Richard Auty, *Resource Abundance and Economic Development* (New York: Oxford University Press, 2001); Auty, "Patterns of Rent-Extraction and Deployment in Developing Countries: Implications for Governance, Economic Policy and Performance," in George Mavrotas and Anthony Shorrocks, eds., *Advancing Development: Core Themes in Global Economics* (London: Palgrave, 2007); and Auty, "The Political Economy of Hydrocarbon Revenue Cycling in Trinidad and Tobago," presented at the workshop Myths and Realities of Commodity Dependence: Policy Challenges and Opportunities for Latin America and the Caribbean, World Bank, September 17–18, 2009.

49. See Stanley Engerman and Kenneth Sokoloff, "Factor Endowments, Institutions, and Differential Paths of Growth among New World Economies: A View from Economic Historians of the United States," in Stephen Haber, ed., *How Latin America Fell Behind* (Stanford, Calif.: Stanford University Press, 1997); Engerman and Sokoloff, "Institutions, Factor Endowments, and Paths of Development in the New World," *Journal of Economic Perspectives* 14:3 (September 2000): 217–32; and Engerman and Sokoloff, "Factor Endowments, Inequality, and Paths of Development Among New World Economies," Working Paper 9259 (October 2002).

50. Iran, for instance. See Hussein Mahdavy, "The Patterns and Problems of Economic Development in Rentier States: The Case of Iran," in M. A. Cook, ed., *Studies in the Economic History of the Middle East* (London: Oxford University Press, 1970); Theda Skocpol, "Rentier State and Shi'a Islam in the Iranian Revolution," *Theory and Society* 11:3 (May 1982): 269; and Benjamin Smith, *Hard Times in the Land of Plenty: Oil Politics in Iran and Indonesia* (Ithaca, N.Y.: Cornell University Press, 2007).

51. See Jonathan Isham, Michael Woolcock, Lant Pritchett, and Gwen Busby, "The Varieties of Resource Experience: Natural Resource Export Structures and the Political Economy of Economic Growth," *The World Bank Economic Review* (New York: Oxford University Press on behalf of the International Bank for Reconstruction and Development, 2005).

52. See Sala-i-Martin and Subramanian, "Addressing the Natural Resource Curse"; Erwin Bulte, Richard Damania, and Robert Deacon, "Resource Intensity, Institutions and Development," *World Development* 33:7 (July 2005): 1029–44.

53. See Halvor Mehlum, Karl Moene, and Ragnar Torvik, "Institutions and the Resource Curse," *Economic Journal* 116:508 (January 2006): 1–20.

54. See Rabah Arezki and Markus Brückner, "Oil Rents, Corruption, and State Stability: Evidence from Panel Data Regressions," IMF Working Paper 09/267 (2009).

55. See Catherine Norman, "Rule of Law and the Resource Curse: Abundance versus Intensity," *Environmental Resource Economics* 43:2 (June 2009): 183–207.

56. See Mehlum, Moene, and Torvik, "Institutions and the Resource Curse"; James Robinson, Ragnar Torvik, and Thierry Verdier, "Political Foundations of the Resource Curse," *Journal of Development Economics* 79:2 (2006): 446–68; Brendan McSherry, "The Political Economy of Oil in Equatorial Guinea," *African Studies Quarterly* 8 (Spring 2006): 23–45; Smith, *Hard Times*; and Paul Collier and Benedikt Goderis, "Commodity Prices, Growth, and the Natural Resource Curse: Reconciling a Conundrum," Centre for the Study of African Economies Working Paper 274 (2007).

57. See Alexeev and Conrad, "The Elusive Curse of Oil." Before the interactive effects, they report significant negative effects of oil or mineral wealth on institutional quality when conditioning on actual initial income, but these effects disappear in their preferred equation, which does not condition on initial income. Institutional quality is measured by a standard rule of law index from the World Bank (and is instrumented by such variables as absolute latitude and fraction of the population speaking English or other major Western European languages).

58. See Rabah Arezki and Frederick van der Ploeg, "Trade Policies, Institutions, and the Natural Resource Curse," from "Can the Natural Resource Curse Be Turned into a Blessing? The Role of Trade Policies and Institutions," IMF Working Paper 07/55 (March 2007).

59. See Jones Luong and Weinthal, *Oil Is Not a Curse*. Their conclusion that private domestic ownership works best sounds convincing until their data point in favor of this ownership structure turns out to be Russia. The alternatives are private foreign ownership (Kazakhstan), state ownership and control (Turkmenistan and Uzbekistan), and state ownership with foreign participation (Azerbaijan).

60. See John Hartwick, "Intergenerational Equity and the Investing of Rents from Exhaustible Resources," *American Economic Review* 67:5 (December 1977): 972–74; and Robert Solow, "On the Intergenerational Allocation of Natural Resources," *Scandinavian Journal of Economics* 88:1 (March 1986): 141–49.

61. See Partha Dasgupta and Geoffrey M. Heal, *Economic Theory and Exhaustible Resources* (Cambridge: Cambridge University Press, 1985).

62. Hardwood forests are a strong example. See James Brander and M. Scott Taylor, "International Trade and Open-Access Renewable Resources: The Small Economy," *Canadian Journal of Economics* 30:3 (1997): 526–52.

63. See Elinor Ostrom and Vincent Ostrom, "Public Goods and Public Choices," in Emanuel Savas, ed., *Alternatives for Delivering Public Services: Toward Improved Performance* (Boulder, Colo.: Westview, 1977), 7–49.

64. See Elinor Ostrom, *Governing the Commons: The Evolution of Institutions for Collective Action* (Cambridge: Cambridge University Press, 1990).

65. See Gary Libecap, "Economic Variables and the Development of the Law: The Case of Western Mineral Rights," *Journal of Economic History* 38:2 (June 1978): 338–62 and Gary Libecap, *Contracting for Property Rights* (Cambridge: Cambridge University

Press, 1989). Libecap emphasizes the superiority of locally grown rules for property rights over federally imposed regimes. Another conclusion is that the establishment of property rights is much easier for mining than for common-pool resources such as fisheries or (less obviously) crude oil.

66. Ronald Findlay and Mats Lundahl study economic development in frontier countries of the late nineteenth and early twentieth centuries. See Ronald Findlay and Mats Lundahl, "Natural Resources 'Vent for Surplus' and the Staple Theory," in Gerald Meier, ed., *From Classical Economics to Development Economics: Essays in Honor of Hla Myint* (New York: St. Martin's, 1994) and Findlay and Lundahl, "Natural Resources and Economic Development: The 1870–1914 Experience," in Richard Auty, ed., *Resource Abundance and Economic Development* (New York: Oxford University Press, 2001).

67. See Lee Alston, Gary Libecap, and Robert Schneider, "The Determinants and Impact of Property Rights: Land Titles on the Brazilian Frontier," *Journal of Law, Economics, and Organization* 12:1 (1996): 25–61. The authors study the coming of land title to agriculture on the Brazilian frontier.

68. See Edward Barbier, "Frontier Expansion and Economic Development," *Contemporary Economic Policy* 23:2 (April 2005): 286–303; Barbier, *Natural Resources and Economic Development* (Cambridge: Cambridge University Press, 2005); and Barbier, "Frontiers and Sustainable Economic Development," *Environmental and Resource Economics* 37:1 (May 2007): 271–95.

69. See Indra De Soysa, "The Resource Curse: Are Civil Wars Driven by Rapacity or Paucity?" International Research Center, Canada, no. 9 (2000); James Fearon and David Laitin, "Ethnicity, Insurgency, and Civil War," *American Political Science Review* 97:2 (February 2003): 75–90; Paul Collier and Anke Hoeffler, "Greed and Grievance in Civil War," *Oxford Economic Papers* 56:4 (2004): 563–95; Macartan Humphreys, "Natural Resources, Conflicts, and Conflict Resolution: Uncovering the Mechanisms," *Journal of Conflict Resolution* 49:4 (August 2005): 508–37; and Paul Collier, *The Bottom Billion: Why the Poorest Countries Are Falling Behind and What Can Be Done About It* (Oxford: Oxford University Press, 2007), chapter 2.

70. See Christa Brunnschweiler and Erwin Bulte, "Natural Resources and Violent Conflict: Resource Abundance, Dependence, and the Onset of Civil Wars," *Oxford Economic Papers* 61:4 (October 2009): 651–74.

71. See Giacomo Luciani, "Allocation Versus Production States: A Theoretical Framework," in Hazem Beblawi and Giacomo Luciani, eds., *The Rentier State* (New York: Croom Helm, 1997); Hussein Mahdavy, "The Patterns and Problems of Economic Development in Rentier States: The Case of Iran," in M. A. Cook, ed., *Studies in the Economic History of the Middle East* (London: Oxford University Press, 1970); and Dirk Vandewalle, *Libya Since Independence: Oil and State-Building* (Ithaca, N.Y.: Cornell University Press, 1998).

Samuel Huntington generalized this principle beyond Middle Eastern oil producers to states with natural resources in other parts of the developing world. See Huntington, *The Third Wave: Democratization in the Late Twentieth Century* (Norman: University of Oklahoma Press, 1991).

72. See Michael Ross, "Does Oil Hinder Democracy?" *World Politics* 53:3 (April 2001): 325–61.

73. See Robert Barro, "Inequality and Growth in a Panel of Countries," *Journal of Economic Growth* 5:1 (March 2000): 5–28; Leonard Wantchekon, "Why Do Resource Dependent Countries Have Authoritarian Governments?" *Journal of African Finance and Economic Development* 2 (2004): 57–77; Nathan Jensen and Wantchekon, "Resource Wealth and Political Regimes in Africa," *Comparative Political Studies* 37:7 (September 2004): 816–41; and Michael Ross, "A Closer Look at Oil, Diamonds, and Civil War," *Annual Review of Political Science* 9 (2006): 265–300.

74. See Smith, "Oil Wealth and Regime Survival"; Smith, *Hard Times*; and Jamy Ulfelder, "Natural Resource Wealth and the Survival of Autocracies," *Comparative Political Studies* 40:8 (August 2007): 995–1018.

75. See Terry Lynn Karl, *The Paradox of Plenty: Oil Booms and Petro-States* (Berkeley: University of California Press, 1997).

76. Loss of statistical power in pure cointegration time series tests might account for this. See Stephen Haber and Victor Menaldo, "Do Natural Resources Fuel Authoritarianism? A Reappraisal of the Resource Curse," presented at the workshop Myths and Realities of Commodity Dependence: Policy Challenges and Opportunities for Latin America and the Caribbean, World Bank, September 17–18, 2009.

77. See Marcus Noland, "Explaining Middle Eastern Political Authoritarianism I: The Level of Democracy," *Review of Middle East Economics and Finance* 4:1 (2008).

78. See Thad Dunning, *Crude Democracy: Natural Resource Wealth and Political Regimes* (New York: Cambridge University Press, 2008).

79. See Romain Wacziarg, "The First Law of Petropolitics," University of California Los Angeles, April 2009.

80. See Robert Barro, "Economic Growth," 407–44.

81. See José Tavares and Romain Wacziarg, "How Democracy Affects Growth," *European Economic Review* 45:8 (August 2001): 1341–78.

82. See Alberto Alesina, Sule Özler, Nouriel Roubini, and Phillip Swagel, "Political Instability and Economic Growth," *Journal of Economic Growth* 1:2 (June 1996).

Sambit Bhattacharyya and Roland Hodler find that natural resource rents lead to corruption but only in the absence of high-quality democratic institutions. See Bhattacharyya and Hodler, "Natural Resources, Democracy, and Corruption," *European Economic Review* 54:4 (August 2010).

Paul Collier and Anke Hoeffler find that when developing countries, as opposed to advanced countries, have democracies, they tend to feature weak checks and balances; as a result, when developing countries also have high natural resource rents, the result is bad for economic growth. See Collier and Hoeffler, "Testing the Neo-con Agenda: Democracy in Resource-Rich Societies," *European Economic Review* 53:3 (April 2009): 293–308.

83. See, for instance, John Helliwell, "Empirical Linkages between Democracy and Economic Growth," *British Journal of Political Science* 24 (April (1994): 225–48; Evelyne Huber, Dietrich Rueschemeyer, and John Stephens, "The Impact of Economic Development on Democracy," *Journal of Economic Perspectives* 7:3 (Summer 1993): 71–85; Seymour Martin Lipset, "The Social Requisites of Democracy Revisited," *American Sociological Review* 59 (February (1994): 1–22; and Jenny A. Minier, "Democracy and Growth: Alternative Approaches," *Journal of Economic Growth* 3 (September 1998): 241–66.

84. See Fareed Zakaria, "The Rise of Illiberal Democracy," *Foreign Affairs* (November 1997) and Zakaria, *The Future of Freedom: Illiberal Democracy at Home and Abroad* (New York: Norton, 2004).

85. R. G. Gregory, W. Max Corden, and Peter Neary and Sweder van Wijnbergen gave us three of the first models. See R. G. Gregory, "Some Implications of Growth in the Mineral Sector," *Australian Journal of Agricultural Economics* 20:2 (August 1976): 71–91; W. Max Corden, "Booming Sector and Dutch Disease Economics: Survey and Consolidation," *Oxford Economic Papers* (New York: Oxford University Press, 1984), 359–80; and Peter Neary and Sweder van Wijnbergen, eds., *Natural Resources and the Macroeconomy* (Cambridge, Mass.: MIT Press, 1986).

The name "Dutch disease"—coined by *The Economist* magazine—was originally inspired by side effects of natural gas discoveries by the Netherlands in the late 1950s. See Jeroen Kremers, "The Dutch Disease in the Netherlands," in Neary and van Wijnbergen, *Natural Resources and the Macroeconomy*, 96–136.

86. See, for example, Sebastian Edwards, "A Commodity Export Boom and the Real Exchange Rate: The Money-Inflation Link," in Neary and van Wijnbergen, *Natural Resources and the Macroeconomy*. During the boom of 2001–11, examples of fixed-rate, oil-producing countries in which the real appreciation came via money inflows and inflation include Saudi Arabia and the Gulf emirates. Examples of floating-rate natural resource countries where the real appreciation took the form of nominal currency appreciation include Australia, Chile, Kazakhstan, Mexico, Norway, Russia, and South Africa. The sensitivity of exchange rates to commodity prices in the cases of Australia and New Zealand is shown by Yu-Chin Chen and Kenneth Rogoff, "Commodity Currencies," *Journal of International Economics* 60:1 (May 2003): 133–60. It holds for South Africa as well: Jeffrey Frankel, "On the Rand: Determinants of the South African Exchange Rate," *South African Journal of Economics* 75:3 (September 2007): 425–41.

87. Osmel Manzano and Roberto Rigobon show that the negative Sachs-Warner effect of resource dependence on growth rates from 1970 to 1990 was mediated through international debt incurred when commodity prices were high. See Manzano and Rigobon, "Resource Curse or Debt Overhang?" *Economia* 9:1 (Fall 2008). Rabah Arezki and Markus Brückner find that commodity price booms lead to increased government spending, external debt, and default risk in autocracies but do not have those effects in democracies. See Arezki and Brückner, "International Commodity Price Shocks, De-

mocracy, and External Debt," IMF Working Paper 10/53 (2010). These authors find that the dichotomy extends also to the effects on sovereign bond spreads paid by autocratic versus democratic commodity producers. See Arezki and Brückner, "Resource Windfalls and Emerging Market Sovereign Bond Spreads: The Role of Political Institutions" (Washington, D.C.: IMF, 2010).

88. See, for instance, Matsuyama, "Agricultural Productivity, Comparative Advantage, and Economic Growth"; and Sweder van Wijnbergen, "The 'Dutch Disease': A Disease After All?" *Economic Journal* 94 (1984): 41–55. The real appreciation is considered to lower long-term growth because the primary sector does not experience "learning by doing" as the secondary sector does, Thorvaldur Gylfason, Tryggvi Thor Herbertsson, and Gylfi Zoega, "A Mixed Blessing," *Macroeconomic Dynamics* 3:2 (June 1999): 204–25.

89. See Graciela Kaminsky, Carmen Reinhart, and Carlos Vegh, "When It Rains, It Pours: Procyclical Capital Flows and Macroeconomic Policies," *NBER Macroeconomics Annual 2004* 19 (2005): 11–82; Carmen Reinhart and Vincent Reinhart, "Capital Flow Bonanzas: An Encompassing View of the Past and Present," in Jeffrey Frankel and Christopher Pissarides, eds., *NBER International Seminar in Macroeconomics 2008* (Chicago: University of Chicago Press, 2009); Michael Gavin, Ricardo Hausmann, Roberto Perotti, and Ernesto Talvi, "Managing Fiscal Policy in Latin America and the Caribbean: Volatility, Procyclicality, and Limited Creditworthiness," Inter-American Development Bank, RES Working Papers 4032 (1996); and Enrique Mendoza and Marco Terrones, "An Anatomy of Credit Booms: Evidence from Macro Aggregates and Micro Data," NBER Working Paper 14049 (May 2008).

90. See John Cuddington, "Commodity Export Booms in Developing Countries," *World Bank Research Observer* 4:2 (July 1989): 143–65; Aaron Tornell and Philip Lane, "The Voracity Effect," *American Economic Review* 89:1 (March 1999): 22–24; Kaminsky, Reinhart, and Vegh, "When It Rains, It Pours"; Ernesto Talvi and Carlos Vegh, "Tax Base Variability and Procyclicality of Fiscal Policy," *Journal of Development Economics* 78:1 (October 2005): 156–90; Alberto Alesina, Filipe Campante, and Guido Tabellini, "Why Is Fiscal Policy Often Procyclical?" *Journal of the European Economic Association* 6:5 (September 2008): 1006–36; Enrique G. Mendoza and P. Marcelo Oviedo, "Fiscal Policy and Macroeconomic Uncertainty in Developing Countries: The Tale of the Tormented Insurer," NBER Working Paper 12586 (October 2006); Ethan Ilzetski and Carlos Vegh, "Procyclical Fiscal Policy in Developing Countries: Truth or Fiction?" NBER Working Paper 14191 (2008); and Paolo Medas and Daria Zakharova, "Primer on Fiscal Analysis in Oil-Producing Countries," IMF Working Paper 56 (March 2009). For Latin America in particular, see Michael Gavin and Roberto Perotti, "Fiscal Policy in Latin America," *NBER Macroeconomics Annual 1997* 12: 11–61.

91. See Cuddington, "Commodity Export Booms in Developing Countries"; and Rabah Arezki, Kirk Hamilton, and Kazim Kazimov, "Resource Windfalls, Macroeconomic Stability and Growth: The Role of Political Institutions," International Monetary Fund (May 2011).

92. See Alan Gelb, "Adjustment to Windfall Gains: A Comparative Analysis of Oil-Exporting Countries," in "Natural Resources and the Macroeconomy: A Theoretical Framework," in Neary and van Wijnbergen, *Natural Resources and the Macroeconomy*, 54–93.

93. See Medas and Zakharova, "Primer on Fiscal Analysis in Oil-Producing Countries."

94. The relationship shown in the figures is statistically significant: Jeffrey Frankel, "On the Tenge: Monetary and Exchange Rate Policy for Kazakhstan," Short-term Consultancy, Republic of Kazakhstan (April 2005). Current government spending increases in boom times but is downward-sticky: Rabah Arezki and Kareem Ismail, "Boom-Bust Cycle, Asymmetrical Fiscal Response, and the Dutch Disease," IMF Working Paper 10/94 (Washington, D.C.: IMF, April 2010).

95. See Jeffrey Davis, Rolando Ossowski, and Annalisa Fedelino, eds., *Fiscal Policy Formulation and Implementation in Oil-Producing Countries* (Washington, D.C.: IMF, et al., 2003); and Sachs, "How to Handle the Macroeconomics of Oil Wealth."

96. See Robert Pindyck, "The Cartelization of World Commodity Markets," *The American Economic Review* 69:2 (May 1979): 154–58 and Christopher Gilbert, "International Commodity Agreements: An Obituary Notice," *World Development* 24:1 (January 1996): 1–19.

97. See Dieter Helm, "Credibility, Commitment, and Regulation," in Bill Hogan and Federico Sturzenegger, eds., *The Natural Resources Trap* (Cambridge, Mass.: MIT Press, 2010).

98. Humphreys, Sachs, and Stiglitz, *Escaping the Resource Curse*, 323.

99. Ron Alquist and Lutz Killian, "What Do We Learn from the Price of Crude Oil Futures?" *Journal of Applied Econometrics* 25:4 (2010): 539–73.

100. Barry Eichengreen and Ricardo Hausmann say that the "original sin" plaguing emerging markets was the reluctance of foreign investors to expose themselves in local currency. See Eichengreen and Hausmann, "Exchange Rates and Financial Fragility," in *New Challenges for Monetary Policy* (Kansas City, Mo.: Federal Reserve Bank of Kansas City, 1999), 329–68.

101. The tendency for official floaters to intervene heavily in practice to dampen exchange rate fluctuations was named "fear of floating" in Guillermo Calvo and Carmen Reinhart, "Fear of Floating," *Quarterly Journal of Economics* 117:2 (May 2002): 379–408.

102. Two qualifications to the apotheosis of the CPI: First, some versions phrase targets in terms of "headline CPI" and some in terms of "core CPI," typically excluding food and energy. Second, proponents often say that it is all right for the central bank to pay attention to the exchange rate (or commodity prices or asset prices) but only to the extent that it helps achieve its longer run objective of price stability. Neither of these nuances matters for present purposes.

103. See Jeffrey Frankel, "A Proposed Monetary Regime for Small Commodity-Exporters: Peg the Export Price ('PEP')," *International Finance* 6:1 (Spring 2003):

61–88. A more moderate variation, for a country already contemplating a peg to a currency basket, is to include the commodity in the basket. Middle Eastern oil exporters, for example, could have a basket peg with one-third weight on the dollar, one-third on the euro, and one-third on a barrel of oil.

104. See Jeffrey Frankel, "Peg the Export Price Index: A Proposed Monetary Regime for Small Countries," *Journal of Policy Modeling* 27:4 (June 2005): 495–508; and Frankel, "Peg the Export Price," CEPR Policy Insight No. 25 (July 2008).

105. See Jeffrey Frankel, "A Comparison of Monetary Anchor Options, Including Product Price Targeting, for Commodity-Exporters in Latin America," NBER Working Paper 16362 forthcoming Economia 2011.

106. See Jeffrey Davis, Rolando Ossowski, James Daniel, and Steven Barnett, "Oil Funds: Problems Posing as Solutions?" *Finance and Development* 38:4 (December 2001); Davis, Ossowski, Daniel, and Barnett, "Stabilization and Savings Funds for Nonrenewable Resources: Experience and Fiscal Policy Implications," IMF Occasional Paper 205 (2001); and Davis, Ossowski, and Fedelino, *Fiscal Policy Formulation and Implementation.*

107. Econometric analysis of these institutions for a relatively large set of countries finds no statistically significant effect on the fiscal stance. This may be partly due to econometric limitations. But it is evidently also in part due to governments that, after having adopted Special Financial Institutions, subsequently find them too rigid in practice and so weaken or abandon them. Recent examples include Ecuador, Equatorial Guinea, and Venezuela. Rolano Ossowski, Mauricio Villafuerte, Paulo Medas, and Theo Thomas, 2008, "Managing the Oil Revenue Boom: The Role of Fiscal Institutions," Occasional Paper No. 260 (International Monetary Fund: Washington, D.C.).

108. See International Monetary Fund, *Chile 2005 Article IV Consultation*, IMF Country Report 05/013 (September 2005): 11.

109. It introduced a Fiscal Responsibility Bill in 2006, which gave legal force to the role of the structural budget. The bill also created a Pension Reserve Fund and a Social and Economic Stabilization Fund, the latter a replacement for the existing Copper Stabilization Funds. For more details and references and tests of hypotheses regarding over-optimism in official forecasts, see Jeffrey Frankel, "A Solution to Fiscal Procyclicality: The Structural Budget Institutions Pioneered by Chile," *Fiscal Policy and Macroeconomic Performance,* Fourteenth Annual Conference of the Central Bank of Chile, NBER WP No. 16945, 2011.

110. See Edwin Truman, *Sovereign Wealth Funds: Threat or Salvation?* (Washington, D.C.: Peterson Institute for International Economics, 2010). Truman gives recommendations for transparency of sovereign wealth funds.

111. See Davis, Ossowski, Daniel, and Barnett, "Stabilization and Savings Funds for Nonrenewable Resources," and Macartan Humphreys and Martin Sandhu, "The Political Economy of Natural Resource Funds," in Humphreys, Sachs, and Stiglitz, *Escaping*

the Resource Curse. In countries with few checks and balances, large yearly changes in oil revenues tend to lead to large yearly changes in government consumption.

112. See Erling Holmøy, "Mineral Rents and Social Policy: The Case of the Norwegian Government Oil Fund," in Katja Hujo and Shea McClanahan, eds., *Financing Social Policy: Mobilizing Resources for Social Development* (London: UNRISD/Palgrave Macmillan, 2010).

113. The political objectives are intended to serve the cause of social responsibility. See Mark Landler, "Norway Keeps Nest Egg from Some U.S. Companies: Proposes to Do Well in Its Investments by Doing Good," *New York Times*, May 4, 2007, C4; Gregory Roth, "Norway Finds Virtue (and Value) in Transparency," *New York Times*, Sept. 27, 2008, B2. Social responsibility apparently includes boycotting stock in Walmart (a company many American economists consider beneficial to people of lower income).

114. See Humphreys and Sandhu, "The Political Economy of Natural Resource Funds."

115. See Sala-i-Martin and Subramanian, "Addressing the Natural Resource Curse."

116. See Nancy Birdsall and Arvind Subramanian, "Saving Iraq From Its Oil," *Foreign Affairs* (July/August 2004): 77–89. See also Michael Ross, "How Mineral-Rich States Can Reduce Inequality," in Humphreys, Sachs, and Stiglitz, *Escaping the Resource Curse*, 236–55.

117. See Lydia Polgreen, "Chad Backs Out of Pledge to Use Oil Wealth to Reduce Poverty," *New York Times*, Dec. 13, 2005, A15; Celia Dugger, "World Bank Suspends Loans to Chad Over Use of Oil Money," *New York Times*, Jan. 7, 2006; David White, "The 'Resource Curse' Anew: Why a Grand World Bank Oil Project Has Fast Run into the Sand," *Financial Times*, January 23, 2006; Lydia Polgreen, "World Bank Ends Effort to Help Chad Ease Poverty," *New York Times*, Sept. 11, 2008; "Breaking the Bank: A Vaunted Model Development Project Goes Awry," *The Economist*, Sept. 26, 2008, 63.

118. See Humphreys and Sandhu, "The Political Economy of Natural Resource Funds," 224–27. During the period when Kuwait was occupied by an Iraqi invasion, access to Kuwaiti bank accounts in London stayed with the exiled Kuwaiti government.

Chapter 2

1. For a typical statement of the oil curse as a universal rule, see Paul Collier and Benedikt Goderis, "Prospects for Commodity Exporters: Hunky Dory or Humpty Dumpty?" *World Economics* 8:2 (April–June 2007): 1–15.

2. Edward Barbier, "Natural Resource-Based Economic Development in History," *World Economics* 6:3 (July–September 2005): 103–52, quote 142.

3. The UAE were referred to as the "Trucial States" before independence from the UK in 1971.

4. Ramon Knauerhouse, *The Saudi Arabian Economy* (New York: Praeger, 1975), 7. One reason the wheel was not used was that even in the early 1950s the country had only forty-five kilometers of asphalted roads (98).

5. K. S. Twitchell, *Saudi Arabia: With an Account of the Development of Its Natural Resources* (Princeton, N.J.: Princeton University Press, 1958), 21.

6. Alexei Vassiliev, *The History of Saudi Arabia* (New York: New York University Press, 2000), 424–25.

7. Kiren Aziz Chaudhry, *The Price of Wealth: Economies and Institutions in the Middle East* (Ithaca, N.Y.: Cornell University Press, 1997), 148.

8. Knauerhouse, *The Saudi Arabian Economy*, 88. Much information from the 1962 survey is found in Thomas Shea, "Measuring the Changing Family Consumption Patterns of Aramco's Saudi Arab Employees—1962 and 1968," in Derek Hopwood, ed., *The Arabian Peninsula: Society and Politics* (London: Allen and Unwin, 1972), 231–54. On the labor unrest that led Aramco to improve workers' conditions in the late 1950s and early 1960s, see Anthony Cave Brown, *Oil, God, and Gold: The Story of Aramco and the Saudi Kings* (Boston: Houghton Mifflin, 1999), 147–54. Brown quotes a 1956 study that found that two-thirds of Aramco's 20,400 employees were Saudis (140). See also Madawi Al-Rasheed, *A History of Saudi Arabia* (Cambridge: Cambridge University Press, 1962), 95–100.

9. George Lipsky et al., *Saudi Arabia: Its People, Its Society, Its Culture* (New Haven, Conn.: HRAF Press, 1959), 277, 279, 328. The first grade was 75 percent Arabic and 14 percent religious studies.

10. Knauerhouse, *The Saudi Arabian Economy*, 215–16, 219. Data on graduates sourced to Saudi Central Department of Statistics, *Statistical Yearbook 1391 AH* (Riyadh, 1971). In 1960–61, there were 544 graduates from secondary school and 8,027 from elementary school.

11. Quoted in Christopher Davidson, *The United Arab Emirates: A Study in Survival* (Boulder, Colo.: Lynne Rienner, 2005), 7. On the role of pearl diving, see page 5–10.

12. Frauke Heard-Bey, *From Trucial States to United Arab Emirates* (London: Longman, 1996), 235–36.

13. World Bank, *The Economic Development of Kuwait* (Baltimore: Johns Hopkins University Press, 1965), 146.

14. Quoted in Rupert Hay, *The Persian Gulf States* (Washington, D.C.: Middle East Institute, 1959), 110. For more on Qatar of this period, see Jill Crystal, *Oil and Politics in the Gulf: Rulers and Merchants in Kuwait and Qatar* (Cambridge: Cambridge University Press, 1990), 112–18.

15. Sief A. El-Wady Ramahi, *Economic and Political Evolution in the Arabian Gulf States* (New York: Carlton Press, 1973), 138. For the revenue estimate, see page 134.

16. The extraordinarily backward character of Oman through the early oil days is told with much color by Ian Skeet, *Oman Before 1970: The End of an Era* (London: Faber and Faber, 1974). Much of the problem was the reactionary attitudes of Sultan

Said, who ruled until 1970. However, see Calvin Allen, Jr., and W. Lynn Rigsbee, II, *Oman Under Qaboos: From Coup to Constitution, 1970–1996* (London: Frank Cass, 2000), 23–26, which suggests Sultan Said did sanction some development activities.

17. Ramahi, *Arabian Gulf States*, 113, which is also the source about 1968. See also Donald Hawley, *The Trucial States* (London: Allen and Unwin, 1970), 234–38.

18. Allen and Rigsbee, *Oman Under Qaboos*, 24, 167.

19. Roger Owen and Şevket Pamuk, *A History of Middle East Economies in the Twentieth Century* (Cambridge, Mass.: Harvard University Press, 1999), 76–82.

20. UN Development Programme, *Human Development Report 2009*, http://origin-hdr.undp.org/en/statistics/.

21. See Christopher Boucek, *Yemen: Avoiding a Downward Spiral*, Carnegie Papers 102, September 2009, http://www.carnegieendowment.org/files/yemen_downward_spiral.pdf.

22. A country-by-country chronicling of physical construction through the early 1990s is in Gwilym Roberts and David Fowler, *Built by Oil* (London: Ithaca Press, 1995).

23. The U.S. Department of Energy's Energy Information Agency issues an annual *OPEC Revenue Fact Sheet* that shows net oil export earnings for each OPEC country in nominal and real dollars. Among the Gulf monarchies, Bahrain and Oman are not OPEC members; data on their export earnings are available in the annual IMF Article IV consultation reports.

24. On the boom years, see Christopher Davidson, *Dubai: The Vulnerability of Success* (New York: Columbia University Press, 2008), 106–33. On the bust, see Davidson, *Abu Dhabi: Oil and Beyond* (New York: Columbia University Press, 2009), 172–75 and especially Davidson, "Dubai: Foreclosure of a Dream," *Middle East Reports* 251 (Summer 2009): 8–13.

25. "Dubai has 30,000 construction cranes," *Gulf News*, 18 June 2006, http://gulfnews.com/business/construction/dubai-has-30-000-construction-cranes-1.241346, accessed 1 April 2010.

26. On the Dubai debt crisis overall, see May Khamis, Abdelhak S. Senhadji, and Maher Hasan, *Impact of the Global Financial Crisis on Gulf Cooperation Council Countries and Challenges Ahead* (Washington, D.C.: IMF, 2010), 20–23. On the March 2010 restructuring, see Simeon Kerr and Andrew England, "Carefully moulded restructuring," *Financial Times*, 26 March 2010, 3.

27. Robin Wigglesworth, "Bondholders have most reason to be happy," *Financial Times*, 26 March 2010, 3.

28. Simeon Kerr and Michael Peel, "Dubai gains as a refuge from regional tensions," *Financial Times*, 25 April 2011, 5; James Gavin, "Dubai cuts spending to repay debts," *MEED* 55:5 (4–10 February 2011), 32–33.

29. World Bank, *Better Governance for Development in the Middle East and North Africa: Enhancing Inclusiveness and Accountability* (Washington, D.C.: World Bank, 2003), 68–71.

30. Owen Kirby, "Want Democracy? Get a King," *Middle East Quarterly* 7:4 (December 2000): 3–12.

31. Maxime Rodinson, *Islam and Capitalism* (Austin: University of Texas Press, 1978).

32. Tim Niblock with Monica Malik, *The Political Economy of Saudi Arabia* (London: Routledge, 2007), 210–15.

33. For "country report cards" comparing the Algerian and Libyan record to that of OPEC- member Gulf monarchies, see Jahangir Amuzegar, *Managing the Oil Wealth: OPEC's Windfalls and Pitfalls* (London: Tauris, 2001), 116–68.

34. This account is based on the single most important book about the Saudi economy, Niblock with Malik, *The Political Economy of Saudi Arabia*. Pages 94–143 analyze 1985–2000 and pages 173–99 discuss 2000–2006.

35. A gloomy and well-informed portrayal of the deep problems facing Saudi Arabia in the mid-1990s is Peter Wilson and Douglas Graham, *Saudi Arabia: The Coming Storm* (Armonk, N.Y.: M.E. Sharpe, 1994). Their account makes clear how easy it would have been for the Saudi economy to have gone seriously off the rails. That this did not happen is actually quite impressive.

36. On the Gulf monarchies' military spending, see Michael Knights, *Troubled Waters: Future U.S. Security Assistance in the Persian Gulf* (Washington, D.C.: Washington Institute for Near East Policy, 2006) and his update, "Changing Conventional Military Balance in the Gulf," *Washington Institute PolicyWatch* 1577 (September 14, 2009).

37. James Gavin, "Riyadh spends to curb unrest," *MEED* 55:15 (15–21 April 2011): 30–31.

38. From IMF Article IV consultation reports available at http://www.imf.org, of which the most recent are IMF Country Reports 10/42 (February 2010) on the UAE and 10/236 (July 2010) on Kuwait. The Article IV consultation reports for Saudi Arabia are not available to the public; instead, a brief Public Information Notice (PIN) is released, of which the most recent is PIN 09/109 (August 2009).

39. Giacomo Luciani, "From Private Sector to National Bourgeoisie: Saudi Arabian Business," in Paul Aarts and Gerd Nonneman, eds., *Saudi Arabia in the Balance: Political Economy, Society, Foreign Affairs* (London: Hurs, 2005), 144–81, quote 178.

40. World Bank, *Doing Business 2010: Country Profile for Saudi Arabia*. The rankings are available at http://www.doingbusiness.org.

41. Amuzegar, *Managing the Oil Wealth*, 102–6.

42. Other than the last sentence, this paragraph is based on David Ottoway, *The King's Messenger: Princer Bandar Bin Sultan and America's Tangled Relationship with Saudi Arabia* (New York: Walker, 2008), 156–65. As cited by Ottoway, Prince Bandar's estimate of payments to royals was in line with that made by the U.S. Embassy in the late 1990s.

43. Niblock with Malik, *The Political Economy of Saudi Arabia*, 36–37.

44. "Saudi 2010 Budget Falls in Line with the Govt's Commitment," *Arab News*, December 26, 2009, http://archive.arabnews.com/?page=6&section=0&article=130230.

45. Peter Salisbury, "Kuwait: State Enters an Era of Change," *MEED*, March 5, 2010, 20–21.

46. Steffen Hertog, "Segmented Clientelism: The Political Economy of Saudi Economic Reform Efforts," in Aarts and Nonneman, eds., *Saudi Arabia in the Balance*, 111–43, quote 116.

47. Foreigners also account for a significant share of the government labor force, especially at the top and the bottom of the skill scale.

48. IMF, Qatar: 2008 Article IV Consultation, Country Report No. 09/28 (January 2009), 29.

49. BP, *BP Statistical Review of World Energy June 2009* (London: BP, 2009), 6, 22, 24.

50. James Gavin, "Delivering Doha's dream"; no author, "Transforming the country"; and Bernadette Redfern, "Avoiding a building boom and bust," *MEED Qatar Projects Supplement* (January 2011), 3–4, 6–7, and 8–9, respectively.

51. Thad Dunning, *Crude Democracy: Natural Resource Wealth and Political Regimes* (Cambridge: Cambridge University Press, 2008). Dunning argues that resource rents have a direct authoritarian effect (by increasing the payoff from controlling power) and an indirect democratic effect (by "moderating the extent to which th[e] poor majority wants to soak the rich by taxing non-resource income," 101). He presents evidence that the latter effect has predominated in several Latin American countries. He argues the direct effect is greater in an economy that is more resource dependent and less egalitarian.

52. Life expectancy and population are from UNDP Human Development Report data, March 2009, http://hdrstats.undp.org/2008/countries/country_fact_sheets/cty_fs_GNQ.html,accessed August 28. Oil exports are from IMF, Republic of Equatorial Guinea: 2008 Article IV Consultation, Country Report. 09/102, 25.

Chapter 3

1. Richard M. Auty, *Resource Abundance and Economic Development* (Oxford: Oxford University Press, 2001).

2. Richard M. Auty, "Elites, Rent Cycling, and Development: Adjustment to Land Scarcity in Mauritius, Kenya, and Cote d'Ivoire," *Development Policy Review* 28:4 (June 2010).

3. David E. Bloom and Jeffrey G. Williamson, "Demographic Transitions and Economic Miracles in Emerging Asia," *World Bank Economic Review* 12:3 (September 1998): 419–55.

4. Shaomin Li, Shuhe Li, and Weiying Zhangb, "The Road to Capitalism: Competition and Institutional Change in China," *Journal of Comparative Economics* 28:2 (June 2000): 269–92.

5. Jonathan Isham, Lant Pritchett, Michael Woolcock, and Gwen Busby, "The Varieties of Resource Experience: How Natural Resource Export Structures Affect the Political Economy of Economic Growth," *World Bank Economic Review* 19:2 (2005): 141–64.

6. Michael L. Ross, "Does Oil Hinder Democracy?" *World Politics* 53:3 (April 2001): 325–61.

7. Nicholas van de Walle, *African Economies and the Politics of Permanent Crisis, 1979–1999* (Cambridge: Cambridge University Press, 2001).

8. Jose G. Montalvo and Marta Reynal-Querol, "Ethnic Diversity and Economic Development," *Journal of Development Economics* 76:2 (April 2005): 294.

9. Robert E. Baldwin, "Patterns of Development in Newly Settled Regions," *Manchester School of Social and Economic Studies* 24:2 (May 1956): 161–79; David Bevan, Paul Collier, and Jean Wilhelm Gunning, "Consequences of a Commodity Boom in a Controlled Economy: Accumulation and Redistribution in Kenya," *World Bank Economic Review* 1:3 (May 1987): 489–513.

10. Paul Collier and Anke Hoeffler, "Testing the Neocon Agenda: Democracy in Resource-Rich Societies," *European Economic Review* 53:3 (April 2009): 293–308.

11. Philip Keefer, "Clientelism, Credibility, and Policy Choices of Young Democracies," *American Journal of Political Science* 51:4 (October 2007): 804–21.

12. Kunle Owolabi, "Politics, Institutions, and Ethnic Voting in Plural Societies: Comparative Lessons from Trinidad and Tobago, Guyana, and Mauritius," Working Paper, University of Notre Dame, 2007.

13. World Bank, "Country Assistance Strategy for the Government of Trinidad and Tobago," *World Bank Report 19052TR* (Washington, D.C.: World Bank, 1999).

14. IMF, "Trinidad and Tobago: Selected Issues," *IMF Staff Country Report 05/06* (Washington, D.C.: IMF, 2005), 3.

15. IMF, "Trinidad and Tobago: Selected Issues," *IMF Staff Country Report 07/08* (Washington, D.C.: IMF, 2007).

16. Alan Gelb and associates, *Oil Windfalls: Blessing or Curse?* (New York: Oxford University Press and World Bank, 1988).

17. BP, *BP Statistical Review of World Energy June 2008* (London: BP, 2008).

18. Gelb et al., *Oil Windfalls.*

19. Gelb et al., *Oil Windfalls.*

20. Richard M. Auty, *Resource-Based Industrialization: Sowing the Oil In Eight Developing Countries* (Oxford: Clarendon Press, 1990), 73.

21. Auty, *Resource-Based Industrialization.*

22. Gelb et al., *Oil Windfalls,* 88.

23. Dudley Seers, "The Mechanism of an Open Petroleum Economy," *Social and Economic Studies* 13:2 (June 1964): 233–42.

24. Benedik Braumann, "Unemployment Persistence and Capital Shortage: The Case of Trinidad and Tobago," IMF Working Paper 97/77 (1997), 5.

25. Daniel Artana, Juan Luis Bour, and Fernando Navajas, "Designing Fiscal Policy to Achieve Development," in Liliana Rojas-Suarez and Carlos Elias, eds., *From Growth to Prosperity: Policy Perspectives for Trinidad and Tobago* (Washington, D.C.: IADB, 2006), 25–64.

26. IMF, "Trinidad and Tobago: Selected Issues," *07/08*, 3.

27. IMF, "Trinidad and Tobago: Selected Issues and Statistical Appendix," *IMF Staff Country Report 99/67* (Washington, D.C.: IMF, 1999), 22.

28. Auty, *Resource-Based Industrialization*.

29. David Small, *Trinidad and Tobago: Natural Gas Monetisation as a Driver of Economic and Social Prosperity* (Port of Spain: Ministry of Energy and Energy Industries, 2006), 6.

30. IMF, "Trinidad and Tobago: Selected Issues," *05/06*.

31. Daniel Johnstone, "Changing Fiscal Landscape," *Journal of World Energy, Law, and Business* 1:1 (2008): 34–54; Emil M. Sunley, Thomas Baunsgaard, and Dominique Sinnard, "Revenue from the Oil and Gas Sector: Issues and Country Experience," in Jeffrey M. Davis, Rolando Ossowski, and Annalisa Fedelino, eds., *Fiscal Policy Formulation and Implementation in Oil-Exporting Countries* (Washington, D.C.: IMF, 2003), 170–71.

32. Graham Kellas, *Taxation of Natural Gas Projects* (Edinburgh: Wood McKenzie, 2008).

33. IMF, "Trinidad and Tobago: Article IV Consultation—Staff Report," *IMF Staff Country Report 09/78* (Washington, D.C.: IMF, 2009).

34. IMF, "Trinidad and Tobago: Selected Issues," *07/08*.

35. Gelb et al., *Oil Windfalls*.

36. Delia Velculescu and Saqib Rizavm, "Trinidad and Tobago: The Energy Boom and Proposals for a Sustainable Fiscal Policy," IMF Working Paper 05/197 (2005), 15.

37. IMF, "Trinidad and Tobago: Article IV Consultation," 24.

38. Inter-American Development Bank, "Country Program Evaluation: Trinidad and Tobago 2000–08" (Washington, D.C.: IDB, 2009), 9.

39. IMF, "Trinidad and Tobago: Selected Issues," *07/08*.

40. Both IMF projections assume oil production holds steady at around 125,000 barrels per day but ceases in 2042 and that gas peaks at 4.2 million cubic feet per day through 2007–21 and then abruptly ceases. The IMF projects that energy prices average around $66 a barrel through 2011 and then fall to $45 over the longer term; the non-energy economy expands at 3 percent annually, and the real interest rate for invested assets is 4 percent. Finally, each sustainable revenue projection sets the baseline for government revenue as 2003–5, when government revenue from the energy sector accounted for 18.2 percent of the total energy revenue stream and the total production revenue from the non-energy sector was around 22.5 percent of non-energy GDP. The IMF then projects that further price increases lift energy taxation to 27 percent of energy revenue, but non-energy revenue holds at 20.7 percent of non-energy GDP.

41. IMF, "Trinidad and Tobago: Article IV Consultation."

42. Ibid., 9.

43. Velculescu and Rizavm, "Trinidad and Tobago."

44. The 2008 fuel subsidy was projected at TT$2.5 billion or 10 percent of non-energy government revenue. See Inter-American Development Bank, "Country Program Evaluation," 7.

45. Priced in U.S. dollars, U.S. gasoline prices rose 50 percent during 2001–3 to around $1.50 per gallon, at which they were frozen, while actual prices in U.S. dollars doubled to over $3 per gallon, with the difference representing the added subsidy.

46. Inter-American Development Bank, "Country Program Evaluation."

47. Ibid.

48. IMF, "Trinidad and Tobago: Article IV Consultation," 20.

49. Trinidad and Tobago Ministry of Finance, *Budget of Trinidad and Tobago 2009* (Port of Spain: Ministry of Finance, 2009).

50. World Bank, *Development Indicators 2009* (Washington, D.C.: World Bank, 2009).

51. Inter-American Development Bank, "Country Program Evaluation."

52. Donald Mitchell, "Sugar in the Caribbean: Adjusting to Eroding Preference," *World Bank Policy Research Working Paper 3802* (Washington, D.C.: World Bank, 2005).

53. Daniel Artana, Sebastian Auguste, Ramiro Moya, Sandra Sookram, and Patrick Watson, *Trinidad & Tobago: Economic Growth in a Dual Economy* (Washington, D.C.: IDB, 2007), 25.

54. Ibid., 7.

55. Inter-American Development Bank, "Country Program Evaluation."

56. Artana et al., *Trinidad & Tobago*, 9.

57. IMF, "Trinidad and Tobago: Selected Issues and Statistical Appendix," *IMF Staff Country Report 99/67* (Washington, D.C.: IMF, 1999), 21–22.

Chapter 4

1. For 2001 to 2008, World Bank figures show Iran's expenditures on subsidies made up 10 to 28 percent of the nation's budget, depending on the difference between domestic and international prices.

2. Iranian Oil Ministry, "Targeting Energy Subsides Policies (in Particular Gas) and Its Effects on Macroeconomic Variables," Planning Division, Strategic Planning Bureau, Economic and Technical Systems Analysis Section, 33 2005, Tehran.

3. In 2008, the United Arab Emirates passed Iran as the third-largest oil exporter in the world. Saudi Arabia and Russia are the world's two largest oil exporters.

4. Each phase is considered a separate field for natural gas production.

5. Ahmad Mojtahed and Masoud Mojtahed, "Evaluation of Iranian Strategy for Energy Use in the Next Decade," 37th Intersociety Energy Conversion Engineering Conference (IECEC), Washington, D.C., July 28–August 1, 2002.

6. Oil Refineries and Distribution Company, "The Study Effect of Gas Price Increase on Consumption in Short and Long Run: Using Auto Regressive Distributed Lag Method (ARDL)," Tehran, 2005.

7. Iranian Oil Ministry, "The Study of Energy Carriers' Price Increase on Inflation and Budget Expenditures of the Urban and Rural Families," Tehran, 2005, 1–49, 63.

8. The Iranian budget is divided into two parts: general budget expenditures and development.

9. For example, see Karimi, S., Jafari, S. A., and Mehnatfard, M., "The Economic Evaluation of Gasoline Subsidies on Inflation Rate in Iran: An Experimental Analysis (1971–2005)," *Journal of Economic Research* 7:1 (2007).

10. BP, *BP Statistical Review of World Energy June 2008* (London: BP, 2008).

11. Because energy efficiency is calculated based on the ratio of production value of one barrel of oil to its price, an increase in oil prices decreases the ratio and improves productivity.

12. *Press TV*, "Iran fuel consumption declines," March 16, 2011.

Chapter 5

1. Ralph Hawtrey, *The Art of Central Banking* (London: Longman, Green, 1932), vi.

2. Jan Dehn, "The Effects on Growth of Commodity Price Uncertainty and Shocks," World Bank Policy Research Working Paper 2455 (2001).

3. "The 1974 and 1979 price increases were not foreseen by consensus forecasts. By the early 1980s, high prices were widely blamed on scarcity, with projections for $50 per barrel or even higher. Instead, the spike of the early 1980s was followed by the oil slump and a sharp price decline. Prices reached an unexpected nadir in 1998 with the shock of the Asia crisis; projections envisaged a slow rebound toward $20 per barrel but failed to pick up the spike of 2000 to levels 50 percent higher." See Benn Eifert, Alan Gelb, and Nils Tallroth, "The Political Economy of Fiscal Policy and Economic Management in Oil Exporting Country," World Bank Research Working Paper 2899 (2002), 3.

4. Pablo Lopez-Murphy and Mauricio Villafuerte, "Fiscal Policy in Oil Producing Countries During the Recent Oil Price Cycle," IMF Working Paper 10/28 (2010).

5. Ben Bernanke, "Nonmonetary Effects of the Financial Crisis in the Propagation of the Great Depression," *American Economic Review* 73:3 (June 1983): 257–76.

6. Heiko Hesse and Tigran Poghosyan, "Oil Prices and Bank Profitability: Evidence from Major Oil-Exporting Countries in the Middle East and North Africa," IMF Working Paper 09/220 (2009).

7. Alex Cukierman, Geoffrey Miller, and Bilin Neyapti, "Central Bank Reform, Liberalization, and Inflation in Transition Economies—An International Perspective," *Journal of Monetary Economics* 49 (2002): 237–64.

8. Ben Bernanke and Mark Gertler, "Monetary Policy and Asset Price Volatility," NBER Working Paper W7559 (2000).

9. Walter Bagehot, *Lombard Street* (London: H.S. King, 1873).

10. Bernanke and Gertler, "Monetary Policy."

11. Hesse and Poghosyan, "Oil Prices and Bank Profitability."

12. Atish Ghosh, "Toward a Stable System of Exchange Rates: Implications of the Choice of Exchange Rate Regime," IMF (2010).

13. Brad Setser, "The Case for Exchange Rate Flexibility in Oil-Exporting Economies," Peterson Institute for International Economics Policy Brief 07-8 (2007).

14. Mohsin Khan, "The GCC Monetary Union: Choice of Exchange Rate Regime," Peterson Institute for International Economics Working Paper 09-1 (2009); Barry Eischengreen and Ricardo Hausmann, "Exchange Rates and Financial Fragility," NBER Working Paper 7418 (2009).

15. Jeffrey Frankel, "A Proposed Monetary Regime for Small Commodity Exporters: Peg to the Export Price (PEP)," *International Finance* 6:1 (2003): 61–88.

16. Thomas Sargent and Neil Wallace, "Some Unpleasant Monetarist Arithmetic," *Federal Reserve Bank of Minneapolis Quarterly Review* 5 (1981): 1–17.

17. See, among many others, Michael Woodford, "Price Level Determinacy Without Control of a Monetary Aggregate," NBER Working Paper 5204 (1995).

18. Mercedes da Costa and Vactor Olivo, "Constraints on the Design and Implementation of the Monetary Policy in Oil Economies: The Case of Venezuela," IMF Working Paper 08/142 (2008).

19. World Bank, *A New Silk Road: Export-Led Diversification*, Azerbaijan Country Economic Memorandum, Report 44365-AZ (Washington, D.C.: World Bank, 2009).

20. Ibid.

21. IMF, *World Economic Outlook* (Washington, D.C.: IMF, October 2009).

22. IMF, *Azerbaijan Article IV Consultation Discussions* (Washington, D.C.: IMF, 2010).

23. Ibid.

24. IMF, *Azerbaijan Country Report* (Washington, D.C.: IMF, 2007)

25. Ibid.

26. Ibid.

27. Cukierman, Miller, and Neyapti, "Central Bank Reform, Liberalization, and Inflation in Transition Economies."

28. Ibid.

29. In fact, my calculations of the LVAW score based on the 1996 law differ slightly from those in Cukierman et al. Their calculations yield an index value of 0.24, and mine yield a score of 0.26. My LVAW is different because Cukierman et al. assign

a score of 0.00 to the item on "Limitations on securitized." I mark it "NA," as there is no record of the relevant item in the law.

30. The total amount can be no higher than 3 percent of state budget average revenues for the past three years. The loan must be repaid in six months.

31. Gerhard Schwödiauer, Vladislav Komarov, and Iryna Akimova, "Central Bank Independence, Accountability, and Transparency: The Case of Ukraine," FEMM Working Paper 30 (December 2006).

Chapter 6

The views expressed in this chapter are those of the author and do not reflect the official policy or position of the National Defense University, the Department of Defense, or the U.S. government. Many thanks to those who have been especially helpful in the development of this article, especially Gavin Helf, the Azerbaijan Diplomatic Academy, Roy Stafford, Rich Andres, Robert Colella, Ken Shreves, and Dan Burghart.

1. For example, the total U.S. asset value in electricity exceeds $800 billion. See U.S. Department of Energy, "GridWorks: Overview of the Electric Grid," Office of Electricity Delivery & Energy Reliability, http://sites.energetics.com/gridworks/grid.html.

2. Venkataraman Krishnaswamy and Gary Stuggins, "Closing the Electricity Supply Demand Gap," World Bank Energy and Mining Sector Board Discussion Paper 20 (January 2007), 3.

3. David S. Brown and Ahmed Mushfiq Mobarak, "The Transforming Power of Democracy: Regime Type and Distribution of Electricity," *American Political Science Review* 103:2 (May 2009): 193.

4. Other chapters in this volume examine the issue of subsidies more fully.

5. Krishnaswamy and Stuggins, "Closing the Electricity Supply Demand Gap," 3.

6. Transparency International, *Corruption Perceptions Index 2009*, http://www.transparency.org/policy_research/surveys_indices/cpi/2009/cpi_2009_table.

7. Government of the Islamic Republic of Iran, "Electric Power Industry in Iran 2008–2009," Office of the Deputy of Human Resources and Researches Management of Information Technology and Statistics (Tehran: Tavanir Iranian Power Generation, Transmission, and Distribution Management Company, 2009), foreword, English version, http://www.tavanir.org.ir/info/stat87/sanatlhtml/s1.htm.

8. World Bank, "Energy Efficiency in Russia: Untapped Reserves," Document 46936, prepared in cooperation with Center for Energy Efficiency (CENEF) and International Finance Corporation (IFC) (Washington, D.C.: World Bank, 2008), 6.

9. National Electricity Regulatory Commission, "Energy Grid Security" and "Understanding the Grid," http://www.nerc.com/page.php?cid=1|15. Some details are from author's personal interviews with NERC representatives, Fall 2009.

10. See Terry Lynn Karl, "Understanding the Resource Curse," in Svetlana Tsalik and Anya Schiffrin, eds., *Covering Oil: A Reporter's Guide to Energy and Development* (New York: Revenue Watch/Open Society Institute, 2005), 25–26.

11. Timothy Irwin and Chiaki Yamamoto, *Some Options for Improving the Governance of State-Owned Electricity Utilities*, World Bank Energy and Mining Sector Board Discussion Paper 11 (February 2004), 3.

12. John E. Besant-Jones, *Reforming Power Markets in Developing Countries*, World Bank Energy and Mining Sector Board Discussion Paper 19 (2006), 14.

13. Ibid., 22.

14. World Bank ESMAP, *Tapping a Hidden Resource: Energy Efficiency in the Middle East and North Africa*, Sustainable Development Network: Middle East and North Africa Region, Energy Sector Management Assistance Program (Washington, D.C.: World Bank Group, February 2009), 51.

15. Ibid., 75.

16. U.S. Department of Energy, "GridWorks."

17. World Bank ESMAP, *Tapping a Hidden Resource*, 4.

18. Ibid., 73.

19. Ibid., 74.

20. Associated Press, "Drought Drives Venezuela to Save Energy," October 27, 2009, http://www.msnbc.msn.com/id/33494234/ns/weather.

21. Ibid.

22. Simon Romero, "Blackouts Plague Energy-Rich Venezuela," *New York Times*, November 11, 2009.

23. Kiraz Janicke, "Chavez Comments Spark Discontent Among Venezuelan Electrical Workers," October 27, 2009, Venezuelanalysis.com, www.venezuelanalysis.com/news/4901.

24. Economist Intelligence Unit, *Country Profile 2009: Venezuela* (London: Economist Intelligence Unit, 2009), 16.

25. EIA, "International Energy Statistics: Electricity, 2009, and Electricity Installed Capacity, 1980–2008," http://tonto.eia.doe.gov/cfapps/ipdbproject/iedindex3.cfm?tid=2&pid=2&aid=7&cid=&syid=2005&eyid=2007&unit=MK.

26. James Suggett, "Venezuela Expands Electricity Production, Conserves Energy amid Shortages," September 22, 2008, Venezuelanalysis.com, www.venezuelanalysis.com/news/3823.

27. Janicke, "Chavez Comments Spark Discontent."

28. Inter-American Development Bank, "Venezuela to Improve Its Electricity Service with a $200 Million IDB Loan," IDB News Release, October 14, 2009.

29. World Bank ESMAP, *Tapping a Hidden Resource*, 1.

30. World Bank, "Benchmarking Data of the Electricity Distribution Sector in the Latin America and Caribbean Region 1995–2005," http://info.worldbank.org/etools/lacelectricity/home.htm.

31. Romero, "Blackouts Plague Energy-Rich Venezuela."

32. "Latin America Realpolitik: Colombia Cuts Electricity to Venezuela, Ecuador," *Latin American Herald Tribune*, October 28, 2009, http://www.laht.com/article.asp?ArticleId=344776&CategoryId=10718.

33. Global Gas Flaring Reduction Initiative 2010 data, http://web.worldbank.org/WBSITE/EXTERNAL/TOPICS/EXTOGMC/EXTGGFR/0,,contentMDK:20297378~menuPK:6296802~pagePK:64168427~piPK:64168435~theSitePK:578069,00.html.

34. Robert Bott, *Flaring Questions and Answers*, 2nd ed. (Alberta: Canadian Centre for Energy Information, 2007), 12.

35. See International Bank for Reconstruction and Development, Global Gas Flaring Reduction Partnership documents, on the Global Gas Flaring Reduction Partnership website, http://web.worldbank.org/WBSITE/EXTERNAL/TOPICS/EXTOGMC/EXTGGFR/0,,contentMDK:20297378~menuPK:6296802~pagePK:64168427~piPK:64168435~theSitePK:578069,00.html.

36. Tavanir Iranian Power Generation, Transmission, and Distribution Management Company, "About Tavanir," "Historical Background of Electric Power Industry in Iran," "Specialized Holding Company of Tavanir and Its Subsidiary Companies," and "The Way That Company Is Run [sic]," http://www.tavanir.org.ir/latin.

37. Timothy Irwin and Chiaki Yamamoto, *Some Options for Improving the Governance of State-Owned Electricity Utilities*. World Bank Energy and Mining Sector Board Discussion paper no. 11 (Washington, D.C.: The World Bank Group, February 2004).

38. Economist Intelligence Unit, *Country Profile 2008: Iran* (London: Economist Intelligence Unit, 2008), 15.

39. Xinhua General News Service, "Tehran Faces Water, Electricity Shortage," January 6, 1991.

40. Associated Press, "Work to Resume on Abandoned Iranian Nuclear Plant," March 11, 1991.

41. Tavanir Iranian Power Generation, Transmission, and Distribution Management Company, "Electric Power Industry in Iran, 2004–2005," Office of the Deputy of Human Resources and Researches Management of Information Technology and Statistics (Tehran: Tavanir, 2005), Foreword and Section 1: Generation, English version, http://www.tavanir.org.ir/latin.

42. Tavanir Iranian Power Generation, Transmission, and Distribution Management Company, "Electric Power Industry in Iran 2008–2009" (Tehran: Tavanir, 2009), Foreword and Section 1: Generation, English version http://www.tavanir.org.ir/info/stat87/sanatlhtml/s1.htm.

43. Ibid.

44. Economist Intelligence Unit, *Country Profile 2008: Iran*, 16.

45. Tavanir Iranian Power Generation, Transmission, and Distribution Management Company, "Electric Power Industry in Iran, 2008–2009."

46. Government of Iran, Ministry of Energy, *World Energy Facts and Figures 2007* (Tehran: Islamic Republic of Iran Ministry of Energy, 2007). The document covers March 21, 2007 to March 21, 2008 (the year 1386 on the Iranian calendar).

47. Economist Intelligence Unit, *Country Profile 2008: Iran*, 16.

48. EIA, "Country Analysis Brief: Iran," February 2009, 10, http://www.eia.doe.gov/cabs.

49. Iranian sources estimate the subsidy to be even higher—on the order of 26.2 percent. For World Bank analysis, see World Bank ESMAP, *Tapping a Hidden Resource*, 53.

50. Ibid., 4.

51. Ibid., 79.

52. Ibid., 19.

53. Economist Intelligence Unit, *Country Profile 2008: Iran*, 16.

54. Oil accounted for 12.5 percent and hydroelectricity for 8.8 percent. Data according to IEA statistics, IEA Statistics Database, http://www.iea.org/stats.

55. Government of Iran Ministry of Energy, *Energy in Iran 2006* (Tehran: Islamic Republic of Iran Ministry of Energy, 2008), official English translation, http://pep.moe.org.ir, 46.

56. Economist Intelligence Unit, *Country Profile 2008: Iran*, 17.

57. Government of the Islamic Republic of Iran, *World Energy Facts and Figures 2007* (Tehran: Islamic Republic of Iran Ministry of Energy, 2007), 39. The document covers the time period from March 21, 2007 to March 21, 2008 (the year 1386 on the Iranian calendar).

58. EIA, "Country Analysis Brief: Iran."

59. World Bank ESMAP, *Tapping a Hidden Resource*, 7.

60. Ibid., 129.

61. Economist Intelligence Unit, *Country Profile 2008: Iran*, 17.

62. BBC Monitoring Middle East, "Analysis: Iranian Media Outlets Face Further Restrictions," *BBC Monitoring Middle East-Political*, July 4, 2007.

63. BBC Monitoring Middle East, "Iran Daily Calls on Reformist Press to Avoid Defamation, Slander," July 19, 2007, reprint of text of report published on the website of the Iranian newspaper *Resalat*, July 1, 2007.

64. Based on 2007 statistics from International Energy Agency (IEA), Statistics Database, http://www.iea.org/stats.

65. Economist Intelligence Unit, *Country Profile 2008: Iran*, 8.

66. World Bank ESMAP, *Tapping a Hidden Resource*, 104.

67. Besant-Jones, *Reforming Power Markets in Developing Countries*, 15.

68. IEA, Statistics Database, data for 2007, http://www.iea.org/stats.

69. EIA, "Country Analysis Brief: Iran," 11.

70. For details, see Theresa Sabonis-Helf, "The Unified Energy Systems of Russia (RAO-UES) in Central Asia and the Caucasus: Nets of Interdependence," *Demokratizatsiya* 15:4 (2007): 429–444.

71. IEA, *Key World Energy Statistics 2009* (Paris: IEA, 2009), 27.

72. In 2007, Russia exported electricity to Azerbaijan, Belarus, Georgia, Kazakhstan, Latvia, Lithuania, Moldova, and Ukraine. For details see Sabonis-Helf, "The Unified Energy Systems of Russia," 431.

73. EIA, "Country Analysis Brief: Russia," May 2008, 14, http://eia.doe.gov/cabs.

74. World Bank, "Potential and Prospects for Regional Electricity Trade in the South Asia Region," Sustainable Development Department South Asia Region, Document 41582 (Washington, D.C.: World Bank Group, June 2007), 16.

75. IEA, Statistics Database, http://www.iea.org/stats.

76. World Bank, "Energy Efficiency in Russia," 19.

77. Ibid., 20.

78. Besant-Jones, *Reforming Power Markets in Developing Countries*, 19.

79. World Bank, "Energy Efficiency in Russia," 27.

80. Ibid., 6.

81. Ibid., 28.

82. EIA, "Country Analysis Brief: Russia."

83. Besant-Jones, *Reforming Power Markets in Developing Countries*, 63.

84. Marshall I. Goldman, *Petrostate: Putin, Power, and the New Russia* (New York: Oxford University Press, 2008), 182.

85. Clifford G. Gaddy and Barry W. Ickes, "Resource Rents and the Russian Economy," *Eurasian Geography and Economics* 46:8 (2005): 565.

86. Steven Mufson, "Belarus Deal Signals Russia's Growing Clout; Gas Monopoly Won a Price Doubling," *Washington Post*, January 2, 2007.

87. Gazprom, "Gazprom Annual Report 2006," English-Language version, 10.

88. Mufson, "Belarus Deal Signals Russia's Growing Clout."

89. Economist Intelligence Unit, *Country Profile 2008: Russia*, 27–28.

90. World Bank, "Energy Efficiency in Russia," 73.

91. According to the Gazprom website. See "History: 15th Anniversary of Gazprom Joint-Stock Company," http://www.gazprom.com.

92. Derek Brower, "Russia: The Heart of the Matter," *Petroleum Economist*, May 1, 2007, 6.

93. World Bank, "Reform of the Russian Natural Gas Sector," Executive Summary by Peter Thompson (Washington, D.C.: World Bank Group, May 2004), 5.

94. Guy Chazen and Gregory L. White, "Russia's Energy Policy Doesn't Match Its G8 Talk," *Wall Street Journal*, July 6, 2006.

95. See Thane Gustafson, *Crisis amid Plenty: The Politics of Energy under Brezhnev and Gorbachev* (Princeton, N.J.: Princeton University Press, 1989).

96. World Bank Azerbaijan, *Country Brief 2009: Azerbaijan* (Baku: World Bank, updated November 2009), http://web.worldbank.org/WBSITE/EXTERNAL/COUN TRIES/ECAEXT/AZERBAIJANEXTN/0,,menuPK:301919~pagePK:141159 ~piPK:141110~theSitePK:301914,00.html.

97. EIA, "Azerbaijan Energy Profile," http://eia.doe.gov/cabs.

98. Ibid.

99. World Bank, *Country Brief 2009: Azerbaijan*.

100. Justin Burke, "Azerbaijan to Ration Electricity," *Azerbaijan Daily Digest*, January 26, 2000, http://www.eurasianet.org/resource/azerbaijan/hypermail/200001/ 0036.html.

101. Author interviews in Baku with energy industry experts and critics, July 2009.

102. Energy Charter, "Dispute Settlement," http://www.encharter.org/index.php ?id=479.

103. UNDP Azerbaijan Development Bulletin, "Barmek Saga Continues," July 14, 2006, http://www.un-az.org/undp.

104. Mina Muradova and Rufat Abbasov, "Azerbaijan: Turkish Investor, Jailed Minister Accused of Embezzlement, Forgery," Eurasianet.org, March 8, 2006, http://www.eurasianet.org/departments/business/articles/eav030806.shtml.

105. Ibid.

106. Krishnaswamy and Stuggins, "Closing the Electricity Supply Demand Gap," 7.

107. World Bank, "Azerbaijan Raising Rates: Short-Term Implications of Residential Electricity Tariff Rebalancing," Report 30749-AZ, Europe and Central Asia Region, Environmentally and Socially Sustainable Development (Washington, D.C.: World Bank, December 10, 2004), 4.

108. Ibid., 5.

109. Ibid., 9.

110. Bruce Hutchinson and Natalia Kulichenko, "Two-Part Wholesale Electricity Tariff Design for Azerbaijan," report prepared by PA Consulting for USAID under Azerbaijan Energy Assistance Project (Washington, D.C.: USAID, September 28, 2006), 6.

111. Author interviews, BakiElectricSebeke, July 2009.

112. Today.Az, "Electricity Quantity Consumed in Azerbaijan in March Revealed," May 1, 2010, Today.Az, report of statistics received from Azerenerji Joint Stock Company, http://www.today.az/news/business/67108.html.

113. Ibid.

114. Today.Az, "Azerbaijan's Sumgait City Ups Electricity Consumption," February 15, 2010, http://www.today.az/news/business/61654.html.

115. ABC.az News Service, "Uroven Abonentskoi Oplati elektroenergii v Azerbaijan podros do 87 percent," May 15, 2010, http://www.abc.az/news_15_05_2010_44993 .html, translation from Russian by the author.

116. European Union Energy Portal, Inogate, accessed May 2011 at http://www .inogate.org/index.php?option=com_inogate&view=countrysector&id=12&Itemid= 63&lang=en.

117. IEA, Statistics Database, data for 2007, http://www.iea.org/stats.

118. Economist Intelligence Unit, *Country Profile 2008: Azerbaijan* (London: Economist Intelligence Unit 2008), 24.

119. See schema from Association of the Power Engineers and Specialists of Azerbaijan (APESA) website, http://www.azenerji.com/az/powersystem/maps/inkishaf_ sxemi.jpg.

120. Milli.Az, "Apreldə 897 milyon 188 min kubmetr qazdan istifadə olunub," May 18, 2010, http://www.milli.az/news/economy/11435.html, translation from Azerbaijani courtesy of Taleh Ziyadov.

121. Author interviews, Asian Development Bank, July 2009.

122. Ibid.

123. Irwin and Yamamoto, *Some Options*, 7.

124. Author interviews with energy sector experts and critics, Baku, July 2009.

125. ABC.az News Service, "Azerbaijan smozhet nachat eksport elektroenergii v Turtsiyu cherez Gruziyu ne ranee 2012 goda,"March 19, 2010, translation from Russian by author.

Chapter 7

1. Alexander Wendt, *Social Theory of International Politics* (Cambridge: Cambridge University Press, 1999), 233–38. Wendt roughly differentiates between four kinds of identities states may have: corporate (or personal), type, role, and collective identities. Corporate identity refers to essential properties that make a particular actor a state; for Wendt, those are (i) an institutional-legal order, (ii) a monopoly on the legitimate use of organized violence, (iii) sovereignty, (iv) a society, and (v) territory. Type identity corresponds to the regime type of a particular state, whereas role identity refers to an identity states take in relation to Others, with Wendt singling out three such roles—those of enemy, rival, and friend. This distinction between Self and Other is blurred in collective identities (202, 224–31).

2. Alexander L. George and Robert O. Keohane, "The Concept of National Interests: Uses and Limitations," in Alexander L. George, ed., *Presidential Decision-Making in Foreign Policy: Making Better Use of Information and Advice* (Boulder, Colo.: Westview Press, 1980), 217–37.

3. Wendt refers collective self-esteem to "a group's need to feel good about itself, for respect or status." Wendt, *Social Theory*, 236. In the case of the post-Soviet states in Central Eurasia, a need for collective self-esteem and physical security worked together to shape and condition their struggle for Western recognition of their individual importance.

4. Sean D. Murphy, "Democratic Legitimacy and the Recognition of States and Governments," *International and Comparative Law Quarterly* 48 (July 1999): 545–46.

5. Alexander Wendt, "Why a World State Is Inevitable," *European Journal of International Relations* 9:4 (2003): 491–542. For a conceptualization of the struggle for recognition, also see Francis Fukuyama, *The End of History and the Last Man* (New York: Avon Books, 1992) and Axel Honneth, *The Struggle for Recognition* (Cambridge, Mass.: MIT Press, 1996).

6. Georg W. F. Hegel, *Phenomenology of Spirit* (Oxford: Clarendon Press, 1977).

7. Wendt, "World State," 511.

8. Ibid., 511–12.

9. Erik Ringmar, "The Recognition Game: Soviet Russia Against the West," *Cooperation and Conflict* 37:2 (2002): 122.

10. Wendt defines cultural selection as "an evolutionary mechanism involving 'the transmission of the determinants of behavior from individual to individual, and thus from generation to generation, by social learning, imitation, or some other similar process'" (*Social Theory*, 324).

11. Ibid., 325.

12. For a detailed conceptualization of the struggle for recognition-imitation nexus, both in theory and in the context of post-Soviet Central Eurasia, see Murad Ismayilov, "Pipeline Politics, the Struggle for Recognition, and Evolutionary Dynamics of Security Relations in a Post-Soviet Central Eurasia" (master's dissertation, University of Cambridge, 2009).

13. Ian Clark, *Legitimacy in International Society* (New York: Oxford University Press, 2007).

14. Throughout the chapter, the concept of knowledge is used in a Foucauldian sense as a discursive form of power. See Michel Foucault, *Archaeology of Knowledge*, 2nd ed. (New York: Routledge, 2002) and Foucault and Alan Sheridan, *Discipline and Punish: The Birth of the Prison* (London: Penguin, 1991).

15. Wendt, *Social Theory*, 326.

16. For the material aspect of the struggle for recognition, see Wendt, "World State," 507–10.

17. For the conceptualization of "brute material forces," see Wendt, *Social Theory*, 109–13, esp. 111.

18. In what is well expressive of this point, Sabir Rustamkhanly, Azerbaijan's information minister at the time, made it clear in 1992 that "we know that many states want to control Azerbaijan in one way or another, but independence is one of the ideals of the Azerbaijani people's fight." Quoted in Brenda Shaffer, *Borders and Brethren: Iran and the Challenge of Azerbaijani Identity*, BCSIA Studies in International Security (Cambridge, Mass.: MIT Press, 2002), 165.

19. Audrey Altstadt, "Azerbaijan's Struggle Toward Democracy," in Karen Dawisha and Bruce Parrot, eds., *Conflict, Cleavage, and Change in Central Asia and the Caucasus* (Cambridge: Cambridge University Press, 1997), 128. Soviet troops withdrew from Lithuania three months later, in August 1993; and in August 1994, the last Soviet troops withdrew from Estonia and Latvia. Georgeta Pourchot, *Eurasia Rising: Democracy and Independence in the Post-Soviet Space* (Westport, Conn.: Praeger, 2008), 55–56. Russia retained its military base at Gyumri and Erebuni in Armenia, as well as those in Ukraine (the Russian Black Sea Fleet naval base at Sevastopol, the Crimea), Georgia, Belarus (at Baranovichi), Kazakhstan (Sary-Shagan training ground and the cosmodrome at Baikonur), Moldova (Tiraspol), Tajikistan (at Nurek and in Dushanbe), and in Kyrgyzstan (Kant airbase, which Moscow upgraded in late 2003). For a detailed account of Russian military bases in a post-Cold War Eurasia, see Zdzislaw Lachowski, "Foreign Military Bases in Eurasia," SIPRI Policy Paper 18 (Stockholm: Stockholm International Peace Research Institute, June 2007), chapter 5.

20. The Russian-run anti-missile radar station at Gabala in the north of the republic remains as the only exception. In 2002, Russia's use of the station, which brings 7 million USD to the Azerbaijani budget, was extended for ten more years.

21. By the end of 1999, Moscow only retained four military bases in Georgian territory: at Vaziani, Gudauta, Batumi, and Akhalkalaki. Following the joint statement Russia and Georgia signed on the sidelines of the OSCE summit in Istanbul in 1999, Russia closed two of its bases: at Vaziani near Tbilisi and at Gudauta in Abkhazia, in June and November of 2001, respectively. On March 31, 2006, a final agreement was reached between Russia and Georgia on the withdrawal of Russian troops from the bases at Batumi and Akhalkalaki by the end of 2008; this was preceded by a joint Russian-Georgian statement issued to that effect on May 30, 2005. See Nicolas Landru, "Georgia: The Evacuation of the Russian Military Base at Akhalkalaki Comes to a Close," *Caucaz Europenews,* May 30, 2007, http://www.caucaz.com/home_eng/breve _contenu.php?id=314; Nikolai Sokov, "The Withdrawal of Russian Military Bases from Georgia: Not Solving Anything," PONARS Policy Memo 363 (June 2005), http://www.csis.org/media/csis/pubs/pm_0363.pdf and Pourchot, *Eurasia Rising,* 107–8. Ahead of the agreed schedule, Russia closed its base in Akhalkalaki in June 2007 and the base in Batumi in November 2007. See Pavel Felgenhauer, "Russian Soldiers Leave South Georgia, Others Deployed in the North," *Eurasia Daily Monitor* 4:212, November 14, 2007, http://www.jamestown.org/single/?no_cache=1&tx_ttnews%5Btt_news %5D=33164. Following the five-day war with Georgia in August 2008 and the subsequent recognition of the latter's two breakaway territories, Russia moved to reinstate its military bases at Gudauta (Abkhazia) and Tskhinvali (South Ossetia). See "Russia Scales Down Plans for Troops in Abkhazia, S. Ossetia," *RIA Novosti,* May 19, 2009, http://en.rian.ru/russia/20090519/155042049.html and Civil Georgia, "Moscow Comments on Gudauta Base in Abkhazia," *Civil Georgia,* May 3, 2006, http://www.civil.ge/ eng/article.php?id=12472. See also Lachowski, "Foreign Military Bases in Eurasia," 58. For a detailed account of Russian military bases in Georgia, see pages 57–59.

22. The Azerbaijan Democratic Republic lasted from May 28, 1918, to April 28, 1920. See Audrey Altstadt, *The Azerbaijani Turks: Power and Identity Under Russian Rule* (Stanford, Calif.: Hoover Institution Press, 1992), 89–107; Tadeusz Swietochowski, *Russian Azerbaijan, 1905–1920* (Cambridge: Cambridge University Press, 2004), chapter 6; Charles Van Der Leeuw, *Azerbaijan: A Quest for Identity* (New York: St. Martin's, 2000), 111–23; and Shaffer, *Borders and Brethren,* 37–39. The Democratic Republic of Georgia lasted from May 1918 to February 1921. See Zourab Avalishvili, *The Independence of Georgia in International Politics 1918–1921* (New York: Hyperion, 1981).

23. Azerbaijanis now commemorate January 20 as "Black January." See, for example, Hafiz Pashayev, *Racing Up Hill: Selected Papers* (New York: Global Scholarly Publications, 2006), 126–32; Altstadt, *The Azerbaijani Turks,* 213–19; Altstadt, "Azerbaijan's Struggle," 122–23; Leeuw, *Azerbaijan,* 160–63; and Reza and Betty Blair, "Black January: Baku (1990)," *Azerbaijan International* 6:1 (Spring 1998): 33–37. In a

symbolic move, Georgians timed the proclamation of their independence from the Soviet Union to the second anniversary of the Soviet assault (April 9, 1991). Georgians now commemorate that day as the Day of National Unity. See Darrell Slider, "Democratization in Georgia," in Dawisha and Parrott, *Conflict, Cleavage, and Change,* 161 and Steven Eke, "Georgia Recalls Soviet Crackdown," *BBC News,* April 8, 2009, http://news.bbc.co.uk/1/hi/world/europe/7986282.stm.

24. E.g., Shaffer, *Borders and Brethren,* esp. chapter 1.

25. Ilham Aliyev, *Azerbaijan's Caspian Oil* (in Russian) (Moscow: Izvestiya, 2003), 151.

26. The most serious among Iran's disruptive efforts so far occurred in July 2001 when, within a week, Iranian jets several times violated Azerbaijan's airspace. It eventually took Turkey to send its military jets "over demonstrative flight over Baku" to have the crisis peacefully resolved. See Shannon O'Lear, "Resources and Conflict in the Caspian Sea," in Philippe Le Billon, ed., *The Geopolitics of Resource Wars: Resource Dependence, Governance, and Violence* (London: Routledge, 2005), 161 and Aliyev, *Azerbaijan's Caspian Oil,* 310.

27. The conflict over Nagorno-Karabakh served to speed up the formation of the Azerbaijani nationalist movement, which spearheaded the anti-Soviet and pro-independence struggle in the country in the late 1980s and early 1990s. See Altstad, "Azerbaijan's Struggle," esp. 118–124. Although a Russia-mediated cease-fire was reached on May 12, 1994, no genuine peace has so far been attained between the parties, who are virtually still in a state of war with each other. For more information on the Nagorno-Karabakh conflict, see, for example, Thomas de Waal, *Black Garden: Armenian and Azerbaijan through Peace and War* (New York: New York University Press, 2003); Kenneth Weisbrode, *Central Eurasia: Prize or Quicksand?* Adelphi Paper 338 (New York: Oxford University Press, 2001), chapter 2; and ICG, "Nagorno-Karabakh: Risking War," *Europe Report* 187 (November 14, 2007).

28. For more on the two conflicts, see Slider, "Democratization in Georgia," 171–73, and Ruth Deyermond, *Security and Sovereignty in the Former Soviet Union* (Boulder, Colo.: Lynne Rienner, 2008), 9–11.

29. Pourchot, *Eurasia Rising,* 8.

30. For Azerbaijan, see Altstadt, "Azerbaijan's Struggle," 137–41; for Georgia, see Slider, "Democratization in Georgia," 190–93.

31. World Bank, *Georgia: Country Brief* (April 2009).

32. Elmira Akhundova, *Moments of Truth* (in Russian) (Baku: Dom Skazki, 2003), 24–25, 30.

33. Wendt, *Social Theory,* 279–97.

34. At the time of their admission, the organization was called the Conference on Security and Cooperation in Europe (CSCE). It was renamed OSCE by a decision of the Budapest Summit in December 1994.

35. The three Baltic states were admitted to the CSCE on September 10, 1991. Armenia, Azerbaijan, Belarus, Moldova, Ukraine, and the five Central Asian states

(Kazakhstan, Kyrgyzstan, Tajikistan, Turkmenistan, and Uzbekistan) became members on January 30, 1992. Georgia became a member on March 24, 1992. The Russian Federation succeeded the USSR as a member of the CSCE.

36. The three Baltic states officially became UN members on September 17, 1991, following their recognition by the Soviet Union on September 6, 1991. Armenia, Azerbaijan, Moldova, and the five Central Asian states (Kazakhstan, Kyrgyzstan, Tajikistan, Turkmenistan, Uzbekistan) became members on March 2, 1992, and Georgia became a member on July 31, 1992. By common consent on behalf of the former Soviet republics, Russia assumed the USSR's position in the UN, a fact of which Boris Yeltsin, Russia's first president, informed the UN in his letter of December 24, 1991. Belarus and Ukraine both had been official members since October 24, 1945.

37. For the text of the Final Act, see http://www.osce.org/documents/mcs/1975/08/4044_en.pdf.

38. An agreement signed between the Russian Federation, Belarus, and Ukraine on December 8, 1991, to establish what came to be known as the Commonwealth of Independent States (CIS) explicitly stated—in its Article 5—that the member-states "recognize and respect the territorial integrity of one another and the inviolability of [the] existing borders," a commitment restated in the Alma-Ata Declaration of December 21, 1991, which extended the CIS to include the five states in Central Asia, plus Azerbaijan, Armenia, and Moldova. In December 1993, Georgia also became a member of the CIS. The Russian text of the first agreement is available at the CIS official website at http://cis.minsk.by/main.aspx?uid=176. Its unofficial English translation is available at http://www.therussiasite.org/legal/laws/CISagreement.html. The English text of the Alma-Ata Declaration is available in the Library of Congress at http://lcweb2.loc.gov/frd/cs/belarus/by_appnc.html.

39. The "war for conquest" (or "constitutive" war), in which the very existence of states is at stake, is different from "positional" war (or "configurative" war), which is limited in its goals by the institution of sovereignty and the parties' mutual recognition thereof and is therefore waged for territory and/or strategic advantage only. See Wendt, *Social Theory*, 283–84.

40. Thomas M. Franck, *The Power of Legitimacy Among Nations* (New York: Oxford University Press, 1990), 8.

41. Rogers Brubaker, *Nationalism Reframed: Nationhood and the National Question in the New Europe* (Cambridge: Cambridge University Press, 1996), 43.

42. That the regional states ended up searching for external sources for the resolution of their domestic security and economic problems was also partly the result of what Altstadt calls "a mentality of control," an "enduring legacy" of the Communist rule that "led the populace as a whole to expect to be controlled by the authorities" who in turn expected to be controlled by "the centre," "Azerbaijan's Struggle," 115. Given that the former "center" in Moscow could no longer deliver on expectations and indeed was itself perceived as a threat to be dealt with, the "mentality of control" pushed the population and the elites alike to search for alternative "centers" that could

be held accountable for the problems of the republic. In what in a remarkable way points to such a mentality of control, Vafa Guluzade, former national security advisor to the president of Azerbaijan, referred to the telephone conversation of October 2, 1995, between Bill Clinton and Heydar Aliyev, which he was translating and in which the U.S. president first voiced the idea of the east-west energy corridor. Guluzade recalls that following the conversation, Aliyev turned to him saying: "We used to have our bosses in Moscow. Now they are in Washington." Personal interview with Vafa Guluzade, Baku, April 24, 2009.

43. Compulsory power refers to social relations, in which one actor exercises direct control over the conditions and actions of another; it is different from what Barnett and Duvall call "institutional power," which refers to actors' indirect control over the conditions of others through the formal and informal institutions. Michael Barnett and Raymond Duvall, "Power in International Politics," *International Organization* 59:1 (Winter 2005): 49–52. Both, however, operate in a social process of interaction (as opposed to that of a constitution).

44. Again, failure to enlist that kind of "recognition of importance"—and consequently, genuine support for their statehood—once already resulted, for both Azerbaijan and Georgia, in the loss of their short-lived independence in 1920–21. In those days, Western powers limited themselves to extending de facto recognition to Azerbaijan, Georgia, and Armenia—the latter three's diplomatic overtures to attain de jure recognition notwithstanding—which eventually resulted in Soviet aggression followed by forceful incorporation of these states into what came to be known as the Soviet Union.

45. In his article in the Russian newspaper *Komsomolskaya Pravda*'s August 1, 1995, edition, Vafa Guluzade, national security advisor to the first three presidents of post-Soviet Azerbaijan, made this link between Azerbaijan's desire for physical security (and indeed independence) and its quest for Euro-Atlantic integration explicit: "Having mighty neighbors to its north and to its south, Azerbaijan views the West as the guarantor of its independence. Azerbaijan needs the support of the United States and Western Europe to protect itself from the influence of Russia and Iran. Given that the interests of the United States and Azerbaijan coincide in that both struggle against the Russian expansionism and Iranian fundamentalism, the two countries should struggle against these forces together." Vafa Guluzade, *Amongst Foes and Friends: Articles, Interviews, Speeches*, in Russian (Baku, 2002), http://www.azeribook.com/politika/vafa_guluzade/sredi_vragov_i_druzey.htm.

46. Although the Commonwealth of Independent States, established in December 1991, was—apart from its other stated and conceived objectives—initially meant to help its members to address post-disintegration problems, including economic hardship, it could not serve as a viable solution because all of its members, including Russia itself, suffered from a severe economic setback following the collapse of the Soviet Union. See Graham Smith, *The Post-Soviet States: Mapping the Politics of Transition* (London: Arnold, 1999), 157.

47. For a conceptual analysis of institutional power, see Barnett and Duvall, "Power in International Politics," 51–52. Also see Stefano Guzzini, "Structural Power: The Limits of Neorealist Power Analysis," *International Organization* 47:3 (Summer 1993): 451–56.

48. Already in December 1991, Azerbaijan's then foreign minister Huseynaga Sadykhov voiced the idea of and the need for Azerbaijan's membership in NATO, viewing the organization as an institutional embodiment of the West and the security guarantees it can provide. See Vladimir Zakharov and Andrei Areshev, *Azerbaijan's Cooperation with NATO and the Situation in Nagorno-Karabakh: Stages, Intentions, Results*, in Russian (Moscow: Centre for Caucasian Research, MGIMO, June 2008), http://www.noravank.am/ru/?page=analitics&nid=1447. Heydar Aliyev, on the other hand, explicitly referred to NATO as a bridge to broader ties with the West in his speech in Brussels after the signing of the Partnership for Peace program on May 4, 1994. In his speech, Heydar Aliyev stressed that "We [Azerbaijanis] view NATO as an organization capable of assisting the young Azerbaijani state in establishing [a] close and multidirectional relationship with the Western world and help[ing] it benefit from the latter's very rich experience." Azerbaijan Presidential Online Library, *Reports, Speeches, Statements, Addresses, Declarations, and Interviews of Heydar Aliyev in 1994*, in Azerbaijani (1994), 149, http://www.elibrary.az/docs/haliyev/1994.pdf.

49. Wendt, *Social Theory*, 226, 291–93.

50. See Altstadt, "Azerbaijan's Struggle," 131–32. The English-language text of the Constitution of the Republic of Azerbaijan is available at http://www.un-az.org/doc/constitution.doc.

51. The English-language text of the Constitution of the Republic of Georgia is available at http://www.parliament.ge/index.php?lang_id=ENG&sec_id=68.

52. Steve LeVinc, *The Oil and the Glory: The Pursuit of Empire and Fortune on the Caspian Sea* (New York: Random House, 2007), 220–23.

53. Pashayev, *Racing Up Hill*, 6. Pashayev follows up by drawing a similar linkage between westward pipelines and his country's independence: "This pipeline [BTC] would also have geo-strategic significance for Azerbaijan; tying into the question of guaranteeing Azerbaijan's independence and its pro-Western foreign policy and of reducing the role of external players, particularly Russia, in the country's internal affairs" (87). In his 1997 speech, he emphasizes this point again: "these oil projects are about providing Azerbaijan [with] the means necessary to maintain its long sought and finally achieved independence" (101).

54. LeVine, *The Oil and the Glory*, 190; also see Joseph Jofi, "Pipeline Diplomacy: the Clinton Administration's Fight for Baku-Ceyhan," *WWS Case Study* 1/99 (Princeton, N.J.: Woodrow Wilson School of Public and International Affairs, 1999), http://wws.princeton.edu/research/cases/pipeline.pdf.

55. Aliyev, *Azerbaijan's Caspian Oil*, 20.

56. Caspian Integration Business Club, "Other Important Projects Following the Baku-Tbilisi-Ceyhan Appear Due to Its Start," *Caspian Integration Business Club*, July

14, 2006, http://www.cibcgroup.com/shab_news_en.shtml?cgi-bin/show_news.pl?lang =en&id=181.

57. President of Georgia, "Public Appearance of the President of Georgia Michael Saakashvili at the Presentation of the Baku-Tbilisi-Ceyhan Oil Pipeline," *Speeches*, July 13, 2006, http://www.president.gov.ge/?l=E&m=0&sm=3&st=100&id=1967.

58. Akhundova, *Moments of Truth*, 30.

59. Aliyev, *Azerbaijan's Caspian Oil*, 153.

60. Pashayev, *Racing Up Hill*, 5.

61. Quoted in Aliyev, *Azerbaijan's Caspian Oil*, 150. Also see Pashayev, *Racing Up Hill*, 120–21. Namik Effendiyev, an Azerbaijani oil official in the early 1990s, concurs: "Baku's onshore industry 'was dead,' its offshore was 'in trouble,' and there was 'no money from Moscow' to fix any of it." Quoted and related in LeVine, *The Oil and the Glory*, 49.

62. With a 34.5 percent growth rate, Azerbaijan became the fastest-growing economy worldwide in 2006. See World Bank, *Azerbaijan: Country Brief*, April 2009, http://web.worldbank.org/WBSITE/EXTERNAL/COUNTRIES/ECAEXT/AZER-BAIJANEXTN/0,,menuPK:301923~pagePK:141132~piPK:141107~theSitePK:301914 ,00.html#econ. The country's growth rate in 2007 averaged 25 percent, in 2008 it was 10.8 percent, and in 2009 it was 9.3 percent. Due to the global economic crisis, the growth in 2010 is projected at 4.3 percent. IMF, *Regional Economic Outlook: Middle East and Central Asia* (Washington, D.C.: IMF, October 2010), 53, http://www.imf .org/external/pubs/ft/reo/2010/mcd/eng/10/mreo1024.pdf.

63. The English-language text of the National Security Concept of the Republic of Azerbaijan is available at http://merln.ndu.edu/whitepapers/Azerbaijan2007.pdf.

64. Explore the ministry's website at http://www.mdi.gov.az/?/en/.

65. UNDP, "Azerbaijan to Start Manufacturing Arms, Military Hardware In 2008," *UNDP Azerbaijan Development Bulletin* 55 (January 2008), http://www.un-az .org/undp/bulnews55/en3.php.

66. E.g., Regnum, "Azerbaijan Starts to Produce Armored Equipment and Unmanned Reconnaissance Aircraft," in Russian, *Regnum*, January 7, 2009, http://www .regnum.ru/news/1107573.html; Sohbet Mammadov, "Baku Is Creating a Military-Industrial Complex. Azerbaijan Is Planning to Become an Arms Exporter," in Russian, *CentralAsia.Ru*, December 29, 2008, http://www.centrasia.ru/newsA.php?st=1230533400.

67. UNDP, "Azerbaijan Military Parade Marks 90th Anniversary of Armed Forces," *UNDP Azerbaijan Development Bulletin* 60 (June 2008), http://www.un-az .org/undp/bulnews60/ms7.php.

68. Quoted in Ia Metreveli, "Baku-Tbilisi-Kars Rail Construction Launched," *Georgian Times*, November 26, 2007, http://www.geotimes.ge/index.php?m=home& newsid=7954.

69. For Armenian arguments to this effect, see Tigran Mkrtchyan, "Armenia's European Future," in Armando García Schmidt, Sibylle Reiter-Zimmermann, and Cortnie Shupe, eds., *The European Union and the South Caucasus: Three Perspectives*

on the Future of the European Project from the Caucasus, Europe in Dialogue Series 1 (Gütersloh: Bertelsmann Stiftung, 2009), 31–32.

70. E.g., Rovshan Ismayilov, "Azerbaijan, Georgia, and Turkey: Building a Transportation Triumvirate?" *EURASIANET.org*, February 7, 2007, http://www.eurasianet .net/departments/insight/articles/eav020707.shtml.

71. Metreveli, "Baku-Tbilisi-Kars Rail," and Lili Di Puppo, "The Baku-Akhalkalaki-Kars Railway Line: Cement for a Strategic Alliance," *Caucaz Europenews*, March 1, 2007, http://www.caucaz.com/home_eng/breve_contenu.php?id=303#.

72. Ismayilov, "Transportation Triumvirate?"

73. According to the contract the two countries signed in 2004, Baku was to buy 4 bcm of Russian gas annually at the price of USD 52 per 1,000 cbm until 2009. The price was unilaterally increased by Moscow in 2006, a measure Azerbaijan agreed to comply with at the time. The price Baku was now asked to pay by Gazprom amounted to USD 235 per 1,000 cbm, more than a twofold increase from the USD 110 that Baku had been charged in 2006. See Sergei Blagov, "Russian Ties with Azerbaijan Reach New Lows," *Eurasia Insight*, January 25, 2007, http://www.eurasianet.org/departments/ insight/articles/eav012507.shtml; Vladimir Socor, "Azerbaijan's President Turns Down Gazprom's 'Blackmail' Price," *Eurasia Daily Monitor* 4:4, January 5, 2007, http://www .jamestown.org/single/?no_cache=1&tx_ttnews%5Btt_news%5D=32360; and Ekho Moskvy, Interview with Ilham Aliyev, in Russian, December 23, 2006, http://www .echo.msk.ru/programs/beseda/48358/. The Russian decision allegedly came after Ilham Aliyev rejected—in early November 2006—Putin's proposal to agree on a "coordinated policy" for energy exports to the West, one that was interpreted as Moscow's attempt to force Baku into siding with it in Gazprom's energy policies vis-à-vis Georgia, Ukraine, and Belarus. See Rovshan Ismayilov, "Baku Banks on Independent Energy Policy," *EURASIANET.org*, December 13, 2006, http://www.eurasianet.org/depart ments/insight/articles/eav121306.shtml.

74. Ekho Moskvy, Interview with Ilham Aliyev.

75. Elmar Mammadyarov, "Protect Us Against Bullies," *Wall Street Journal*, January 19, 2007, http://online.wsj.com/article/SB116916219589980825.html?mod=opinion _main_europe_asia.

76. Ekho Moskvy, Interview with Ilham Aliyev; Blagov, "Russian Ties with Azerbaijan Reach New Lows"; and Socor, "Azerbaijan's President Turns Down Gazprom's 'Blackmail' Price."

77. Ekho Moskvy, Interview with Ilham Aliyev.

78. Karl Rahder, "Azerbaijan Looks Westward," *ISN Security Watch*, February 22, 2007, http://www.isn.ethz.ch/isn/Current-Affairs/Security-Watch/Detail/?ots591=4888 CAA0-B3DB-1461-98B9-E20E7B9C13D4&lng=en&id=52948.

79. Beginning in January 2007, following the Gazprom-demanded double increase in the price Georgia was to pay for Russian gas, Azerbaijan started to supply Georgia with natural gas at a preferential rate of 120 USD per 1,000 bcm. This move,

combined with SOCAR's move late in 2008 to purchase some important parts of Georgia's gas distribution system and the five-year November 14 (2008) agreement between Azerbaijan and Georgia on the supply of Azerbaijani natural gas to Georgia, prompted some to compare "the Azerbaijani use of its energy wealth" with "the Russian take-over of Armenian energy assets," with economic subsidies and control being effectively translated into political influence. See Ismayilov, "Baku Banks on Independent Energy Policy"; Mamuka Tsereteli, *The Impact of the Russia-Georgia War on the South Caucasus Transportation Corridor* (Washington, D.C.: Jamestown Foundation, 2009), 17; and Heidi Kjaernet, "The Energy Dimension of Azerbaijani-Russian Relations: Maneuvering for Nagorno-Karabakh," *Russian Analytical Digest* 56 (March 3, 2009): 3, http://www.fni.no/russcasp/RAD-56.pdf.

80. World Bank, *Georgia: Country Brief* (April 2009).

81. Altstadt, "Azerbaijan's Struggle," 123. For a fine overview of the Western reaction to the January 20 events and for similarities with previous Soviet invasions in Eastern Europe (Hungary, Czechoslovakia) and USSR (Baltic countries, Georgia) as perceived in Baku, see Pashayev, *Racing Up Hill*, 126–32. Also see Pourchot, *Eurasia Rising*, 43.

82. Pourchot, *Eurasia Rising*, 69.

83. "Elkhan Nuriyev, "Azerbaijan Does Not Need an Exclusively Pro-American or Pro-Russian Policy," in Russian, *Day.az*, April 28, 2009, http://www.day.az/news/politics/155199.html.

84. E.g., "Baku Announced the Capital of Islamic Culture in 2009," in Russian, *Day.az*, September 15, 2008, http://www.day.az/news/culture/130508.html. Interestingly, however, Baku, while seeking to instrumentalize Islamic knowledge and the power of institutions in which the latter is embedded, in a pragmatic pursuit of its national interests moved to resist deeper levels of penetration of that knowledge among the Azerbaijan society, a policy that manifested itself, among other things, in the government's recent moves to close down, or suspend the work of, numerous mosques in the capital on different grounds. E.g., Mina Muradova, "Azerbaijan: Mosques Close in Baku, 'Capital of Islamic Culture,'" *Eurasia Insight*, May 27, 2009, http://www.eurasianet.org/departments/insightb/articles/eav052709b.shtml and Islam Online.Net, "Azeri Muslims Decry Suppressive Government," *IslamOnline.Net*, October 14, 2008, http://www.islamonline.net/servlet/Satellite?c=Article_C&cid=1223905206798&pagename=Zone-English-News/NWELayout. For discussions on the Islamic penetration in post-Soviet Azerbaijan, see for example Sofie Bedford, *Islamic Activism in Azerbaijan: Repression and Mobilization in a Post-Soviet Context*, Stockholm Studies in Politics (Stockholm: Dept. of Political Science, Stockholm University, 2009); Arzu Geybullayeva, "Is Azerbaijan Becoming A Hub of Radical Islam?" *Turkish Policy Quarterly* 6:3 (Summer 2007): 109–16; and Liz Fuller and Badek Bakir, "Azerbaijan: Why Is 'Alternative' Islam Gaining Strength?" *Eurasia Insight*, August 12, 2007, http://www.eurasianet.org/departments/insight/articles/pp081207.shtml.

85. Elmar Mammadyarov, "Azerbaijan Will Step up Support for Islamic States in Zones of Conflict,'" in Russian, *Day.az*, May 24, 2009, http://www.day.az/news/politics/158480.html.

86. E.g., Mevlut Katik, "Turkic Summit to Explore Commonwealth Possibility," *Eurasia Insight*, November 15, 2006, http://www.eurasianet.org/departments/insight/articles/eav111506.shtml.

87. The first Turkic summit was initiated by the late Turkish President Turgut Ozal and was summoned in 1992 in Ankara. After the seventh Turkic summit convened in Istanbul in 2001, however, the process of "Turkic integration" was stalled only to be revived in 2006. See Igor Torbakov, "Strengthening the 'Eastern Vector': Ankara Hosts Turkic Summit," *Eurasia Daily Monitor* 3: 214, November 17, 2006, http://www.jamestown.org/single/?no_cache=1&tx_ttnews%5Btt_news%5D=32247, and Shirin Akiner, "Political Processes in Post-Soviet Central Asia," in Mehdi P. Amineh and Henk Houweling, eds., *Central Eurasia in Global Politics: Conflict, Security, and Development*, 2nd ed. (Leiden: Brill, 2005), 137.

88. Quoted in Mevlut Katik, "Spirit of Cooperation Dominates Turkic Summit," *Eurasia Insight*, November 20, 2006, http://www.eurasianet.org/departments/insight/articles/eav112006.shtml.

89. The new Turkic TV channel is on air twenty-four hours a day. Every Turkic country (Turkey, Azerbaijan, Kazakhstan, Uzbekistan, Kyrgyzstan, and Turkmenistan) is allocated four hours daily.

90. Saban Kardas, "Turkey Pushes for Closer Political Ties within the Turkic-Speaking World," *Eurasia Daily Monitor* 5:225, November 23, 2008. The first regular meeting of the Parliamentary Assembly took place in Baku, Azerbaijan, on September 28–29, 2009. In August 2010, the Parliamentary Assembly launched its own website (http://www.turk-pa.org) currently available in two languages, Azerbaijani and English.

91. Suleyman Kurt, "Turkic World to Put Ties in Institutional Framework in Nakhchivan," *Today's Zaman*, October 3, 2009.

92. Yossi Shain and Aharon Barth, "Diasporas and International Relations Theory," *International Organization* 57:3 (Summer 2003): 459.

Chapter 8

The author is grateful for funding and research support from the Azerbaijani Diplomatic Academy in Baku and for research support from the National Center for Scientific and Technical Information in Almaty. The author would like to thank the editors, Brent Durbin, Marcy McCullaugh, and Tobias Schulze-Cleven for their comments and suggestions on previous drafts.

1. Human capital and education have important roles to play in civil society, democratic politics, community building, and governance, which are not the focus of this paper.

2. For a typology of various types of capital (physical, human, social, financial), see Eric Sievers, *The Post-Soviet Decline of Central Asia: Sustainable Development and Comprehensive Capital* (London: RoutledgeCurzon, 2003).

3. For more on the economic and political dimensions of boom and bust cycles in petrostates, see Terry Lynn Karl, *The Paradox of Plenty: Oil Booms and Petro-States* (Berkeley: University of California Press, 1997) and Kiren Chaudhry, *The Price of Wealth: Economics and Institutions in the Middle East* (Ithaca, N.Y.: Cornell University Press, 1997).

4. For an intellectual history of studies by economists and others on the relationship between education, human capital, and development, see *The Road Not Traveled: Education Reform in the Middle East and Africa*, MENA Development Report (Washington, D.C.: World Bank, 2008), chapter 2.

5. Nancy Birdsall, David Ross, and Richard Sabot, "Education, Growth, and Inequality," in Nancy Birdsall and Frederick Z. Jaspersen, eds., *Pathways to Growth: Comparing East Asia and Latin America* (Washington, D.C.: Inter-American Development Bank, 1997), 93–130.

6. Task Force on Higher Education and Society, *Higher Education in Developing Countries: Perils and Promise* (Washington, D.C.: World Bank, 2000). For an overview of the types of higher education institutions and the broader system of higher education including financing, governance, political, and legal systems in which they are embedded, see Chapter 3. For an overview of the role education plays in science and technology, see Chapter 5.

7. *Higher Education in Kazakhstan*, OECD Review of National Policies for Education (Washington, D.C.: OECD and World Bank, 2007).

8. Javier Corrales, "The Politics of Education Reform: Bolstering the Supply and Demand; Overcoming Institutional Blocks," Education Reform and Management Series 2, 1 (World Bank, 1999).

9. Task Force on Higher Education and Society, *Higher Education in Developing Countries*.

10. World Bank EdStats database. For the remainder of the chapter, all statistics referenced in this chapter are from the World Bank EdStats database, unless otherwise noted. The definition of gross enrollment ratio is the total enrollment at a given educational level, regardless of age, divided by the population of the age group that typically corresponds to that level of education. The specification of age groups varies by country, based on different national systems of education and the duration of schooling at the first and second levels. For tertiary education, the ratio is expressed as a percentage of the population in the five-year age group following the official secondary school leaving age. Gross enrollment ratios may exceed 100 percent if individuals outside the age cohort corresponding to a particular educational level are enrolled in that level.

11. In contrast, signs of low education quality include rote memorization, corruption and cheating in education assessments, and outdated books, resources, and information sources.

12. To the extent that humanities and social sciences are taught to the exclusion of science, engineering and vocational skills, labor market demands will often not be met. See *The Road Not Traveled*.

13. For example, see Paul Pierson, *Dismantling the Welfare State: Reagan, Thatcher, and the Politics of Retrenchment* (Cambridge: Cambridge University Press, 2002) and Evelyne Huber and John D. Stevens, *Development and Crisis of the Welfare State: Parties and Policies in Global Markets* (Chicago: University of Chicago Press, 2001).

14. As of 1950, almost all OECD countries had publicly funded higher education systems limited to a small fraction of the population. Ansell identifies three types of higher education systems that emerged after World War II: partially private, mass public, and elite systems. Ben Ansell, "University Challenges: Explaining Institutional Change in Higher Education," *World Politics* 60 (January 2008): 189–230.

15. Isabela Mares and Matthew E. Carnes, "Social Policy in Developing Countries," *Annual Review of Political Science* 12 (2009): 94.

16. A summary of these differences is as follows: "East European welfare systems, though increasingly strained, provided comprehensive protections and services to almost all of their populations. East Asian welfare systems offered minimal social insurance, but a number placed a high priority on investment in education. In Latin America, the urban middle class and some blue-collar workers enjoyed access to relatively generous systems of public protection, but peasants and informal-sector workers were generally excluded or underserved." Stephan Haggard and Robert Kauffman, *Development, Democracy, and Welfare States: Latin America, East Asia, and Eastern Europe* (Princeton, N.J.: Princeton University Press, 2008), 1. For variation in post-Communist social welfare policy, see Linda Cook, *Postcommunist Welfare States: Reform Politics in Russia and Eastern Europe* (Ithaca, N.Y.: Cornell University Press, 2007) and Cook, "Negotiating Welfare in Postcommunist States," *Comparative Politics* 40:1 (October 2007): 41–62.

17. For a broad overview on the role of human capital, human agency, and institutions in development, see Peter Gourevitch, "The Role of Politics in Economic Development," *Annual Review of Political Science* 11 (2008): 137–59.

18. International pressures include the influence of global capital and multinational companies, multilateral financial institutions, the global spread of ideas, and economic competition with other states. Domestic initiatives can be a result of desires to promote nationalism, to neutralize domestic political rivals, or to reward supporters via clientelism. Javier Corrales, "The State Is Not Enough: The Politics of Expanding and Improving Schooling in Developing Countries," in Aaron Benavot, Julia Resnick, and Javier Corrales, eds., *Global Educational Expansion: Historical Legacies and Political Obstacles* (Washington, D.C.: American Academy of Arts and Sciences, 2006), chapter 2.

19. Ben W. Ansell, "Traders, Teachers, and Tyrants: Democracy, Globalization, and Public Investment in Education," *International Organization* 62 (Spring 2008): 306.

20. In *Development, Democracy, and Welfare States*, Haggard and Kaufman also find that democracies—due to electoral competition and interest group pressure—are more likely to provide greater social welfare spending and better outcomes than short-lived democracies or authoritarian regimes. See Chapter 1 and Appendix 1 for a summary and discussion of dozens of studies investigating the link between democracy and social policy and social outcomes.

21. Ansell, "Traders, Teachers, and Tyrants," 2008.

22. Birdsall et al., "Education, Growth, and Inequality."

23. Nancy Birdsall, Thomas Pinckney, and Richard Sabot, "Natural Resources, Human Capital, and Growth," Carnegie Endowment for International Peace Global Policy Program Working Paper 9 (February 2000).

24. Regarding the comparison between East Asia and Latin America, the former's superior performance in education was not a result of greater expenditures on education per se; rather Birdsall et al. in "Education, Growth, and Inequality" find that it was attributed to three factors: "the positive feedback from more rapid growth to larger expenditures on education; the allocation of substantially larger shares of public expenditure to basic education; and the markedly slower growth rates of the school age population," 125.

25. Task Force on Higher Education and Society, *Higher Education in Developing Countries*, conclusion.

26. Policy entrepreneurs often have more success with other policy arenas such as macroeconomic reform in part because the benefits in such areas are more immediate.

27. Corrales, in *The Politics of Education Reform*, shows that there are important exceptions to these trends. Successful reform adoption is thus contingent on addressing the following political hurdles: (1) concentration of costs on a few actors; (2) low incidence of policy entrepreneurship (shortcomings in the supply side of reform); (3) political disengagement of potential beneficiaries (shortcomings in the demand side); and (4) political advantages of cost-bearing groups.

28. Corrales contrasts initiatives to increase access to education with improvements in education quality. The former are easier to implement as they entail favorable outcomes for all, but improvements in quality often entail distinct opponents and losers. Middle-class beneficiaries of improved education quality are often not a vocal political force because they can opt for private education or tutoring opportunities (6).

29. Birdsall et al., "Education, Growth, and Inequality, 96. Indicators that suggest problems in school quality in Latin America include reductions in per-pupil expenditures (books, equipment, and teachers); high repetition rates; high dropout rates; and poor test scores in subjects such as reading, math, and science skills.

30. UNRISD Research Agenda 2005–2006, *Financing Social Policy in Mineral-Rich Countries*, Proposal, December 27, 2007, Social Policy and Development Programme.

31. Thorvaldur Gylfason, "National Resources, Education, and Economic Development," *European Economic Review* 45 (2001): 858.

32. Birdsall et al., "Natural Resources, Human Capital, and Growth."

33. Ibid., 1, 9.

34. Gylfason, "National Resources, Education, and Economic Development," 856.

35. Specifically, Indonesian leadership during this time granted Western-trained economists significant leeway and control over economic policy and development decisions. See Karl, *The Paradox of Plenty*, 208–13. For a comparison of education policies in Southeast Asia that is more critical of presumed education achievements in these countries, see Anne Booth, "Education and Economic Development in Southeast Asia: Myths and Realities," in Jomo K. S., ed., *Southeast Asian Paper Tigers? From Miracle to Debacle and Beyond* (London: RoutledgeCurson, 2003), 173–95. More broadly, the differences between Indonesia and Nigeria have been studied, leading to the following conclusion: "Many commentators have argued that the big difference between the Nigerian and Indonesian response to oil windfalls was the ability of the Indonesian government to keep the exchange rate competitive and ensure the health of the agricultural sector through investments in technology, access to inputs, and the provision of extension services." Xavier Sala-i-Martin and Arvind Subramanian, "Addressing the Natural Resource Curse: An Illustration from Nigeria," IMF Working Paper WP/03/139 (July 2003), 16. See also Peter M. Lewis, *Growing Apart: Oil, Politics, and Economic Change in Indonesia and Nigeria* (Ann Arbor: University of Michigan Press, 2007).

36. For a typology and an elaboration on the five types of political regimes found in resource-rich countries, see Benn Eifert, Alan Gelb, and Nils Borje Tallroth, "The Political Economy of Fiscal Policy and Economic Management in Oil-Exporting Countries," in Jeffrey M. Davis, Rolando Ossowski, and Annalise Fedolino, eds., *Fiscal Policy Formulation and Implementation in Oil-Producing Countries* (Washington, D.C.: IMF, 2003), 82–122. The types include mature democracy (Norway), fractional democracy (Venezuela and other Latin American countries), paternalistic autocracy (Saudi Arabia and Kuwait), reformist autocracy (Indonesia), and predatory autocracy (Nigeria). For a more general discussion on the differences between predatory and developmental states, see Peter Evans, "Predatory, Developmental, and Other Apparatuses: A Comparative Political Economy Perspective on the Third World State," *Sociological Forum* 4:4 (1989): 561–87.

37. In the 1980s and 1990s, the UAE spent 2 percent on education, still much lower than MENA averages. Despite low populations and the vast energy wealth of small Gulf countries such as the UAE and Qatar, education spending and quality remain low though recent initiatives discussed below are attempting to address these problems. For more on the challenges in reforming education in these states, see Joan Muysken and Samia Nour, "Deficiencies in Education and Poor Prospects for Economic Growth in the Gulf Countries: The Case of the UAE," *Journal of Development Studies* 42:6 (2006): 957–80 and Gabriella Gonzalez, Lynn A. Karoly, Louay Constant, Hanine Salem, and Charles A. Goldma, "Facing Human Capital Challenges of the 21st Century: Education and Labor Market Initiatives in Lebanon, Oman, Qatar, and the United Arab Emirates," *RAND*, 2008.

38. Keith Hinchliffe, "Public Expenditures on Education in Nigeria: Issues, Estimates and Some Implications," Africa Region Human Development Working Paper, Human Development Sector (World Bank, 2002), vii. The most recently reported statistic on education spending as a percent of GDP in the World Bank Edstats database is from 1995 at 1 percent.

39. A wide range of scholars considers Nigeria to be a neopatrimonial rentier state. See Eifert et al., "The Political Economy of Fiscal Policy and Economic Management," and Atul Kohli, *State-Directed Development: Political Power and Industrialization in the Global Periphery* (Cambridge: Cambridge University Press, 2004).

40. Birdsall et al., "Natural Resources, Human Capital, and Growth," 8.

41. Gylfason, "National Resources, Education, and Economic Development," 850.

42. Kohli, *State-Directed Development*, 331.

43. In Nigeria, the broader problem of fiscal federalism between the national, state, and local governments has made data collection on education problematic and erratic. Between 1960 and 1991, there were sixteen changes made to the constitution to resolve the problems; however, there is still "no credible estimate of the total amount of public expenditure which is spent by federal, state and local governments on education." Hinchliffe, "Public Expenditures on Education in Nigeria," 1.

44. Henry Bienen, "Oil Revenues and Policy Choice in Nigeria," World Bank Staff Working Paper 592 (1983), 22–23. Regarding the choice to invest in education and infrastructure, Bienen argues that this was due to the weakness of class-based and other sectoral divisions in Nigerian society: ethnic and regional differences were most important, and policy decisions in terms of expanding the number of states and investing in education institutions and infrastructure reflected this. Moreover, people sought to exit from agriculture and move to urban areas to improve their social mobility and employment options, which meant that the demand for support of the agricultural sector was low. See also Karl, *The Paradox of Plenty*, 206–7.

45. Bienen, "Oil Revenues and Policy Choice in Nigeria," 19.

46. Kohli, *State-Directed Development*, 358.

47. Sala-i-Martin and Subramanian, "Addressing the Natural Resource Curse," and Bienen, "Oil Revenues and Policy Choice in Nigeria," 31–33.

48. Eifert et al., "The Political Economy of Fiscal Policy and Economic Management," 112.

49. Kohli, *State-Directed Development*, 348.

50. Ibid., 359.

51. Kohli, *State-Directed Development*, and Karl, *The Paradox of Plenty*.

52. Karl, *The Paradox of Plenty*, 208.

53. Onyinye Nwachukwu, "Nigeria's Unemployment Rises to 10 million," *Business-Day*, May 28, 2010, http://www.businessdayonline.com/index.php?option=com_content&view=article&id=11422:nigerias-unemployment-rate-rises-to-10m-&catid=85:national&Itemid=340.

54. Jean-Philippe Stijns, "Natural Resource Abundance and Human Capital Accumulation," *World Development* 34:6 (2006): 1060–83.

55. Eifert et al., "The Political Economy of Fiscal Policy and Economic Management." Although this strategy has served important political and social goals, it has made administrative reform and control more difficult. There are, however, pockets of relatively efficient and capable bureaucracies within the system, a finding not often cited in the rentier state literature. See Steffen Hertog, *Princes, Brokers, and Bureaucrats: Oil and the State in Saudi Arabia* (Ithaca, N.Y.: Cornell University Press, 2010).

56. Mordechai Abir, *Saudi Arabia: Government, Society, and the Gulf Crisis* (London: Routledge, 1993).

57. Ibid., 90–93.

58. Ibid., 215–25.

59. Ibid., 19–20, 62.

60. Gawdat Bahgat, "Education in the Gulf Monarchies: Retrospect and Prospect," *International Review of Education* 45:2 (1999): 127–36, quote 131. One quote from a young Saudi journalist summarizes the problem: "We cannot have 80 percent of our college students graduating in history, geography, Arabic literature, and Islamic studies, and we barely have enough students graduating in science, engineering, or from the medical schools." Roger Hardy, "Unemployment: The New Saudi Challenge," *BBC News*, October 4, 2006. Another reason for the big gap between educational attainment and labor market outcomes lies in the role of women in Saudi society: although they are becoming increasingly educated (over 55 percent of the graduates), opportunities in the labor market remain limited and women constitute 5–20 percent of the workforce.

61. *The Road Not Traveled.* According to Prokop, between 1995 and 1999, out of the 120,000 graduating from Saudi universities, only 10,000 had technical degrees. Michaela Prokop, "Saudi Arabia: The Politics of Education," *International Affairs* 79:1 (2003): 87. See also Richard Auty, "The Political State and the Management of Mineral Rents in Capital-Surplus Economies: Botswana and Saudi Arabia," *Resources Policy* 27 (2001): 79.

62. Ali N. Alghafis, *Universities in Saudi Arabia: Their Role in Science, Technology, and Development* (University Press of America, 1992), 12.

63. Statistics are difficult to verify given uncoordinated data collection among government agencies, but estimates put this number between 10 percent and 33 percent of employment age population. See Alghafis, *Universities in Saudi Arabia*, 132, and Hertog, *Princes, Brokers, and Bureaucrats*, 187.

64. Eifert et al., "The Political Economy of Fiscal Policy and Economic Management," 107. Another source claims that in the early 2000s, there have been 200,000 graduates entering the job market each year, with newly available jobs only numbering 20,000 annually. Hertog, *Princes, Brokers, and Bureaucrats*, 188.

65. Roger Hardy, "Unemployment: The New Saudi Challenge," *BBC News*, October 4, 2006, http://news.bbc.co.uk/2/hi/business/5406328.stm.

66. Bahgat, "Education in the Gulf Monarchies," 127–36.

67. The exact percentage is unclear (see Hertog, *Princes, Brokers, and Bureaucrats*, 187); however, the World Bank estimates this at about 80 percent. See *The Road Not Traveled*, 53.

68. Abir, *Saudi Arabia*, 148–151.

69. Suzanne Maloney, "The Gulf's Renewed Oil Wealth: Getting It Right This Time?" *Survival* 50:6 (December 2008–January 2009): 133.

70. Jamil Salmi, *The Challenge of Building World Class Universities* (Washington, D.C.: The World Bank, 2009). This marriage of being attentive to local demands within a country and also renowned around the world leads to the motto Salmi uses: "locally relevant yet globally engaged."

71. Karin Amos et al., "The Research University in Context: the Examples of Brazil and Germany," in David P. Baker and Alexander W. Wiseman, eds., *The Worldwide Transformation of Higher Education* (Bingley: Emerald, 2008), 112.

72. David Turner, "World University Rankings," in Baker and Wiseman, eds., *The Worldwide Transformation of Higher Education*, 27–61.

73. Salmi, *The Challenge of Building World Class Universities*, 1.

74. The first wave of Western-oriented universities in the Middle East included American University in Cairo, Egypt, and others in Beirut and Damascus. Also, other developing countries around the world have been forging relationships with Western and other internationally renowned institutions and building new institutions.

75. Katherine Zoepf, "In Qatar's Education City, U.S. Colleges Build Atop a Gusher," *Chronicle of Higher Education*, April 28, 2008.

76. For more information about the Dubai Initiative, see http://belfercenter.ksg .harvard.edu/project/53/dubai_initiative.html; for the DSG, see http://www.dsg.ae/ ACADEMICPROGRAMS/Introduction.aspx.

77. Zvika Krieger, "An Academic Building Boom Transforms the Persian Gulf," *Chronicle of Higher Education*, March 28, 2008.

78. Zvika Krieger, "Saudi Arabia Puts Its Billions Behind Western-style Education," *Chronicle of Higher Education*, September 14, 2007.

79. One academic and consultant who visited the new institutions in Saudi Arabia remarked that although the physical buildings and infrastructure existed, significant challenges remained in building the knowledge and learning to take place within the buildings.

80. Krieger, "An Academic Building Boom."

81. Altbach as quoted in Salmi, *The Challenge of Building World Class Universities*, 4.

82. Maloney, "The Gulf's Renewed Oil Wealth."

83. John Wakeman-Linn, Paul Mathieu, and Bert van Selm, "Oil Funds in Transition Economies: Azerbaijan and Kazakhstan," in Jeffrey M. Davis, Rolando Ossowski, and Annalisa Fedelino, eds., *Fiscal Policy Formulation and Implementation in Oil-Producing Countries* (Washington, D.C.: IMF, 2003), 349–50.

84. Eifert et al., "The Political Economy of Fiscal Policy and Economic Management," 106.

85. Birdsall et al., "Natural Resources, Human Capital, and Growth," 7, 9–11.

86. *The Road Not Traveled*. See Table 5.1 for the categorization of types of education reform initiatives.

87. Auty, "The Political State," 79. For more on the myriad ways in which corruption occurs in the contracting of education-related services and the red flags associated with these trends, see Jacques Hallak and Muriel Poisson, *Corrupt Schools, Corrupt Universities: What Can Be Done?* (UNESCO, 2007), chapter 6.

88. Richard Auty, "Mining Enclave to Economy Catalyst: Large Mineral Projects in Developing Countries," *Brown Journal of International Affairs* 13:1 (Fall/Winter 2006): 138.

89. Data from World Bank World Development Indicators (WDI) database.

90. Eifert et al., "The Political Economy of Fiscal Policy and Economic Management," 111.

91. Mark S. Johnson, "The Legacy of Russian and Soviet Education and the Shaping of Ethnic, Religious, and National Identities in Central Asia," in Stephen Heyneman and Alan J. DeYoung, eds., *The Challenge of Education in Central Asia* (Greenwich: Information Age, 2004), 21–36.

92. Ibid. For more on the history of education in Azerbaijan and Kazakhstan under Tsarist and Soviet rule, see Audrey Altstadt, *The Azerbaijani Turks* (Stanford, Calif.: Hoover Institution Press, 1992) and Martha Brill Olcott, *The Kazakhs* (Stanford, Calif.: Hoover Institution Press, 1987).

93. Jack Bielasiak, "Policy Choices and Regional Equality among the Soviet Republics," *The American Political Science Review* 74:2 (June 1980): 394–405.

94. Mikk Titma and Ellu Saar, "Regional Differences in Soviet Secondary Education," *European Sociological Review* 11:1 (May 1995): 37–58, and Donna Bahry and Carol Nechemias, "Glass Half Full or Half Empty? The Debate over Soviet Regional Inequality," *Slavic Review* 40:3 (Autumn 1981): 366–83.

95. Johnson, "The Legacy of Russian and Soviet Education."

96. Hallak and Poisson, *Corrupt Schools, Corrupt Universities*. Certain private institutions across the region have good reputations for quality of education and absence of corruption, including Qafqaz and Khazar in Azerbaijan, KIMEP and KBTU in Kazakhstan, and the American University of Central Asia in Kyrgyzstan.

97. John C. Weidman and Adiya Enkhjargal, "Corruption in Higher Education," in Baker and Wiseman, eds., *The Worldwide Transformation of Higher Education*, 63–88; Ararat L. Osipian, "Corruption Hierarchies in Higher Education in the Former Soviet Bloc," *International Journal of Educational Development* 29 (2009): 321–30 and Eric Lepisto and Elimina Kazimzade, "Coercion or Compulsion? Rationales Behind Informal Payments for Education in Azerbaijan," *European Education* 40:4 (Winter 2008-9): 77–92.

98. Mark S. Johnson, "Historical Legacies of Soviet Higher Education and the Transformation of Higher Education Systems in post-Soviet Russia and Eurasia," in Baker and Wiseman, eds., *The Worldwide Transformation of Higher Education*, 160–61.

99. Martha Finnemore, "International Organizations as Teachers of Norms: The UNESCO and Science Policy," *International Organization*, 47:4 (Autumn 1993): 565–97.

100. Karen Mundy, "Educational Multilateralism in a Changing World Order: UNESCO and the Limits of the Possible," *International Journal of Educational Development* 19 (1999): 27–52.

101. For more on the World Bank's approach to education investments beginning in the 1960s and how lending is done, see S. P. Heyneman, "The History and Problems in the Making of Education Policy at the World Bank," *International Journal of Education Develoment* 23 (2003): 315–37: Karen E. Mundy, "Retrospect and Prospect: Education in a Reforming World Bank," *International Journal of Educational Development* 22 (2002): 483–508; Christopher S. Collins and Robert A. Rhoads, "The World Bank and Higher Education in the Developing World: The Cases of Uganda and Thailand," in Baker and Wiseman, eds., *The Worldwide Transformation of Higher Education*, 177–221; and Corrales, "The State Is Not Enough."

102. Jazira Asanova, "Emerging Regions, Persisting Rhetoric of Educational Aid: The Impact of the ADB on Educational Policy Making in Kazakhstan," *International Journal of Educational Development* 26 (2006): 660–66.

103. Examples include the United States through USAID, Japan through JICA, Sweden through SIDA, Germany through GTZ, and Turkey through the Cag Foundation. Each country has its own "donor logic" or set of priorities and incentives, often representing what the donor knows best or believes to be the best path forward.

104. The Soros Foundation is promoting community involvement and civic participation in education at the primary and secondary levels and funding universities in Central Asia and Eastern Europe (American University in Central Asia [AUCA] in Bishkek, Kyrgyzstan, and Central European University [CEU] in Budapest, Hungary).

105. The Aga Khan Foundation together with the governments of Kazakhstan, Tajikistan, and Kyrgyzstan has also been working to launch a private higher education institution called the University of Central Asia with campuses in mountainous (non-capital) regions of each Central Asian republic. The university will have degree programs that focus on particular skills and professions that will advance the socioeconomic development of these regions as well as opportunities for professional development and research in these areas. Aiming to be operational in 2012, the university expects to have 3,000 students in all programs (undergraduate and graduate) with over 300 faculty across the three campuses. More information is available at the university's website, http://www.ucentralasia.org/.

106. Sarah Amsler, "Higher Education Reform in Post-Soviet Kyrgyzstan: The Politics of Neoliberal Agendas in Theory and Practice," in Joyce E. Canaan and Wesley Shuma, eds., *Structure and Agency in the Neoliberal University* (New York: Routledge, 2008), 101.

107. Murad Ismayilov and Michael Tkacik, "Nation-Building and State-Building in Azerbaijan: The Challenges of Education Abroad," *Turkish Policy Quarterly* 8:4 (2009): 93.

108. Johnson, "Historical Legacies of Soviet Higher Education," 172.

109. Interviews were conducted in Baku, Azerbaijan, and Almaty, Kazakhstan.

110. For a broader discussion of rentier states in the post-Soviet region, see Anja Franke, Andrea Gawrich, and Gurban Alakbarov, "Kazakhstan and Azerbaijan as Post-Soviet Rentier States: Resource Incomes and Autocracy as a Double 'Curse' in Post-Soviet Regimes," *Europe-Asia Studies* 61:1 (2009): 109–40; Shannon O'Lear, "Azerbaijan's Resource Wealth: Political Legitimacy and Public Opinion," *Geographical Journal* 173:3 (September 2007): 207–23; and Pauline Jones Luong and Erika Weinthal, "Rethinking the Resource Curse: Ownership Structure, Institutional Capacity, and Domestic Constraints," *Annual Review of Political Science* 9 (2006): 241–63.

111. Richard M. Auty, "Optimistic and Pessimistic Rent Deployment Scenarios in Azerbaijan and Kazakhstan," in Richard M. Auty and Indra de Soysa, eds., *Energy, Wealth, and Governance in the Caucasus and Central Asia: Lessons Not Learned* (London: Routledge 2006), 67.

112. Ibid., 68.

113. Public education expenditure per student as a percent of per capita GDP for all education levels is available for Azerbaijan in 2006 and totals 7 percent. Other countries such as Iran, Kuwait, Singapore, Georgia, and Mexico range from 14–18 percent, and the U.S. and UK range between 24 and 26 percent.

114. Data for this indicator are not in the World Bank Edstats database and are compiled from *Higher Education in Kazakhstan* 2007, 83. Data for Azerbaijan from ADA briefing, November 1, 2009.

115. These are: Program for International Student Assessment (PISA), Progress in International Reading Literacy Study (PIRLS), and Trends in International Mathematics and Science Study (TIMSS).

116. For an analysis of the 2006 PISA scores in Azerbaijan, see Turgut Mustafayev, "Highlights of PISA 2006," *Context: Quarterly Journal* (Winter 2010).

117. Kazakhstan has not participated in an international test on reading/comprehension.

118. Most of the students who passed the threshold of 200 points got places in the university (about 28,000). About half got accepted under the condition that they pay fees to attend, and about 40 percent got scholarships that allow them to study for free. Twelve percent got into private institutions. See TQDK. *Abituriyent* 12, November 2009, http://www.tqdk.gov.az/Content/statistic/PDF/abit12_2010.pdf.

119. "Higher Education in Kazakhstan," OECD Review of National Policies for Education, 2007.

120. Interview with former employee of the Bolashak program, July 13, 2009, Almaty, Kazakhstan.

121. Interview with director of the State Students Admission Commission, July 7, 2009, Baku, Azerbaijan. She recounted a visit to a design museum in the United States where she saw phones and other electronic equipment displayed as part of a 1970s col-

lection. She remarked that such devices are still used in Azerbaijan today, indicating the disadvantages that Azerbaijani students face in competing in the global labor market.

122. Data for these two countries available from education ministry websites. The increase in Azerbaijan during this period (2001–2009) was from AZN 202 million to AZN 1.1 billion. The increase in Kazakhstan during this period (2004–2008) was from 190 billion tenge to 641 billion tenge.

123. World Bank Project, Appraisal for a Credit of $25 million to Azerbaijan for a Second Education Sector Development Project, Report No: 40973-AZ, March 26, 2008. For more on what Azerbaijan has been doing in terms of the Bologna process, see Turgut Mustafayev, "Integrating Azerbaijan's Higher Educational System Into European Higher Education Area: Accomplishments, Challenges, And Future Prospects," *Azerbaijan in the World* I:20 (November 15, 2008).

124. "Education Minister Gives Status Report to Kazakh President," *Kazakhstan General Newswire*, September 2, 2009, accessed via Lexis-Nexis on September 25, 2009. The education reforms are part of a broader government strategy entitled "100 Schools, 100 Hospitals." The article states: "About 25 new schools were put into service by September 1, 2009, and another 19 schools will have been ready by the end of the year. 27 billion tenge (current FOREX rate is 150.75/$1) has been allocated this year to repair about 7,000 schools. 58 new preschools have been put in service." See also Joanna Lillis, "Kazakhstan: Astana Strives to Overhaul the Education System," *Eurasianet*, September 29, 2008, http://www.eurasianet.org/departments/insight/articles/eav093008.shtml.

125. National Research Council of the National Academies, *Science and Technology in Kazakhstan: Current Status and Future Prospects*, (Washington, D.C.: National Academics Press, 2007). In addition, another new university was constructed in the new capital, Astana—the Eurasian National University—in 1996. http://www.enu.kz/en/about/.

126. ADA brochures and interviews with administrators, Baku, July 2009. More information on ADA is available at http://ada.edu.az/.

127. Interview with rector of the tourism university, July 6, 2009, Baku, Azerbaijan.

128. Additional examples in Azerbaijan include: "The State Oil Academy now has a joint MBA program with Georgia State University and is involved in an international collaboration project with Germany's University of Siegen. Azerbaijan Technical University is cooperating with Cologne Technical University on a joint program. And several other institutions, among them Azerbaijan University of Architecture and Construction, Azerbaijan University of Languages, Azerbaijan State Economic University, Baku State University, have joint programs with tertiary institutions in France, Italy, Russia, Turkey, and other countries." See Mustafayev, "Integrating Azerbaijan's Higher Educational System."

129. Glenn E. Schweitzer, "Science Policy in Kazakhstan," *Science* 322 (December 5, 2008): 1474–5.

130. World Bank Project Information Document Appraisal Stage, Report AB3574 (January 17, 2008), 3.

131. "Shortage of Qualified Labor Impedes Industrial Production Growth," *Kazakhstan Mining Weekly*, September 8, 2008, accessed via Lexis Nexis. Accessed May 9, 2011.

132. Both Azerbaijan and Kazakhstan have a vocational training plan for 2008–12.

133. Interview with American education NGO specialist, July 5, 2009, Baku, Azerbaijan.

134. For example, students from families with money can study abroad independently. Governments around the world also offer fellowships to study in their countries. For example, the U.S. government funds the UGRAD and the Muskie programs administered by IREX, which sends twelve to fifteen students on each program annually in both countries and a handful of Fulbright scholars from each country annually. The Soros Foundation also sponsors students from the region to study at the Central European University in Budapest, Hungary.

135. David Mikosz, "Academic Exchange Programs in Central Asia: The First Eight Years," in Heyneman and DeYoung, eds., *The Challenge of Education in Central Asia*, 117–25 and interview with education specialist at education NGO, July 14, 2009, Almaty, Kazakhstan.

136. Official brochure of the Bolashak program, 2005.

137. Dilyara Teshebayeva, "Kazakhstan Plans Vast Expansion of Payments to Elderly, Students, and State-Sector Employees," *Eurasianet*, May 5, 2005.

138. Interview with representative of CIP, July 15, 2009, Almaty, Kazakhstan.

139. Ibid.

140. Data from official Bolashak website: http://www.edu-cip.kz/eng/index.php?option=com_content&task=view&id=258&Itemid=361.

141. Interview with former administrator of Bolashak, July 13, 2009, Almaty, Kazakhstan.

142. An exception is a group of students who studied in the U.S. on U.S. government-funded programs, such as the FLEX program, a high school exchange administered by the American Councils that sends about 100 students a year to America for one year of high school. These students have good English due to their experience in the U.S. This synergy between U.S. government-funded programs and Bolashak, however, only provides for a fraction of applicants to the Bolashak program.

143. Interveiw with former administrator of Bolashak, July 14, 2009, Almaty, Kazakhstan. In confirming that the biggest challenges for many students in Kazakhstan was English language skills, she also mentioned that in the past parents used to send their children to Russia, but with the recent rise in fears over ethnic/xenophobic sentiments, some parents are less supportive of this destination.

144. Decree Number 2090 of the President of the Azerbaijan Republic, "On State Scholarship Program for Education of Azerbaijani Youth Abroad in 2007–2015."

145. Interview with American education NGO specialist, July 5, 2009, Baku, Azerbaijan, and interview with education specialist of the World Bank, Baku, Azerbaijan, July 6, 2009.

146. Information in Azerbaijani is available at the government's website, http://xaricdetehsil.edu.gov.az. See also Paul Goble, "Baku Increases Funding for Study Abroad Program," *ADA Biweekly* 3:2 (January 15, 2010), http://www.ada.edu.az/biweekly/issues/vol3no2/20100118035138698.html; and interview with El'mar Gasymov, "Otradno, shto nasha molodezh' posle okonchaniia obucheniia za granitsei bozbrashchaetsia na Rodinu,"*1st News*, April 5, 2010. One government official in summer 2009 suggested that it was not required that students return to the home country upon completion of studies and unlike Kazakhstan, this was more "democratic." Since then, however, official statements suggest that students return to work in the public or private sector in Azerbaijan. Interview with official of the Ministry of Education, Baku, July 2009.

147. Mikosz, "Academic Exchange Programs," and interview with former administrator of Bolashak program, July 13, 2009, Almaty, Kazakhstan.

148. Prominent examples include Azamat Abdymomunov, former vice minister for science and education and Alzhan Braliev, former vice minister of environmental protection.

149. Ismayilov and Tkacik, "Nation-Building and State-Building in Azerbaijan."

150. Data from World Bank's WDI database.

151. Data from the International Labor Organization (ILO) labor statistics database except for Kuwait, Saudi Arabia, and Bahrain, which are from the World Bank's *The Road Not Traveled*, 53.

152. Ibid., 102.

153. One recent Fulbright recipient—a doctor and specialist in occupational health and medicine—recounted that she would have had to pay $10,000 to work in a hospital in Baku, describing this as "envelope money." She chose instead to work in the private sector. Moreover, she lamented that no one in government contacted her or seemed to care about what she learned and how she could apply her knowledge to Azerbaijan's challenges. Discussion in Baku, Azerbaijan, July 5, 2009.

154. Cook, *Post-Communist Welfare States*.

155. For example Qafqaz and Khazar Universities.

156. As of 2009, six rectors—including those of Baku State University and the Azerbaijan Economic University—were simultaneously members of Parliament. The full list is: Rector of the Baku State University, Abel Maharramov; Rector of the University of Languages, Samad Seidov; Rector of the Azerbaijan Economic University, Shamsaddin Haciyev; Rector of the Azerbaijan Physical Culture and Sports Academy, Aghacan Abiyev; Rector of the Nachchivan State University, Isa Habibbayli; and Rector of 'Odlar Yurdu' University, Ahmad Valiyev.

157. Both debates were mentioned in an interview with an employee of the Ministry of Education, July 8, 2009, Baku, Azerbaijan, and subsequently confirmed by others.

158. Konstantin M. Simis, *The Corrupt Society: The Secret World of Soviet Capitalism* (New York: Simon and Schuster, 1982), 229–42. Simis describes the logic of corruption in the education sector across the Soviet Union and highlights that bribes were often higher in the Caucasus and Central Asia.

159. The YOK is the Higher Education Council, and the idea is that the state controls education to guarantee that it is fair and secular. The YOK appoints rectors, administers state exams, and controls bylaws. The goal is for state institutions to be independent of politicians and ministers. The president appoints the head of the YOK.

160. Hallak and Poisson, *Corrupt Schools, Corrupt Universities*. Indeed, standardized test taking in many parts of the world, including the U.S., Turkey, Japan, and Korea, has spurred entire industries of test-prep services. In the case of the SAT in the United States, one important difference is that the SAT is at most only one of many requirements in a university application. Each university and college has its own application requirements, usually including SAT score, essays, and letters of recommendation. Concerns about the ill-effects of the SAT have prompted some several hundred universities, institutes, and colleges, such as Bard, Bates, Bowdoin, Bryn Mawr, Colby, and Middlebury Colleges; George Mason University; and the California State University and University of Arizona systems, to no longer require the SAT as part of admissions applications.

161. Interview with Director of the State Students Admission Commission, July 7, 2009, Baku, Azerbaijan.

162. In contrast to Azerbaijan, where the Minister of Education has been working in his position for over a decade, Kazakhstan—under the direction of President Nursultan Nazarbaev—has actively practiced a policy of cadre rotation for government officials in higher posts. For example, the Minister of Education has been rotated very often, between 1994 and 2004 about twelve times and between 2004 and 2009 about three times. In addition, the president of the Bolashak program has also been frequently rotated. There are allegations of serious corruption in education in Kazakhstan as in Azerbaijan, and one analyst writes that frequent changes in ministerial leadership impacted ability to coordinate negotiation and monitor development assistance and led to loss of institutional memory. Asanova "Emerging Regions," 656–57; interview with specialist of education NGO, July 14, 2009, Almaty, Kazakhstan; and interview with Professor of Kazakh State University (KazGU), July 14, 2009, Almaty, Kazakhstan. As the professor stated, "the minister changes, and everything comes to a halt." An alternative hypothesis is that the strategy of rotating education ministers actually helps break the entrenchment of a long-standing minister of education.

163. Interview with American education NGO specialist, July 5, 2009, Baku, Azerbaijan, and interview with education specialist of the World Bank, Baku, Azerbaijan, July 6, 2009.

164. Auty, "Optimistic and Pessimistic Rent Scenarios," 74.

165. Evelyn Dietsche, "Institutional Change and State Capacity in Mineral-Rich Countries," forthcoming in *Mineral Rents and Social Development,* UNRISD, 2011.

166. As Gourevitch, "The Role of Politics in Economic Development," succinctly stated, "No agency, no politics, no policy. With some agency, there can be politics, and policy could matter—for ill as well as for good."

Chapter 9

1. Thorvaldur Gylfason and Gylfi Zoeaga, *Natural Resource and Economic Growth: The Role of Investment* (World Economy, 2006).

2. Erling Holmøy and Kim Massey Heide, *Is Norway Immune to Dutch Disease?* Paper 413 Statistics Norway, Research Department (2005).

3. Svein S. Andersen, *The Struggle over the North Sea: Governmental Strategies in Denmark, Britain, and Norway* (Oslo: Scandinavia University Press, 1993); Ole Andreas Engen, "Rhetoric and Realities: The NORSOK Programme and Technical and Organisational Change in the Norwegian Petroleum Industrial Complex," Dissertation for degree of Dr. Polit., University of Bergen, 2002; and Ole Gunnar Austvik, *The Norwegian State as an Oil and Gas Entrepreneur: The Impact of the EEA Agreement and EU Gas Market Liberalisation* (Oslo: Verlag Dr. Müller, 2009).

4. Hydro Oil & Gas was the name of the petroleum division in Norsk Hydro in 2007. It was this division that became a part of Statoil. After the merger Norsk Hydro continued its operation as a Norwegian aluminum and renewable energy company.

5. U.S. President Dwight D. Eisenhower introduced the term in his valedictory speech in 1960. His intention was to warn against the network of informal alliances that had been developed between U.S. industry and the U.S. Army. Such strong connections of common interest could, according to the president, become a powerful, independent, antidemocratic force within the society.

6. The NGU view as late as 1958 was that "The chances of finding coal, oil, or sulphur on the continental shelf off the Norwegian coast can be discounted."

7. Andersen, *The Struggle over the North Sea*.

8. Robert Dahlstrøm and Arne Nygaard, "Multinational Corporate Strategy and Host Country Control," *Scandinavian Journal of Management* 8:1 (1993): 3–13.

9. Olav Wicken, *The Layers of National Innovation Systems: The Historical Evolution of a National Innovation System in Norway*, TIK Working Papers on Innovation Studies (Oslo: University of Oslo, 2007).

10. Even Lange, "The Concession Laws of 1906–1909 and Norwegian Industrial Development," *Scandinavian Journal of History* 2 (1977).

11. Michael Porter, *The Competitive Advantages of Nations* (London: Macmillan, 1990).

12. Øyvind Ihlen, "The Oxymoron of Sustainable Oil Production: The Case of the Norwegian Oil Industry," *Business Strategy and Environment* 18:1 (November 2006): 53–63.

13. Jan Erik Karlsen and Preben H. Lindøe, "The Nordic OHS Model at a Turning Point?" *Policy and Practice in Health and Safety* 4:1 (2006): 17–30; and Daniel Felming, Pauli Kettunen, Henrik Søborg, and Christer Thörnqvist, eds., *Global Redefining of Working Life* (Copenhagen: Nordic Council of Ministers, 1998).

14. Oddbjorn Knutsen, "From Old Politics to New Politics: Environmentalism as a Party Cleavage," in Kaare Strøm and Lars Svåsand, eds., *Challenges to Political Parties: The Case of Norway* (Ann Arbor: University of Michigan Press, 1997), 229–62.

15. Andreas Tjernshaugen and Oluf Langhelle, "Technology as Political Glue: CCS in Norway," in James Meadowcroft and Oluf Langhelle, eds., *Caching the Carbon: The Politics and Policy of Carbon Capture and Storage* (Cheltenham: Edward Elgar, 2009), 98–124.

16. World Commission on Environment and Development, *Our Common Future* (Oxford: Oxford University Press, 1987).

17. Tjernshaugen and Langhelle, "Technology as Political Glue."

18. Eivind Hovden and Gard Lindseth, "Discourses in Norwegian Climate Policy: National Action or Thinking Globally?" *Political Studies* 52:1 (March 2004): 63–81.

19. Tjernshaugen and Langhelle, "Technology as Political Glue."

20. Ibid.

21. The SINTEF Group is the largest independent research organization in Scandinavia.

22. Tjernshaugen and Langhelle, "Technology as Political Glue."

23. Olav Mosvold Larsen and Audun Ruud, "HydroKraft: Mapping the Innovation Journey in Accordance with the Research Protocol of CondEcol," Working Paper 3/05 (Oslo: ProSus, 2005).

24. Tjernshaugen and Langhelle, "Technology as Political Glue."

25. Ibid.

26. Ibid. and Meadowcroft and Langhelle, eds., *Caching the Carbon*.

27. Ove Heitmann Hansen and Mette Ravn Midtgard, "Going North: The New Petroleum Province of Norway," in Aslaug Mikkelsen and Oluf Langhelle, eds., *Arctic Oil and Gas: Sustainability at Risk?* (London: Routledge, 2008), 200–239.

28. Ibid.

29. Ibid.

30. Oluf Langhelle and Ketil Fred Hansen, "Perception of Arctic Challenges: Alaska, Canada, Norway, and Russia Compared," in Mikkelsen and Langhelle, eds., *Arctic Oil and Gas*, 317–49.

Chapter 10

1. The IEA is an autonomous body within the framework of the OECD, the economic policy forum of the world's developed economies. All but six OECD member countries (Iceland, Mexico, Chile, Slovenia, Israel, and Estonia) are now members of the IEA, which includes most European Union states, Australia, Canada, Japan, South Korea, New Zealand, Norway, Switzerland, Turkey, and the United States.

2. The Organization of Arab Petroleum Exporting Countries was created in 1968 for political as much as economic reasons. Most Arab countries are members. Seven (Algeria, Libya, Saudi Arabia, Iraq, Kuwait, Qatar, and the UAE) are also members of OPEC.

3. Dr. Kissinger played a leading role in founding the IEA.

4. I was the note taker at the meeting where the exiled emir of Kuwait presented the letter requesting U.S. assistance in enforcing the UN embargo on exports of stolen Kuwaiti oil and oversaw its translation and transmission to Washington.

5. These included Finland, France, and Iceland, not IEA member countries at that point. Finland and France joined in 1992.

6. The official lowest price for West Texas Intermediate oil was $8.25 a barrel; some shipments of crude reportedly changed hands at less than $7 a barrel.

7. Norway participates as an IEA member in a special membership agreement.

8. Indonesia resigned from OPEC in 2008; it ceased to be an exporter in 2004.

9. Angola became an OPEC member in 2007.

10. In this early phase of the IEA, OPEC dominance of the oil trade and the tightness of the global oil market made it difficult to set the terms for a successful dialogue. The French government, which declined to join the IEA in 1974 because it saw it as confrontational, organized an ambitious Conference on International Economic Cooperation, which took place in Paris from mid-1976 to autumn 1977. The United States, which transitioned from the Ford to the Carter administration during this period, joined the conference. However, there was little enthusiasm for it, at least in the State Department's Bureau of Economic and Business Affairs. A subcommittee co-chaired by an American and a Saudi official was set up to discuss energy markets but never reached agreement on contentious issues, such as oil production and prices. In the end, the conference developed into another north-south trade conference rather than the producer-consumer dialogue its organizers had intended.

Chapter 11

1. David R. Mares, "Resource Nationalism and Energy Security in Latin America: Implications for Global Oil Supplies," James A. Baker III Institute for Public Policy Working Paper, January 2010. http://www.bakerinstitute.org/publications/EF-pub-MaresResourceNationalismWorkPaper-012010.pdf.

2. IEA, *World Energy Outlook 2008* (Paris: IEA, 2008), 323.

3. IEA, *World Energy Outlook 2009* (Paris: IEA, 2009), 145.

4. Matthew Chen and Amy Myers Jaffe, "Energy Security: Meeting the Growing Challenge of National Oil Companies," *Whitehead Journal of Diplomacy and International Relations* (Summer/Fall 2007): 4.

5. Amy Myers Jaffe, "Iraq's Oil Sector: Past, Present and Future," James A. Baker III Institute for Public Policy, March 2007. http://bakerinstitute.org/programs/energy-forum/publications/energy-studies/docs/NOCs/Papers/NOC_Iraq_Jaffe.pdf.

6. Amy Myers Jaffe and Jareer Elass, "Saudi Aramco: National Flagship with Global Responsibilities," James A. Baker III Institute for Public Policy, March 2007, http://bakerinstitute.org/programs/energy-forum/publications/energy-studies/docs/NOCs/Papers/NOC_SaudiAramco_Jaffe-Elass-revised.pdf.

7. Sergei Guriev, Anton Kolotilink, and Konstantin Sonin, "Determinants of Expropriation in the Oil Sector: A Theory and Evidence from Panel Data," CEPR Discussion Paper 6755 (March 2008).

8. Constitution Text, Coded by Marc Becker, http://ilstu.edu/class/hist263/docs/1917const.html.

9. Ian Bremmer and Robert Johnston, "The Rise and Fall of Resource Nationalism," *IISS Survival* 51:2 (April 2009): 149–58, quote 150.

10. For a brief history of how BP got license, see http://www.tnk-bp.com/operations/exploration-production/projects/kovykta/.

11. Abrahim Lustgarten, "Shell Shakedown," *Fortune Magazine*, February 1, 2007, and Derek Brower, "From Russia with Tough Love," *Offshore Engineer*, October 2007.

12. Timothy Fenton Krysiek, "Agreements from Another Era: Production Sharing Agreements in Putin's Russia, 2000–2007," *Geopolitics of Energy*, July 2007.

13. Ibid.

14. Bremmer and Johnston, "The Rise and Fall of Resource Nationalism."

15. Jose L. Valera, "Special Report: Changing Oil and Gas Fiscal and Regulatory Regimes in Latin America," *Oil and Gas Journal* (December 3, 2007).

16. Alberto Cisneros-Lavalier, "Resource Nationalism Now and Then in Latin America: Demystifying Its Comparison," *Geopolitics of Energy* 29:12 (December 2007).

17. Yelena Kalyuzhnova and Christian Nygaard, "Resource Nationalism and Credit Growth in FSU Countries," *Energy Policy* 37 (2009): 4700–4710.

18. See analysis by David R. Mares, "Resource Nationalism and Energy Security in Latin America: Implications for Global Oil Supplies," James A. Baker III Institute for Public Policy Working Paper, January 2010. http://www.bakerinstitute.org/publications/EF-pub-MaresResourceNationalismWorkPaper-012010.pdf.

19. Rhuks T. Ako and Patrick Okunmah, "Minority Rights in Nigeria: A Theoretical Analysis of the Historical and Contemporary Conflicts in the Oil-Rich Niger Delta Region," *International Journal on Minority and Group Rights* 16 (2009): 53–65.

20. "Shell Nigeria Capacity Still Shut," *Oil Daily*, November 5, 2009.

21. Amy Myers Jaffe, "Chavez the Pragmatist? Forget About It," *The Argument* (blog), Foreignpolicy.com, January 19, 2009, http://experts.foreignpolicy.com/blog/3062.

22. "Iraq: The Mother of All Oil Stories," Global Markets Research Co., Deutsche Bank, October 4, 2010, 14.

23. "CNPC Signs Al-Ahdab Field Development Contract," *Middle East Economic Survey*, Vol. LI, No. 46, November 17, 2008.

24. For example, see the position taken by the Partido de lay Revolucion Democratica (PRD) on Mexico's energy reform, "La Izquierda Mexicana Está Unida en la

Defensa del Petróleo Nacional: Sandoval," Nota 3760, Fundar: Centro de Análisis e Investigación, September 20, 2009. http://www.fundar.org.mx/c_e/notas.htm.

25. James A. Baker III Institute for Public Policy, "The Changing Role of National Oil Companies in International Oil Markets," Baker Institute Policy Report, no. 35, April 2007. http://bakerinstitute.org/programs/energy-forum/publications/energy-studies/nocs.html/?searchterm=noc.

26. Miranda Ferrell Wainberg, Michelle Michot Foss, et al., "Commercial Frameworks for National Oil Companies," CEE-UT, www.beg.utexas.edu/energyecon/new-era/, 30.

27. Christian Wolf and Michael G. Pollitt, "Privatizing National Oil Companies: Assessing the Impact on Firm Performance," Cambridge Working Paper in Economics 0811 (University of Cambridge, February 2008).

28. Stacy Eller, Peter Hartley, and Kenneth Medlock, "Empirical Evidence of the Operational Efficiency of National Oil Companies: The Changing Role of National Oil Companies in International Energy Markets," Baker Institute Working Paper 2007, http://www.rice.edu/energy.

29. Michael L. Ross, "Blood Barrels: Why Oil Wealth Fuels Conflict," *Foreign Affairs* 87:3 (May/June 2008): 5, http://www.sscnet.ucla.edu/polisci/faculty/ross/Blood-BarrelsFA.pdf.

30. See Andreas Goldthau and Jan Martin White, "Back to the Future or Forward to the Past? Strengthening Markets and Rules for Effective Global Energy Governance," *International Affairs* 85:2 (2009): 373–90.

31. Jeff Mason and Darren Ennis, "G20 Agrees on Phase-Out of Fossil Fuel Subsidies," *Reuters,* September 25, 2009, http://www.reuters.com/article/idUSTRE58O18U20090926.

Chapter 12

1. Theda Skocpol, "Rentier State and Shi'a Islam in the Iranian Revolution," *Theory and Society* 11 (April 1982): 265–83.

2. Michael L. Ross, "Does Oil Hinder Democracy?" *World Politics* 53:3 (2001): 325–61.

3. Jeffrey D. Sachs and Andrew M. Warner, "Natural Resource Abundance and Economic Growth," NBER Working Paper W5398 (December 1995).

4. James D. Fearon, "Why Do Some Civil Wars Last So Much Longer Than Others?" *Journal of Peace Research* 41:3 (2004): 275–303; Macartan Humphreys, "Natural Resources, Conflict, and Conflict Resolution: Uncovering the Mechanisms," *Journal of Conflict Resolution* 49:4 (2005): 508–37; and Michael Ross, "A Closer Look at Oil, Diamonds, and Civil War," *Annual Review of Political Science* 9 (2006): 265–300.

5. Thomas F. Homer-Dixon, *Environment, Scarcity, and Violence* (Princeton, N.J.: Princeton University Press, 1999), and Michael T. Klare, ed., *Resource Wars: The New Landscape of Global Conflict* (New York: Henry Holt, 2001).

6. Philippe Le Billon, "The Geopolitical Economy of Resource Wars," *Geopolitics* 9:1 (2004): 17.

7. Hevina S. Dashwood, *Zimbabwe: The Political Economy of Transformation* (Toronto: University of Toronto Press, 2000).

8. Kenneth N. Waltz, *Theory of International Politics* (New York: McGraw-Hill, 1979). According to Waltz, miscalculation is one of the (immediate) reasons nations go to war, but he maintains that miscalculation results in wars only because the anarchical nature of international relations permits (permissive cause) it in the first place. In this chapter I slightly modify the meanings of these phrases.

9. Paul Collier and Anke Hoeffler, "On Economic Causes of Civil War," *Oxford Economic Papers* 50:4 (1998): 563–73.

10. Indra De Soysa, "Paradise Is a Bazaar? Greed, Creed, and Governance in Civil War, 1989–1999," *Journal of Peace Research* 39:4 (2002): 395–416; Fearon, "Why do Some Civil Wars Last So Much Longer Than Others?"; Humphreys, "Natural Resources, Conflict, and Conflict Resolution"; and Ross, "A Closer Look at Oil, Diamonds, and Civil War."

11. Homer-Dixon, *Environment, Scarcity and Violence*; John W. Maxwell and Rafael Reuveny, "Resource Scarcity and Conflict in Developing Countries," *Journal of Peace Research* 37:3 (2000): 301–22; Klare, ed., *Resource Wars*; and Mary Kaldor, Terry Karl, and Yahia Said, *Oil Wars* (London: Pluto Press, 2007).

12. Jacques Delacroix, "The Distributive State in the World System," *Studies in Comparative International Development* 15:3 (1980): 18.

13. See James D. Fearon and David D. Laitin, "Ethnicity, Insurgency, and Civil War," *American Political Science Review* 97:1 (2003): 81; Michael P. Moore, "Political Underdevelopment: What Causes Bad Governance?" *Public Management Review* 3:3 (2003): 385–418; Terry Lynn Karl, *The Paradox of Plenty: Oil Booms and Petro States* (Berkeley: University of California Press, 1997); and Giacomo Luciani, "Allocation vs. Production States: A Theoretical Framework," in Hazem Beblawi and Giacomo Luciani, eds., *The Rentier State* (London: Croom Helm, 1987), 63–82.

14. Dirk Vanderwalle, "Political Aspects of State Building in Rentier Economies: Algeria and Libya Compared," in Beblawi and Luciani, eds., *The Rentier State*, 160.

15. Hal B. Lary, *Imports of Manufacturers from Less Developed Countries* (New York: Columbia University Press, 1968), and Gobind Nankani, "Development Problems of Mineral Exporting Countries," Staff Working Paper 354 (Washington, D.C.: World Bank, 1979).

16. Luciani, "Allocation vs. Production States," 67.

17. Karl, *The Paradox of Plenty*, 237. This insight is helpful in understanding the difference between "Norways and Nigerias," a juxtaposition one may encounter in almost every work related to resource curse literature.

18. Ibid.

19. Daron Acemoglu, Simon Johnson, and James A. Robinson, "The Colonial Origins of Comparative Development," *American Economic Review* 91:5 (2001): 1369–1401.

20. Hussein Mahdavy, "The Patterns and Problems of Economic Development in Rentier States: The Case of Iran," in Michael A. Cook, ed., *Studies in Economic History of the Middle East* (London: Oxford University Press, 1970); Hazem Beblawi and Giacomo Luciani, "Introduction," in Beblawi and Luciani, eds., *The Rentier State*.

21. James D. Fearon, "Primary Commodity Exports and Civil War," *Journal of Conflict Resolution* 49:4 (2005): 487.

22. Ibid.

23. Carmen M. Reinhart and Peter Wickham, "Commodity Prices: Cyclical Weakness or Secular Decline?" IMF Staff Paper 41 (1994): 175–213; Thad Dunning, "Resource Dependence, Economic Performance, and Political Stability," *Journal of Conflict Resolution* 49:4 (2005): 451–82; and Humphreys, "Natural Resources, Conflict, and Conflict Resolution," 511.

24. Benjamin Smith, "Oil Wealth and Regime Survival in the Developing World, 1960–1999," *American Journal of Political Science* 48:2 (2004): 233.

25. Humphreys, "Natural Resources, Conflict, and Conflict Resolution," 511.

26. Richard M. Auty, *Resource Abundance and Economic Development* (Oxford: Oxford University Press, 2001), and Sachs and Warner, "Natural Resource Abundance and Economic Growth."

27. Karl, *The Paradox of Plenty*, 4.

28. T. Clifton Morgan and Kenneth N. Bickers, "Domestic Discontent and the External Use of Force," *Journal of Conflict Resolution* 36:1 (1992): 25–52; Ross A. Miller, "Domestic Structures and the Diversionary Use of Force," *American Journal of Political Science* 39 (1995); and Alastair Smith, "Diversionary Foreign Policy in Democratic Systems," *International Studies Quarterly* 40:1 (1996).

29. Jackie Cilliers and Peggy Mason, *Profits or Plunder? The Privatization of Security in War-Torn African Societies* (Pretoria: Institute for Strategic Studies, 1999).

30. Le Billon, "The Geopolitical Economy of Resource Wars."

31. Arthur Westing, ed., *Global Resources and International Conflict: Environmental Factors in Strategic Policy and Action* (Oxford: Oxford University Press, 1986), 206.

32. Humphreys, "Natural Resources, Conflict, and Conflict Resolution," 517.

33. The associations mentioned above are what the mainstream political science literature has defined as the intervening effect. For the sake of clarity, i.e., to distinguish them from the intervening effects of the preceding section, I will refer to this kind of interaction as mediation. One of the potential ways for testing such indirect effects could be multiplicative terms. As Robert Friedrich argues, "the most common simplification in quantitative analysis is the assumption of additivity." That is, the effect of an independent variable on a dependent variable is assumed to be the same,

whatever the levels of other variables are. In the face of the complexity of many political phenomena, however, "it often makes sense to admit the possibility of nonadditivity of interaction" where "the effect of an independent variable on a dependent variable may vary, depending on the level of some other variable." Robert Friedrich, "In Defense of Multiplicative Terms in Multiple Regression Equations," *American Journal of Political Science* 26:4 (1982): 797–98.

34. Faten Ghosn and Glenn Palmer, *Codebook for the Militarized Interstate Dispute Data, Version 3.0* (State College, Penn.: Correlates of War 2 Project—The Pennsylvania State University, 2003), http://cow2.la.psu.edu (accessed December 20, 2008).

35. Ibid., 171.

36. Kirk Hamilton and Michael Clemens, "Genuine Savings Rates in Developing Countries," *World Bank Economic Review* 13:2 (1999): 333–56.

37. Ross, "A Closer Look at Oil, Diamonds, and Civil War," 273.

38. Monty G. Marshall and Keith Jaggers, *Polity IV Project, Political Regime Characteristics and Transitions, 1800–2003,* 2003, http://www.cidcm.umd.edu/inscr/polity. University of Maryland, College Park, Md.

39. Level of Income is divided by 10,000 to make the interpretation of the coefficients intelligible; i.e., one unit equals 10,000 $US.

40. Arthur S. Banks, *Cross-National Time-Series Data Archive*, CD-ROM, Databanks International, 2004.

41. Reuben M. Baron and David A. Kenny, "The Moderator-Mediator Variable Distinction in Social Psychological Research: Conceptual, Strategic, and Statistical Considerations," *Journal of Personality and Social Psychology* 51:6 (1986): 1173–82, and Duane F. Alwin and Robert M. Hauser, "The Decomposition of Effects in Path Analysis," *American Sociological Review* 40 (February 1975): 37–47.

42. Baron and Kenny, "The Moderator-Mediator Variable Distinction."

43. Ross, "Does Oil Hinder Democracy?" and M. Steven Fish, "Islam and Authoritarianism," *World Politics* 55:1 (2002): 4–37.

44. The time range of the analysis is from 1970 to 2004. There are 144 countries and about 3,500 country-years, the latter being the unit of analysis. Main models involving Force Use Onset as the dependent variable utilize population average logit with robust standard errors. In order to estimate the effect of the temporal dependence I create a dummy variable counting the number of peace years since the previous failure (see Nathaniel Beck, Jonathan N. Katz, and Richard Tucker, "Taking Time Seriously: Time-Series-Cross-Section Analysis with a Binary Dependent Variable," *American Journal of Political Science* 42:4 (1998): 1260–88). To account for the nonlinearity of the logistic regression, this variable is included together with three cubic splines. All independent variables are lagged to mitigate the endogeneity problem. All models are run in Stata 10 statistical software.

45. Westing, *Global Resources and International Conflict*; Klare, ed., *Resource Wars*; and Paul R. Hensel, "Contentious Issues and World Politics: Territorial Claims in the Americas, 1816–1996," *International Studies Quarterly* 45:1 (2001): 81–109.

46. Luciani, "Allocation vs. Production States," 76.

47. Smith, "Oil Wealth and Regime Survival."

48. Ibrahim Elbadawi and Nicholas Sambanis, "How Much War Will We See? Explaining the Prevalence of Civil War in 161 Countries, 1960–1999," *Journal of Conflict Resolution* 46:3 (2002): 307–34, and Patrick M. Reagan and Daniel Norton, "Greed, Grievance, and Mobilization in Civil Wars," *Journal of Conflict Resolution* 49:3 (2005): 319–36.

49. Thomas Brambor, William Roberts Clark, and Matt Golder, "Understanding Interaction Models: Improving Empirical Analyses," *Political Analysis* 14:1 (2006): 63–82.

50. Dashwood, *Zimbabwe, the Political Economy of Transformation*; Andrew Meldrum, "Good-bye," the website of *The New Republic*, April 17, 2000; and Bjørn Willum, "Foreign Aid to Rwanda: Purely Beneficial or Contributing to War?" (doctoral dissertation, University of Copenhagen, 2001).

51. United Nations, *Report of the Panel of Experts on the Illegal Exploitation of Natural Resources and Other Forms of Wealth of the Democratic Republic of Congo*, S/2001/357 (New York: United Nations Security Council, 2001).

52. Collier and Hoeffler, "On Economic Causes of Civil War."

Chapter 13

1. See, inter alia, Halvor Mehlum, Karl Moene, and Ragnar Torvik, "Institutions and the Resource Curse," *Economic Journal* 116 (2006): 1–20; Xavier Sala-i-Martin and Arvind Subramanian, "Addressing the Natural Resource Curse: An Illustration from Nigeria," NBER Working Paper 9804 (June 2003); and Adnan Vatansever and Alexandra Gillies, "The Political Economy of Natural Resource Management for Development: A Framework for Operational Research," manuscript, World Bank (2009).

2. Following scholarly convention, I refer to East Timor by its anglicized name, rather than its official name (in Portuguese), Timor-Leste.

3. See, inter alia, Richard Auty, *Sustaining Development in Mineral Economies: The Resource Curse Thesis* (London: Routledge, 1993); Thad Dunning, *Crude Democracy: Natural Resource Wealth and Political Regimes* (New York: Cambridge University Press, 2008); Terry L. Karl, *The Paradox of Plenty: Oil Booms and Petro States* (Berkeley: University of California Press, 1997); and Michael L. Ross, "The Political Economy of the Resource Curse," *World Politics* 51:2 (1999): 297–322.

4. Thad Dunning, "The Political Economy of the Resource Paradox: An Overview," Draft, World Bank (2008), 6.

5. Ibid.

6. Moore provides a discussion of rentier states and their conformity to the propositions of fiscal sociology. Mick Moore, "Revenues, State Formation, and the Quality of Governance in Developing Countries," *International Political Science Review* 25 (2004): 297–319.

7. Robert H. Bates, *When Things Fell Apart: State Failure in Late-Century Africa* (New York: Cambridge University Press, 2008).

8. Karl, *The Paradox of Plenty*, 16.

9. Dunning, "The Political Economy of the Resource Paradox," 2.

10. See, for example, Michael Woolcock, Lant Pritchett, and Jonathan Isham, "The Social Foundations of Poor Economic Growth in Resource-Rich Countries," in Richard Auty, ed., *Resource Abundance and Economic Development* (New York: Oxford University Press, 2001), 76–92; Pauline Jones Luong and Erika Weinthal, "Rethinking the Resource Curse: Ownership Structure, Institutional Capacity, and Domestic Constraints," *Annual Review of Political Science* 9 (2006): 241–63; and Vatansever and Gillies, "The Political Economy of Natural Resource Management." McPherson and MacSerraigh also enumerate the special features of the petroleum industry that render it particularly susceptible to corruption. Charles McPherson and Stephen MacSearraigh, "Corruption in the Petroleum Sector," in J. Edgardo Campos and Sanjay Pradhan, eds., *The Many Faces of Corruption: Tracking Vulnerabilities at the Sector Level* (Washington, D.C.: World Bank, 2007), 191–220.

11. Vatansever and Gillies, "The Political Economy of Natural Resource Management," 22–23.

12. Terry L. Karl, "Ensuring Fairness: The Case for a Transparent Fiscal Social Contract," in Macartan Humphreys, Jeffrey D. Sachs, and Joseph E. Stiglitz, eds., *Escaping the Resource Curse* (New York: Columbia University Press, 2007), 259.

13. Karl, *Paradox of Plenty*, articulates this as the core logic of the "petro-state," and Moore, "Revenues, State Formation, and the Quality of Governance," further explains the link between fiscal sources and accountability.

14. Known as the "voracity effect," this has been modeled in Aaron Tornell and Philip R. Lane, "The Voracity Effect," *American Economic Review* 89:1 (1999): 22–46.

15. Robinson et al. have modeled a country with weak institutional controls where a resource boom creates incentives for politicians who want to stay in power to spend resource windfalls on public programs and employment. James A. Robinson, Ragnar Torvik, and Thierry Verdier, "Political Foundations of the Resource Curse," *Journal of Development Economics* 79:2 (2006): 447–68.

16. See, for example, Naazneen Barma, "Strengthening Political Economy Analysis on the Resource Paradox: Terms of Reference for Country *X* Case Study," manuscript, World Bank (October 2008) and Naazneen Barma, Kai Kaiser, Tuan Le, and Lorena Viñuela, *Rents to Riches? The Political Economy of Natural Resource-led Development* (Washington, D.C.: World Bank, forthcoming 2011).

17. For a thorough description of the approach and its components, see Eleodoro Mayorga Alba, "Extractive Industries Value Chain: A Comprehensive Integrated Approach to Developing Extractive Industries," Oil, Gas, and Mining Policy Division Working Paper 3 and Africa Poverty Reduction and Economic Management Department Working Paper 125, World Bank (2009). For a related discussion of the sector

value chain approach in diagnosing corruption in the petroleum sector, see McPherson and MacSearraigh, "Corruption in the Petroleum Sector."

18. Often a fifth link in the value chain is included, which addresses implementation of sustainable development projects and policy. In this chapter, I fold this concern into the four links mentioned where possible but focus on the four prior links to retain the emphasis on the interaction of natural resource revenues with governance and institutional quality.

19. The brief description of Cambodia's contemporary political and institutional context is adapted from Naazneen Barma, "Crafting the State: Transitional Governance and the International Role in Post-Conflict Peacebuilding," Ph.D. dissertation (University of California, Berkeley, 2007).

20. David W. Ashley, "The Failure of Conflict Resolution in Cambodia," in Frederick Z. Brown and David G. Timberman, eds., *Cambodia and the International Community: The Quest for Peace, Development, and Democracy* (New York: Asia Society, 1998).

21. Philippe Le Billon describes how this took place in Cambodia's forestry sector in a commodity chain analysis similar to that pursued here. Philippe Le Billon, "The Political Ecology of Transition in Cambodia 1989–1999: War, Peace, and Forest Exploitation," *Development and Change* 31 (2000): 785–805.

22. Author's interviews with donor officials, Phnom Penh, Cambodia, May and October 2005.

23. Ashley, "The Failure of Conflict Resolution in Cambodia."

24. Le Billon develops this concept of the "shadow state," arguing that the Cambodian political elite used the forestry sector for these purposes. "The Political Ecology of Transition in Cambodia," 798–99.

25. Graham Lees, "Cambodia Set for Oil and Gas Development Bonanza," *World Politics Review*, December 4, 2006.

26. The IMF defines a country as "resource-dependent" if an average of 25 percent or more of its government revenues over the past three years derived from oil, gas, or mining.

27. Geoffrey Cain, "The Curse of Oil Looms for Cambodia," *Far Eastern Economic Review*, June 5, 2009.

28. World Bank, *Cambodia: Energy Sector Strategy Review*, Issues Paper (2006).

29. Global Witness, "Country for Sale: How Cambodia's Elite Has Captured the Country's Extractive Industries," *Global Witness*, 2009, http://www.globalwitness .org/media_library_detail.php/713/en/country_for_sale.

30. The Cambodian government has elected not to join the Extractive Industries Transparency Initiative (EITI), which would have required full disclosure of petroleum revenues.

31. Global Witness, "Country for Sale."

32. Department for International Development, *Cambodia Country Governance Analysis* (London: Department for International Development, 2007).

33. The rule-of-thumb estimate that has emerged from Collier et al.'s research on the causes of renewed conflict is that approximately half of countries that emerge from civil war return to violent conflict within five years. See, in particular, Paul Collier, Lani Elliot, Håvard Hegre, Anke Hoeffler, Marta Reynal-Querol, and Nicholas Sambanis, *Breaking the Conflict Trap: Civil War and Development Policy* (Washington, D.C. and New York: World Bank and Oxford University Press, 2003).

34. The brief description of East Timor's contemporary political and institutional context is adapted from Barma, "Crafting the State."

35. Author's interviews with East Timorese government officials in civil service human resource management and public financial management, Dili, East Timor, April 2005.

36. Anthony Goldstone, "UNTAET with Hindsight: The Peculiarities of Politics in an Incomplete State," *Global Governance* 10 (2004): 84.

37. Author's interviews with academics, East Timorese provincial officials, and World Bank and other donor officials, Dili, East Timor, 2005. One Timorese official reported that Fretilin was the only party that had a presence in his (relatively large) province.

38. Author's interviews with East Timorese NGO representatives and journalists, Dili, East Timor, April 2005.

39. IMF, "Democratic Republic of Timor-Leste: 2009 Article IV Consultation—Staff Report," IMF Country Report 09/219 (2009). Only two other countries have hydrocarbon revenues exceeding non-oil GDP—Equatorial Guinea (around 120 percent) and Congo (around 103 percent). On average, other petroleum-producing countries have hydrocarbon revenues at around 50 percent of fiscal revenues and 20 percent of GDP. See also McPherson and MacSearraigh, "Corruption in the Petroleum Sector."

40. Production and revenue figures taken from IMF, "Democratic Republic of Timor-Leste."

41. The discussion on institutional and governance arrangements in East Timor's petroleum sector draws from a research trip to East Timor in November 2009 sponsored by the World Bank as well as Catherine Anderson, Naazneen Barma, and Douglas Porter, "The Political Economy of Natural Resource Management in Timor-Leste: A Value Chain Perspective," World Bank, draft (2009).

42. McPherson and MacSearraigh, "Corruption in the Petroleum Sector."

43. These plans are referred to as the "Petroleum Industry Corridor" concept in the 2010 budget submission of the Secretariat of State for Natural Resources.

44. The NPA was created as the successor to the Timor Sea Designated Authority, which was responsible for all petroleum activities occurring in the JPDA.

45. Author's interviews with petroleum sector experts, Dili, East Timor, November 2009. At issue is where the gas pipeline will be landed, with the Timorese government having expressed a clear preference for it to come to East Timor; on the other hand, Woodside, the international petroleum company that currently holds the production

rights to the field, has only prepared detailed feasibility studies for a floating LNG plant or for the pipeline to be landed in Darwin, Australia.

46. Democratic Republic of Timor-Leste Petroleum Fund Law, Law 9/2005. Accessed at: http://timor-leste.gov.tl/wp-content/uploads/2010/03/Law_2005_9_petro leum_fund_law_.pdf on May 6, 2011.

47. Anderson, Barma, and Porter, "The Political Economy of Natural Resource Management."

48. See McPherson and MacSearraigh, "Corruption in the Petroleum Sector," and Silvana Tordo with David Johnston and Daniel Johnston, "Petroleum Exploration and Production Rights: Allocation Strategies and Design Issues," Working Paper No. 179, World Bank (2009).

49. This would not be permissible under the current Petroleum Fund Law, which explicitly states that all petroleum revenue, including revenue from equity participation in petroleum production, must be channeled into the fund; but this could be amended in the current revision cycle.

Conclusion

1. This classification is from Andrew Rosser, "The Political Economy of the Resource Curse: A Literature," IDS Working Paper 268 (2006), 8.

2. Ragnar Nurkse, *Equilibrium and Growth in the World Economy* (Cambridge, Mass.: Harvard University Press, 1961), 242–43, 305; also see Irving B. Kravis, "Trade as a Handmaiden of Growth: Similarities Between the Nineteenth and Twentieth Centuries," *Economic Journal* 80:320 (1970): 850–72.

3. Nurkse, *Equilibrium and Growth in the World Economy*, 299. Nurkse thought the demand for goods and services originated from these countries in relative terms was not as high as it was a century ago. But Kravis notes, "Nurkse did not oppose trade in principle as an engine of growth for today's developing countries, but he was pessimistic about its availability to the developing countries. The world's industrial centres were no longer 'exporting' their own growth rates to primary producing countries, owing to such factors as low income elasticities of demand, the rise of synthetics, and the importance of home primary product output in the advanced countries (especially in the United States). Prospects for exports of manufactures from the developing countries to the industrial centres were also poor, both because of the 'formidable' obstacles to the attainment of a minimum level of efficiency in the former countries and because of unfavourable commercial policies in the latter" ("Trade as a Handmaiden of Growth," 851–52).

4. Nurkse, *Equilibrium and Growth in the World Economy*, 301.

5. See Sweder van Wijnbergen, "Inflation, Employment, and the Dutch Disease in Oil-Exporting Countries: A Short-Run Disequilibrium Analysis," *Quarterly Journal of Economics* 99:2 (1984): 233–50; Sweder van Wijnbergen, "The 'Dutch Disease': A Disease After All?" *Economic Journal* 94:373 (1984): 42–55; Alan Gelb and associates,

Oil Windfalls: Blessing or Curse? (New York: Oxford University Press and World Bank, 1988); Richard M. Auty, *Resource-Based Industrialization: Sowing the Oil in Eight Developing Countries* (New York: Oxford University Press, 1990); Jeffrey D. Sachs and Andrew M. Warner, "Natural Resource Abundance and Economic Growth," NBER Working Paper 5039 (1995); and Terry L. Karl, *The Paradox of Plenty: Oil Booms and Petro-States* (Berkeley: University of California Press, 1997).

6. Gobind T. Nankini, "Development Problems of Nonfuel Mineral Exporting Countries," *Finance and Development* 17 (January 1980). In his study of hard-rock-exporting developing countries between 1960 and 1976, Nankini revealed a slower growth rate for these countries than resource-poor developing countries. Similar studies by David Wheeler and Alan Gelb found a negative relationship between economic growth and mineral dependence. See David Wheeler, "Sources of Stagnation in Sub-Saharan Africa," *World Development* 12:1 (January 1984), and Gelb et al., *Oil Windfalls*; also see Richard M. Auty, *Sustainable Development in Mineral Economies* (London: Routledge, 1993). For a counterargument disputing these results, see Graham A. Davis, "Learning to Love the Dutch Disease: Evidence from the Mineral Economies," *World Development* 23:10 (October 1995).

7. Sachs and Warner, "Natural Resource Abundance and Economic Growth."

8. For an extended literature review, see Michael L. Ross, "The Political Economy of the Resource Curse," *World Politics* 51:2 (January 1999): 297–322, and Andrew Rosser, "The Political Economy of the Resource Curse: A Literature," IDS Working Paper 268 (2006).

9. Thorvaldur Gylfason, "Nature, Power, and Growth," *Scottish Journal of Political Economy* 48:5 (2001): 585.

10. Christa N. Brunnschweiler, "Cursing the Blessings? Natural Resource Abundance, Institutions, and Economic Growth," *World Development* 36:3 (March 2008): 399–419; Christa N. Brunnschweiler and Erwin H. Bulte, "The Resource Curse Revisited and Revised: A Tale of Paradoxes and Red Herrings," *Journal of Environmental Economics and Management* 55:3 (May 2008): 248–64.

11. Rosser, "The Political Economy of the Resource Curse." Rosser underlines the inconclusive nature of previous studies and points to some aspects of the phenomenon that have yet to be explained adequately, stating that the hitherto offered evidence linking a lack of growth to resource abundance "is by no means conclusive." Similarly, Ragnar Torvik, writes that, "[we] still simply do not know to what extent resource abundance causes *slow* growth" (emphasis original). Torvik, "Why Do Some Resource-Abundant Countries Succeed While Others Do Not?" *Oxford Review of Economic Policy* 25:2 (2009): 254.

12. Ross, "The Political Economy of the Resource Curse." Ross notes that qualitative studies on the resource curse have rarely been tested, which resulted in scholars being "unable to produce a cumulative body of knowledge about the policy failures of resource exporters" and "their arguments are often left underspecified—with nebu-

lous variables, ambiguous domains of relevant cases, and fuzzy causal mechanisms" (307–8).

13. See Torvik, "Why Do Some Resource-Abundant Countries Succeed While Others Do Not?" 254–55.

14. Ross, "The Political Economy of the Resource Curse." Ross lists the four most common economic explanations for the resource curse as "a decline in the terms of trade for primary commodities, the instability of international commodity markets, the poor economic linkages between resource and non-resource sectors, and an ailment commonly known as the 'Dutch Disease'" (298).

15. Charles P. Kindleberger, *The Terms of Trade: A European Case Study* (New York: MIT Press and John Wiley, 1956), and Nurkse, *Equilibrium and Growth in the World Economy*, 245.

16. Raul Prebisch, *The Economic Development of Latin America and Its Principal Problems* (New York: UN Economic Commission for Latin America, 1950), and H. W. Singer, "The Distribution of Gains Between Investing and Borrowing Countries," *American Economic Review* 40:2 (1950): 473–85.

17. For discussion and critique of the import substitution approach in the neoclassical and dependency theories and their application in the newly industrializing countries (NICs), see Stephan Haggard, *Pathways from the Periphery: The Politics of Growth in the Newly Industrializing Countries* (Ithaca, N.Y.: Cornell University Press, 1990). Also see Bela Balassa, *The Process of Industrial Development and Alternative Development Strategies* (Washington, D.C.: World Bank, 1980).

18. Hans Singer, Neelambar Hatti, and Rameshwar Tandon, *Export-Led Versus Balanced Growth in the 1990s* (Delhi: B.R. Publishing, 1998), 1.

19. See Andrew P. Thirlwall and James Bergevin, "Trends, Cycles and Asymmetries in the Terms of Trade of Primary Commodities from Developed and Less Developed Countries," *World Development* 13:7 (July 1985). For example, Thirlwall and Bergevin record "substantial and convincing evidence" that the terms of trade for primary products have deteriarated in the post-World War era, except for minerals and oil.

20. Singer et al., *Export-Led Versus Balanced Growths*, 3.

21. William Easterly, Michael Kremer, Lant Pritchett, and Lawrence H. Summers, "Good Policy or Good Luck?" *Journal of Monetary Economics* 32:3 (December 1993): 459–83.

22. See Ross, "The Political Economy of the Resource Curse," for further references on the ongoing debate in the literature on the role of export instability and resource curse.

23. J. Peter Federer, "Oil Price Volatility and Macroeconomy," *Journal of Macroeconomics* 18 (1996): 1–26. Also see Robert B. Barsky and Lutz Kilian, "Oil and the Macroeconomy Since the 1970s," *Journal of Economic Perspectives* 18:4 (Autumn 2004): 115–34.

24. For discussion on hydrocarbon versus the manufacturing sector, see Macartan Humphreys, Jeffrey Sachs, and Jospeh Stiglitz, eds., *Escaping the Resource Curse* (New York: Columbia University Press, 2007), 3–4; and Egil Matsen and Ragnar Torvik, "Optimal Dutch Disease," *Journal of Development Economics* 78:2 (December 2005): 495.

25. See Mancur Olson, "The Productivity Slowdown, The Oil Shocks, and the Real Cycle," *Journal of Economic Perspectives* 2:4 (Autumn 1988): 43–69; Stanley Fischer, "Symposium on the Slowdown in Productivity Growth," *Journal of Economic Perspectives* 2:4 (Autumn 1988), 3–7; and Dan Ben-David and David H. Papell, "Slowdowns and Meltdowns: Postwar Growth Evidence From 74 Countries," *Review of Economics and Statistics* 80:4 (November 1998): 561–71.

26. James D. Hamilton, "Oil and the Macroeconomy since World War II," *Journal of Political Economy* 91:2 (April 1983): 228–48.

27. Lutz Kilian, "The Economic Effects of Energy Price Shocks," *Journal of Economic Literature* 46:4 (December 2008): 871–909. Kilian argues that "the nature of the energy price shocks has evolved and that recent energy price shocks have been qualitatively different from earlier shocks." He states that "an energy price increase driven by strong global demand for industrial commodities (including crude oil) . . . may have far less adverse consequences for U.S. real output than the same energy price increase driven by adverse global oil supply shocks or by expectations-driven shocks to the precautionary demand for oil" (26).

28. Ibid., 33.

29. For more detailed discussion of Dutch disease, also see Christine Ebrahim-Aade, "Back to Basics: Dutch Disease. Too Much Wealth Managed Unwisely," *Finance and Development* 40:1 (March 2003): 50–51.

30. Joscph Stiglitz, *Making Globalization Work* (London: Penguin, 2006), 148.

31. For earlier discussions on the limited and detrimental impact of export-driven growth, see Kravis, "Trade as a Handmaiden of Growth," 886.

32. See Richard M. Auty, "The Economic Stimulus from Resource-Based Industry in Developing Countries: Saudia Arabia and Bahrain," *Economic Geography* 64:3 (July 1988). Auty points to a muted and lagged economic stimulus from resource-based industry in early years but notes that if effectively implemented, the stimulus could be great in the long run.

33. Jeffrey D. Sachs and Andrew M. Warner, "The Curse of Natural Resources," *European Economic Review* 45:4–6 (March 2001): 837.

34. See Gershon Feder, "On Export and Economic Growth," *Journal of Development Economics* 12:1–2 (1982): 59.

35. Matsen and Torvik, "Optimal Dutch Disease," 495.

36. S. M. Murshed, "Short-Run Models of Contrasting Natural Resource Endowments," in Richard M. Auty, ed., *Resource Abundance and Economic Development* (Oxford: Oxford University Press, 2001), 114–15. Murshed notes that "resource booms cause *hysteresis*," which can sometimes result in "a permanent loss of competitive-

ness." Especially for resource-rich developing states, Dutch disease impedes "their future potential for exporting manufactured goods and diversifying the production base."

37. Khalid Yousif Khalafalla and Alan J. Webb, "Export-Led Growth and Structure Change: Evidence from Malaysia," *Applied Economics* 33:13 (October 2001); Thorvaldur Gylfason, "Natural Resources and Economic Growth: From Dependence to Diversification," Discussion Paper 4804 (London: Centre for Economic Policy Research, 2004); and Torvik, "Why Do Some Resource-Abundant Countries Succeed While Others Do Not?"

38. World Bank, *Azerbaijan Country Economic Memorandum—A New Silk Road: Export-Led Diversification* (Washington, D.C.: World Bank, 2009). The report (22) cites successful experiences of several previously export-dependent states that have managed to diversify their economies and grow at the same time. It notes that in early oil booms, the governments of resource-rich states should "take concentrated action to reverse the unfavorable trends in non-oil private investment, non-oil exports, and non-oil FDI" (28).

39. This is particularly true for many Sub-Saharan African resource-rich countries that made poor policy choices during boom cycles and ended up borrowing excessively to sustain the over-expanded public sector and inefficient public projects. For discussion see Matthias Basedau, "Context Matters: Rethinking the Resource Curse in Sub-Saharan Africa," Working Papers Series 1, German Overseas Institute (2005), and Michael L. Ross, "The Natural Resource Curse: How Wealth Can Make You Poor," in Ian Bannon and Paul Collier, eds., *Natural Resources and Violent Conflict: Options and Actions* (Washington, D.C.: World Bank, 2003).

40. Auty, *Resource Abundance and Economic Development*, 317–21. Auty points out that the structural changes in resource-poor countries that start their competitive industrialization early lead to self-reinforcing economic and social circles, but in countries that rely on exports of single or few primary products, this process is delayed, making it difficult to catch up later.

41. For more on "white elephant" projects, see James A. Robinson and Ragnar Torvik, "White Elephants," *Journal of Public Economics* 89:2–3 (February 2005): 197–210.

42. See Basedau, "Context Matters." With respect to trade policy, resource-poor countries tend to be less prone to protectionism and closure than resource-rich states and more likely to abandon protectionist policies earlier than the latter ones; see Richard M. Auty and A. H. Gelb, "Political Economy of Resource-Abundant States," in Auty, ed., *Resource Abundance and Economic Development*, 129.

43. Jahangir Amuzegar, *Managing the Oil Wealth: OPEC's Windfalls and Pitfalls* (London: Tauris, 1999), 48–115. Amuzegar notes that this behavior has been common to almost all OPEC member countries.

44. Nigeria is a good case study of a mismanaged public sector and debt crisis during the bust period. See Amuzegar, *Managing the Oil Wealth*, 89–93.

45. Murshed, "Short-Run Models of Contrasting Natural Resource Endowments," 114–15. Murshed notes that "a country whose manufacturing base is eroded during a [resource] boom can irreversibly lose competitiveness, even when the [real] exchange rate reverts to [its initial level] after the boom has subsided."

46. Amuzegar, *Managing the Oil Wealth*, 49.

47. For detailed discussion on the role of energy subsidies see Douglas F. Barnes and Jonathan Halpern, "The Role of Energy Subsidies," in Energy Sector Management Assistance Program (ESMAP), eds., *Energy Services for the World's Poor* (Washington, D.C.: World Bank, 2000): 60–66, and also Taimur Baig, Amine Mati, David Coady, and Joseph Ntamatungiro, "Domestic Petroleum Product Prices and Subsidies," IMF Working Paper–WP/07/71 (March 2007).

48. Amuzegar, *Managing the Oil Wealth*, 48–49.

49. For example, in the early 1990s, the richest 20 percent of the population of Venezuela "received six times more in fuel subsidy per person than the poorest third of the population." Baig et al., "Domestic Petroleum Product Prices and Subsidies," 9.

50. For example, since 1965, India has provided low-cost electricity to farmers for agricultural pumping and irrigation systems. Despite the fact that this subsidy is no longer necessary, a strong farm lobby has managed to keep the existing subsidies in place. See Barnes and Halpern, *The Role of Energy Subsidies*. Also see the discussion on factors affecting the modification of behavior of rent seekers in countries applying import substitution in Michael Lusztig, "The Limits of Rent Seeking: Why Protectionists Become Free Traders," *Review of International Political Economy* 5:1 (1998): 38–63.

51. Humphreys et al., *Escaping the Resource Curse*, 178–79. The authors note that the allocation of public investment is conditioned by the level of development of oil-rich countries. That is, they argue that in the poorest oil-rich countries, oil revenues should be used "to enable the economy to meet basic needs . . . and to put in place the infrastructure"; in the middle-income oil-rich countries, oil revenues should be used "to promote the transition from a resource-based rural economy . . . to a human-capital and knowledge-based urban economy"; and in the high-income oil countries that already have solid infrastructure in place, revenues should be used "to support the budget burdens of social insurance."

52. See Anne O. Krueger, "The Political Economy of the Rent-Seeking Society," *American Economic Review* 64:3 (1974): 291–303.

53. Karl, *The Paradox of Plenty*, 16.

54. Kevin M. Murphy, Andrei Shleifer, and Robert W. Vishny, "Why Is Rent-Seeking So Costly to Growth?" *American Economic Review* 83:2 (1993): 409–14, contend that "an increase in rent-seeking activity may make rent-seeking more (rather than less) attractive relative to productive activity," which in turn could lead to "'bad' equilibria exhibiting very high levels of rent-seeking and low output."

55. Humphreys et al., *Escaping the Resource Curse*, 3–4.

56. Karl, *The Paradox of Plenty*, 16.

57. See Mick Moore, "Revenues, State Formation, and the Quality of Governance in Developing Countries," *International Political Science Review* 25:3 (2004): 297–319. Also see Karl, *The Paradox of Plenty.*

58. Karl views the resource curse as a political phenomenon and claims that petrostates turn into "honey pots," which are raided by both domestic and external actors in the pursuit of resource rents. Too often resource-rich states find themselves in the middle of external interventions and pressures by foreign actors or multinational companies. Terry Karl, "Ensuring Fairness: The Case for a Transparent Fiscal Social Contract," in Humphreys et al., *Escaping the Resource Curse,* 262.

59. James A. Robinson, Ragnar Torvik, and Thierry Verdier, "Political Foundations of the Resource Curse," *Journal of Development Economics* 79:2 (2006): 466.

60. For example, Xavier Sala-i-Martin and Arvind Subramanian, "Addressing the Natural Resource Curse: An Illustration from Nigeria," NBER Working Paper 9804 (2003), 24–25. The authors maintain that "wasted and poor institutional quality stemming from oil rather than the Dutch Disease has been primarily responsible for [Nigeria's] poor long-run economic performance."

61. Moore, "Revenues, State Formation, and the Quality of Governance in Developing Countries."

62. Daniel Kaufmann and Aart Kraay, "Growth Without Governance," World Bank Working Paper 2928 (2002).

63. Brunnschweiler and Bulte, "The Resource Curse Revisited and Revised," 248–64.

64. Thorvaldur Gylfason, "Natural Resources, Education, and Economic Development," *European Economic Review* 45 (2001): 847–59.

65. Robinson, Torvik, and Verdier, "Political Foundations of the Resource Curse," 447. For the literature review on institutions and governance, see Chapter 1.

66. See Michael D. Shafer, *Winners and Losers: How Sectors Shape the Developmental Prospects of States* (Ithaca, N.Y.: Cornell University Press, 1994).

67. For example, Terry Karl states that resource-rich governments in time develop a "differentiated and efficient bureaucratic apparatus in the areas necessary to extract revenues from the international oil industry, especially in powerful energy ministries and national oil companies," see Karl, "Ensuring Fairness," 263.

68. Karl, *The Paradox of Plenty,* 16.

69. Richard Auty and Alan Gelb, "Political Economy of Resource-Abundant States," in Auty, ed., *Resource Abundance and Economic Development.*

70. Christa N. Brunnschweiler, "Oil and Growth in Transition Countries," OxCarre Research Paper 29 (CER-ETH Center of Economic Research at ETH Zurich and OxCarre, University of Oxford, 2009), 11.

71. Pauline Jones Luong and Erika Weinthal, *Oil Is Not a Curse: Ownership Structure and Institutions in Soviet Successor States* (Cambridge: Cambridge University Press, 2010). See, for example, Brunnschweiler, "Oil and Growth in Transition Countries." Brunnschweiler tests Luong and Weinthal's theory and finds contradictory

results, concluding that "State-controlled oil assets [in the oil-rich republics of the former Soviet Union] in fact seem to have given the greatest positive effects, reminiscent of the positive experience in Norway."

72. The Norwegian State Oil Company (StatOil) was only privatized in 2001. Thanks to already existing institutions in Norway and effective management, the state ownership of the natural resource industry has not been a major problem.

73. Thorvaldur Gylfason, "Institutions, Human Capital, and Diversification of Rentier Economies," prepared for Workshop on Transforming Authoritarian Rentier Economies, at the Friedrich Ebert Foundation in Bonn, Germany, September 21–24, 2005. Available online at http://notendur.hi.is/~gylfason/_private/Bonn%20Paper%202005%20Rev%20IOES.pdf.

74. Thorvaldur Gylfason, "A Nordic Perspective on Natural Resource Abundance," in Auty, ed., *Resource Abundance and Economic Development*, 301–2.

75. Gylfason, "Natural Resources, Education, and Economic Development," 850.

76. Erika Weinthal and Pauline Jones Luong, "Combating the Resource Curse: An Alternative Solution to Managing Mineral Wealth," *Perspectives on Politics* 4:1 (2006): 38–42.

77. Sala-i-Martin and Subramanian, "Addressing the Natural Resource Curse," 25.

78. Jesper Jensen and David Tarr, "Trade, Foreign Exchange, and Energy Policies in the Islamic Republic of Iran," World Bank Working Paper 2768 (January 2002).

79. Thomas Palley, "Oil and the Case of Iraq," *Challenge* 47:2 (2004): 96.

80. Sachs, "How to Handle the Macroeconomics of Oil Wealth," 177–78, 188–89; also see Ross, "How Mineral-Rich States Can Reduce Inequality," 242–44.

81. The parliamentary redistribution system of Papua New Guinea is a type of direct distribution. "Its democracy encourages MPs to siphon [mineral] rent to their constituents. But the extreme fragmentation of the vote (too many candidates per parliamentary constituency) means MPs actually 'represent' a couple of hundred people (those who actually voted for the winner rather than one of his dozens of rivals) and they invariably offload the central government revenue to this lucky group through parties (cultural tradition), which is not the best use of rent from a developmental perspective. The MPs do not expect to gain re-election, so another group gets a chance. It ends up being like a National lottery." From the author's personal communication with Richard Auty (June 2010).

82. For more about the experience of Papua New Guinea see Richard M. Auty and R. F. Mikesell, *Sustainable Development in Mineral Economies* (Oxford: Clarendon Press, 1998), 212.

83. Kirk Hamilton, "The Sustainability of Extractive Economies," in Auty, ed., *Resource Abundance and Economic Development*, 36–56.

84. From the author's personal communication with Auty (June 2010).

85. Richard Auty, "A Growth Collapse with High Rent Point Resources: Saudi Arabia," in Auty, ed., *Resource Abundance and Economic Development*, 196–97.

86. Weinthal and Luong, "Combating the Resource Curse," 39.

87. Ibid., 40–41.

88. From the official website of the Extractive Industries Transparency Initiative (EITI), http://eiti.org/.

89. See Khalafalla and Webb, "Export-Led Growth and Structure Change"; Gylfason, "Natural Resources and Economic Growth"; and Torvik, "Why Do Some Resource-Abundant Countries Succeed While Others Do Not?"

90. World Bank, *Azerbaijan Country Economic Memorandum*, 28.

91. Rosser, "The Political Economy of the Resource Curse," 7.

92. Karl, *The Paradox of Plenty*, 5.

93. Sachs, "How to Handle the Macroeconomics of Oil Wealth," 173.

CONTRIBUTORS

Richard M. Auty is Professor Emeritus of Economic Geography at Lancaster University. He researches industrial policy, resource-driven development, and the political economy of development. His books include: *Resource Abundance and Economic Development* (Oxford University Press, 2004); *Sustainable Development in Mineral Economies* (Oxford University Press, 1998); *Resource Endowment, Development Policy and Economic Growth* (Edward Arnold, 1995).

Naazneen H. Barma is Assistant Professor of National Security Affairs at the Naval Postgraduate School in Monterey, California. Her research focuses on the political economy of development and on international interventions in post-conflict states. Barma previously worked at the World Bank on governance and institutional reform in East Asia and the Pacific. She is co-author of *Rents to Riches? The Political Economy of Natural Resource-Led Development* (World Bank, 2011).

Reidar Bratvold is a professor at the University of Stavanger and at the Norwegian Institute of Technology and Science where he is teaching and supervising graduate students engaging in research in uncertainty assessment, risk management, investment analysis, decision sciences, and market-based valuation. He holds a PhD in petroleum engineering and an MSc in mathematics, both from Stanford University. Reidar is the author of the book *Making Good Decisions* (Society of Petroleum Engineers, 2010).

Patrick Clawson is the Director of Research at the Washington Institute for Near East Policy. He is the author or editor of sixteen books and monographs about the Middle East. He previously served at the International Monetary Fund, the World Bank, the U.S. National Defense University, and the Foreign Policy Research Institute.

Ole Andreas Engen is a professor at SEROS (Centre for Risk Management & Societal Safety), University of Stavanger, Norway. He holds a master's degree (MPhil) in Economics and a PhD in Sociology. He is also employed part time as a senior researcher at International Research Institute of Stavanger (IRIS).

Jeffrey Frankel is Harpel Professor at Harvard University's Kennedy School of Government. He directs the program in International Finance and Macroeconomics at the National Bureau of Economic Research, and is on its Business Cycle Dating Committee, which officially dates US recessions. He served on President Clinton's Council of Economic Advisers, 1996–99.

Murad Ismayilov is a research fellow at the Azerbaijan Diplomatic Academy (ADA). He is also the editor of ADA's publication *Azerbaijan in the World*. His research interests include international relations, international security, political theory, energy security, national identity, and state-society relations (with a regional focus on Azerbaijan and post-Soviet Eurasia), as well as sociology and security of the Middle East. He has authored a number of academic articles and book chapters.

Amy M. Jaffe is the Wallace S. Wilson Fellow in Energy Studies and director of the Energy Forum at the James A. Baker III Institute For Public Policy at Rice University. Jaffe's research focuses on oil and gas geopolitics, strategic energy policy, and energy economics. Among her publications she served as co-editor of *Energy in the Caspian Region: Present and Future* (Palgrave, 2002) and *Natural Gas and Geopolitics: From 1970 to 2040* (Cambridge University Press, 2006), and as co-author of *Oil, Dollars, Debt and Crises: The Global Curse of Black Gold* (Cambridge University Press, January 2010 with Mahmoud El-Gamal).

Richard Jones is the Deputy Executive Director of the International Energy Agency, a post he has held since October 2008. Jones has been a career U.S. diplomat, serving as the U.S. Ambassador to four countries: Israel (2005–2008), Kuwait (2001–2004), Kazakhstan (1998–2001), and Lebanon (1996–1998). He has academic degrees from Harvey Mudd College (BS, Mathematics with Distinction) and the University of Wisconsin, Madison (MS, PhD in Business/Statistics).

Oluf Langhelle is a professor at the University of Stavanger. He holds a Dr. Polit. in political science and teaches sustainable development and corporate social responsibility (CSR). He has co-edited a number of books, among them *Caching the Carbon: The Politics and Policy of Carbon Capture and Storage*, together with James Meadowcroft.

Ahmad Mojtahed is professor of Economics at Allameh Tabatabai University and vice president of Saman bank in Tehran, Iran. Previously, he served as president of Monetary and Banking Research Academy of Central Bank of Iran.

Elkin Nurmammadov is Assistant Professor of Economics at the Azerbaijan Diplomatic Academy. He holds a BA in Business Administration from Bogazici University and a PhD in Economics from the University of Georgia. His research interest is in the fields of economic growth and development, and financial development in transition economies.

Theresa Sabonis-Helf is Professor of National Security Strategy at the National War College in Washington, D.C., where she has taught mid-career government and military professionals since 2001. She is also an adjunct professor at Georgetown University in the School of Foreign Service. She has lived and worked in seven countries of the former Soviet Union, and has been a policy analyst for think tanks in the United States and in Russia, examining matters of energy, economic transition, and environment.

Brenda Shaffer is a faculty member at the School of Political Science in the University of Haifa. She is also a Visiting Professor at the Azerbaijan Diplomatic Academy. Dr. Shaffer previously served as the Research Director of the Caspian Studies Program at Harvard University. She is the author of the books *Energy Politics* (University of Pennsylvania Press, 2009) and *Borders and Brethren: Iran and the Challenge of Azerbaijani Identity* (MIT Press, 2002). She is also the editor of the book *Limits of Culture: Islam and Foreign Policy* (MIT Press, 2006). She has published numerous academic articles, including recent publications in the journals *Energy Policy* and *Post-Soviet Affairs*. She serves as a lecturer and consultant on the Caucasus and Caspian region to a number of public organizations, governments, and regional security organizations.

Elnur Soltanov is Assistant Professor of Political Science at the Azerbaijan Diplomatic Academy. His research focuses on international security and political economy, comparative politics, methodology and energy politics. He received his PhD in Political Science from Texas Tech University (2009). Between 2000 and 2003, Dr. Soltanov worked as a researcher at the Center for Eurasian Strategic Studies (ASAM) think-tank in Ankara. Among his publications is the book *A Political Economy of Russian Foreign Policy* (VDM Verlag, 2009). Prior to joining ADA, Dr. Soltanov served as Assistant Professor of Political Science at the Truman State University, Missouri.

Regine A. Spector teaches courses in comparative politics, development, and Eurasian studies at Smith College and the University of Massachusetts, Amherst. Dr. Spector organizes the Central Eurasian Studies Speaker Series at the Woodrow Wilson Center's Kennan Institute in Washington, D.C., where she was previously a visiting research scholar.

Taleh Ziyadov is research fellow at the Azerbaijan Diplomatic Academy (ADA) and a PhD candidate at the University of Cambridge. He specializes in energy security and transportation issues in Central Eurasia. He holds a master's degree from the School of Foreign Service, Georgetown University.

INDEX

Abdullah (King of Saudi Arabia), 74–75, 291
Abkhaz Autonomous Republic (Georgia), 208, 404n21
Abu Dhabi, 61–62, 66, 67–68, 237, 292, 293, 300. *See also* United Arab Emirates
Acemoglu, Daron, 31, 32, 317
Aga Khan Foundation, 242, 421n105
Ahmadinejad, Mahmoud, 111, 183
Alaska, 54, 57, 289, 368
Alesina, Alberto, 38
Alexeev, Michael, 28, 34, 379n57
Algeria, 72, 88, 139, 172, 285, 291, 292, 294, 298, 306, 318, 319, 324, 357, 376n31
Aliyev, Heydar, 207–9, 215, 406n42, 408n48
Aliyev, Ilham, 218, 410n73
Aliyev, Natiq, 215
Alkatiri, Mari, 347–48
Amuzegar, Jahangir, 361
Anglo-Iranian Oil Company, 298
Anglo-Persian Petroleum. *See* British Petroleum (BP)
Angola, 18, 289, 307, 314, 319, 329, 350, 429n9
Ansell, Ben, 228
Antalya Declaration, 222
Arab Oil Embargo (1973), 11, 26, 45, 283–85, 371n6. *See also* OPEC
Arab-Israeli War (1973), 11, 285, 299
Aramco, 59, 267, 299, 309, 387n8
Arezki, Rabah, 33–34
Argentina, 45, 143, 353
Armenia: Azerbaijan and, 217; education in, 240–41, 244, 246; electricity sector in, 185, 191, 194; Iran and, 116, 184–85; public sector in, 255; Russia and, 221
Asian Development Bank (ADB), 242
Australia, 29, 289–90, 301, 345
Auty, Richard, 18, 33, 363

Azerbaijan: Armenia and, 217; Azerbaijan Diplomatic Academy (ADA), 249–50; Azerbaijan Tourism Institute, 250; banking sector in, 146–49; Caspian region and, 113; constitution of, 212; corruption in, 164, 197–98; economic conditions in, 147, 190–91, 208–9; economic development and, 94, 215–16; education in, 240–41, 243–58; electricity sector in, 164–65, 167–68, 172–74, 185, 190–99; energy exports and, 6, 10, 191, 243; European Union and, 151, 217–18; exchange rates and, 139, 150–52; foreign investment in, 300; foreign policy of, 221; Georgia and, 197–98; global financial crisis (2008) and, 141, 147; governance in, 94; international oil companies and, 214–15; Iran and, 116, 184, 207–8; Islamic identity in, 220–22; military spending in, 216–17; Ministry of Defense Industry, 216; Ministry of Education, 253, 256–57; Nagorno-Karabakh and, 10, 191, 208–9, 215; natural gas and, 172, 191, 197–98, 218; oil and, 191, 197, 214–15, 289; oil prices and, 147; pipelines and, 213–14, 219–20, 223, 366–67; public sector in, 254–55; railroad projects in, 216–18; Russia and, 151, 191–92, 197, 207–8, 214, 216, 218; state oil fund in, 253, 368, 370; Soviet legacy in, 203–4, 207, 240, 251; Tariff Council, 151; Turkey and, 151, 192, 197–98, 217, 222, 253; Turkic culture and, 221–22; United Kingdom and, 215; United States and, 151, 215, 217–18; Western imitation and, 219–20, 223. *See also* Central Bank of Azerbaijan (CBA)
Azerenerji, 191, 195

ACKNOWLEDGMENTS

The idea of *Beyond the Resource Curse* was first conceived at a research workshop organized and sponsored by the Azerbaijan Diplomatic Academy (ADA), July 10–12, 2009, in Baku, Azerbaijan. We would like to thank ADA for its generous support and assistance throughout the making of this volume. Special thanks go to ADA Rector, Ambassador Hafiz Pashayev—a scholar and intellectual who understands very well the importance of this volume for his country and other resource-rich states. We are also grateful to a number of colleagues from ADA for their support and encouragement, especially Galib Mammad, and Fariz Ismailzade.

A number of people at the University of Pennsylvania Press made an important contribution to *Beyond the Resource Curse*. Bill Finan, editor of Public Policy and International Relations, led the pack with his professional input and guidance. Bill also was always kind and upbeat. Dr. Alison Anderson, Managing Editor at UPENN Press gave critical suggestions and advice at important junctures in the production process. UPENN's input greatly improved this volume. Thanks also go to the two anonymous reviewers.

We would like to thank the authors who participated in this research and book project. They are a very interesting and diverse group of people from different disciplines, who not only did great research but were a pleasure to work with. We also thank John Grennan for his research assistance, editing of some of the chapters of the book, and preparation of the index.

We especially thank Omri, Yael, and Oghuz.

Brenda Shaffer and Taleh Ziyadov

Lightning Source UK Ltd.
Milton Keynes UK
UKHW040848291022
411273UK00003B/95/J

9 780812 244007